The Techniques of Reading

*An Integrated Program for
Improved Comprehension and Speed*

THIRD EDITION

THIRD EDITION **The**
Techniques
of Reading

An Integrated Program for
Improved Comprehension and Speed

Horace Judson

in consultation with
William S. Schaill
The Reading Laboratory, Inc.

 Harcourt Brace Jovanovich, Inc.
New York   Chicago   San Francisco   Atlanta

For Grace,
with the memory of teaching you to read

PROGRESS PROFILE

Enter your score for each Reading Speed exercise in the place provided at the bottom of the chart. To construct your Progress Profile, draw a bar from the base line of the graph up to the words-per-minute speed you reached when reading that selection. Use a contrasting color (for example, a red pencil) for the exercises on the *difficult* level. If your score on the comprehension questions was 70 per cent or better, draw a solid bar; if below 70 per cent, indicate that by drawing a hatched or hollow bar.

Do not expect to show steady progress. Your greatest gains in speed are likely to take place early in the series of exercises—though some students are exceptions to this pattern—while in later exercises you should be able to consolidate those gains and improve your comprehension at the new levels of speed. The interest, familiarity, and degree of freshness or fatigue with which you approach each exercise will also affect your performance: therefore, it is the trend over several exercises that is most important. As Chapter 3 explains more fully, repeated *high* comprehension scores may mean that you are not stretching for the limits of your potential reading speed on material of similar difficulty; these "measured miles" offer the opportunity to experiment more boldly.

A clear and important indication of progress is the development of a marked difference—perhaps a 50 to 150 w.p.m. difference—between your reading speed on materials at the average level and at the difficult level. Chapter 4 discusses the reasons for this difference.

W.P.M.

	650
	625
	600
	575
	550
	525
	500
	475
	450
	425
	400
	375
	350
	325
	300
	275
	250
	225
	200
	175
	150
	125

W.P.M.

COMPRE-
HENSION
SCORE (%)

EXERCISE	AV. #1	DIF. #1	AV. #2	AV. #3	DIF. #2	AV. #4	AV. #5	DIF. #3	AV. #6	DIF. #4	AV. #7

PREFACE

The chief problem in reading improvement—given almost any sensible, coherent teaching method—lies beyond the method itself: the most effective techniques are worthless unless the student carries them over into his day-to-day reading. Thus, as I said in the previous edition, *The Techniques of Reading* is a book for the serious student who needs to learn how to understand more, and more quickly and pleasantly, in his nonfiction reading at the college level—which is to say, at the adult level. *The Techniques of Reading* offers a proven balance of methods by which the student can increase his reading comprehension and his speeds. For speed, the methods of improvement are based on the two principles of reading by phrases and flexibility of reading rate. For comprehension, the book shows the student how to analyze workaday prose in terms of his own reading purpose and the writer's organization and overall rhetorical technique. Speed and comprehension are kept in balance by the insistence that methods of understanding are prerequisite to speed, while better speeds, once they are possible, themselves become an aid to comprehension.

The third edition conserves those aims. But it goes beyond them in the effort to open up the book so that it reaches into all the student's other reading. The result is perhaps not so neat and self-contained but is much more relevant and persuasive. Chapter texts now carry a new emphasis on demonstrations, questions, and suggestions that are relevant to the student's own reading. The reading exercises, heavily revised and updated, use many more questions of the open-ended, short-essay, or sentence-completion form than before; as the book moves forward, multiple-choice questions are abandoned stage by stage. A change like this does not necessarily make a textbook any easier to teach or use; but it makes the exercises more like real-life reading problems. Most importantly, I have introduced a new series of bridging exercises. In each chapter, the section of reading-practice material now begins with a Reading Journal assignment, which asks the student to apply the techniques of reading, as they are introduced, to his daily work, and to keep detailed self-analytical notes about this application in a separate notebook. Moreover, a new cycle of "carry-over exercises" now guides the student in applying techniques—notably pre-reading, summarizing, paragraph analysis, and reading speed—to materials he selects from his current outside reading.

Another, more modest aim of this revision is to extend some of the techniques into reading other than the practical prose that has always been the book's chief concern. Thus, the sections and chapters having to do with critical reading are considerably strengthened, and a beginning is made at breaking down the distinction we created in the first edition between practical prose and other kinds of reading. The assumption here is simple: structural and rhetorical analyses—tactfully applied—have a place in the reading of literature, criticism, history, even fiction and poetry. It is therefore our duty at least to introduce such reading, and the new final chapter does so.

We asked many users of the second edition to answer some questions about how the book could be improved. Suggestions we have adopted range from simplifications of format (such as placing the questions on each exercise immediately after the reading selection and including an answer key for the multiple-choice questions) to more and stronger material on research, concentration, memory, and vocabulary development. But like its predecessors, the third edition of *The Techniques of Reading* is founded in large part on The Reading Laboratory's experience with students — by now tens of thousands of students at college level.

My association with The Reading Laboratory's founder and president, William S. Schaill, has been long and always bracing; it is a duty, surely, and a great delight to thank him for his friendship and help. My friendships at Harcourt Brace Jovanovich have proved solid and gratifying too. A book about reading has many general debts to acknowledge, but although I recognize their weight, I find these hard to identify, for reading, after all, has been a primary, *the* primary, intellectual concern for thousands of years.

Horace Judson

CONTENTS

CHAPTER 3   Pre-reading   62

CHAPTER 4   The Mechanics of Reading Speed   91

1

Fundamentals

Your Lifetime of Reading

> *Wait!* Better reading starts now—with this interruption of your usual plunge into the stream of a new book. Before reading this introductory chapter, please read the table of contents carefully. It starts on page xi. Reading the table of contents and introduction of a book is part of an important technique called *pre-reading,* discussed in detail in Chapter 3.

Max Perutz is a molecular biologist at Cambridge University. He has won a Nobel Prize for unraveling the atomic structure of hemoglobin. He is also a man with a reading problem, which he defined in a recent interview: "Is my field of science still growing? Look at *The Journal of Molecular Biology.* It started as a slim pamphlet which came out every two months, and now it's a volume of 400 pages, coming out every other week. I first read it from cover to cover. Then I read at least all the summaries. Now I hardly have time to read all the titles!"

This is one reading problem everybody has: the unstoppable, rising flood of the written word. You must learn to read better because there is so much reading to do. It is as simple as that. The amounts are staggering. For the rest of your life, you will have hardly a waking hour when you do not read something, if only a few words. Many times a day you will read a paragraph or more— a news story, lab report, business memorandum, or letter from a friend. Once or twice almost every day you will read for concentrated periods of half an hour or more. Painter or professor, scientist or storekeeper, lawyer, merchant, or political activist, few people read less than that. Many people, you as a student certainly among them, read much more.

Much of this reading is inessential, of course, even irritating—the visual equivalent of noise. But inextricably mixed with the noise is the signal you want, the message you need to read. Driving down the highway? You are surrounded by reading. DRINK CAFFEINE-COLA, screams the billboard. That's noise. But there are signals, too. OIL PRESSURE, whispers the gauge that lights up red on the dashboard. SERVICE 500 YARDS, says the sign by the road. It is the same with a newspaper or *The Harvard Law Review,* a shelf of references for a paper you must write or a stack of correspondence you must answer—you must filter, as the engineers would say, to increase the signal-to-noise ratio. But even after the most ruthless selection, the reading you should do and want to do is overwhelming in its sheer bulk. So you must learn to handle it efficiently, with at least a little more speed and with a lot more understanding.

After all, you learned to read in grade school. But what have you learned about reading since?

The question is worth thought. Compare your reading with your writing. You learned writing in grade school too. At least, you began to put words and sentences on paper. But you have learned a lot more about writing since then. On the mechanical side, you may have learned new, faster ways of putting words on paper: typing, shorthand. (Reading has its mechanical side too, offering faster ways of getting words off paper.) More importantly, your skills of prose composition, from punctuation and grammar through organization and outlining, all the way perhaps to the finer points of style, have been the object of regular instruction and incessant correction all through school and college, and sometimes beyond.

For every book, or article, or memorandum, or report, or letter you will ever write, how many will you read? Yet the skills of reading do not get the same kind of detailed, systematic, how-to-do-it training. To be sure, you will have been introduced to such auxiliary matters as how to take notes and how to use a library. Also, training in writing should have sharpened your awareness, as you read, of sentence and paragraph structures. But otherwise, as you moved up through the years, it was reading in a different sense that got increasing attention in your English classes: the reading of literature.

Meanwhile, you have been doing all that other reading that is hardly great literature. Instead, it is what we shall call *practical prose:* nonfiction you read primarily for information, rather than for enjoyment or for aesthetic or philosophic appreciation. Each year, not only the quantity, but also the variety and difficulty of your practical prose reading have grown. Of course your reading skills have grown too, for instance, your vocabulary. But most of the things you have learned about reading since grade school you have picked up along the way, without thought and without system. Among the things you have picked up are some bad habits.

It is now time to learn to read practical prose with mature proficiency. That means gaining important new skills. It means organizing your present skills and the new ones into a reliable system for mastering various types of reading matter. It means suppressing bad habits. It also means increasing your reading speeds somewhat, and increasing very much the flexibility and control with which you use different reading speeds.

It is now time to learn to read like a professional, because you now face the months and years of your greatest reading load. There are 586 words on this page. They take the average reader about two and one half minutes to read. There are:

276,000 words in this book;

239,050 words in *Writing with a Purpose,* 4th edition, by James M. McCrim-mon, a typical textbook for the first-year college composition course;

522,665 words in *How We Live: Contemporary Life in Contemporary Fiction,* a fat, interesting anthology of literature, edited by Penney C. and L. Rust Hills;

621,640 words in *Life: An Introduction to Biology,* 2nd edition, by George Gaylord Simpson and William S. Beck;

362,400 words in *Introduction to Psychology,* 5th edition, by Ernest R. Hilgard and Richard C. Atkinson;

583,260 words in *The National Experience: A History of the United States,* 2nd edition, by John M. Blum *et al.*

A first year's college course load might well include these six textbooks: upwards of 2,500,000 words, just as basic reading.

The quantity and difficulty of the reading to be done at college level are a shock to most entering students (and this despite the obvious fact that high school students who plan to go to college have been finding the competitive pressures greater every year). That first 2,500,000 words in assigned texts is just the beginning. "Supplementary" reading lists may contain five to fifty or more titles, ranging from articles of 5,000 words to books of half a million words. *War and Peace* is famous for its 635,000 words, but it is outranked, say, by Gunner Myrdal's pioneering treatise on the Negro in our history and society, *An American Dilemma,* at 700,000 words. Not all the titles on a supplementary bibliography may be required reading; instead, what you are asked to do is in some ways even more difficult, that is to explore on your own, following the trails that lead from book to book, from a problem to the various possible solutions. Books and articles mount up quickly that way. At the inescapable minimum, for each volume of required text, the extras add up to another two volumes. The total easily reaches 8,000,000 words in the first college year. Better students read more. Later years require more. Relentlessly, each year the loads get heavier: when the first edition of this book was published, our estimate was 4,000,000 words in a freshman's year of reading.

8,000,000 words of college-level practical prose: is that, in fact, a lot? To get through it just once, an average adult reader who works attentively, without interruptions or distractions, without taking any notes, without reviewing — without even stopping to question or reflect — would have to read for ten full hours a day for sixty-two days. And by the end, how much, out of those 8,000,000 words, would he have learned?

Three Case Histories

Your years of greatest reading load only start at the university. What will your career be: professional — doctor or lawyer? Academic — teacher or researcher? Politician? Businessman? Scientist? Journalist? There's no letup to the reading. Not even at the top. The idea that adults need reading lessons was emphatically publicized when John F. Kennedy took training in reading because only with better-organized comprehension and much greater speeds could he master the reading necessary to stay on top of his presidential work load. At less exalted levels, consider the reading problems experienced by three people: a college student, a scientist, and a magazine writer.

A college student

Simon Burke had just finished his freshman year at the main campus of a state university on the West Coast when he enrolled for the summer in a reading course. The year had been tough, for many reasons. In high school, Burke had gotten excellent grades, not without work but without real difficulty. He had been a competition swimmer; he had played rhythm guitar in a pop group with three friends. In his last year he was active in a student chapter of the youth wing of one of the political parties, which took him debating all over the state, and once to picket the legislature. He had enjoyed it all, the work as well as the action, and had known shrewdly enough that his record looked promisingly "well rounded." He had breezed into his first year at the university with the same energy, enthusiasm, and interests. By Christmas, he knew he was in trouble.

Burke's grief was not the studying alone, though that was where trouble was obvious. True, he found the 8,000,000 words a rude awakening, but what daunted him was the unrelenting combination of difficulty and quantity. Burke also faced some unsettling, though not unusual, problems of adjustment. There were more than 15,000 students on his campus. He knew only two fellow students when he arrived, and none of the instructors. Lecture classes were often huge; even in workshops and discussion groups, as he said to a meeting of students that spring, "Contact with instructors is what Hobbes called man's life in the state of nature—'poor, nasty, brutish, and short.'" As unsettling as the size of the place, the unfamiliarity, and the chilly freedom of living away from home, was the fact that he had stepped from the top of the high school ladder to the bottom rung of a new ladder, with all the climbing to be done again.

Worst, Burke came to a typical crisis of the college student. He found himself unsure of what he wanted to do. He had thought seriously of physics, but now realized he did not have the mathematical flair. Law? He had enjoyed his state-wide debating: perhaps law and politics? But he found literature the only reading he could concentrate on. He liked songwriting, and was doing well in composition—maybe he was a writer? One thing he was for certain: directionless.

The problems showed in his grades, but long before that he felt them in his reading. He was rushed, and often late, with assigned readings. He read less and less from the supplementary lists. He found great difficulty in concentrating, and often felt hopelessly sleepy when trying to study; he was seized by panic, would sit up late trying to catch up with the aid of caffeine pills, then would sleep too late in the mornings. He would sometimes find himself compulsively reading a science fiction magazine—or, slightly better, a piece of fiction assigned for next week—when he should have been reading biology for the next morning.

Burke was shaken enough to let the facts discipline him. He dropped out of extras, put his guitar away, and settled into the rhythm of long hours. His first semester grades were mediocre. His second semester was satisfactory, but no more. Because he wanted to do better, and wanted time for more than study, he spent the following summer reading ahead the books for his main subjects the next year. And he took a course in reading.

A scientist

By learning to read at four years old, Doc Jenkins had earned his nickname by the time he was eight. By thirty-two, he had earned the title in earnest, with both an M.D. and a Ph.D., and full charge of a new biological research laboratory at a major university. He was already a good reader when he enrolled in a reading improvement course. By the end of the course he had become remarkably fast and skillful. One thing about him, though, was average: the vast quantity of reading he had to do as a scientist.

Jenkins' branch of biology happens to be developing fast. Laboratories all over the world race into print with discoveries. One weekly publication and five monthlies (three American, two British) in this field of biology report the most significant new work. Other reports are exchanged among some of the laboratories on an almost weekly basis. In terms of reading to be done, all of this averages more than 400 pages per week. Most of it makes a hard subject harder with dull writing.

As for the projects in Jenkins' own laboratory, he commented that they "generate paper faster than results." This day-to-day work gives him 150 additional pages of reading in an average week.

Reports in that branch of biology are also published in German, French, and Russian. (The laboratories in Japan fortunately publish their most important results in the English-language journals.) English-language summaries of Russian publications are available; full translations can be had. When it comes to reading technical German and French, Jenkins gets along by himself, as most scientists must try to do. All told, foreign-language reports add 120 pages a week.

Outside Jenkins' immediate field, there are half a dozen other monthlies and quarterlies in subjects so closely related that he must read them with careful attention for the clues they provide for his own work. Thus the weekly stack grows by another 100 pages. Then there is the interest and responsibility, felt by most scientists, to try to be aware of important work going on in other fields of science (ideally in all fields of science). This devotion to the unity of knowledge costs Jenkins another 50 or more pages a week.

The total: upwards of 1,000 pages, or the equivalent of *War and Peace* every week.

The problem: how to read that much when reading is not the central part of Jenkins' work. It is indispensable, but only preliminary. Rather, Jenkins' job is to do a kind of thinking perhaps best described as disciplined, highly informed speculation — and then to devise and carry out techniques to check the accuracy of his speculations. This work demands time, in great chunks, regularly. As another scientist describes it, "The art is never to confuse hard work and hard thinking. It is so easy to fill up time with hard work; it is difficult to leave time for thinking."

A magazine writer

John Lippincott is a journalist now writing for a weekly news magazine. His specialty is law, but he has written about education and about politics; with each subject he faced the same reading problems. He writes three or four short articles each week, spending Wednesday and Thursday at the typewriter until well past midnight; the rest of the week is devoted to research, which means reading. He reads *The New York Times* and *The Washington Post* every day, often *The Los Angeles Times* as well, selectively but carefully, not only for their reporting of law cases but also for the political and social background of the law, civil rights and liberties, police work, and so on. His writing is based on three kinds of material. In answer to queries he sends out, the magazine's own reporters in the field teletype detailed "files" on cases, running six to thirty pages. The press, and the Associated Press wire service, may carry further details. Beyond that, for the legal significance of a story, Lippincott draws on the formidable mass of professional publications for lawyers. His aim is to cover all the law, as the most important legal happenings of each week put one or another aspect of the law into the news. Civil rights, insurance claims, obscenity trials, tax law, Supreme Court decisions, how police get evidence, a sensational defense lawyer in a murder trial: Lippincott must be ready to make himself an instant expert on any of these, for his audience of millions of readers includes thousands of lawyers who will challenge any error.

As he discovered when he took a reading improvement course, Lippincott must read in three quite different ways in the course of his work. Hundreds of pages of newspapers and journals must be combed, roughly and as fast as possible, to keep in the most general touch with what is developing and to locate material that must be read carefully. Perhaps two to six pieces must be read carefully each week, even though he is not writing about them. Then the research for each story will run 30 to 100 pages, in the most varied forms, mastered so totally that when he turns to the typewriter the most important facts and implications integrate themselves smoothly into his final article.

Notice how Lippincott's reading problem resembles Doc Jenkins', not only in the extent of the reading to be done, but also in the fact that reading is necessary but is not their main work — at once indispensable and a terrible obstacle. This description of professionals' reading problems applies to most scientists, to some engineers, and to a variety of other people in technical work. Even when their immediate aims may be more obviously "practical," the pressures of reading are similar. For example, doctors: it is notorious that men ten years out of medical school may be practicing obsolete medicine unless they keep up with the almost overwhelming load of medical publications. Lawyers, tax accountants, other professionals face the same problems.

What This Book Tries to Do

Thus, the first problem of practical prose is its sheer bulk. Indeed, such practical prose will probably make up 70 per cent or more of your reading during the next fifty years. Second, the subject matter of practical prose is often difficult. Material from physics, economics, law, history, and biology is often abstruse, demanding background and a high degree of reading skill if you are to comprehend it as thoroughly as you need or want to do.

Third, practical prose is often written badly. Gobbledygook in government writing, jargon in technical and scientific writing, wordy "businessese," and the mile-long formulas with which legal phraseology tries to plug all loopholes — these are the most notorious examples of the windy, self-important ways that authors can make reading more difficult than need be. Here is a juicy example from a source as everyday as a college catalogue:

COURSE TITLE: Man and His Environment   UNITS 3–3

PREREQUISITES: None

The subject of this course is man and his relationships to his environment. It is concerned with the total needs of man, and it seeks to identify the relationships of life that are basic to an ecology of man in harmony with his own nature and with the ecologies of other living things.

The purpose of this course is to create a context which is broad enough, deep enough, and relevant enough to provide a framework within which the search for human fulfillment is worthwhile. It seeks to provide the student with experiences which will enable him to become an aware, cogent, functioning, person.

Efficient reading of practical prose must get you through bad writing, as well as that which is terse and straightforward.

The Techniques of Reading will help the already literate person become a more skilled reader. With detailed explanations and extensive practice material, this book instructs and drills you in the methods that skilled readers use when they want to understand practical prose accurately and efficiently. *The Techniques of Reading* is built on the experience of specialists at The Reading Laboratory who have improved the reading skills of over 80,000 students. If you are a reader of average intelligence and ability, this book should enable you to improve, markedly, your understanding of practical prose, while increasing your reading speeds by 20 to 50 per cent, perhaps more. What does that mean in practice? Just take that minimum of 20 per cent improvement in speed, with increased comprehension. Apply it to the 8,000,000 words facing a college freshman: it is as if they were cut to 6,666,000 words—and made easier at the same time. Again, apply that 20 per cent to your lifetime of reading, the tens of millions of words we have mapped out: for every ten books you read, you will have time for two more, month after month, year after year.

Speed is just a small part of the improvement you will discover. You will begin by measuring the quality of your present reading, in the Reading Skills Survey that follows this chapter. In the succeeding chapters, you will learn:

How to look material over before reading it thoroughly, making a map to guide you through the unknown territory ahead. This is the important technique we have already mentioned, called *pre-reading.*

How to define your precise *purpose* in reading.

How and when to *skim.*

How to recognize passages that are safe for you to *skip* entirely.

How to build your *reading vocabulary.*

How to *summarize.*

Several ways to take *notes* most usefully without wasting time.

How to read *newspapers* most efficiently.

Several ways to approach difficult and *specialized reading,* such as law or science.

How to help your *concentration,* even when the reading doesn't interest you.

How to read with *questions* in mind—an approach that can become your most important tool for critical, reflective, comparative reading on the highest levels.

Each chapter of this book explains in detail one aspect or technique of skillful reading. Although the techniques are closely related and often used in combination, obviously each one must be treated somewhat independently. However, immediately after each chapter, exercises give you practice in *many* of the techniques introduced up to that point.

Speed and comprehension exercises are an important part of these practice materials. Your scores on these exercises will chart your Progress Profile (the frontispiece of this book, page vi). At the start, your Progress Profile will show gains that come just from your conscious effort to push along faster with more careful attention. Practice will extend those gains; and special exercises are designed to help you carry the techniques of reading over to all your day-to-day encounters with practical prose.

Three Objections, with Answers

Near the beginning of a course of reading improvement, students often raise several troubling questions.

When speed goes up, doesn't understanding come down? There is an almost universal fear among untrained readers that reading speeds cannot increase very much without causing a loss in understanding. *This fear is largely unfounded.* On the contrary, most readers find that their comprehension improves as they learn to read faster. Dramatic gains in speed involve system, discipline, concentration, absorbing the author's ideas more efficiently and in larger chunks—all explained and taught in later chapters. You will find that reading is like typing or tennis: a sudden spurt of speed just makes for wildness and mistakes, but with practice and instruction, speed and accuracy both improve, reinforcing each other.

What about reading simply for the enjoyment of plot, humor, suspense, freshness, surprise—isn't all that spoiled by "techniques"? One of the chief techniques is to ask yourself explicitly, before you start to read something, just what your purpose is. When you answer, "enjoyment, plot, suspense . . ." then of course you will not apply reading techniques that would spoil those qualities. The skillful reader selects the reading method appropriate to the work at hand, choosing, consciously, from many methods; the average reader has very few methods and applies them indiscriminately. The technique called pre-reading, for example, has you read the first *and last* chapters of a book, before reading all the chapters in between. Would anybody seriously propose following that method with a detective story?

Do these techniques for speed and understanding in reading practical, factual prose also apply to poetry, or philosophy, or great fiction? For many, this is more than a question; it is an instinctive protest that arises from their respect for great literature. They fear that simple-minded "efficiency" in reading will render the student imperceptive to precise shades of meaning, implication, or beauty; or unfit to read works of great complexity or originality.

In the same way, many people without much formal training in music believe that to learn how to analyze music technically would have the undesirable effect of inserting, between them and the music, a muffling screen of self-conscious analytical perceptions. But that need not happen: great violinists and great conductors have found themselves overwhelmed to the point of weeping when they hear works they know perfectly because they have performed them. One amateur in music reports that twenty years ago he took a course in which four weeks were spent in technical dissection of a single symphony of Mozart's; still today, whenever he hears it played well, it moves him profoundly.

The musical analogy suggests that analysis ("technique") is not entirely out of place in that all-important 10 to 30 per cent of your reading that includes philosophy, drama, poetry, the best fiction, biography, and history. Nonetheless, this manual does not pretend to teach you any system for such reading. No system could presume to claim that it prepares you for the original, even elusive, reading problems that such works often present. Rather, this book is primarily concerned with the problems of reading practical prose efficiently, that is, with the degrees of understanding you need or want, and with the highest possible speeds.

With greater efficiency in reading practical prose, you will at least gain more time for the "impractical." You will find, too, that from time to time the individual techniques you learn from this manual will help you with that reading: certainly the ability to summarize, and to read comparatively and critically. Perhaps most importantly, the emphasis on practical prose organization, which runs throughout this book, will make you more sensitive to organization while reading for pleasure or for aesthetic or philosophic appreciation.

How to Use This Book

To benefit most fully from *The Techniques of Reading,* remember these slogans:

Short and frequent. Practice for a short time every day is better than long periods once or twice a week.

Do it all. Work through this book thoroughly; complete all the exercises for one chapter before going on to the next.

Steady pace. If you are using this book for independent study, it is particularly important not to skip around; rather, go through a little every day over a period of about six weeks.

Apply it. For all readers, the most important step is to use the new skills in all your everyday reading.

Application of the new techniques will never become as automatic as are your present reading habits. Indeed, we have certainly implied that the new methods make the reading of practical prose more deliberate, more planned, and more controlled. As you apply these new methods in your daily work, however, you will quickly find that they become easy to remember and pleasant to use.

READING SKILLS SURVEY

Your Reading Inventory

Summarizing
"The Community Centered School," by Preston R. Wilcox

Skimming for a Fact

Pre-reading
Table of Contents from *Introduction to Psychology,* by Ernest R. Hilgard, Richard C. Atkinson, and Rita L. Atkinson

Reading Speed Exercise: Average Level 1
"From Plankton to Whales," from *Kon-Tiki,* by Thor Heyerdahl

Reading Speed Exercise: Difficult Level 1
"Culture," from *Society: An Introduction to Sociology,* by Ely Chinoy

This book is one-third instruction and two-thirds practice materials. The chapter texts provide the instructions, explanations, suggestions, and techniques. After each chapter is a set of practice materials, the exercises. Most of the exercises are passages of practical prose. They have been drawn from a variety of sources; a few have been chosen because they are samples of the pedestrian, or even bad, writing you will often meet. Some of the exercises require you to time your reading. Most of them ask you to answer questions after reading, to measure your understanding. Speed and comprehension, measured regularly, will help you gauge the development of your reading skills.

To gauge your development, you must first know where you are now. This initial set of exercises, the Reading Skills Survey, is designed to measure several important aspects of your present level of reading ability. The meaning of your scores on these exercises—and the sorts of improvement you should accordingly be able to make by following the suggestions in this book—will be brought out in the next several chapters. If you are taking the Reading Skills Survey in class, your instructor may add other tests to it, such as a vocabulary test and a test of general verbal ability.

Your Reading Inventory

Having read this far, you know what this book asserts about the importance of reading and about the amounts of reading that people must get through; you must also have a feeling for the point of view about reading from which the book is written. Do you find that these reading loads are accurate for you? Do you agree with that point of view? What is your own reading case history? This first section of the Reading Skills Survey is intended to help you assess your present reading habits and attitudes. Answer the questions thoughtfully and completely. There are no "right" answers. There is no score. This section is for your eyes only.

A: Problems and Skills

How do you rate your own performance as a reader? What are your strengths and weaknesses?

PRESENT PERFORMANCE

1. Overall, how well do you think you read?
   ☐ Very well   ☐ Well   ☐ Average   ☐ Poorly   ☐ Very poorly
2. If you were required to read extensively in books that were considerably more difficult than most of those you now read, how well do you think you could do?
   ☐ Well   ☐ Adequately   ☐ Poorly
3. How fast do you think you read?
   ☐ Very fast   ☐ Fast   ☐ Average   ☐ Slowly   ☐ Very slowly
4. Do you read different kinds of prose at different speeds?
   ☐ Yes   ☐ No, mostly the same speed   ☐ Don't know
5. How would you rate your vocabulary?
   ☐ Excellent   ☐ Good   ☐ Poor

PROBLEMS

	Often	*Sometimes*	*Rarely*
6. Do you find you must reread material to understand it?	☐	☐	☐
7. Do you have trouble concentrating when you read? What kind of trouble?	☐	☐	☐

_____

_____

_____

	Often	*Sometimes*	*Rarely*
8. Do you have trouble remembering what you have read, a day or a week later?	☐	☐	☐
9. After you have read something, are you uncertain or anxious about whether you have gotten what you need from it?	☐	☐	☐
10. Do you have trouble remembering the meanings of new words, even after you look them up in the dictionary?	☐	☐	☐

SKILLS

	Often	*Sometimes*	*Rarely*
11. When you start to read an article or book, do you pause to state your purpose in reading it?	☐	☐	☐
12. Do you read the tables of contents of nonfiction books?	☐	☐	☐
13. When you start to read an article or book, do you write out a short list of questions you expect your reading to answer?	☐	☐	☐
14. When you have just finished reading an article, or a book chapter, do you write out a short summary of it?	☐	☐	☐
15. When you have just read a paragraph, would you be able to pick out its most important sentence?	☐	☐	☐
16. Do you know how to skim? ☐ Yes ☐ No Do you skim?	☐	☐	☐
17. Can you take notes quickly and skillfully? ☐ Yes ☐ No Do you take notes on your reading?	☐	☐	☐

B: Do You Give Yourself a Chance?

How well do you help your eyes and reading environment to make reading easier for you?

1. Do you wear glasses? Yes_____ No_____ When was the prescription last

   changed? (Date)_____

2. Have your eyes been examined this last year? Yes_____ No_____ When do

   you plan to have them examined again? (Date)_____

3. Have you any feeling of eye strain or discomfort when you read? Yes_____

No_____ Do you have headaches during prolonged periods of reading?

Yes_____ No_____ Does it seem comfortable to hold most reading mate-

rial about 14 inches away? Yes_____ No_____

4. Do you make a practice of doing your serious reading in just one or two

locations — at the same desk or chair each time? Yes_____ No_____ Is the

chair upright and firm? Yes_____ No_____ Do you use a bookrest, tilted
so that the top and bottom of the page are about an equal distance from

you? Yes_____ No_____

5. Is there a firm surface at hand for writing or taking notes, and are there pen

and paper always handy? Yes_____ No_____

6. Does the lamp have at least a 100-watt bulb? Yes_____ No_____ Does
the light fall over the opposite shoulder from the hand you write with, so

that you can write without casting a shadow? Yes_____ No_____ Is the

rest of the room lit evenly, free from glare? Yes_____ No_____

C: Your reading load

How much reading do you do now? How much will you do in the future?

For each type of reading listed, enter in column 1 the number of hours
you now read, each week. When you have finished the column, add up the
totals — and if necessary go back to adjust. Then go down column 2, putting a
check mark wherever you think you should, or would like to, read more. In the
last column, estimate how many hours per week you expect to spend reading
this type of material five years from now.

Type of reading	1 Your load: hours per week now	2 Should you (or would you like to) read more now?	3 Hours per week in 5 years
PERIODICALS			
a. Newspapers			
Which? _____	_____	☐	_____
b. News magazines			
Which? _____	_____	☐	_____

Type of reading	**1** Your load: hours per week now	**2** Should you (or would you like to) read more now?	**3** Hours per week in 5 years
c. Other general magazines	_____	☐	_____
d. Specialized scientific or professional magazines, journals or newspapers	_____	☐	_____
e. Specialized trade or business magazines or newspapers	_____	☐	_____
BOOKS			
f. "Light" fiction	_____	☐	_____
g. "Serious" fiction	_____	☐	_____
h. Nonfiction, including textbooks			
1. Biology, physical sciences	_____	☐	_____
2. Social sciences: psychology, economics, sociology, political science, anthropology	_____	☐	_____
3. History, biography, current affairs	_____	☐	_____
4. Mathematics	_____	☐	_____
5. Law	_____	☐	_____
6. Foreign languages	_____	☐	_____
Totals	_____		_____

D: Attitudes

You have rated yourself as a reader; now, how do you rate reading itself?

1. Do you enjoy reading? _____

2. What kinds of reading do you like best? _____

   Least? _____

3. What book have you enjoyed most in the past year? _____
4. What are the titles of the two books you have read most recently? What sort of book is each one, history, fiction, etc.?

a. _____

b. _____

5. What sorts of reading do you find most difficult? _____
   _____

6. Does difficult reading challenge you and interest you, or does it make you

   uncomfortable, so that you want to put it off? _____
   _____

7. Do you find that difficult reading leaves you with the confused feeling that
   you have pushed through it mechanically, without really grasping it?

   _____

8. Do you prefer to learn from discussions, lectures, conversations, rather than

   reading? _____

9. How many books do you own? _____ When did you last buy one? _____
10. Would you say that you read *actively*, for example by making notes in the
    margin when you disagree with an author, and by looking up words or
    facts you are not sure of; or do you read *passively*, starting at the beginning
    of an article or book and submerging yourself in the words until you reach

    the end? _____
    In general and overall, what do you think about reading? about its impor-

    tance to you? about yourself as a reader? _____

    _____

    _____

    _____

Summarizing

A public school in any of America's cities stands at the intersection of at
least four of the nation's most grave problems: race, poverty, education, and
the city itself. Where these problems meet are the children themselves; and
right there, some educators argue, the community must make its schools work
for its needs. One educator who argues this passionately is Preston R. Wilcox
of New York City. The following article is taken from a longer piece by him.
For this exercise, your purpose in reading the article is to summarize each
paragraph and then the entire passage. The questions follow the passage.

This is not a timed exercise. You may refer to the article as you answer
the questions.

"The Community Centered School"[1]
by PRESTON R. WILCOX

A

Why do black people seek control over their local schools? After watching the failures of the present school system, they have concluded that those in control of that system define its objectives in terms of white America. The present authorities use such phrases as "the entire system" or "Negroes aren't the only ones who need better schools." Activists, however, recognize these as euphemisms for maintenance of the degrading *status quo*. The tragic fact is that, regardless of intentions, black Americans are treated not as full participants in the society but essentially as a group to be considered after the interests of others are attended to. So long as this remains true, school programs will continue to draw heavily on white, middle-class assumptions.

B

The essence of the struggle, therefore, has been to help the black and poor residents of the ghettoes understand that the present system, in the last analysis, was organized for the protection of "others" — not black Americans. Indeed, it has been established fairly conclusively on the basis of ethnic composition, performance scores, per capita expenditures, teacher turnover and assignments, and the figures on upgrading of minority-group staff, that many large urban complexes have, in fact, dual school systems — one white and one black, but both controlled by whites.

C

The minority-group student thus finds himself in the curious position of being miseducated by a system that represents everybody's interest but his. Such students are ordered to attend school under compulsory education laws seemingly for the express purpose of being convinced of their own uneducability. Those black students who were able to negotiate the schools had to adopt the views of their oppressors. They had to listen to discussions of history that highlighted the honesty of George Washington but not the fact that he was a slaveowner. In short, the Wasp model was substituted for one with which black students could more readily identify.

D

It is this tendency to deliver *generalized* white products into *specialized* black communities that set the stage for the thrust by black communities to take control of the schools set up to serve their children. The issue was engaged at one New York school, I.S. 201. But it quickly spread to at least four other sites in New York, and to Washington, Boston, and Columbus, Ohio. It can be expected to break into the open in the South, as well, before long. In every instance, a confrontation has occurred between the black and/or poor and the school system. Note the word "poor," for this thrust is quite unlike the middle-class-oriented drive for quality, integrated education outside the ghetto. It is based on the poor, not the middle class. It seeks to build a constituency among parents and community leaders who, unlike the "black bourgeoisie," recognize that their own destiny is tied to the plight of the black poor in a society in which it pays to be neither black nor poor.

E

The new thrust for community control of ghetto schools thus represents an important shift in emphasis: from a desire to replicate that which is American to a desire to reshape it. There is in this drive less concern with social integration than with effective education. To bring about effective education, however, it is necessary to do more than simply transfer control or change the ratio of white to black on the teaching staff. It is necessary to take a revolutionary view of the role of the school in the community. This brings us to the concept of the community-centered school — the school that functions as an acculturation tool, an educational instrument, and a community center.

For each of the five paragraphs in the article, pick out below the *best* summary. The last question asks you to choose a summary statement for the complete passage. You may refer to the article as you answer the questions.

A
1. Black people seek to control their local schools because otherwise they will be run by the whites.
2. Blacks' efforts to control local schools spring from belief that — whatever the official phrases — their educational needs are given lowest priority by white America.
3. Black Americans, not treated as full participants in American society, have no alternative but to set up their own society, starting with the schools.

ANSWER _____

B
1. All the statistics seem to agree that when whites are in control of the educational systems of large cities, they give blacks what is in practice a separate and very unequal school system.
2. The first step in seizing control of the local schools is to convince ghetto residents that the inequalities of white-controlled education are great, systematic, and intentional.
3. Action on ghetto schools begins with teaching the community that in large city school systems controlled by whites, educational inequalities are built into what amounts to two separate school systems.

ANSWER _____

C

1. Ghetto schools not controlled locally give black pupils a distorted education, so that they either seem uneducable or are forced to accept white values and biasses.
2. Compulsory education laws compound the pressure of the system that represents Wasp values and interests, to the point that blacks cannot identify with the system, sometimes cannot even be educated.
3. The effect of compulsory attendance at schools built on white models is to make black children either dolts or sheep, uneducable or brainwashed.

ANSWER _____

D

1. In reaction, a movement is spreading among the ghettoes to take control of local schools away from the school system, so that they can be made to serve the particular needs of the poor blacks, which are unlike those of the middle class and the whites.
2. Confrontation between black activists and the white-run school systems began in New York on a small scale but is spreading rapidly, wherever the blacks and the poor respond to leadership loyal to them.
3. Because both blacks and the poor have needs that are different from and denied by the white middle-class school systems, an alliance of blacks and the poor is beginning to seize the local schools.

ANSWER _____

E

1. But once local schools are locally controlled, their role in the community demands revolutionary change.
2. Seized by the community, the school must serve the community as an instrument of revolutionary educational progress.
3. Local control also revolutionizes the educational aims of the school, making it the center of changes in the entire community.

ANSWER _____

Now choose, from the following, the best summary of the entire passage.

1. The needs of the black poor, not met by an educational system whose inequalities are built in by the whites, explain why ghetto residents are trying to gain control of their local schools to revolutionize their educational role within the entire community.
2. Black ghetto schools now do less than schools in middle-class white areas, but they need to do far more; the necessary responsiveness to local needs requires local control.
3. Black schools in large cities are now effectively separate; if actually controlled by the communities they supposedly serve, they could meet their real —and revolutionary—needs for quality education rather than the irrelevant aims whites have built into the systems.

ANSWER _____

Now go on to the rest of the Reading Skills Survey. When you have completed it, check all your answers against the key, page 480, and enter your scores in the appropriate spaces.

Skimming for a Fact

Five paragraphs follow. You are to skim each one to find one particular piece of information. You are to work for speed, recording your total time on the five paragraphs. *Keep clearly in mind the fact, stated at the beginning of each paragraph, for which you are skimming.* Put a pencil check in the margin of the page next to the fact when you find it. After you have skimmed and checked all the paragraphs, note your total time; then enter your time and the sentence number of each fact in the proper blank of the answer space on page 23.

Since this is your first skimming exercise, review these instructions carefully before beginning. Remember that the objective is not to read thoroughly, but only to find the one fact in each paragraph as quickly as possible. Work with pencil in hand. If you are taking the exercise on your own, time yourself by following the first three steps of the Instructions for Timing on page 474. In class, follow your instructor's directions for timing.

Begin timing here.

A

LOOK FOR: the percentage of manufacturing employment accounted for by the giant firms in 1944

1   It is quite clear that it was the industrial giants, the biggest of the
2   big firms, which made the greatest gains during the war. In each of the
    war industries, with but one exception, firms with 10,000 or more em-
3   ployees grew in relative importance. In manufacturing as a whole, these
    few giants accounted for 13 per cent of total employment in 1939, and
    for fully 31 per cent of the total in 1944.[2]

B

LOOK FOR: the most important field where small enterprise predominates

1   The analysis of the list of largest administrative units can disclose
     the types of activities in which large enterprise plays a significant role
     but can throw little light on the fields in which really small enterprise
2,3 predominates. Of these, agriculture is by far the most important. In 1935
     there were nearly 7 million farm units, less than 42,000 of which involved
4   the gainful activity of more than 5 persons. The 7 million farm units each
     engaging the activities of only 2 to 5 persons accounted for well over
     half of the total number of producing units in the country and together
     they accounted for 97 per cent of the persons engaged in agriculture.[3]

C

LOOK FOR: the total per cent of decline in the stock of money from peak to the January 1922 bottom

1   From the peak reached in September 1920, the stock of money declined fairly steadily until the reference trough in July 1921, then
2   flattened out, and reached bottom in January 1922. The total decline was
3   9 per cent. Although the magnitude of decline was much less than in prices or value of output, it was a major decline in terms of the historical behavior of the stock of money, which tends ordinarily to rise during
4   mild business contractions as well as during business expansions. It was, indeed, the largest percentage decline recorded in our series up to that time, though only slightly larger than that before resumption in 1879.
5   True, our data before 1907 are annual and semiannual and so understate the amplitude of change but it is extremely doubtful that monthly data
6   would alter this conclusion. Furthermore, there is only one larger decline in the subsequent record—that accompanying the contraction of 1929–33.[4]

D

LOOK FOR: the rate of the first United States income tax

1,2   The income tax was first used during the Civil War. It was abandoned soon after the war ended, but during the ensuing years of depression and economic readjustment rural and debtor groups which objected to a high protective tariff argued for the reestablishment of an income tax as a way to collect from the more prosperous interests in the country
3   their just share of federal taxes. Requirement of an income tax provided one of the important planks in the platform of the Populist party during
4   the early 1890's. The Democratic party took over this plank for its own use, and, in a measure which reduced tariff levels, provided for a tax of
5   two per cent on all incomes above $4,000. This was the period when the so-called "robber barons" were ruthlessly acquiring their industrial and commercial empires and propertied interests were frightened by the
6   spread of radicalism. The advocates of the unlimited printing of paper money and unlimited coinage of silver and other panaceas for the ills of the unfortunate kept businessmen and their lawyers profoundly uneasy.
7   Dreams of the horrors of socialism and communism disturbed the slumbers of the fearful.[5]

E

LOOK FOR: the source of any evidence that manufacturers have been appropriating more for capital projects

1   Early surveys of business plans have in the past often proved wide of the final mark; for example, three years ago McGraw-Hill turned out
2   9 percent too low, and two years ago it was over 3 percent too high. But

as they stand, current surveys would suggest that capital-goods volume will rise about 5 percent over the course of the next year, which would make investment quite a plus in the over-all business outlook; significantly more than 5 percent would tend to spell boom in the 1969 economy.

3   The biggest increase in capital spending is indicated in the manu-
4 facturing area. Here the McGraw-Hill survey projects an 11 percent
5 advance. More telling evidence is that manufacturers have actually been appropriating more for capital projects — 15 percent more in the summer (excluding oil firms), according to the National Industrial Conference
6 Board. And, a sampling of large companies indicated intentions to keep
7 increasing appropriations in the autumn. This sudden rise in appropriations was accompanied by a sharp summer increase in new contracts for industrial construction (other business contracts went up to a lesser degree) and also by an advance in new orders for machinery and equip-
8 ment, much of which goes to manufacturers. Thus an upturn in manufacturing investment is now a tangible fact.[6]

Stop timing here.

For each paragraph, enter the number of the sentence that contains the fact you were to find. (The sentences are numbered in the left margin.)

Skimming time in seconds for all items: _____

A: _____   B: _____   C: _____   D: _____   E: _____

Pre-reading

We have reprinted below the table of contents from a standard text for the first college course in psychology. Here the organizational skeleton of the book is laid out. Look over this material to see what you can discover about the organization of the book and its parts. Then answer the questions that follow. This is not a timed exercise. You may refer to these pages as you answer the questions.

Table of Contents from *Introduction to Psychology*[7]
by ERNEST R. HILGARD, RICHARD C. ATKINSON, and RITA L. ATKINSON

contents

IV LEARNING AND THINKING

VII CONFLICT, ADJUSTMENT, AND MENTAL HEALTH

VIII SOCIAL BEHAVIOR

After reading the table of contents from *Introduction to Psychology,* answer the following questions. Note that not all the questions are in the usual multiple-choice form; some ask you to supply *page numbers* or *chapter numbers* from the table of contents. You may refer to the material as you answer.

1. Studying the table of contents before reading a book enables you to spot material within the book that performs a special function: introductory, transitional, or concluding chapters (or sections). Judging from the table of contents to *Introduction to Psychology,* which of the following *sections* (groups of chapters) seems to be introductory, transitional, or concluding? (a) "I   The Science of Psychology"; (b) "III   Perceptual Processes"; (c) "IV Learning and Thinking"; (d) "V   Motivation and Emotion"; (e) "VII   Conflict, Adjustment, and Mental Health.

ANSWER _____

2. Which particular *chapters* might have such special functions? (Give *chapter numbers* for your answer.)

ANSWER _____

3. In reading the book you might find the technical vocabulary sometimes difficult. To which page would you turn for help? (Give *page number* for your answer.)

ANSWER _____

4. How are the fourth and fifth sections of the book ("Learning and Thinking" and "Motivation and Emotion") related to each other? (a) Section IV discusses common student problems and Section V explains what can be done about them; (b) Section IV discusses the "rational" or "thinking" aspects while Section V goes on to the "emotional" aspects of individual psychology; (c) broadly speaking, Section IV discusses "rational" or "thinking" aspects and Section V deals with "emotional" aspects of behavior; in addition, each section begins with basic introductory chapters and then goes on to particular problem areas; (d) both sections are primarily designed for students who intend to go into teaching as a profession; (e) the two sections cannot really be compared.

ANSWER _____

5. What chapter would you read to get an understanding of the relation of the science of psychology to contemporary social and political problems? (Give the *chapter number*.)

ANSWER _____

6, 7, 8. After reading this *Introduction to Psychology,* a student might go on to study other more advanced and specialized areas of psychology. Several of these are listed below, each followed by chapter references to the table of contents. Please select the set of chapters that would provide the most adequate introduction to each of the more advanced areas of psychology.

6. Educational Psychology: (a) Chapters 8 through 11; (b) Chapters 3, 4, and 8 through 11; (c) Chapters 3, 4, 8 through 11, and 15; (d) Chapters 3, 4, 8 through 11, and 18 through 20.

ANSWER _____

7. Social Psychology (that is, the psychology of groups, and of individuals as they are influenced by groups to which they belong): (a) Chapters 15, 16, and 22; (b) Chapters 4, 5, 12, 22, and 23; (c) Chapters 3, 4, 16, 22, and 23.

ANSWER _____

8. Psychiatry: (a) Chapters 20 through 22; (b) Chapters 3, 4, 7, 13, 14, 16, 17, and 19 through 21; (c) Chapters 1, 6, 7, 14, and 21; (d) Chapters 7, 20, 21, and 23.

ANSWER _____

Reading Speed Exercise: Average Level 1

Six Scandinavians adrift on a balsa-wood raft in the southern Pacific, risking their lives to prove an anthropological theory about the way early South

American Indians might have migrated across the ocean to the islands of Polynesia: this is science that is high adventure, too. When the leader of the expedition, Thor Heyerdahl, published his book about the voyage, it became an immediate best seller, and has remained one of the great classics of exploration ever since. The following passage is reprinted from that book. The difficulty of content and style is about average. That is, skilled readers read it at the same speed they use for material of a factual nature, popularly written.

You are to read the selection against time. If you are taking the exercise in class, follow your instructor's directions for recording accurately the time you require to read it. If you are taking the exercise on your own, follow the Instructions for Timing on page 474.

After reading the selection and recording your time, go on to the ten questions beginning on page 32. There is no time limit for the questions, but it will invalidate the exercise if you refer to this passage while you answer them.

Begin reading and timing here.

"From Plankton to Whales"[8]
from *Kon-Tiki* by THOR HEYERDAHL

It is certain that there must be very nourishing food in these almost invisible plankton which drift about with the current on the oceans in infinite numbers. Fish and sea birds which do not eat plankton themselves live on other fish or sea animals which do, no matter how large they themselves may be. Plankton is a general name for thousands of species of visible and invisible small organisms which drift about near the surface of the sea. Some are plants (*phyto*-plankton), while others are loose fish ova and tiny living creatures (*zoo*-plankton). Animal plankton live on vegetable plankton, and vegetable plankton live on ammoniac, nitrates, and nitrites which are formed from dead animal plankton. And while they reciprocally live on one another, they all form food for everything which moves in and over the sea. What they cannot offer in size they can offer in numbers.

In good plankton waters there are thousands in a glassful. More than once persons have starved to death at sea because they did not find fish large enough to be spitted, netted, or hooked. In such cases it has often happened that they have literally been sailing about in strongly diluted, raw fish soup. If, in addition to hooks and nets, they had had a utensil for straining the soup they were sitting in, they would have found a nourishing meal — plankton. Some day in the future, perhaps, men will think of harvesting plankton from the sea to the same extent as now they harvest grain on land. A single grain is of no use, either, but in large quantities it becomes food.

The marine biologist Dr. A. D. Bajkov told us of plankton and sent us a fishing net which was suited to the creatures we were to catch. The "net" was a silk net with almost three thousand meshes per square inch. It was sewn in the shape of a funnel with a circular mouth behind an iron ring, eighteen inches across, and was towed behind the raft. Just as in other kinds of fishing, the catch varied with time and place. Catches diminished as the sea grew warmer farther west, and we got the best results at night, because many species seemed to go deeper down into the water when the sun was shining.

If we had no other way of whiling away time on board the raft, there would have been entertainment enough in lying with our noses in the plankton net. Not for the sake of the smell, for that was bad. Nor because the sight was appetizing, for it looked a horrible mess. But because, if we spread the plankton out on a board and examined each of the little creatures separately with the naked eye, we had before us fantastic shapes and colors in unending variety.

Most of them were tiny shrimplike crustaceans *(copepods)* or fish ova floating loose, but there were also larvae of fish and shellfish, curious miniature crabs in all colors, jellyfish, and an endless variety of small creatures which might have been taken from Walt Disney's *Fantasia.* Some looked like fringed, fluttering spooks cut out of cellophane paper, while others resembled tiny red-beaked birds with hard shells instead of feathers. There was no end to Nature's extravagant inventions in the plankton world; a surrealistic artist might well own himself bested here.

Where the cold Humboldt Current turned west south of the Equator, we could pour several pounds of plankton porridge out of the bag every few hours. The plankton lay packed together like cake in colored layers — brown, red, gray, and green according to the different fields of plankton through which we had passed. At night, when there was phosphorescence about, it was like hauling in a bag of sparkling jewels. But, when we got hold of it, the pirates' treasure turned into millions of tiny glittering shrimps and phosphorescent fish larvae that glowed in the dark like a heap of live coals. When we poured them into a bucket, the squashy mess ran out like a magic gruel composed of glowworms. Our night's catch looked as nasty at close quarters as it had been pretty at long range. And, bad as it smelled, it tasted correspondingly good if one just plucked up courage and put a spoonful of it into one's mouth. If this consisted of many dwarf shrimps, it tasted like shrimp paste, lobster, or crab. If it was mostly deep-sea fish ova, it tasted like caviar and now and then like oysters.

The inedible vegetable plankton were either so small that they washed away with the water through the meshes of the net, or they were so large that we could pick them up with our fingers. "Snags" in the dish were single jellylike coelenterates like glass balloons and jellyfish about half an inch long. These were bitter and had to be thrown away. Otherwise everything could be eaten, either as it was or cooked in fresh water as gruel or soup. Tastes differ. Two men on board thought plankton tasted delicious, two thought they were quite good, and for two the sight of them was more than enough. From a nutrition standpoint they stand on a level with the larger shellfish, and, spiced and properly prepared, they can certainly be a first-class dish for all who like marine food.

That these small organisms contain calories enough has been proved by the blue whale, which is the largest animal in the world and yet lives on plankton. Our own method of capture, with the little net which was often chewed up by hungry fish, seemed to us sadly primitive when we sat on the raft and saw a passing whale send up cascades of water as it simply filtered plankton through its celluloid beard. And one day we lost the whole net in the sea.

"Why don't you plankton-eaters do like him?" Torstein and Bengt said contemptuously to the rest of us, pointing to a blowing whale. "Just fill your mouths and blow the water out through your mustaches!"

I have seen whales in the distance from boats, and I have seen them stuffed in museums, but I have never felt toward the gigantic carcass as one usually feels toward proper warm-blooded animals, for example a horse or an elephant. Biologically, indeed, I had accepted the whale as a genuine mammal, but in its essence it was to all intents and purposes a large cold fish. We had a different impression when the great whales came rushing toward us, close to the side of the raft.

One day, when we were sitting as usual on the edge of the raft having a meal, so close to the water that we had only to lean back to wash out our mugs, we started when suddenly something behind us blew hard like a swimming horse and a big whale came up and stared at us, so close that we saw a shine like a polished shoe down through its blowhole. It was so unusual to hear real breathing out at sea, where all living creatures wriggle silently about without lungs and quiver their gills, that we really had a warm family feeling for our old distant cousin the whale, who like us had strayed so far out to sea. Instead of the cold, toadlike whale shark, which had not even the sense to stick up its nose for a breath of fresh air, here we had a visit from something which recalled a well-fed jovial hippopotamus in a zoological gardens and which actually breathed—that made a most pleasant impression on me—before it sank into the sea again and disappeared.

Now note your reading time. Record it below and go on to the questions.

YOUR READING TIME: _____MIN. _____SEC. _____W.P.M. COMPREHENSION SCORE: _____%
(WORDS PER MINUTE FROM THE TABLE ON PAGE 475.)

Please do not read these questions until you have read the selection itself against time. Do not refer to the selection as you answer the questions. Choose the *one best* answer to each question and enter the corresponding letter in the proper answer space.

1. Individual plankton are invisible.   (T) True; (F) False

ANSWER _____

2. The net with which the author caught plankton was a funnel of fine silk, almost 300 meshes per square inch.   (T) True; (F) False

ANSWER _____

3. Plankton seems to be more plentiful in colder waters.   (T) True; (F) False

ANSWER _____

4. Not all plankton are edible. (T) True; (F) False

ANSWER _____

5. The definition of plankton that emerges from the article is (a) strongly diluted, strongly smelling, brilliantly colored fish soup; (b) the basic food for every creature that moves in or over the sea; (c) a general name for thousands of species of minute organisms, both vegetable and animal, which drift near the surface of the sea; (d) tiny animals that live in the sea, mostly fish ova, larva, and shrimp, with an occasional jelly fish; (e) whale food.

ANSWER _____

6. Plankton may be important in the future, the author suggests, because (a) it can save the lives of castaways at sea; (b) it provides the basic food for edible fish in commercially important quantities; (c) we may learn to harvest it; (d) its presence or absence provides a "map" of the currents of the ocean; (e) none of the above is correct.

ANSWER _____

7. Which of the following was *not* a characteristic of plankton? (a) Phosphorescence; (b) great variety of forms and colors; (c) a foul smell; (d) uniformity of flavor; (e) delicious flavor once you nerved yourself to try it.

ANSWER _____

8. To the *author*, the most memorable feature of the whale they sighted was (a) its size; (b) its blow-hole, shiny as a polished shoe; (c) its breathing; (d) its jovial, harmless disposition; (e) its sudden, silent disappearance into the sea.

ANSWER _____

9. To the *reader,* the most remarkable feature of the story of the encounter with the whale is (a) the danger the raft was in; (b) the surprising safety of the raft; (c) the contrast between the danger the reader can imagine, and the light, matter of fact way in which the story is told; (d) the way the whale's "personality" is rapidly sketched; (e) the off-hand bravery of the members of the expedition.

ANSWER _____

10. The logical connection between plankton and whales, which explains why the author discusses them together in this passage, is (a) the fact that humans will learn to strain plankton out of the sea for food as whales have always done; (b) the fact that both whales and plankton are marine animals; (c) the contrast between the smallest marine life and the largest; (d) the fact that whales, the largest marine life, depend for food completely on plankton, the smallest; (e) the fact that the whale appeared immediately after the men's first experience with plankton.

ANSWER _____

Reading Speed Exercise: Difficult Level 1

The next exercise is the last in the Reading Skills Survey. The subject of the reading selection is sociology; the source is a highly regarded college-level introductory text. The passage is on a difficult level of content and style.

You are to read the selection against time. If you are taking the exercise in class, follow your instructor's directions for recording accurately the time you require to read it. If you are taking the exercise on your own, follow the Instructions for Timing on page 474.

After reading the selection and recording your time, go on to the ten questions that begin on page 36. There is no time limit for the questions, but it will invalidate the exercise if you refer to this passage while you answer them.

Begin reading and timing here.

"Culture"[9]
from *Society: An Introduction to Sociology* by ELY CHINOY

Culture, as used in sociological inquiry, has a much wider meaning than it is usually given. In conventional usage it refers to the "higher" things in life — painting, music, poetry, sculpture, philosophy; the adjective "cultured" stands close to cultivated or refined. In sociology, culture refers to the totality of what is learned by individuals as members of society; it is a way of life, modes of thinking, acting, and feeling. Edward Tylor's old (1871) but still widely cited definition indicates its scope: "Culture is that complex whole which includes knowledge, belief, art, morals, law, custom, and any other capabilities and habits acquired by man as a member of society." The technique of brushing one's teeth, the Ten Commandments, the rules of baseball or cricket or hopscotch, the procedures for choosing a President or Prime Minister or members of the Supreme Soviet are as much a part of culture as the latest volume of avant-garde poetry, Beethoven's *Ninth Symphony,* or the *Analects* of Confucius.

Regularities in human behavior do not in themselves constitute culture. They occur in large part because men possess culture, because they have common standards of good and bad, right and wrong, appropriate and inappropriate, and possess similar attitudes and share a fund of knowledge about the environment — social, biological, and physical — in which they live. Culture, George Murdock has noted, is to a large extent "ideational": it refers to the standards, beliefs, and attitudes in terms of which people act. Because our culture is so much a part of us we take it for granted, frequently assuming that it is a normal, inevitable, and inherent characteristic of all mankind. (This assumption, known as "ethnocentrism," has important implications for the study of society and culture.) Anthropologists have often reported that when they ask members of small preliterate groups why they act in some particular fashion they receive an answer which amounts to "That's just the way it's done" or "It's customary." "When

Captain Cook asked the chiefs of Tahiti why they ate apart and alone, they simply replied, 'Because it is right.' " Habituated to their own way of life, men frequently can conceive of no other. Among Americans, the expression "It's just human nature" is a characteristic explanation for many actions — competing for fame and power, profit-seeking, marrying for love or for money. Yet this "explanation," which by seemingly explaining everything explains nothing, is itself a manifestation of the ethnocentrism of Americans.

The importance of culture lies in the fact that it provides the knowledge and techniques that enable mankind to survive, both physically and socially, and to master and control, insofar as it is possible, the world around him. Man seems to possess few if any instinctive skills and no instinctive knowledge which might enable him to sustain himself, either singly or in groups. The salmon's return from the sea to spawn and die in fresh water, the annual migration of birds from one part of the world to another, the nest-building of the mud wasp, the complex living patterns of ants and bees are all inherited forms of behavior which seem to appear automatically at the appropriate times. They are not learned from parents or from other members of the species. Man, on the other hand, survives only by virtue of what he learns.

Man is not, however, the only animal that learns to act instead of responding automatically to stimuli. Dogs can be taught a good deal and can learn from experience, as can horses and cats, monkeys and apes, and rats and white mice. But by virtue of his greater brain power and his capacity for language, man can learn more and therefore possesses greater flexibility of action than other animals. He can transmit a great deal of what he learns to others, including his young, and he can in part control the world around him — even to the point of transforming much of it. Man is the only animal to possess culture; indeed, this is one of the crucial distinctions between man and other animals.

Of central importance in the definition of culture is the fact that it is both *learned* and *shared*. Men, we have said, do not inherit their habits and beliefs, their skills and knowledge; they acquire them during the course of their lives. What they learn comes from the groups into which they are born and in which they live. The habits acquired by an infant are likely to be patterned on those of its family and of other persons close at hand. (Not all habits reflect customs or culture, however, for some are merely personal idiosyncrasies.) In an endless number of ways — via explicit instruction, the application of punishment and the offering of rewards, identification with elders and imitation of their behavior — each generation learns from its predecessors. Behavior which is universal, though not learned, or is peculiar to the individual, is not part of culture.

The learned and shared character of culture has led to its occasional identification as the "superorganic" or as man's "social heritage." The former term, created by Herbert Spencer, emphasizes the relative independence of culture from the realm of biology and its distinctive quality as a product of social life. "Social heritage" calls attention to culture's historical character and therefore to the possibilities of change and growth; it suggests the need for analyzing and understanding its temporal dimensions.

Culture is clearly so inclusive a concept that its component elements must be identified, labeled, analyzed, and related to one another. These components can be grouped roughly in three large categories: institutions, the rules or norms which govern behavior; ideas, that is, knowledge and belief of all varieties — theological, philosophical, scientific, technological, historical, sociological, and so on; and the material products or artifacts which men produce and use in the course of their collective lives.

Now note your reading time. Record it below and go on to the questions.

YOUR READING TIME: _____MIN. _____SEC. _____W.P.M. COMPREHENSION SCORE: _____%
(WORDS PER MINUTE FROM THE TABLE ON PAGE 475.)

Please do not read these questions until you have read the selection itself against time. Do not refer to the selection as you answer the questions. Choose the *one best* answer to each question and enter the corresponding letter in the proper answer space.

1. The author's overall purpose in the passage is (a) to contrast man with the other animals, which do not possess culture; (b) to make the reader aware that many things he takes for granted are cultural, not universal; (c) to define the term *culture* as used in sociology; (d) to define the aim of sociology, namely the study of culture; (e) to contrast culture, by implication, with the other key concept of sociology, society (which term forms the title of his book).

ANSWER _____

2. The term *culture*, in sociology, (a) refers to the "higher" aspects of life, those that must be learned and shared, like music, poetry, or philosophy; (b) overlaps, but is much more extensive than, the conventional usage of the term; (c) refers to the totality of what is learned by individuals as members of society; (d) refers to the totality of what is learned by individuals as members of society, and thus contrasts with the conventional usage of the term; (e) refers to the totality of techniques that enable man to survive with few if any instinctive skills.

ANSWER _____

3. The author's extended definition of the term *culture* is a sequence of several parts; these are listed here, but out of the correct order. What is their actual sequence in the article? (a) How the conventional usage of the word *culture* is more limited than the sociologist's; (b) the three major components of culture, broadly classified; (c) how cultures are taken for granted by those who grow up in them, including Americans just as typically as primitive tribesmen; (d) the implications of the fact that culture is shared; (e) the contrast between man's learning of culture and the learned behavior of other animals.

ANSWER _____

4. Which of the following are not, in themselves, culture? (a) The latest poetry or music; (b) the rules of baseball, cricket, or hopscotch; (c) common standards of good and bad, right and wrong, appropriate and inappropriate; (d) knowledge, belief, art, morals, law, custom; (e) regularities of human behavior.

ANSWER _____

5. By *ethnocentrism* sociologists mean (a) the assumption that one's own culture is the only conceivable human way of living and set of attitudes; (b) the knowledge and techniques, learned not instinctive, that enable man to survive; (c) the inability even to perceive one's own culture objectively; (d) the habit of ignoring those parts of culture that are not among the "higher" things of life; (e) each generation learning from its predecessors.

ANSWER _____

6. The author holds that typical American attitudes and actions like marrying for love, competing for power and fame, seeking profit, are (a) explainable as "just human nature"; (b) often explained as "human nature," but that that explanation is nothing but an example of ethnocentrism; (c) comparable to the culture-bound actions of primitive tribes; (d) unintelligible or even shocking to the noncompetitive cultures of many primitive tribes; (e) comparable to the migration of birds or the nest-building of mud wasps.

ANSWER _____

7. Culture is both *learned* and *shared,* the author stresses, which means that (a) it must be based on language; (b) what men learn comes from the groups they are born in and live in; (c) infants' habits are patterned on those of its family; (d) it is inseparable from the particular society in which it is found, whether primitive or modern; (e) it is a by-product of social life.

ANSWER _____

8. The description of culture as "superorganic" was made by (a) Herbert Spencer, and emphasizes that culture is relatively independent from biology; (b) Edward Tylor, and calls attention to culture's historical character; (c) George Murdoch, and points out the all-inclusive character of the concept; (d) Herbert Spencer, and stresses that culture is ideational; (e) George Murdoch, and means that culture binds individuals together like the cells in an organism.

ANSWER _____

9. The author groups the many components of culture into several large categories. Which of the following is *not* one of these categories? (a) Material products and artifacts men make and use in their collective lives; (b) ideas, including knowledge and belief of all varieties; (c) the means of transmitting ideas, knowledge and belief, from formal education and its tools, to rewards and punishments within the family; (d) institutions, the norms which govern behavior; (e) choose this answer if all four of the above *are* among the author's categories.

ANSWER _____

10. In the course of the passage, the author defines briefly a number of key terms. Which of the following does he *not* define? (a) Ethnocentrism; (b) "social heritage"; (c) instinctive behavior; (d) society; (e) institutions.

ANSWER _____

After completing the Reading Skills Survey, check your answers against the Key, page 480. Enter the scores for the two Reading Speed Exercises on your Progress Profile, page vii.

CHAPTER 2

There's More to Reading Than Meets the Eye

Better reading starts with pre-reading. Follow these steps before reading this chapter thoroughly. They will give you the general plan of the chapter, which will help you understand the details better when you go on to read thoroughly. Pre-reading is explained fully in Chapter 3; but now—

Read normally the first three paragraphs of the chapter;

then read *the first sentence only* of each of the remaining paragraphs;

but when you reach the last three paragraphs, read them thoroughly.

Begin pre-reading here.

We can divide reading skills in two: the eyes track across the page, and the mind takes in what the eyes see. The two are of course closely, frogthigl interdependent—as you have just demonstrated by the way your eyes stopped on that nonsense word when your mind stumbled on it. But it happens that speed improvement is largely concerned with how your eyes move, and is relatively simple and well understood. It is more difficult to know (and to improve) how the mind goes about comprehending what the eyes perceive. Of the sixteen chapters in this book, speed gets attention here and in all of Chapter 4, while skimming is discussed in Chapter 6. All the other thirteen chapters discuss aspects of comprehension. That emphasis corresponds truly to the relative importance of improvements in comprehension compared to speed and to the relative difficulty of making those improvements.

How does reading speed relate to comprehension? Most people think that if you increase your reading speed to any extent, you will understand less — or, to put it the way it feels in practice, that in order to boost comprehension, you must slow down. Yet the experience of tens of thousands of students clearly demonstrates that the average reader need fear no loss of comprehension when training raises his comfortable reading speeds considerably, and permanently, above what they have been. For most students, new habits of speed, once they are learned thoroughly, in fact increase comprehension, sometimes remarkably. There are at least four reasons why:

> Speed becomes a tool that you control to get the comprehension you require.

> A faster pace helps keep your attention centered on your reading.

> Part of your gains in speed will come from improved *rhythm* in reading. Rhythm helps comprehension as well.

> Most important, to develop higher speeds you must learn to read *by phrases* rather than word by word.

Pre-reading: Begin reading only the first sentence of each paragraph.

Look back now to your scores on the Reading Skills Survey at the end of the last chapter: how much difference was there between your reading speeds on the last two exercises, the one at the difficult level, the other at average level? It is a striking fact that most readers vary their speed little, often not at all, between easy and difficult prose. Thus, untrained readers — even those who insist, in theory, that they can improve comprehension by slowing down — do not, in practice, use changes of speed to help their understanding. In contrast, the speeds of the skilled reader are not only higher, but show great sensitivity to variations in difficulty, so that he may read some materials even twice as fast as others. When you gain this kind of flexibility, then you will be using speed as a major technique for comprehension.

Second, when you read with the conscious intention of pushing your speed to your top comfortable level, you will find that this effort necessarily brings with it closer attention to the material. Like the man who strolls along a rough country lane, the average reader leaves plenty of opportunity for his mind to wander; when his purpose (as always with practical prose) is to get to the end of the road as quickly as possible without stumbling, he finds that going faster also greatly intensifies his concentration on the details of the terrain.

Third, an important part of your gains in reading speed through use of this book will come from smoothing out the rhythm of the movements of your eyes across the lines of print. We will explain in a moment precisely how this works. Improved rhythm makes reading not only faster but more accurate, for reading is in this way similar to such other physical activities as swimming, skiing or tennis. Perhaps the closest parallel is with typing, where smooth rhythm is essential for the achievement of speed with accuracy.

Control of reading speeds for comprehension, better concentration, smoother rhythm—all these are ways in which speed training can help you understand what you read. But speed training will help your comprehension most of all because fast reading requires you *to read by phrases* rather than word by word.

Here is what reading by phrases means. Do you remember how you learned to read as a child? Some children even teach themselves, perhaps by learning to recognize signs in the street or the words in favorite storybooks. As if following the example of such children, much elementary reading instruction for many years has begun directly with recognition of whole words. Or, in first grade you may have been taught to read letter by letter, that is, first by learning the sounds of the alphabet, and then how to puzzle out words by combining the sounds. There has recently been new interest in alphabetic methods for teaching children to read; to make the first steps easier, speſhul alfabets ɑr ɛɛvn bɛɛiŋ tried, liek ſhis wun kauld ſhe iniſhial tɛɛ(hiŋ alfabet. But whichever way you first learned, today you would find comprehension extremely difficult if you had to read letter by letter. You can see this if you take a piece of heavy paper with a small notch in one edge, and slide the notch along the line of print so that only one or two letters are exposed at a time, like this:

Letter by letter

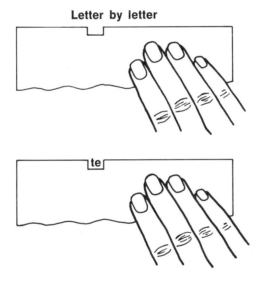

Obviously, comprehension as well as speed improves when you proceed not letter by letter but by recognizing whole words at a time. Words are larger "units" of reading. We can even take them in by overall shape without being sure of all the letters:

comprehension and speed

comprehension and speed

high phrase visibility

high phrase visibility

But the eye can take in more than one word at a time. At least by late high school or college, the reader is usually ready to take the second and final step in this process of enlarging his units of reading: he is ready to read, not just word by word, but by phrases.

Phrase reading is by far the most important ability that distinguishes fast readers from average. Just as words are easier to understand than individual letters, so phrase reading, once mastered, offers dividends of comprehension as well as speed. Some gifted individuals develop into phrase readers on their own. Alexander Hamilton, for example, apparently equalled the highest reading speeds that have been achieved by modern training methods. But most of us require specialized instruction to take this step.

What Kind of Speed Improvement Can You Make?

Once again, recall your speed scores on the Reading Skills Survey. It is highly probable that you read both the average and the difficult speed exercises at a rate of from 200 to 250 words per minute. This range is not merely average, it is all but universal. You can talk nearly that fast.

Furthermore, as noted earlier, many a beginning student will find that the difference between his speed scores on the average and the difficult material is very slight, less than ten or fifteen words a minute. This means, for example, that if you read the selection from *Kon-Tiki* at 225 words per minute, you may well have read the sociology selection, "Culture," somewhere between 210 and 235 w.p.m.

When the reader whose usual speed falls between 200 and 250 w.p.m. tries all at once to read much faster than that, say in the 300 to 350 w.p.m. range, naturally he is uncomfortable, uncertain about his understanding; he may indeed do badly on questions about the material. Guided practice makes the difference: after three months of training, that same student may be reading difficult prose at something like 325 w.p.m.; he will score as well as ever on questions about the material, and he will feel confident at that pace. Further, his comfortable speed on easier prose will probably be over 400 w.p.m.

Those are cautious, sensible forecasts for speed improvement. You may have read claims for speeds many times higher. A few readers are indeed able to read considerably faster. Reading speeds of 600 w.p.m. on difficult, and 800 to 1,000 w.p.m on average material are not rare among highly trained readers. Perhaps one student in a thousand is able to reach consistent speeds of 1,300 w.p.m. or higher, with good comprehension, on practical prose of average difficulty. Against these readers, however, must be balanced the occasional student whose intelligence, general abilities, and reading skills all test out well at the beginning of training, but who for one of several reasons is unable to improve his speed significantly.

Thus, obviously, no one could reasonably *guarantee* that you will double your present reading speed. But if your reading rate is average — as defined above — or higher, with fairly good comprehension, you can reasonably expect to increase your reading speeds for practical prose by 20 to 50 per cent, and perhaps more, with marked gains in comprehension as well — *if you apply fully the techniques of this book.* You will also learn to adjust your reading speed to the difficulty of what you read, and you will find the gap between reading rates for easy and difficult selections widening until it approaches 80 to 120 w.p.m.

How Speed Improvement Works

When you read a line of print, you have the feeling that your eyes move smoothly across the page. Actually, however, your eyes make a series of stops on the line. You see the words *only when your eyes are not moving.*

This essential fact about eye movements in reading is the basis for a great deal of the work you will be doing to increase your speeds. You can see for yourself how your eyes move by performing a simple experiment.

Demonstration: Eye Movements in Reading

Step 1. Punch a hole with a pencil, through the center of this page, at the black dot.

Step 2. Have a friend read this page as he normally would, while you hold the book up and watch his eye movements from the other side of the page, through the hole. You will need to put your own eye close to the hole and watch very carefully, because the eye movements are small and quick.

Step 3. What kinds of eye movements do you see? With a little practice you will be able to distinguish the *jig-jig-jig* of the eye movements from the reader's left to right (but of course from your right to left as you face him), and the longer *flick* back to the beginning of the next line. You may notice an occasional hesitation or rereading of a word or two. You may even be able to count the number of stops per line, if you remember to include the first stop, at the end of the *flick* to the first word on the line. However, the movements are so fast that it is hard to analyze their meaning without the help of a special eye-movement camera, as described in Chapter 4.

You spend approximately 90 per cent of your reading time looking at a word or a group of words, and the other 10 per cent jumping from one word to another. Taking in whole phrases as units, the highly trained reader makes few stops on the line, and equally important, he makes them smoothly — as the numbers show in the following lines:

> Hate spewed across the galaxy in a high crusade. Metal ships
>   1   2   3   4   5
> leaped from world to world and hurtled across space . . .
>   6   7   8   9

The unskilled reader, on the other hand, stops as often as once on each word. Furthermore, he may often reread, jumping back several words to do so. In extreme cases he may have trouble finding his way from the *end* of one line to the *beginning* of the next, stopping twice or more on the way back rather than making a quick and accurate return leap. The eye-movement pattern of such a not-very-good reader might look like this:

> Hate spewed across the galaxy in a high crusade. Metal ships
> 1   2   3   4 5 8 6 9 7   10   11 12
> leaped from world to world and hurtled across space to farther
> 13   14   15 16 17 18   20   19   21 22 23
> and farther stars. Planets surrendered their ores to sky-reaching
> 25 24   26   27   28   29   30   31 32 33   34
> cities, built around fortress temples and supported by vast net-
> 35   36   37   38   39   40   41 44 42 43 45
> works of technology.
> 47 46   48

Obviously the first reader of space opera is faster than the second. Just as important, you can see why the *second reader* may well be uncertain about the meaning of what he has read.

Can Better Comprehension Help Speed?

As the average reader slogs along the line of print, not only is his speed inflexible, his methods of comprehension are unresourceful as well. The skilled reader attacks factual prose with many methods for extracting what he needs. All these many methods, however, are related to two concepts that are as essential to better comprehension as phrase reading is to greater speed. These two keys are *the reader's purpose* and *the writer's organization.*

Many purposes are possible in reading. At one time you may be chasing a specific fact: when you use any standard reference book it is frequently for a purpose as narrow as this, but many kinds of reading matter could be searched for a similar reason. It is also possible to read, not for any specific information, but to see whether the author says anything that is new to you: you don't know what it is until you find it. Technical, scientific, and business publications are often read for this reason. At the other extreme your purpose may be, as is often true with textbooks, to soak up every detail the author offers.

Again, you may be reading to determine an author's conclusions and opinions, or you may be more interested in his method of arriving at them. In science, for example, your interest in reading *Molecular Biology of the Gene,* by James D. Watson, would probably be first of all for its overall presentation of the basics of his science; the author is a Nobel prize winner and a world authority on his subject, but the book itself, you would quickly discover, is intended as a textbook for students beginning that advanced subject. On the other hand, if you saw a research report by Watson in the current issue of a leading professional journal like *Science*, your initial interest would doubtless be in the conclusions — the new discoveries — he was announcing; after seeing what they were, your interest would naturally turn to the methods he used to make the discoveries. But you would read a classic of science like William Harvey's *On the Motion of the Heart and Blood*, not to discover his conclusions (which are stated succinctly in any biology text), but rather to follow the details of his method, which after three hundred years are still fascinating and instructive.

Without analyzing further at this point the many purposes for which you may read practical prose, we can understand some reasons why you will read better, and often be free to read faster, if you always begin with a clear notion of your purpose. Awareness of your purpose tells you when you can skim and what you can safely skip. A conscious purpose is a wonderful tonic for your concentration. It enables you to sort out what is important for you to remember, and then helps you to remember: as one student put it when she first discovered this "sorting" effect, "It's as if the points I'm after were printed in boldface type." Purpose lets you know when to take notes, and when you must reread. In short, a clear purpose in reading controls your choice of most of the other techniques of reading.

Perhaps most important, a clear purpose lets you know when you have finished reading. You would be surprised how many untrained readers go far more slowly than they need, waste time on material that cannot help them, reread more often than necessary, and in general seem reluctant to decide they have finished a job of reading, all because they have no way to tell when they have mastered the material adequately. A clear purpose acts as a yardstick by which you can measure the adequacy of your comprehension. Thus it attacks one of the most common causes of confusion and discomfort in reading, and one of the most common obstacles to speed.

The second master key to comprehension is the writer's organization. From sentence to sentence, paragraph to paragraph, and chapter to chapter, a writer organizes his material according to some plan of development. The organization may not be easy to grasp. For example, some tables of contents are uninformative to the point of rudeness; even a book whose overall plan is supremely clear and logical may turn out to be dense and difficult to follow from one paragraph to the next. But if you can discover in detail how the work is put together, you will find it easier and faster to take apart. By understanding the organization, through pre-reading and other methods, you will command a framework that puts the details, as they develop, in relation to each other. As you read you will know more clearly where you have been and where the author is taking you.

Pre-reading: Now read the last paragraphs thoroughly.

When you have learned to use your purpose and the writer's organization as tools for comprehension, you will discover that they are also tools for speed. Indeed, greater reading efficiency is possible because most methods for developing better understanding also allow you to use higher reading speeds.

Up to a point the reverse is true: many techniques for greater speed will help you with comprehension as well.

We have analyzed the many differences between the average and the skilled reader, and have mapped out the directions your improvement can take. One contrast sums up these many differences and states the goal you are working toward. Most readers read passively: they treat each work like every other and bob along from one sentence to the next, three-quarters submerged in the stream of the author's words. But the skilled reader is in tension with his book: he reads actively and varies his methods to suit his book and his purpose in reading it.

EXERCISES FOR CHAPTER 2

Reading Journal

Eye Span

Phrase Flashing

Summarizing

"Misunderstandings About Children's Reading," by Leonard Bloomfield, from the preface to *Let's Read: A Linguistic Approach*

Phrase Sense

Eye Movements in Reading

Reading Speed Exercise: Average Level 2

"The Survival of Slavery," from *The National Experience: A History of the United States*, by John M. Blum, *et al.*

Reading Journal

To carry new reading techniques over into your day-to-day work is, of course, essential: without that any gains are meaningless. Yet some students find just this change of habits to be the most difficult part of reading improvement. To make the transition easier, keep a **Reading Journal:** in a separate notebook, record the reading you do and the problems of speed and comprehension you encounter.

To start that Reading Journal, please list in the notebook:

1. Today's date, and the heading **current reading.**
2. Everything you have read in the past forty-eight hours, including title,

author, type of material or subject, approximate length, and time you spent on it. For example:

Current Reading

Thursday- <u>Los Angeles Times</u>, news section, browsed ten minutes, especially article on student demonstrations breaking up political speech by governor. Two columns. Sports page, five minutes; theater review of new play by Ionesco, five minutes.

Chapter 2 of <u>Techniques of Reading</u>, 23 pages, fifteen minutes, plus exercise materials.

<u>Newsweek</u>, ten minutes, mostly national political news, especially current California election and student protests.

<u>Moby Dick</u>, Herman Melville, 65 pages in one hour, ten minutes, rereading for American Lit. class tomorrow.

3. Add to each item on that list in your Reading Journal your exact purpose in reading it. In some cases you will have noted this already, as the *Moby Dick* item in the sample suggests.

Eye Span

The following material is designed to extend the width of phrase you are able to take in at a single glance. Use a 3 x 5 card to cover the column you are working with. Move the card rapidly down the column, one line at a time. As each line is exposed, read it, looking at it only once and approximately at the center as shown by the dots between the words. Try to take in the entire width of the line. At first you may have to focus for several seconds on each set of dots before you are able to perceive all the words on the line.

In the	....	machinery	capital.	....	This
and	....	equipment	has	....	caused
industries,	....	firms	no	....	large
making	....	capital	dismissals	....	of
goods	....	or	labor.	....	Firms
repairing	....	capital	making	....	goods
equipment	....	are	for	....	the
still	....	short	consumer	....	are
of	....	working	continuing	....	to

acquire	....	larger	be	....	assured
liquid	....	assets	of	....	more
and	....	are	speedy	....	payment.
placing	....	orders	The	....	iron
for	....	both	and	....	steel
passenger	....	cars	firms	....	have
and	....	trucks	had the	....	worst
in	....	great	capital	....	shortage
numbers.	....	Less	but	....	even
interest	....	is	here	....	levels
reported	....	in	of	....	production
exports.	....	Firms	are	....	being
prefer	....	to	maintained.	....	Bridge
concentrate	....	on	building	....	and
internal	....	sales	other	....	construction
for	....	which	work	....	is
they	....	can	proceeding	....	well.

Phrase Flashing

This exercise is designed to help you develop the quick and accurate perception of *phrases as units* upon which efficient reading speeds depend. The materials for this practice have been grouped together at the back of the book so that you can return to them repeatedly as you work through the chapters, progressing to longer and longer phrases. Please turn to page 476 and follow the instructions.

Summarizing

The passage below is excerpted from an unusual and effective book for teaching children to read. The bulk of the book is made up of a system of carefully graduated reading materials for the children; in the preface for teachers and parents, Leonard Bloomfield, one of the creators of the system, explains why it should work better than many methods of primary reading instruction now widely used. For this exercise, your purpose in reading the article is to summarize each paragraph (or group of short paragraphs) and then the entire passage. The questions follow the passage.

This is not a timed exercise. You may refer to the article as you answer the questions.

"Misunderstandings About Children's Reading"[1]

by LEONARD BLOOMFIELD

from the preface to *Let's Read: A Linguistic Approach*

A

The child does his first reading out loud. Then, under the instruction or example of his elders, he economizes by reading in a whisper. Soon he reduces this to scarcely audible movements of speech; later these become entirely inaudible. Many adults who are not very literate move their lips while reading. The fully literate person has succeeded in reducing these speech movements to the point where they are not even visible. That is, he has developed a system of internal substitute movements which serve him, for private purposes, such as thinking and silent reading, in place of audible speech sounds. When the literate adult reads very carefully — as when he is reading poetry or difficult scientific matter or a text in a foreign language — he actually goes through this process of internal speech; his conventional way of reporting this is that he internally pronounces or "hears himself say" the words of the text. The highly-skilled reader has trained himself beyond this: he can actually shunt out some of the internal speech movements and respond to a text without seeing every word. If you ask him to read aloud, he will often replace words or phrases of the printed text by equivalent ones; he has seized only the high spots of the printed text. Now this highly skilled adult has forgotten the earlier stages of his own development and wants the child to jump directly from an illiterate state to that of an overtrained reader.

B

The marks in a piece of American Indian picture writing represent *things*, or, if you prefer, *ideas*. The characters in a piece of Chinese writing do not represent things (or ideas) but words. The letters in a piece of English writing do not represent things, or even words, but *sounds*. The task of the reader is to get the *sounds* from the written or printed page. When he has done this, he must still, of course, perform a second task: he must understand the meaning of these sounds. This second task, however, is not peculiar to reading, but concerns all use of language; when we are not reading, but hearing spoken words, we have the same task of appreciating the content of what is said. The ideational methods, in short, show us the age-old confusion between the use of writing and the ordinary processes of speech.

C

It is true, of course, that many children in the upper grades — and even, for that matter, many postgraduate students in the university — fail to seize the content of what they read. It was this unfortunate situation which led to the invention of ideational methods in reading instruction. This, however, meant confusing two entirely different things. A person who can read aloud a text that is before his eyes, but cannot reproduce the content or otherwise show his grasp of it, lacks something other than reading power, and needs to be taught the proper response to language, be it presented in writing or in actual speech. The marks on the page offer only sounds of speech and words, not things or ideas.

D

Even the most elementary understanding of systems of writing suffices to show the fallacy of "ideational" reading. The kind of writing which can be read ideationally is picture writing. There the visible marks directly represent the content and do not presuppose any particular wording. In word writing and in alphabetic writing, the visible marks are tokens for speech forms and not for "ideas." The visible word marks tell the Chinese reader to speak (out loud or internally) such and such words of his language. The visible letters of alphabetic writing tell us to speak (out loud or internally) such and such phonemes of our language. If the Chinese reader or we choose to skip the less important of these directions and to notice only the high spots, we can go all the faster, but we do not accurately reproduce the author's words; as soon as the exact wording is important, as in a poem or a difficult exposition, we do in fact accurately follow the visible signals to speech. In short, the black marks on paper which represent an English word, say,

h o r s e

do not represent the shape or smell or any other characteristics of a horse, or even the "idea" (whatever that may be) of a horse; they merely direct us to utter the speech sounds which make up the English word *horse*. These speech sounds, in turn, are connected for us as a kind of signal, with the animal, and it is only through these speech sounds that the black marks

h o r s e

on the paper have any connection with the animal, or, if you will, with the "idea" of the animal. The adult's instantaneous step from the black marks to the "idea" is the result of long training.

E

The circumstances which lead the more intelligent but linguistically untrained schoolman to seek an "ideational" method is the distressing fact that many older students and adults are unable to get the content from a printed text. We have all heard of the devastating results of experiments in which pupils or adults are given a paragraph to read, and then are asked to reproduce the content; a large proportion of the persons tested are unable to make anything like a correct statement of what the author was trying to tell them. The schoolman concludes that these people were not properly taught to read, and therefore seeks to make elementary reading instruction bear more directly on the content. In this, however, he confuses two entirely different things—the ability to respond to visible marks by uttering speech sounds and the ability to respond correctly to speech. The child who is laboring to find out what words or phrases he must utter when he sees certain printed marks cannot be expected at the same time to respond correctly to the meaning of these words or phrases. If he has spelled out the words *Bill hit John,* we need not be surprised that we can trap him with the question "Whom did John hit?" His problem is to say the correct word or phrase when he sees the black marks, and, indeed, this is enough of a problem; it takes a sophisticated but linguistically untrained adult to underestimate its difficulty. The other problem, which the schoolman confuses with ours, is the problem of responding correctly to speech, and it concerns actual speech just as much as reading. When one tests graduate university students by making a simple oral statement and asking them to reproduce it, the result is just as discouraging as that of similar reading tests. This is a problem which our schools have to face, and the beginning will doubtless have to be made in the earliest grades, but the one place where this problem most certainly cannot be solved is in the elementary instruction in reading, where the child has all he can do to pass from the visual symbols to the spoken words.

F

In fact, an understanding of the latter difficulty will lead us to see our problem in its simplest terms. Aside from their silliness, the stories in a child's first reader are of little use, because the child is too busy with the mechanics of reading to get anything of the content. He gets the content when the teacher reads the story out loud, and later on, when he has mastered all the words in the story, he can get it for himself, but during the actual process of learning to read the words he does not concern himself with the content. This does not mean that we must forego the use of sentences and connected stories, but it does mean that these are not essential to the first steps. We need not fear to use disconnected words and even senseless syllables, and, above all, we must not, for the sake of a story, upset the child's scarcely-formed habits by presenting him with irregularities of spelling for which he is not prepared. Purely formal exercises that would be irksome to an adult are not irksome to a child, provided he sees himself gaining in power. In the early stages of reading, a nonsense syllable like *nin* will give pleasure to the child who finds himself able to read it, whereas at the same stage a word of irregular spelling, such as *gem*, even if introduced in a story, will discourage the child and delay the sureness of his reactions.

For each of the paragraphs in the article, pick out below the best summary. Put the number of this summary in the answer space for that paragraph. The last question asks you to choose a summary statement for the *entire* passage. You may refer to the article as you answer the questions.

A
1. Children read more slowly than adults because they say the words to themselves, but the highly trained adult reader may not remember that.
2. Highly trained readers got that way by a long process of internalizing their spoken response to written words, sometimes eliminating the "hearing" so successfully that they think children should learn to read that way directly.
3. Children will be likely to have trouble learning to read when adults forget

that reading begins out loud, then as whispers, then unconscious internal speech.

ANSWER _____

B

1. Writing systems may refer to *things,* to *words,* or to *sounds,* three possibilities that have often been confused, as by those who advocate "ideational" reading.
2. Reading, like any other form of communication, involves grasping the meaning of the words or sounds communicated.
3. In English, contrasted to some other systems of writing, what's on the page represents sounds, which the reader must get right before understanding can follow.

ANSWER _____

C

1. "Ideational" methods of teaching reading were invented because so many children, and even adults, don't grasp what they read, and therefore need to be taught the proper response to language.
2. True, many people fail to understand what they read, but this won't be corrected by confusing the marks on the paper with ideas when they represent only sounds.
3. Misunderstanding the meanings of language is only made worse by misunderstanding the differences between things, ideas, sounds and words.

ANSWER _____

D

1. Alphabetic writing, as in English, uses the marks on paper as signals to which the sounds of speech are the response; it takes long training to be able to go at once from the word on paper to the idea.
2. If the child can make the correct verbal response when he sees the letters on paper, for example *horse*, he knows how to read; to get from there to being able to "understand" the "idea" of *horse* instantly from the letters on paper is merely a matter of sufficiently long time.
3. Though readers of Chinese may have the advantage of dealing with whole words, they too deal with marks on paper as primary cues to speech, which proves that "ideational" reading, though the goal of adults, is in English an impossible way to start children.

ANSWER _____

E

1. The other problem, failure to get the content of what is read, is also a serious problem that will need to be faced in the earliest years of school, but not by mixing it into the first problem, difficult enough anyway, of first teaching children to read.
2. Whether words are read or spoken, not only children but also adults may fail to understand them, which proves that the problem of comprehension will only get worse if made part of elementary reading instruction.
3. "Ideational" methods of teaching reading would be justified as a solution to the comprehension problem, if only they were possible.

ANSWER _____

F

1. In fact, children do not need or want meaning in their first steps to learn to read.
2. In fact, reproducing speech sounds is such a challenge to the child first learning to read that meaning may be irrelevant.
3. In fact, reproducing speech sounds is so totally absorbing a problem for the child, and can be so rewarding, that content is not essential.

ANSWER _____

Now choose the best summary for the entire article.

1. The jump from letters on paper to meaning is one that literate adults make so easily that they forget that the child finds it difficult; hence the vogue for "ideational" reading.
2. Though meaning is the object of reading, it is not the first object in teaching a child to read, and should not be allowed to get in the way of his learning to translate the marks on the page into speech sounds.
3. For Western languages, the alphabet is, despite the fallacious theories of "ideational" reading, still the basis on which children must learn to read; and the alphabet is concerned with reproducing speech sounds, from which the child will later learn — or fail to learn — to extract "meaning."

ANSWER _____

Phrase Sense

The purpose of this next exercise is to increase your "phrase sense" — your understanding of whether or not a group of several words within a sentence hangs together as a meaningful unit. Read through the passage, dividing each sentence into phrases by circling them or by marking a "slash" (/) between them. The first several phrases have already been marked correctly, to show you what you are to do.

When the Americans / arrived in Berlin / in 1945, / they found / that the police / and fire departments / then in existence / had been recruited / by the Soviets / almost from nothing. In their recruitment the Russians had placed a hard core of Communists in most of the strategic positions, as well as a considerable number in the rank and file.

The first two years were devoted to sorting out the mass of raw recruits and training them in their professions. This was a prodigious task. The uniformed police, for example, numbered 11,000 men; in the first two years there was a turnover of 10,000 in this group alone.

Of these 10,000 policemen approximately 25% were men who had entered the police force because they needed employment quickly, and who left because they found other jobs more to their liking. Another 25% were discharged, either for misdemeanors committed while policemen or because their previous criminal records were discovered. The remaining 50% were discharged because of former participation in Nazi activities.

Buildings were found or repaired to house police stations; telephone and teletype systems were installed; the first true uniforms replaced the original pieced-together clothing; some means of transportation were obtained, though not enough.

Training was started with short lectures at the stations where the men reported for duty. This later developed into two schools, one in the Soviet sector and one in the British Sector.

Eye Movements in Reading

The exercise that follows has been set up to help you improve the mechanics of moving your eyes across the page. It works primarily to reduce the number of stops your eyes make on each line of print, and to smooth out the rhythm of those stops. At the same time, if your reading habits include any uncertainty in eye movement returning from the end of one line to the beginning of the next, this exercise will help you eliminate that uncertainty.

"Read" these pages by glancing very briefly at each bar, moving from left to right along each line. Work very quickly, or you will, without being aware of it, make more stops on the line than there are bars. Be especially careful to make a fast return sweep from the end of one line to the beginning of the next.

You will not feel that the exercise is comfortable until you have tried it on several occasions. However, one "reading" is enough on any occasion.

Practice with this material just before reading each speed exercise in this manual.

Of course, in normal reading the stops you make on the line will be determined partly by the phrases read, which may not be spaced as evenly as the bars here.

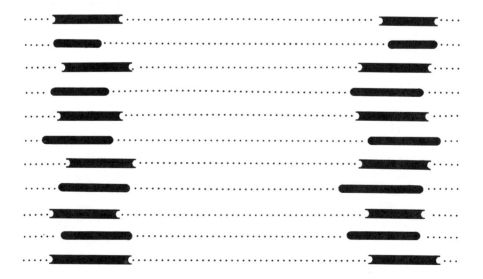

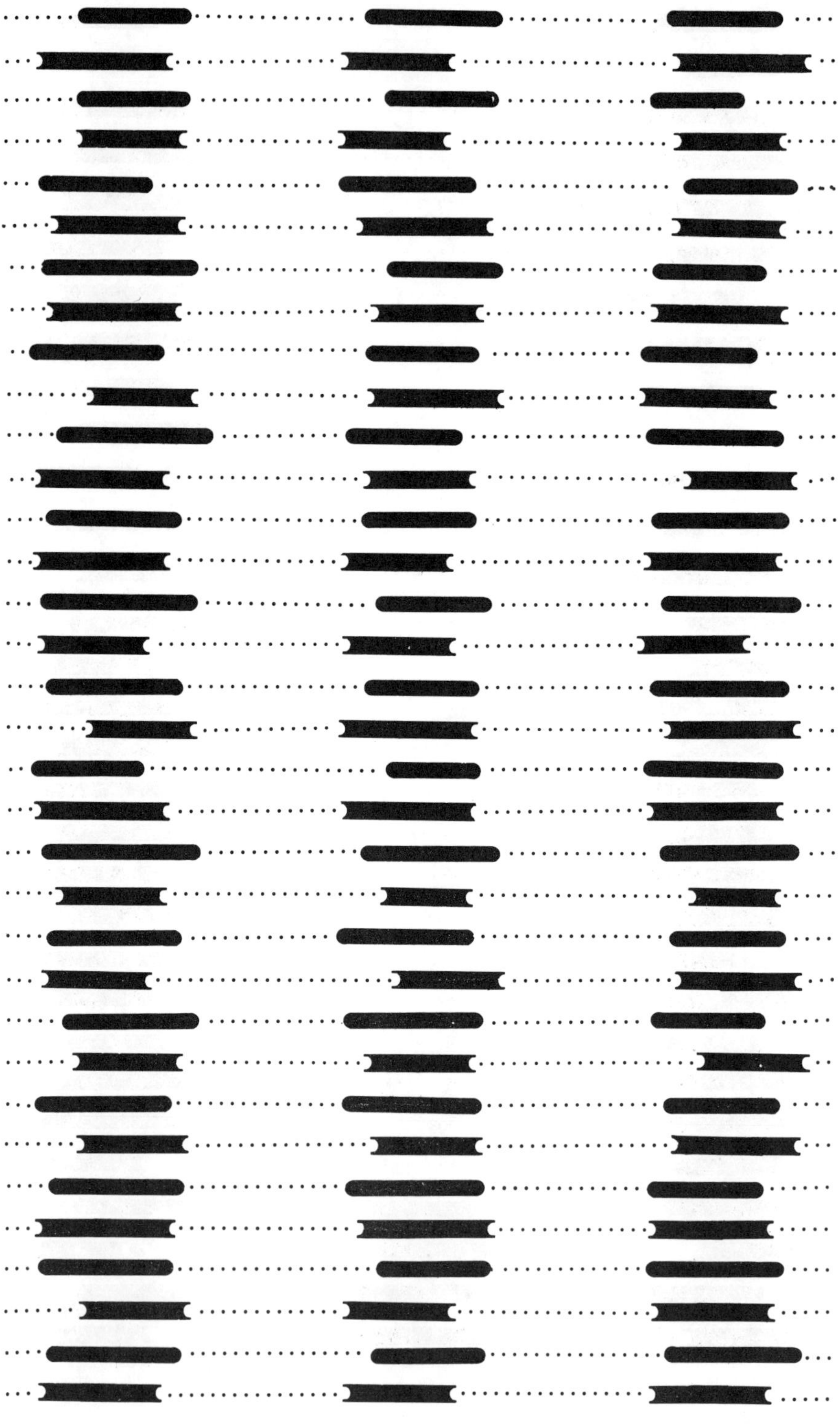

Reading Speed Exercise: Average Level 2

Slavery: nobody would seriously maintain that it was a desirable institution, yet it persisted in the American South until destroyed by the Civil War. Why did it survive? At what cost? These questions are examined in the next article, which is taken from a standard college-level textbook in American history. The difficulty of content and style is about average. That is, skilled readers read it at the same speed they use for material of a factual nature, popularly written.

You are to read the selection against time. Follow your instructor's directions in class, or the Instructions for Timing on page 474.

Before reading the selection, practice with the Eye Movements in Reading exercise on the preceding pages.

Do not pre-read the selection; the timed reading exercises are designed to measure improvements in speed alone.

After reading the selection and recording your time, go on to the ten true-false and multiple-choice questions beginning on page 60. There is no time limit for the questions, but it will invalidate the exercise if you refer to this passage while you answer them.

Begin reading and timing here.

"The Survival of Slavery"[2]
from *The National Experience: A History of the United States*
by JOHN M. BLUM, *et al.*

. . . What was it that made the Old South unique? Not physical isolation, for it lacked natural frontiers separating it from the rest of the country; nor geographic and climatic uniformity, for it had great diversity of soils, topography, mean temperatures, growing seasons, and average rainfalls. Not a difference in population origins, for the South, like the North, was originally settled by middle- and lower-class people; nor contrasts in religion or political philosophy, for here, too, the similarities outweighed the differences. Not even the economies of North and South were altogether unlike, for, although there were important differences, the majority of the white people of both sections were independent yeomen farmers who worked their own lands. In contrast to the Western farmers, however, few Southern farmers benefited from improved transportation and became part of the national market economy. Wealth was less evenly distributed in the South than in the West; less money was invested in education; and the rate of illiteracy was higher. Fewer towns and less local industry developed, with the result that much of the income of the cotton-planters flowed out of the region to pay for goods and services provided by the West and Northeast. In short, the Old South remained more rural and economically less diversified than the North, and a larger proportion of its small farmers lived a life of pioneer self-sufficiency.

But all these differences between North and South were of secondary importance. By far the most significant difference was the presence and survival in the South of Negro slavery, which Southerners themselves called their "peculiar institution." More than anything else, it was slavery, with all its ramifications, that eventually gave the Old South its identity and Southerners their feeling of separateness from the rest of the Union.

In the eighteenth century, of course, Southern slavery had not been a peculiar institution, for it existed in the Northern colonies and throughout the Western Hemisphere. During or soon after the Revolution, however, the Northern states abolished it; and in the first half of the nineteenth century slaves gained their freedom in most of Central and South America. Many Southerners of Washington's and Jefferson's generation also were critical of slavery; as late as the 1820's there were numerous emancipation societies in the Upper South that carried on a discreet but steady agitation. In Virginia, in the late eighteenth and early nineteenth centuries, a prolonged agricultural depression resulting from low tobacco prices and soil exhaustion led some to believe, or hope, that slavery would soon die. In August 1831, Southampton County, Virginia, was the scene of the South's bloodiest slave insurrection, led by a bondsman named Nat Turner, in which sixty whites and scores of Negroes (including Turner) were killed. This event precipitated an earnest debate in the Virginia legislature the following January during which various legislators denounced slavery as a social canker, an economic blight, and a moral evil, and demanded a program of gradual emancipation. But the Virginia emancipationists, like those in other Southern states, were defeated; and soon after 1832 Southern critics were either silenced or driven into exile.

Southern slavery, then, did not die of natural causes; it did not even decline. Instead, with the rise of the Cotton Kingdom and the eventual improvement of agriculture in the seaboard states, it flourished and seemed to have the vitality to survive indefinitely. Since the federal Constitution recognized slavery as a local institution within the jurisdiction of individual states, Southerners saw nothing to prevent them from introducing it into the Southwest. Some moved there with their Negroes, while others stayed behind and operated new plantations as absentee owners. Still others took advantage of high slave prices resulting from the labor shortage in the Southwest and sold a portion of their Negroes to professional traders who took them to the busy markets in New Orleans and Natchez. There at the slave auctions the self-made men of the Cotton Kingdom, some of whom had started with no slaves at all, purchased "prime field hands" to work their growing estates.

Negro slaves thus became an important element in the migration to the Southwest and played a major role in clearing the land for cultivation. By 1840 almost half the population of Alabama and Louisiana and more than half the population of Mississippi (by then the leading cotton-producing state) consisted of Negro slaves. Yet at all times nearly three-fourths of the white families in the South as a whole held no slaves and depended on their own labor alone. Moreover, the great majority of slaveholders owned just a few slaves; as late as 1860 only ten thousand Southern families belonged to the planter aristocracy operating large estates with slave gangs numbering more than fifty.

Why did Southern slavery survive far into the nineteenth century? Not because Negroes were natural slaves; nor because white labor could not adjust to the Southern climate and successfully cultivate the Southern crops; nor because the Negroes' health was not adversely affected by living in the malarial swamps, where the sugar and rice plantations and many of the cotton plantations were located. The reasons the South clung so tenaciously to slavery are to be found in the fears, ambitions, and aspirations of Southern white men.

By the nineteenth century the South's peculiar institution was two hundred years old, and to abolish it would have brought painful changes in long-established habits and attitudes. Those who would destroy slavery, warned a Georgian, "would have to wade knee-deep in blood"; indeed, slavery is "so intimately . . . mingled with our social conditions that it would be impossible to eradicate it." To some, who thought that Negroes were naturally shiftless and immoral, slavery was a system of controlling an inferior race. To nonslaveholders slavery symbolized their link with the privileged caste of white men and the Negroes' social and legal subordination. "Now suppose they was free," explained a poor Southern farmer to a Northern visitor, "you see they'd all think themselves as good as we." To the master class the possession of slaves brought great prestige, for in the South the ownership of a plantation worked by slave labor was the sign of success and high social position.

But, above all, slavery survived because it was a viable and profitable labor system and because it represented an enormous investment of Southern capital. Slavery, of course, did not make every master a rich man, nor did every master strive to wring the last ounce of profit from his toiling bondsmen. Nevertheless, most slaveholders earned good returns on their investments—and this accounts for the generally heavy demand for slaves and for their high price in the market. The system, moreover, was highly adaptable. Slaves were employed, not only in agriculture and as domestics, but as skilled artisans, as laborers in construction gangs, and as workers in iron foundries, textile mills, and tobacco factories. In short, the master class had no compelling economic reason for wanting to abolish slavery.

White men paid a high price for slavery: artisans and yeoman farmers suffered from the competition of cheap slave labor; most white Southerners were more or less distressed by the obvious paradox of slavery in a republic whose moral commitment was to individual freedom and natural rights; and all were bedeviled by a nagging fear of slave rebellions, a fear that is endemic wherever bondage exists. But the Negro paid an even higher price. Apart from his exposure to cruelty and his meager rewards, slavery afforded him little opportunity for cultural advancement. It gave him some vocational training, indoctrinated him with a crude form of

Christianity that provided more emotional release than spiritual nourishment, and exposed him to some of the external forms of white civilization. But slavery also made the Negro family unstable, encouraged sexual promiscuity, and exposed Negro women to the lust of white men. It robbed the Negro of his manhood, encouraged infantile and irresponsible behavior, and put a premium on docility. In short, slavery deprived a whole race of the opportunity to develop its potentialities and of the freedom that white men treasured so highly.

Now note your reading time. Record it below and go on to the questions.

YOUR READING TIME: _____MIN. _____SEC. _____W.P.M. COMPREHENSION SCORE: _____%
(WORDS PER MINUTE FROM THE TABLE ON PAGE 475.)

Please do not read these questions until you have read the selection itself against time. Do not refer to the selection as you answer the questions. Choose the *one best* answer to each question and enter the corresponding letter in the proper answer space.

1. Even apart from the question of slavery, the economic and social differences between the Old South and the North and pioneer West far outweighed the similarities.   (T) True; (F) False

   ANSWER _____

2. Slavery was the South's "peculiar institution," even in the eyes of Southerners, since the eighteenth century.   (T) True; (F) False

   ANSWER _____

3. The South had many citizens opposed to slavery, but these were silenced or driven away by the middle of the nineteenth century.   (T) True; (F) False

   ANSWER _____

4. The principal reason for the survival of slavery well into the nineteenth century was that the system was economically successful.

   ANSWER _____

5. The authors mention several differences setting off the Old South from the rest of the United States at that time. Which of the following is *not* one of those differences? (a) A degree of physical isolation behind natural frontiers; (b) wealth distributed less evenly in the South; (c) greater illiteracy among whites, and lower expenditures on education; (d) industry less diversified in the South; (e) fewer towns in the South.

   ANSWER _____

6. Before the time of the Revolution, slavery was (a) already peculiar to the South; (b) two hundred years old in the South; (c) under attack by leading Southerners such as Washington and Jefferson; (d) in existence in the Northern colonies as well; (e) being abolished in the American North, though still in existence in Latin America.

   ANSWER _____

7. In the South, sentiment in favor of emancipation (a) grew stronger as the nineteenth century progressed; (b) persisted, though surreptitiously, even until the Civil War; (c) was defeated and silenced before 1840; (d) was crushed in reaction against the bloody Nat Turner slave insurrection; (e) declined as tobacco prices became depressed while cotton prices rose.

ANSWER _____

8. The development of what was then the Southwest (Alabama, Mississippi and Louisiana) brought with it (a) the spread of slaveholding to a much larger percentage of the Southern farming class; (b) the growth of the slave trade from Africa; (c) a significant increase in the number of Negroes to more or less half the total population of the Cotton Kingdom states; (d) a marked strengthening of repression and even cruelty; (e) immense wealth to plantation owners who bred slaves for market.

ANSWER _____

9. Which of the following was *not* mentioned as a reason for the survival of slavery? (a) The labor shortage in the Southwest; (b) the inability of white labor to adjust to the Southern climate and to cultivating the Southern crops; (c) the belief of some slaveholders that Negroes were an inferior race; (d) the social status that the Negroes' subordination gave even to nonslaveholding whites; (e) the great prestige and social position that slaveholding gave to the master class.

ANSWER _____

10. The economic advantages of slavery, however, were (a) great for most whites, which is after all the main reason slavery persisted; (b) largely confined to the master class, who thus had no compelling economic reason to abolish the system; (c) largely confined to the master class, while other whites paid a high price for it economically as well as morally; (d) largely confined to the master class, while the costs were great for all whites and of course still greater for the Negroes; (e) unevenly distributed, as were the degrading costs of slavery for both whites and Negroes.

ANSWER _____

Now check your answers and enter your score on your Progress Profile, page vii.

CHAPTER 3

Pre-reading

In this chapter we explain pre-reading, an important technique for comprehending practical prose. Pre-reading gives you a map of what's ahead, so that when you read thoroughly you can go faster because you know the general framework into which the details fit. To understand this chapter better, pre-read it:

Read normally the first three paragraphs of the chapter;

then read the *first sentence only* of each of the remaining paragraphs;

but when you reach the last three paragraphs, read them thoroughly.

Begin pre-reading here.

Consider practical prose from the writer's point of view for a moment. He wants above all to communicate with you, to help you in every way to understand him. He may be skillful about it, or he may be fumbling. But he is on your side. So how can you take advantage of the fact that the writer is on your side? The basic techniques for improving comprehension are all answers to that one question.

The writer has several strategies he can call on to make his writing clear and memorable. The most important of these have to do with the way he organizes his material and the way he warns you in advance of the organization he has chosen. The more skillful a writer is, the more you can rely on him to use these basic strategies.

The most important strategy is called *introduction, development, conclusion.* A time-worn saying has it that the key to memorable writing is "first tell them what you're going to tell them, then tell them, then tell them what you told them." Simple? Yes. Yet the point is remembered by most writers of non-fiction: begin with an overall statement of what it's about, where it's going, how it's going to get there; then deliver what has just been promised; and end by summarizing what has been said and by pointing out the consequences.

Pre-reading: Begin reading first sentences only.

A second essential strategy of the writer is *transition*, which means traffic signs for the reader. In short passages these may be only a word or a phrase; but in any work longer than a few pages, the author should pause in his development from time to time to summarize what he has already said and to point out the twists and turns in the road ahead.

Thus practical prose tends toward certain uniform patterns of organization. And as the flood of practical prose rises ever higher, as writers grow more skillful and their editors more demanding, these uniform patterns become all but mandatory. Today, as you might expect, scientific journals exhibit the most rigid use of these patterns. College textbooks come next: over the past decade, textbooks have become ever more elaborate in their use of chapter openings, concluding summaries, headings, and even special sections set off in contrasting typefaces, to make the organization of the material clear even to the most unskillful reader.

These patterns are there to be used, to increase understanding. The skilled reader seeks them out. He pays special attention to introductory material; he looks for transitions within the development; he puts concluding material to work.

The reader does this with the technique we call *pre-reading*. The remarkable fact about pre-reading is that you apply it *before you begin to read thoroughly*. Pre-reading takes advantage of the patterns of practical prose to spy out *in advance* the book's organization and general content. Pre-reading is a new habit for most readers. Like most new habits, at first it will be bothersome to remember and apply. But once established, this habit makes reading simpler.

Pre-reading makes comprehension easier and better, because it provides a framework into which you fit details during your later thorough reading. The more difficult the material, the more pre-reading will help your comprehension.

Pre-reading is an essential step in defining your precise purpose in reading a particular work.

Pre-reading provides an advance sampling of the book's style and content. This sampling makes it easier in subsequent thorough reading to maintain the most efficient speed, that is, the highest speed at which you can obtain the desired degree of comprehension.

Pre-reading, though not intended as a substitute for thorough reading, will sometimes show you that you should skip all or part of a selection, if (a) the content is familiar; (b) it is irrelevant to your immediate purpose; or (c) you need more background before you can master the material.

Pre-reading, because it makes clear to you the author's overall point of view and conclusions, helps you to read the work more critically when you come to read thoroughly.

Pre-reading is indispensable even to the most thorough form of thorough reading, which is study reading with note-taking. Written notes cannot be organized accurately without the advance understanding of the material's structure that pre-reading provides.

To pre-read anything, you start with careful examination of all detectable introductory material. Then you give the development of the work a highly selective, systematic looking over; and then you examine thoroughly all concluding material. The check list below shows how these steps apply to different kinds of material.

THE STEPS TO PRE-READING

An article or chapter of a book

1. *Introduction.* Read the opening paragraphs thoroughly. This usually means from two to five paragraphs.

2. *Development.* Read only the first sentence of each remaining paragraph, and any subheadings, until you reach the last few paragraphs.

3. *Conclusion.* Read the final paragraphs thoroughly. This usually means from one to four paragraphs.

A book

1. *Introduction.*
   a. Examine carefully the table of contents and the index.
   b. Note the date of publication.
   c. Read the prefatory material.
   d. Pre-read, then read thoroughly, the first chapter.

2. *Development.* Returning to the table of contents, try to find any chapter between the first and the last that seems to be a summary or transition. Pre-read each such chapter, then read it thoroughly.

3. *Conclusion.* Pre-read, then read thoroughly, the last chapter.

In your later thorough reading of the book, pre-read each chapter as you come to it.

An Article or Chapter of a Book

An article, technical paper or report, the chapter of a book, or any piece of practical prose of similar length, will almost universally use the first several paragraphs to introduce its subject in general terms. Professional writers often call these paragraphs the *lead* of their piece, and they sometimes spend as much time writing these leading paragraphs as they then use to write all the rest. As a variation on this pattern, particularly in magazine journalism, a writer will sometimes use an anecdote ("narrative lead"), a startling fact, or some other interest-catching device. The introduction proper will then begin just after the interest-arouser.

The job of the introductory paragraphs is to tell you the nature, the importance, and perhaps something of the structure of what follows. There are several ways the opening paragraphs can do this. Usually they state the main subject, theme, or problem of the following material; they may in effect state the author's purpose. They may define important terms or concepts. (For an excellent example of such a definition see the reading selection "On the Unpopularity of Intellect," by Richard Hofstadter, page 404.) Less frequently, the introductory paragraphs abstract or survey the principal points that will follow.

Concluding paragraphs, like introductory ones, give a general view of the article's or chapter's content and organization, though in a somewhat different manner. They are likely to summarize or recapitulate what has been said in the body of the article or chapter. They may also round out the matter by offering conclusions that bring out the importance or significance of what has been said. Concluding paragraphs in chapters of books may provide a transition to the next chapter.

These formulas for constructing an article or chapter of a book are followed with great rigidity by scientific publications (*see pages 66 and 67*). Some textbooks are just as rigid in their formulas for introductory and concluding paragraphs. For example, *Life: An Introduction to Biology,* by George Gaylord Simpson and William S. Beck, follows an intricate pattern in which each group of three or four chapters is introduced by two pages that explain what those chapters are about and just how they progress; each chapter then has from one paragraph to a page of introductory material; and each chapter ends with a summary which is in effect an outline or check list for review. Similar patterns are followed by most modern textbooks, in subjects as divergent as educational psychology, sociology, and government.

The first and third steps in pre-reading an article or the chapter of a book, then, simply take advantage of a nearly universal pattern of organization of practical prose. These divisions are not always so crisply separated as in textbooks or scientific papers, but they exist in all competent writing.

The middle step in pre-reading a chapter or article is, as you have seen, to read the first sentence of each paragraph between the introduction and the conclusion. In these middle paragraphs the author develops what he has to say. Your reading of first sentences lets you get at the skeleton of this development by taking advantage of still another rule of organization followed by most authors.

Demonstration: Predigested Pre-reading

Many professional journals do your pre-reading for you. Most scientific publications begin each article with an *abstract*. An extreme case is *The British Medical Journal,* where an article always begins with a brief, boldface Summary, then an Introduction, proceeds through Method to Results, and always ends with Discussion.

Cardiovascular State of Newly Discovered Diabetic Women*[1]

J. A. WEAVER,† M.D.,M.R.C.P. ; S. K. BHATIA,‡ M.B., B.S., M.R.C.P.ED. ; D. BOYLE,† M.D., M.R.C.P.

D. R. HADDEN,† M.D., M.R.C.P.ED. ; D. A. D. MONTGOMERY,† M.D., F.R.C.P.

British Medical Journal, 1970, **1**, 783-786

Summary: A cardiovascular study of a group of 90 newly diagnosed diabetic women aged 35 to 75 years was begun in 1965 and a repeat examination was carried out on the same patients in 1968. A high prevalence of ischaemic heart disease was found in these patients at the time of diagnosis, and this finding had some predictive value as regards prognosis over the three-year period.

A comparative study with general medical outpatients and long-established diabetics (greater than 10 years' duration of disease) confirmed the high prevalence of ischaemic heart disease in late-onset mild diabetics controlled by diet or oral drugs. It is suggested that this type of milder diabetic patient contributes in undue proportion to the high prevalence of ischaemic heart disease in diabetes.

Introduction

The general association between diabetes mellitus and cardiovascular disease is well established, both from pathological reports (Warren and LeCompte, 1952) and from clinical studies (Bradley and Bryfogle, 1956). These observed concerned groups of diabetic patients with of some duration, but the card the time of initial cli studied in de a gr

Patients and Methods

Ninety consecutive women patients aged 35 to 75 years were first examined in 1965 at the same time as the diagnosis of diabetes mellitus was established (group A). The clinical history paid attention to the occurrence of angina, intermittent claudication, details of smoking habits, and parity. The examination included the measurement of body weight, blood pressure in the supine position, and the presence of posterior tibial artery pulsation. A 12-lead electrocardiogram was carried out in all patients, and the tracing was analysed according to the Minnesota classification (Blackburn et al., 1960) by a cardiologist (D.B.), who did not know the clinical data. He was also unaware whether the tracing was from patient or a control subject (see below trocardiograms was recorded on glucose tolerance test estimation of An i

Giant Brain Cells in Mollusks[2]

Study of the neurons of a large mollusk with a stereotyped pattern of behavior yields a picture of what each cell does and how the cells interact to produce the behavior pattern

by A. O. D. Willows

The quest for detailed understanding of how the brain controls behavior can be pursued today at the primary level of the performance of individual brain cells. Although this kind of study is not yet feasible in mammals, with their enormously complex brains consisting of billions of minute cells, present techniques enable us to carry out such investigations in certain simple animals that have a brain consisting of a relatively small number of giant cells. In the University of Washington's Friday Harbor Laboratories, with a convenient mollusk as the subject, I ' been investigating the con⁺ tive behaviors, ⸱⸱ ' escape h⸱⸱

these various investigations, I decided in 1964 to undertake a study of cell systems within the brain itself, with a view to examining the control of an animal's complex, integrated behavior.

The first problem was to find a suitable animal. What was wanted was a subject with (1) large brain cells that could be identified individually, (2) a well-centralized nervous system co⁻ trating most of the nerv⸱ brain and (3) a re⁻ behavior⸱'
⸱'

and oral veil into paddle-like structures and make swimming movements with its body. These movements, although clumsy and poorly directed, are vigorous enough to remove *Tritonia* fro⁻ clutches of the starfish. Th⸱ ' tivity is thorouᵍʰ' cludes a ⸱
⸱⸱

The point of such a rigid form is to facilitate your initial evaluation of the piece, and to make possible selectively more thorough reading. Even a magazine aimed at a more general audience, such as *Scientific American,* prefaces every article with a carefully written three-line description.

Demonstration: The Topic Sentence Skeleton

To show the power of pre-reading topic sentences, here is the skeleton of this chapter created simply by listing the first sentences of paragraphs.

Consider practical prose from the writer's point of view for a moment.

The writer has several strategies he can call on to make his writing clear and memorable.

The most important strategy is called *introduction, development, conclusion.*

A second essential strategy of the writer is *transition,* which means traffic signs for the reader.

Thus practical prose tends toward certain uniform patterns of organization.

These patterns are there to be used, to increase understanding. The reader does this with the technique we call *pre-reading.*

To pre-read anything, you start with careful examination of all detectable introductory material. . . .

An article, technical paper or report, the chapter of a book, or any piece of practical prose of similar length, will almost universally use the first several paragraphs to introduce its subject in general terms.

The job of the introductory paragraphs is to tell you the nature, the importance, and perhaps something of the structure of what follows.

Concluding paragraphs, like introductory ones, give a general view of the article's or chapter's content and organization, though in a somewhat different manner.

These formulas for constructing an article or chapter of a book are followed with great rigidity by scientific publications. . . .

The first and third steps in pre-reading an article or the chapter of a book, then, simply take advantage of a nearly universal pattern of organization of practical prose.

The middle step in pre-reading a chapter or article is, as you have seen, to read the first sentence of each paragraph between the introduction and the conclusion.

Topic sentences are not an exciting subject, until you see what power they give you over practical prose.

After pre-reading, stop for a moment's thoughtful review of what you have discovered.

After pre-reading, you choose what to do next with the article or chapter of a book.

Stay flexible. . . .

Tables of contents are meant to be read: they are an incomparable tool for opening up the organization of most books.

Here is an example of the usual form of tables of contents, from *Middletown,* by Robert S. and Helen M. Lynd. . . .

The next example is from a current text for an introductory-level college course, *Anthropology: The Study of Man,* by E. Adamson Hoebel. . . .

Clearly, close analysis of a table of contents can tell you a great deal about the book itself, though usually you will ask more questions than the table of contents alone will be able to answer.

Topic sentences are not an exciting subject, until you see what power they give you over practical prose. They are so essential for good comprehension that we spend Chapter 5 discussing them. There you will see that the first sentence is very often the topic sentence of a paragraph, containing its principal thought. By reading the first sentence of each paragraph between the introduction and the conclusion, therefore, you will obtain a clear, though highly simplified, notion of what the author's principal thoughts are. But more important, you will know quite accurately the sequence in which these thoughts are developed. Knowledge of the author's organization is a key to comprehension.

After pre-reading, stop for a moment's thoughtful review of what you have discovered. There are several general questions to ask yourself at this point: What do you now say is your purpose in reading the piece? What are the author's main concerns? What are his conclusions? What is the sequence in which he develops his ideas? Can you see any reason why the author chose *this* sequence of development, rather than a different organization? Besides these general questions, the particular selection should provoke other specific questions to bear in mind while reading thoroughly. Questions asked immediately after pre-reading are remarkably helpful for comprehension and concentration, and also for reading speed. We will discuss them in more detail in Chapter 7.

After pre-reading, you choose what to do next with the article or chapter of a book. You may decide that pre-reading itself gave you all the information you need. You may decide to go back to one or two passages for a second helping. You may well decide to read the whole piece thoroughly, because pre-reading by itself can hardly give thorough comprehension. Even when you do read thoroughly, pre-reading should have saved you time: since you know how the author organizes and develops his discussion, and since you have assessed the difficulty of style and content, you should be able to read at high speed.

Stay flexible. Once you become practiced in the technique, pre-reading an article or chapter of a book of average length should take you only one or two minutes. As you accustom yourself to pre-reading, you will find that in some cases, especially in journal or magazine articles, the process can be abbreviated. Often you will not need to read every first sentence, but only the first and last few paragraphs, with a brief sampling of what lies between.

Books

Tables of contents are meant to be read: they are an incomparable tool for opening up the organization of most books. Realizing this, authors and editors have been making tables of contents work harder than they did in older books; indeed, there is almost a fashion now for texts or technical books to have two tables of contents, one short "survey" or "synoptic" table that puts all the parts and chapters on a page, and the second, longer table, which shows the parts, the chapters, and then all the subdivisions within each chapter.

Here is an example of the usual form of tables of contents, from *Middletown*, by Robert S. and Helen M. Lynd. The book was a pioneering study in American sociology. Read the table of contents carefully; then turn to the pre-reading analysis that follows.

Table of Contents from *Middletown*[3]
by ROBERT S. and HELEN M. LYND

CONTENTS

VI. Engaging in Community Activities

This table of contents is easy to pre-read—indeed, it is self-explanatory. The first three chapters (take a look) are labeled as the introduction and are a statement of problems the writers deal with and of methods they use to solve the problems. The last chapter, labeled "Conclusion," undoubtedly has a summarizing function. Remember that introductory and concluding chapters are read as part of pre-reading. Are there any other chapters in *Middletown* that have a summarizing function, as far as you can tell from this table of contents?

The body of the book is divided into six sections, each with several chapters. Evidently each section deals with one aspect of life in "Middletown"; chapters within each section analyze that aspect.

On closer examination, one can formulate some fruitful questions. Why is "Getting a Living" treated as the first main topic instead of later in the book? The title of the first chapter in that section ("The Dominance of Getting a Living") makes the authors' reason clear: this topic is treated first because it is first in importance in "Middletown." But in that case, what does the title of that section's *last* chapter ("Why Do They Work So Hard?") suggest about the authors' attitude toward the people of "Middletown"?

Again, since children are usually thought to be a vital part of the home, why are Sections II and III treated separately? Here too, the chapter titles within each section reveal possible reasons: apparently Section III largely deals with schools. But from the chapter titles of Section III, what do you think the authors concluded about the importance of the home in training children in "Middletown"?

For two more examples of what a table of contents can tell you, look at Section VI. First, do these chapter titles suggest a complete list of the community activities you would hope to find in a town where you lived? There may be an indication here that the authors found community activities somewhat limited in "Middletown"—including, perhaps, even the highly typical activities discussed in Sections IV and V. Second, does Chapter XXVIII seem to belong with Section VI? Or is it perhaps a chapter that contains some of the authors' conclusions about the subjects discussed throughout the book?

The next example is from a current text for an introductory-level college course, *Anthropology: The Study of Man,* by E. Adamson Hoebel. Again, read it carefully, then turn to the analysis which follows. The analysis will also suggest that you compare this table of contents to that of the introductory psychology text you examined in the pre-reading exercise in the Reading Skills Survey, pages 24–28.

Table of Contents
from *Anthropology: The Study of Man*[4]
by E. ADAMSON HOEBEL

Contents

Part 4 *Primitive culture and society*

Part 5 *Anthropology today and tomorrow*

What is anthropology about? What is its central concern? What are its key terms? The table of contents of this text makes two things clear at once. Begin with the largest divisions of the book, the five parts. The most important single term is *culture,* appearing in four of the part titles and many chapter titles as well. The particular kind of culture that anthropology is concerned with is primitive culture, for Part 4 alone, "Primitive Culture and Society," takes up fully half the book (check the page totals), and Part 2, as shown by its chapter titles, is also concerned with the primitive.

Reading through the chapter titles, you can see that Part 1 amounts to a long definition of culture itself. This observation suggests that in pre-reading this book further, after reading the preface and Chapter 1 you would do well to include Chapter 2, which by its title and position in relation to the rest of the book should prove to have an introductory, general, subject-defining function. Chapter 6, the last of Part 1, launches what appears to be a second key concept of the book, *evolution of culture,* which gets the entire next part to itself. Chapter 6, therefore, is clearly transitional, leading out of the introductory part into the next.

Part 2, then, is primitive culture in the historical view. There is no chapter with a clearly transitional function to fill, bridging the gap between parts 2 and 3, yet that gap is one of thousands of years, from "The Dawn of Civilization" to the human races of the present day. Nonetheless, what Part 3 describes must have come to be through the processes of Part 2, which suggests that the relation between the evolution of culture and the evolution of race may be spelled out in the last few pages of Chapter 12 or in the opening of Chapter 13.

Part 4, the meat of the book, progresses through several subsidiary parts that are not labeled as such. Read through the chapter titles again. The author begins with the simplest productive activities, food gathering and so on, which culminate in the more complicated production of art – to which he gives one of the longest chapters in the part. (Which one is longer?) From material concerns he moves to human relationships, and quickly to *marriage, the family,* and *kinship,* which are clearly three more key terms. Chapters 26 and 27 discuss, briefly, other kinds of social groups. The next group of chapters treats institutions, from economic ones through law and politics to religion. Significantly, in the title of Chapter 34 the key term *culture* reappears after an absence, and yoked to a notion of overall outlook: this chapter must be a summing-up, with as much importance as Chapter 36, and you must include it in pre-reading.

Chapter 35 is the recruiting talk that seems almost obligatory at the end of introductory texts in social sciences. This hybrid two-chapter final part recalls the similar last section of the *Introduction to Psychology.* Turn back to the table of contents of that book (page 24): the parallels between the two books, in their organization, are many. Do you see how both texts begin by defining their subject at length? How each then takes up the way things develop – individual growth in the one book, the evolution of culture in the other?

Consider Part 4 of *Anthropology* as if its subdivisions were labeled: what portion of *Introduction to Psychology* fills the same general structural position? Again, what emerge as the key terms in psychology, the way *culture,* *kinship* and so on can be seen to be keys in anthropology? Finally, in the light of the discussions of the contents pages of *Middletown* and *Anthropology,* review your answers to the questions about the table of contents in the Reading Skills Survey (pages 28–29).

Clearly, close analysis of a table of contents can tell you a great deal about the book itself, though usually you will ask more questions than the table of contents alone will be able to answer. Not all tables of contents are as considerate of the reader as the one we have just examined. Books printed in German, French, and other European languages even put their tables of contents at the back rather than up front. But even when the chapter titles at first seem uninformative, thoughtful questioning at this point in pre-reading will lay bare much of the basic structure of a book. Your later comprehension will thus be directed and improved; details within the book will be more significant and memorable; and the various parts of the book, as you read them, will be held in better relation to each other. As you read the book thoroughly, you will find that an occasional return to the table of contents will help, for the same reasons.

Your next step in pre-reading a book is to note the date of publication (normally found on the reverse side of the title page, but sometimes on the title page itself), and then to examine the index. The index is of course valuable for finding particular bits of information. But beyond that, the index of most books is worth a glance when pre-reading, because it may supplement the table of contents in telling you approximately how much space the author devotes to each of his major topics.

Pre-reading: Read these last paragraphs thoroughly.

Looking over prefatory material is the next step. Though sharp distinctions among *introduction, preface,* and *foreword* are not always observed, any of these, read selectively, can tell you much that will help later. An *introduction* will often prove most useful in giving information about the subject covered and the overall structure, and in texts or technical works may contain important suggestions for using the book. Sometimes the author will tell you what first impelled him to write the book, how he planned it, what its central question is. Occasionally the author will, in his prefatory material, suggest implications of his work that reach too far—or are too tentative—to be part of the book proper. Prefatory material written by someone other than the author may tell you the history and importance of the book and the author. Where prefatory material becomes less useful, for example where the author starts interminable thanks to his friends, obviously you will skip on ahead.

The last step in pre-reading a book is to pre-read and then read the first and last chapters. These chapters are of course similar in function to the first and last paragraphs of an article or chapter, and should be read as part of pre-reading for the same reasons that introductory and concluding paragraphs are read. Where the table of contents indicates that other chapters, besides the first and last, have the function of introducing any part of the book, of summarizing, or of providing a transition, those chapters should also be pre-read and then read thoroughly at this stage in your examination of the book.

This book has many exercises with which you will practice all these steps in pre-reading. These exercises, because they have questions to guide you, will enable you to measure your understanding of how to pre-read. But adequate pre-reading practice really requires leafing through many whole chapters and entire books. Space limits the number of examples that can be reprinted here, but the suggestions for your Reading Journal and other application exercises are designed to carry your pre-reading into active use exactly where it is most useful — in your day-to-day reading.

EXERCISES FOR CHAPTER 3

Reading Journal

Eye Span

Phrase Flashing

Pre-reading
Table of Contents from *Principles of Art Appreciation,* by Stephen C. Pepper

Summarizing
From the Introduction to *Ten Modern Masters,* by Robert Gorham Davis

Phrase Sense

Reading Speed Exercise: Average Level 3
"Foreign Correspondent," from *Personal History,* by Vincent Sheean

Reading Journal

In the separate notebook that you were asked to start after Chapter 2, please add the following:

current reading
1. Under today's date, list everything you have read since your last entry in the Reading Journal, including title, author, type of material or subject, approximate length, and time spent on it.
2. Add to each item your purpose in reading it.
3. Then add to each item a brief summary — one or two sentences — of the content of the piece, and of your opinion of it.

future reading
Start this new heading as a separate section of the notebook. List the titles and authors of every piece of reading you now know that you expect to do — or will be required to do — in the next three months. To each item, add the subject or type of material, and the number of pages. You will return to this list

repeatedly over the coming weeks to add notes and comments, so be sure to allow at least half a page of space for each item.

Eye Span

The following material is designed to extend the width of phrase you are able to take in at a single glance. Use a 3 x 5 card to cover the column you are working with. Move the card rapidly down the column, one line at a time. As each line is exposed, read it, looking at it only once and approximately at the center as shown by the dots between the words. Try to take in the entire width of the line. At first you may have to focus for several seconds on each set of dots before you are able to perceive all the words on the line.

The	. . . .	thousand	with	. . . .	impunity.
injuries	. . . .	of	A	. . . .	wrong
Fortunato	. . . .	I	is	. . . .	unredressed
had	. . . .	borne	when	. . . .	retribution
as I	. . . .	best	overtakes	. . . .	its
could:	. . . .	but	redresser.	. . . .	It
when he	. . . .	ventured	is	. . . .	equally
upon	. . . .	insult,	unredressed	. . . .	when
I vowed	. . . .	revenge.	the	. . . .	avenger
You,	. . . .	who	fails	. . . .	to make
so well	. . . .	know	himself	. . . .	felt
the	. . . .	nature	as such	. . . .	to him
of my	. . . .	soul,	who has	. . . .	done
will	. . . .	not	the	. . . .	wrong.
suppose,	. . . .	however,	It	. . . .	must
that	. . . .	I	be	. . . .	understood,
gave	. . . .	utterance	that	. . . .	neither
to a	. . . .	threat.	by	. . . .	word
At	. . . .	*length*	nor	. . . .	deed
I	. . . .	would	had I	. . . .	given
be	. . . .	avenged;	Fortunato	. . . .	cause
this	. . . .	was	to	. . . .	doubt
a	. . . .	point	my	. . . .	good-will.
definitely	. . . .	settled	I	. . . .	continued,
—but	. . . .	the	as was	. . . .	my wont,
very	. . . .	definitiveness	to	. . . .	smile
with	. . . .	which	in	. . . .	his face,
it was	. . . .	resolved,	and he	. . . .	did not
precluded	. . . .	the idea	perceive	. . . .	that
of	. . . .	risk.	my smile	. . . .	*now*
I	. . . .	must	was	. . . .	at
not only	. . . .	punish,	the	. . . .	thought
but	. . . .	punish	of his	. . . .	immolation.

Phrase Flashing

This exercise is designed to help you develop the quick and accurate perception of *phrases as units* upon which efficient reading speeds depend. The materials for this practice have been grouped together at the back of the book so that you can return to them repeatedly as you work through the chapters, progressing to longer phrases. Please turn to page 476 and follow the instructions.

Pre-reading

From a book that surveys the field of art appreciation—in an introductory way for the serious nonspecialist reader—we reprint below the table of contents. Here the organizational skeleton of the book is laid out. Here you would pre-read with thoughtful attention, to gain both speed and understanding in your later reading of the whole book.

See what you can discover from this table of contents about the organization of the book and its parts. Then answer the questions that follow. This is not a timed exercise. The questions assume you are examining the table of contents because you intend eventually to read the book itself.

Table of Contents
from *Principles of Art Appreciation*[5]
by STEPHEN C. PEPPER

CONTENTS

Enter the answer for each question in the corresponding space. You should refer to the material as you answer the questions. Note that some of these questions require you to supply *page numbers* or *chapter numbers* from the reprinted table of contents.

1. Enter in the answer space the numbers of the chapters that should be read as part of the pre-reading process. Include all chapters that seem clearly— from their titles, lists of subtopics, or positions in the book—to have an introductory, transitional, or concluding function.

ANSWER _____

2. Music, painting, poetry, ballet, the movies—all these and many more are called "arts." Which of the following best defines the arts with which *this* book is most concerned? (a) All the arts; (b) all the arts that are appreciated *visually;* (c) arts appreciated visually, but not including those where *physical motion* is important; (d) all the arts where design, pattern, type, and emotion are important; (e) painting and sculpture.

ANSWER _____

3. Some people maintain that to analyze or think too closely about a work of art will ruin one's appreciation of it; that, for example, one should "experience" a piece of music or a painting as "directly" as possible, without ever "tearing it down" into its various parts and artistic techniques. What would seem to be this author's opinion? (a) He would agree; (b) he would disagree, at least to the point of maintaining that often one's ability to analyze has a part to play in making a work of art more enjoyable; (c) he would disagree, because he clearly believes that the "direct" approach is itself virtually worthless; (d) clearly, he insists that each person must approach works of art in his own way; (e) there is no way to infer the author's opinion, because this book is in no way concerned with this question.

ANSWER _____

4. Judging from the subtopics listed for each chapter, where would you be most likely to find the author's discussion of the problem raised in question 3, above? (Give a chapter number for answer.)

ANSWER _____

5. "It's all a matter of taste"—or so many people will state when asked why they like or dislike an object of art. What would this author seem to think about that statement? (a) He would simply agree; (b) he would agree, but say that some have good taste while others do not; (c) he would point out that taste can be developed and educated to make use of certain general principles; (d) he would disagree, because he holds that matters of taste are always subject to the fundamental rules of appreciation; (e) he would say that his book is not about taste at all, but about artistic psychology and technique.

ANSWER _____

6. Which of the following is the best statement of how the four major *parts* of this book are related? (a) Introduction, followed by a survey of three different approaches to art appreciation; (b) general principles in the first half, followed in the second half by discussions that apply the principles to various specific types of art; (c) specific examples discussed in the first half, from which the second half develops general principles; (d) three parts analyzing different general areas of art appreciation, followed by a fourth part that applies these analyses to the individual visual arts; (e) four completely separate methods of analyzing art to increase one's appreciation.

ANSWER _____

7. Within each chapter, judging from the subtopics, what can we tell about the author's usual pattern of organization? (a) He usually moves from one or more examples to a general statement of principle; (b) as shown by the

wording of the first subtopic in many chapters, he often (perhaps always) begins with a definition; (c) as shown by the wording of the first, contrasted with the later, subtopics in each chapter he states a problem and then works toward the solution; (d) he proceeds always from general principles to specific applications with particular objects of art; (e) he follows no regular plan.

ANSWER _____

8. Chapter 1 is clearly an introduction to the general subject matter of the book. What special function can we be fairly sure Chapter 2 performs? (a) It discusses how taste is formed and may change or be changed; (b) it justifies the author's attempts to change the reader's taste; (c) it applies the general philosophizing of Chapter 1 to specific problems; (d) it relates the unchanging principles of art appreciation to the styles and fads of particular times; (e) it discusses, as Chapter 1 fails to do, the subject matter of Part One, the psychology of art appreciation.

ANSWER _____

Summarizing

The passage below is taken from the critical introduction to *Ten Modern Masters,* an anthology of modern short stories. In his general introduction, the editor discusses what the short story is; how modern short story writers differ from earlier ones; and what general characteristics the reader should be aware of as he reads and thinks about the stories in the anthology. For this exercise, your purpose in reading the passage is to summarize each paragraph and then the entire passage. The questions follow the passage.

This is not a timed exercise. You may refer to the passage as you answer the questions.

From the Introduction to *Ten Modern Masters*[6]
edited by ROBERT GORHAM DAVIS

A

Modern short-story writers do not tell *about* events. They present experience in its most immediately sensuous, concrete and graphic form. This makes the story more vivid, of course, but that is not their only reason. They are not trying primarily to entertain or excite or convince, but to show what life is like. Atmosphere, moods, feelings, sensuous details are essential ingredients of our sense of life at any given moment. If a story is to be completely faithful to life, it must render these essentials insofar as they can be rendered in words. This holds even for a writer like Hemingway, who seems at times to write so objectively, so much from the outside. We know from his statement printed in the appendix of this book, that he takes great pains to describe external events and details in such a way that they will create in the reader precisely the inner feeling which it is his purpose to express.

B

In being at once objective and subjective, general and particular, social and personal, the short story views life with a double vision. It gives us the illusion of immediate experience, and yet at the same time permits us to see this experience in perspective, to understand its meaning in a way that is seldom possible while we are in the midst of life. Sometimes this double view is represented dramatically in the story itself, as in the eyes of the old men looking down on the shining table in Conrad's "Youth."

C

Though an author deals with particular events happening to particular people, he is interested in them, as we have seen, for their representative character. He is not so much concerned with what literally occurred as a matter of history on some given occasion, as with the kind of event that is likely to occur, that is probable, and therefore has meaning for everyone.

D

The classic distinction between fiction and history appears in Aristotle's treatise on poetry. It was written in the fourth century B.C., but still holds good. In fact, most modern textbooks on short stories can add little to what Aristotle said about plot construction. Aristotle said that poetry — by which he meant imaginative literature generally — "is a more philosophic and higher thing than history: for poetry tends to express the universal; history, the particular." The business of the poet, he said, is not to state what *did* happen, but to describe what *may* happen; that is, how a person of a certain type will behave and feel in a certain situation "according to the laws of probability."

E

What Aristotle says is consistent with ordinary experience. History does not repeat itself. The mere fact that a thing has happened once does not mean that it will happen again. No science of history has yet been developed that enables us to predict the future certainly, nor does the science of psychology enable us to predict certainly the behavior of our friends. How many historians anticipated the pact in 1939 between Hitler and Stalin? Who could tell that Edward VIII would renounce his throne for Mrs. Simpson?

F

And yet in living our lives, in planning for the future, we have to try to predict. In making the decisions that constantly face us, we ask what is *likely* to happen, what consequences, moral and otherwise, are *likely* to follow from our decisions, how people are *likely* to feel about it, how the values we cherish or the larger ends we seek are *likely* to be affected. These are the probabilities of which Aristotle spoke, and these are the probabilities of which the plots of short stories are made. This is also what is meant by verisimilitude or plausibility. Given this beginning, what is likely to follow?

Given this complication, how is it all likely to end? Another way of putting it is to say that authors choose to write about consequential actions, that is, actions which make a difference. The nature of that difference is what they are communicating to the reader.

For each of the six paragraphs in the selection, choose the best summary. The last question asks you to choose a summary statement for the complete passage. You may refer to the passage as you answer the questions.

A
1. The sensuous, concrete, graphic detail of modern short stories makes them vivid and lifelike.
2. Modern short story writers use particular details to create a general, but vivid, impression about the people and events they portray.
3. Modern short story writers use particular detail to create in you a faithful sense of what life is like in its many aspects.

ANSWER _____

B
1. The modern short story creates an illusion of immediate experience, but also shows how that experience can be generally interpreted.
2. A double view of life is one of the most characteristic features of the modern short story.
3. The particular graphic detail of a short story is important only as it helps you understand the meaning of the experiences portrayed.

ANSWER _____

C
1. The literal detail of the events and experiences in a modern short story is not the author's main concern.
2. The graphic details of people and events are chosen by the author to give the story meaning for everyone.
3. The short story writer creates an immediate sense of life, yes; but at the same time his people and events are chosen to represent what is probable and meaningful.

ANSWER _____

D
1. Aristotle's distinction between history and poetry can have little added to it today.
2. Aristotle's distinction, still good today, is that history relates what did happen in particular cases; but that imaginative literature ranks higher because it describes more generally what most probably would happen.
3. Poetry, by which Aristotle meant imaginative literature generally, describes how certain types of people will behave and feel in certain situations.

ANSWER _____

E
1. We can see that Aristotle was right to say history deals with particular events that do not happen the same way again.

2. Our ordinary experience bears out what Aristotle said about the difference between history and fiction.
3. Because we cannot predict the future from history, historical writing is less useful to us than fictional writing.

ANSWER _____

F
1. In contrast with the particular details of history, which do not allow us to predict, the vivid and concrete in fiction provide the basis from which we can predict the probable consequences.
2. The plots of short stories must be probable and plausible.
3. Just as we plan for the future by trying to predict the probable outcomes of our different actions, so, as Aristotle meant, the writer of fiction builds his plot around actions that make a difference.

ANSWER _____

Now choose, from the following, the best summary of the entire passage.

1. Most modern short story writers follow the tradition, started by Aristotle, that they must build their plots with events and psychological types that are universally or very widely likely to occur; we can see this better if we realize that history deals only with events that did in fact occur, but will not recur with any likelihood.
2. History is convincing because it deals with truth and fact; fiction is convincing because it deals with illusion built on details that are vivid, probable, and plausible.
3. We understand short stories better when we realize how fiction differs from history; both are concerned with the concrete detail of events, but, as Aristotle was first to point out, history tells us only what particular events did happen, while fiction deals more generally with events that would be most likely to happen.

ANSWER _____

Phrase Sense

As you will remember from Chapter 2, the purpose of this next exercise is to increase your understanding of what groups of several words within a sentence hang together as a meaningful unit. Therefore, after you have completed the Summarizing exercise above, you are to go back to those same paragraphs and divide each sentence by circling the phrases or marking a "slash" (/) between them. Work as quickly as you can, without stopping to reason out or ponder over the phrases. You are working for the *sense* of what words clump together. The first sentence of the article above is reprinted again here, marked correctly.

Modern short-story writers / do not tell / *about* events. / They present experience / in its most / immediately sensuous, / concrete and graphic form.

Reading Speed Exercise: Average Level 3

The next article is an excerpt from *Personal History,* by the foreign correspondent and political commentator, Vincent Sheean. The book itself is an autobiography, dealing for the most part with the period between the two World Wars. The author, as a journalist, was close to many of the major events of that period. These events, and the author's ability to convey in vigorous prose how they struck him just as they unfolded, have made the book a minor classic. In the passage reprinted here, Sheean tells how he first became a foreign correspondent. The difficulty of content and style is about average. That is, skilled readers read it at the speed they use for material of a factual nature, popularly written.

You are to read the selection against time. Follow your instructor's directions in class, or the Instructions for Timing on page 474.

Before reading, practice with the *Eye Movements in Reading* exercise on pages 54–56.

Do not pre-read the selection; the timed reading exercises are designed to measure improvements in speed alone.

After reading the selection and recording your time, go on to the ten true-false and multiple-choice questions beginning on page 88. There is no time limit for the questions, but it will invalidate the exercise if you refer to this passage while you answer them.

Begin reading and timing here.

"Foreign Correspondent"[7]
from *Personal History*
by VINCENT SHEEAN

When the money did come I took the first train to Paris. On the night I left Rome the young men in black shirts were thronging to the railway station, singing and shouting, with banners; they were on their way to the Fascist Congress at Naples. In a week's time they would be on their way back again, moved by a collective fever, marching on Rome: the *Giovinezza* of 1922, which I had so inadequately understood or appreciated. Before I reached Paris they had already shown unmistakable signs of their intention, and I read in the newspapers at the Gare de Lyon, with surprise and unbelief, that these noisy children in their fancy dress claimed the right to control the powers of the state.

I had gone to Paris to get a job. Even if this had not been economically necessary I should probably have done it just the same, for I had no talent for leisure and wanted something definite—tasks with a beginning and an end—to fill the hours. The only kind of work I knew anything about, or had ever been able to perform even half well, was journalism, and Paris was the centre of American journalism in Europe. When I reached Paris one day in that cold, wet October, I went to the office of the Chicago *Tribune*—drawn there by the notion that anything connected with Chicago must be vaguely all right for me—and was received by a laconic, keen-eyed, wooden-faced man who talked out of the corner of his mouth: Mr. Henry Wales. By what method he arrived at his conclusions I never knew; there must have been dozens of stray newspaper men drifting into that office every week, some of them far more experienced than I was; I had no special qualification to offer, except an acquaintance with certain foreign languages. But whatever the reasons, he determined to take me on, at first as a sort of general handy-man, to be used either in his own office or in the office of the European Edition of the *Tribune,* printed in Paris; and afterwards as his assistant. Thus, in a click of time, I became what was called a "foreign correspondent" — a role I was to fill, in the service of that vigorous newspaper, for the next three years.

My suitability for the job of foreign correspondent — as distinguished from my specific qualifications, which were dubious — must have been considerable. Little though I had known about the affairs of the world during my fox-trotting undergraduate days, in New York I had rapidly acquired a wider interest; and now, after five or six months in France and Italy, much reading of the political press in three languages, and that sharper interest in events which comes of an acquaintance with their physical scene, I was prepared (in interest and self-confidence, at least) to deal with the largest doings of the great, their words and deeds and gestures, as a journalist should — that is, without unduly yielding to their persuasions, believing in their beliefs, or crediting their enthusiasms. M. Poincaré awed me at first, it is true, as any old man of immense power and prestige must awe an insignificant youth of twenty-two; but this particular kind of awe evaporated once its instrument was removed, and when I sat down at the typewriter, an instrument even colder and more impersonal than M. Poincaré, I was already, at the outset of my experience in the trade, a "correspondent": that is, I was able to treat M. Poincaré exactly as I might have treated any other element in the news of the day, a beggar who had been enriched by an eccentric millionaire, a film star in a motor accident, or a prize fighter who was going to America. This professional indifference to the material of journalism did not endure. As months and years passed, as I acquired a steadier, more intimate acquaintance with the struggles going on under the surface of smooth black print on white paper, the craft itself (i.e., the art of putting those struggles into the smooth-running print) lost its fascination, political interest deepened to political passion, and I came in time to "take sides" and have opinions, feel them as deeply and express them as violently as any amateur. In so doing I only reversed the familiar procedure by which a good many of my colleagues, having begun with beliefs and enthusiasms, ended in callous indifference towards all human effort.

My job was not easy: I had to be "on duty" from noon until two or three o'clock the next morning, an unhuman *corvée* made tolerable by the fact that for some of these hours there was little or nothing to do; but the extension of what might be called public preoccupations — politics and journalism — through the whole waking time of an inexperienced young man drove out private interests entirely, so that such figures as M. Poincaré became more consistently real to me, day in and day out, than most of my transient colleagues on the Chicago *Tribune* or my acquaintances in the bars and cafés of Paris. A good many newspaper men of the time and place could have been said to be without private lives, or to treat their private lives with indifference — to marry and beget absent-mindedly, see their wives sometimes once a week, and live, in all the keener hours of their existence, in the "office," a place taken to comprise most of the other offices, bars, cafés and meeting places of the press and politicians; and this absorption in work was especially uncompromising with me, to whom it was all new and upon whom, for a long time, it exercised a fascination without precedent. I fell into political journalism as a water spaniel falls into a river, and was quickly so taken up with the new element that the days before I had made its acquaintance seemed to me dry, cramped and distant.

It was, even in the beginning, a political job. In objective fact I was an ignorant but active youth of twenty-two, earning a minuscular salary, living in a small and dirty hotel behind the offices of the Chicago *Tribune* in the Rue Lamartine; but such circumstances did not keep me from dealing magisterially with the policies and leaders of nations as they were shown in events. The power of the press, in one important aspect, was this: that its anonymity enabled such fragments of humanity as myself to exert, in spite of youth, poverty or obscurity, a kind of suffrage, at least in opinion, so that the course of events was never wholly regulated by the desires or machinations of the powerful. In the single case of M. Poincaré, the first politician I ever saw at close range, it was unquestionably people like myself who brought him to grief: he lost the friendly opinion of the world because he lost the respect of its press, and he lost our respect because we saw, with the utmost sickening clearness, week after week for two solid years, how incapable that nervous little provincial lawyer was of rising above the parochial hatreds of his native village.

Now note your reading time. Record it below and go on to the questions.

YOUR READING TIME: _____MIN. _____SEC. _____W.P.M. COMPREHENSION SCORE: _____%
(WORDS PER MINUTE FROM THE TABLE ON PAGE 475.)

Please do not read these questions until you have read the selection itself against time. Do not refer to the selection as you answer the questions. Choose the *one best* answer to each question and enter the corresponding letter in the proper answer space.

1. The Fascist seizure of power in Italy, just after the author left Rome, came as a complete surprise to him.   (T) True; (F) False

    ANSWER _____

2. The author went to Paris to get a job because it was one of the two centers of American journalism in Europe.   (T) True; (F) False

    ANSWER _____

3. The author's specific qualifications for the job of foreign correspondent were few and dubious.   (T) True; (F) False

ANSWER _____

4. As a correspondent, the author was "on duty" from early morning to late afternoon or early evening.   (T) True; (F) False

ANSWER _____

5. As he started, the author's first reaction toward professional political journalism was one of (a) interest; (b) great interest, to the point of pre-occupation; (c) indifference, as he was merely seeking the best way to keep close to active politics; (d) indifference, as he was already, at the outset of his experience in the trade, an impersonal "correspondent"; (e) indifference, as he was merely seeking tasks to fill the hours.

ANSWER _____

6. According to the author, the professional journalist believes he should write of the doings of the great (a) without being unduly influenced by their beliefs, persuasions, and enthusiasms; (b) after careful evaluation and judgment of them; (c) with total objectivity; (d) objectively while providing the background information for readers to evaluate the events correctly; (e) with frank admission of his own beliefs and convictions, since total freedom from bias is impossible.

ANSWER _____

7. Many foreign journalists in Paris at that time were forced by the nature of their jobs (a) to live a totally routine existence in the midst of important events; (b) to be as indifferent to their private lives, through lack of time, as they were to great events as a matter of professional viewpoint; (c) to be indifferent to their private lives because of their total and passionate absorption in the significance of the great issues; (d) to live a transient existence in the bars and cafés, which were the only places where a newsman could meet with the great; (e) to use their influence on public opinion as the only available way to take an active part in politics.

ANSWER _____

8. The author uses the example of M. Poincaré to show (a) how his "professional" journalistic attitude worked in practice; (b) how the professional coldness and impersonality of journalists could actually create considerable political effect; (c) the attitudes of his employers, the newspaper publishers and editors, as distinct from the indifference of working journalists; (d) how his attitude had changed since he started as a correspondent; (e) what event caused his attitude to change.

ANSWER _____

9. Compared with the experience of most journalists, the author says that his experience with journalism was (a) similar, in that he became progressively more concerned with the people and events that journalism deals with; (b) similar, in that he became progressively more indifferent to the people and events that journalism deals with; (c) unusual, in that he became progressively more concerned with the people and events that journalism deals with; (d) unusual, in that he became progressively more indifferent

to the people and events that journalism deals with; (e) not comparable, at least as far as one can tell from the article.

ANSWER _____

10. Would you anticipate from this article that the author eventually gave up the profession of journalism? (a) No; (b) the article does not say enough to permit an answer either way; (c) yes, for in fact he says so; (d) yes, because it is evident from the tone of his remarks that he feels he has "grown out of" his interest in journalism; (e) yes, because it is evident from his remarks that he now dislikes journalism intensely.

ANSWER _____

Now check your answers, and enter your score on your Progress Profile, page vii.

CHAPTER 4

The Mechanics of Reading Speed

Pre-read this chapter as your first step in reading.

Read normally the first several paragraphs;

then read the first sentence only of each remaining paragraph;

but when you reach the concluding paragraphs, read them thoroughly.

At the end of the chapter you will find several questions that you should be able to answer from what you learn by pre-reading.

Begin pre-reading here.

You will remember that in Chapter 2 we suggested that you watch, through a hole punched in the page, the eye movements of a friend as he read the other side of the page. If you did not try this experiment when you read Chapter 2, please go back and try it now. More vividly than we can describe, this simple experiment demonstrates an important fact: although your reading feels like a smooth, unbroken sweep from left to right across the line of print, actually your eyes make a series of brief stops on the line. You see words only when your eyes are *not* moving. As we also said then, most readers take in only one word at a time, which means they stop many times on each line.

Specialists have learned how to record and analyze eye movements. One way to do this is to bounce a thin beam of light off each eyeball so that as the person reads, the movements of the reflected beams can be captured on movie film. Figure 1 shows two such photographic records of eye movements in reading four lines of print. Pauses of the reader's eyes on the line, during which he sees to read, are called *fixations*. A *regression* is a special type of fixation that occurs when one jumps from *right to left* on the line to reread one or several words. The *return sweep* takes the eyes from the last fixation at the end of one line to the first fixation on the next line.

Demonstration: Where Speed Improvement Comes From

The two film strips show gains achieved through developmental reading training by a college freshman who was a poor reader when he started training (left strip), and an excellent reader three months later (right strip).

Figure 1

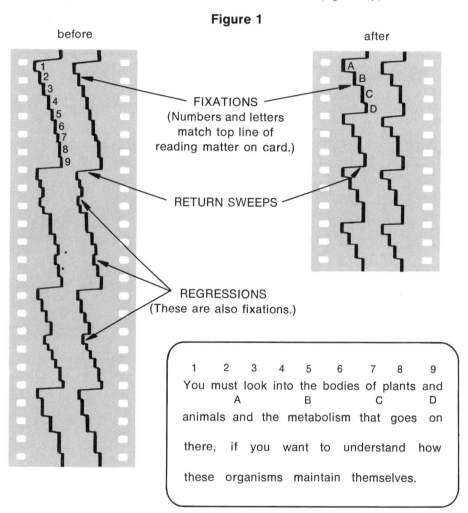

before   after

FIXATIONS
(Numbers and letters match top line of reading matter on card.)

RETURN SWEEPS

REGRESSIONS
(These are also fixations.)

```
1    2    3    4    5    6    7    8    9
You must look into the bodies of plants and
          A         B         C         D
animals and the metabolism that goes on

there; if you want to understand how

these organisms maintain themselves.
```

The film strips demonstrate three ways you can improve your speed:

Fixations: you can make fewer stops on the line; as pointed out in Chapter 2, this means learning to *read by phrases* rather than by single words. This is the secret of the greatest gains in speed.

Regressions: you can, with suitable practice materials, cut down the number of regressions you make.

Rhythm: you can smooth out the rhythm of your eye movements, so that you spend closer to the same amount of time on each fixation; cutting out regressions helps rhythm too.

Pre-reading: Begin reading first sentences only.

How Phrase Reading Is Possible: Peripheral Vision

Right now you can try a second simple test that will demonstrate another important fact about your eyes in reading. Spread your arms to both sides, with your hands at ear level, as if you were trying to touch the left and right walls of the room both at once. Look directly in front of you, focusing your eyes on the wall ahead. Now snap the fingers of both hands at once, several times. Still looking directly ahead, and moving your hands six or eight inches forward if necessary, if you concentrate you should be able to see your fingers snap — both hands at once.

You have just demonstrated that your eyes are capable of seeing a much wider span than you utilize in reading.

The vision you use for closely focused work, like threading a needle or examining a ten-dollar bill to see if it is counterfeit, is called *macular* vision. As you see in Figure 2, macular vision uses only a small part of the retina. Here the eye's light receptors are densely crowded together, and are capable of very fine discrimination. Vision outside the macular area is called *peripheral* (that is, "around the edge"). Outward from the macular area of the retina, light receptors become progressively more thinly spaced; focusing and visual discrimination become progressively less sharp. But peripheral vision in the immediate neighborhood of the macular area can be put to work in reading. *It is this that makes phrase reading possible.*

Figure 2.   Peripheral vision: the eye takes in more than most people use in reading.

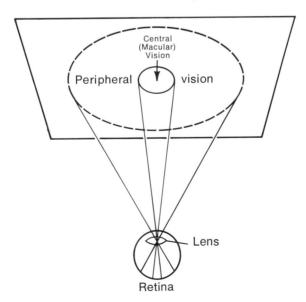

Demonstration: The Eye-span Pyramids

Here is a third simple experiment to make. The pyramids below will show you that the peripheral vision you want to use in reading is even now quite accurate over a span equal to a long phrase. To "read" the pyramids, focus carefully on the number at the center of each line; start with the top line and move down. By concentrating hard you should be able to read the numbers and the nonsense syllables at both ends simultaneously, even of quite long lines.

4	1	6		x	1	f
28	2	59		ad	2	bo
55	3	70		pe	3	tu
18	4	46		om	4	id
92	5	11		fit	5	hop
67	6	23		ro	6	am
71	7	88		ak	7	la
80	8	39		fun	8	may
12	9	41		he	9	it

Most students discover, with practice material of this sort, that they are more accurate at the left end of the span than at the right. This is because years of reading have trained people to pay attention from left to right as they look at almost anything, from a signpost to a map to a painting. People whose reading language runs from right to left, like Arabic, are more accurate at the right side of an eye-span pyramid. Students also find the extreme outside numbers or letters on the longer lines easier to read than the inside numbers. You will observe these things yourself as you work with the exercises in this book that are intended to increase your use of peripheral vision.

Demonstration: Square-span, Spaced Units, Boustrophedon: Three Attempts to Use Peripheral Vision

Many methods	have been suggested	to take advantage	of the eye's capacity	to take in more
than one word	at a single glance.	This odd way to set type	is called *square-span.*	Square-span tries to fit
groups of words	together into units	to be read with one	fixation on each.	The idea is neat

in theory   because the eye   can, of course,   see more than one
word up and down   as well as sideways.   But, in fact,   square-span
is awkward,   bulky,   and expensive.   Another idea
is spaced-unit   presentation,   which breaks   the text
into natural phrases.   This, too, takes   more space,
both between the phrases   and between the lines.   Furthermore

some readers can take in wider phrases than others. Another method
sometimes mentioned is this one, called *boustrophedon*, where alternate
lines run the opposite way to gain efficiency by making return sweeps
unnecessary. Boustrophedon began with the Sumerians. Most readers
today find it about as easy to read as Greek.

All these ideas ignore the crucial question: how can we read faster in the millions of books already in print?

Four different types of exercises in this book work directly with the way you use your eyes in reading. Perhaps the most important of these is *Phrase Sense*, important because it relates comprehension to the mechanics of phrase reading by improving your awareness of how words are correctly grouped into *meaningful* reading phrases. The notion of a meaningful phrase is important to fast and accurate reading, as you will see from the following sentence which is improperly broken into phrases:

Airline / terminals have / noticed that / large banks of luggage / lockers fill / up first from the / left end.

The words do not group meaningfully that way, which makes the sentence harder to understand than in the next version, correctly phrased for reading:

Airline terminals / have noticed / that large banks / of luggage lockers / fill up first / from the left end.

A very fast reader would combine several of the correct groupings:

Airline terminals have noticed / that large banks of luggage lockers / fill up first from the left end.

Exactly what makes up a meaningful phrase will be discussed in more detail in Chapter 8.

Two types of exercises, *Eye Span* and *Phrase Flashing,* help you stretch your use of peripheral vision. The Eye Span exercises do with words essentially the kind of thing done with numbers and nonsense syllables in the pyramids above. These exercises progress through wider and wider spacings of words on the line, thus stretching progressively farther your ability to recognize words by using peripheral vision. And after Chapter 3, at page 78, you first began to use the Phrase Flashing materials to practice reading, with a single fixation, phrases that in later chapters will grow progressively wider; for flexible use, and to save space, these materials are grouped together on pages 476 through 479.

Fourth, the *Eye Movements in Reading* exercise gives you practice in the fixation patterns used by highly skilled readers. By "reading" the nonmeaningful shapes of this exercise as a warm-up before practicing speed with normal reading matter, you learn how it feels to move your eyes with few fixations per line, with an even rhythm along the line, and with a sure return sweep from the end of one line to the beginning of the next.

Two Eye-movement Techniques to Try in Your Daily Reading

To break the strongly developed habit of focusing on almost every word in the line, many readers find it very helpful to practice reading "between the lines." You do this by fixating, not on the line of print itself, but on the white space just above each line. The bars between the lines of this paragraph show you what we mean, though you will find when you try it that this technique works on every paragraph except this one, because the way it has been set up to demonstrate the idea may make you too conscious of your fixations. In actual practice—with normal spacing of the lines of type—you will discover after a few moments of "reading between the lines" that you do become aware of the space between the lines as a solid bar of white, along which your eyes travel. Also, although you should never try to "feel" your fixations, when you read between the lines you will probably be aware of a difference, a new sensation of freedom from the individual words as fixation points. This sensation can be disquieting at first, but will lead to considerable increases of speed as your practice with Eye Span and Phrase Flashing exercises works to decrease the number of fixations you need for each line.

Reading "between the lines" in this fashion is a technique perfectly suited for regular use in much of the reading you do each day. Another technique, which for some students produces speed gains immediately, is to "shorten" each line at both left and right. That is, if the last fixation you make on each line falls at the extreme right end, there is nothing but blank margin for your peripheral vision to take in on the right side; similarly, if your return sweep carries you *all* the way to the extreme left of each new line, there is nothing but blank margin to the left of your first fixation. For this reason, at the beginning and end of each line, many readers use only one side of their peripheral vision. Thus you may be able to eliminate a total of one full fixation each line, simply by starting the line about three-quarters of an inch inside the left margin, and ending it half an inch before the right margin. The lines down the sides of this paragraph show approximately where your first and last fixations should fall. (What have we said earlier in this chapter that explains why you can leave more for your peripheral vision to do at the beginning of the line than at the end?)

You will find it helpful, the first several times you try this technique, to draw similar lines in pencil down the sides of the page, as reminders to your eyes until you learn the habit. If you now make seven or eight fixations on an average line, by cutting out just one fixation per line with this simple technique you can gain more than 10 per cent in speed.

Subvocalizing: Barrier to Reading Speed

Fixations, reading word by word, regressions—all of these are difficult to feel in one's own reading. *Subvocalizing,* closely associated with word-by-word reading, is something everyone can feel in his reading, can "hear" in his reading: it is the small voice that says the words in your head. Subvocalizing is an inescapable habit when you are thinking. We think in words; often we think in words almost out loud: do you remember the last time you were angry with a friend, and went away rehearsing in your mind what you might have retorted? or the last time you wrote a paper, and debated with yourself the exact wording of the opening paragraph? While you thought, you heard the words in the imagination's ear. That is subvocalizing, or part of it.

In reading, subvocalizing is a useless habit, usually left over from child-hood lessons; for many adults it is a severe barrier to speed. Subvocalizing consists of tiny movements of the lips, tongue, and throat muscles. The reader is just on the verge of reading out loud, so that his speaking muscles get set to pronounce each word. There are several degrees of subvocalizing. Even the fastest reader probably does it sometimes: for example, when reading a tele-phone number, or a word he has never seen before. At its worst, subvocalizing includes visible motions of the lips. You should be able to discover an example of lip reading if you watch newspaper readers the next several times you ride a bus or subway. Now, the fastest professional television or radio announcers rarely speak more than 150–160 words per minute, and for most of us the top speaking speed is about 135 w.p.m. Therefore, the lip reader is limited to read-ing about 180 w.p.m. maximum, even though he does not pronounce the words completely.

Few people are visibly lip readers. But experiments using sensitive elec-trodes placed on the skin to detect minute muscle movements have shown that a high percentage of us, when reading, do demonstrate some muscular activity, at least at the voice box in the throat. Many also show similar invisible activity of the lips and tongue. But the experiments that discovered it also found that about 30 per cent of the readers tested seemed to be free of these tiny muscle movements. Precisely these readers were fastest of those tested.

If you subvocalize without being an obvious lip reader, there is no simple way to know about it directly. The tiny muscle movements occur without your being able to feel them. However, you probably are aware, if you stop to think about it, that as you read you "hear" the words internally, or at least some of them, with that tiny voice of the imagination. "Hearing" the words is apparently directly connected with subvocalizing. As your reading gets faster, you will "hear" fewer and fewer of the words.

As we said, the obvious lip reader is limited in speed to somewhere near 180 w.p.m. Speed barriers of less obvious subvocalizers cannot be fixed so precisely, but we can say that the invisible movements of lips and tongue limit the reader to less than 225–250 w.p.m. Above that there is simply no time for these movements to take place. Throat movements apparently drop out at a a speed slightly higher still. "Hearing" words seems not to disappear completely until somewhere between 275 and 400 w.p.m.

You will note that these last speed ranges are where phrase reading replaces word-by-word reading.

Two Ways to Break Subvocalizing: Knuckle-biting and Number-mumbling

Fortunately, in most cases subvocalizing is fairly easy to correct. For many readers it corrects itself as they push their speed and learn to read by phrases. But if your speeds were below 200 w.p.m. on exercises of average difficulty—or if you do not seem to be able, no matter how hard you try, to go faster than 250 w.p.m. on exercises of average difficulty—you should suspect subvocalizing as a barrier.

In either case, you will find the following technique helpful: during the next three weeks, every time you start to read anything, put the knuckle of your forefinger between your teeth, and grip it—and then, every time, push your reading speed until you are going uncomfortably fast. Besides giving you an air of furious concentration, the knuckle between the teeth throws your lips and tongue into an unusual position, upsetting the physical pattern of subvocalizing. You take advantage of this by accelerating at the same time, to move beyond the speed levels at which lip and tongue movements are possible.

When you can read in the neighborhood of 300 w.p.m. fairly comfortably, you will find it enlightening to try a second technique. Each day for a week, use this on two or three pages of fairly simple reading matter, such as light fiction. Read at your top comfortable rate and, *at the same time,* mumble or whisper to yourself over and over again the numbers "seventeen-eighteen-nineteen-twenty, seventeen-eighteen-nineteen-twenty." You will find it very difficult to understand the first several paragraphs you read this way, or even the first few pages. But with practice you will be able to mumble the numbers and at the same time understand the reading matter.

At this point you will find the effect very startling: probably for the first time you will be reading without any opportunity to subvocalize, and furthermore without being able to "hear" internally any of the words. You will be aware of a sense of detachment from the words, but you will still understand what you read. Probably for the first time you will be taking in the printed symbols with no subvocal filter between the page, your eyes, and your mind. Some readers find this uncomfortable or disquieting at first, because they are accustomed to the subvocal filter as one part of the comprehension process. Most readers, however, soon find that freedom from subvocalizing and internal "hearing" allows them considerably greater speed — with comprehension quickly restored.

Caution

An average golfer or tennis player will be "off his stroke" if he tries to analyze the individual muscle movements as he plays. However, if his game is to improve, he must learn the elements of a good stroke and must practice specific exercises to perfect certain of these elements. As he practices, he will be unusually aware of each movement he makes; but as he improves, this awareness recedes and he pays attention again to the overall object of each play and the entire game.

The average reader is in somewhat the same situation. In this chapter we have explained in some detail exactly what goes on when you read. These details are important so that you can understand and apply the many techniques for improving the various elements of the physical or muscular side of reading skill. But at this point it is important to warn you that, like the golfer, you will be "off your stroke" if you try to concentrate too closely on individual fixations, for example, as you read. True, certain exercises and techniques do ask you to pay attention to individual elements of the reading process, but, except when practicing those exercises, your attention should be on the reading matter itself, on your specific purposes in reading it, and on the overall objective of skillful reading of practical prose — which is to get the full necessary comprehension at the highest possible speed. The rest of this chapter will show you ways to practice, in the speed exercises and in your daily reading, to attain this overall objective.

As you know, the Reading Speed Exercises in this manual are separated into average and difficult levels. The two levels help you learn flexibility in speed. As you progress through the exercises, you should find that the gap will widen between the speeds you use on the two levels. You should eventually approach an 80 to 120 w.p.m. difference in speed, like that of the highly skilled reader.

The retention and comprehension questions that are part of the Reading Speed Exercises will give you a measure of your best, most effective reading speeds for each level. In two respects, however, the questions have you at a disadvantage: first, since you do not pre-read the speed exercises, you are reading them "cold"; and second, the selections are drawn from so many sources that the general subject matter of many of them will be new to you. (For these reasons, 70 per cent or better is defined as an adequate score on the comprehension check.)

Because there are questions to measure your retention and comprehension, you can experiment with speeds when taking timed reading exercises. Whenever your Progress Profile shows that you have read two consecutive speed exercises with comprehension at 70 per cent or above, take the next exercise *with the intention of reading too fast* for adequate comprehension. You will be surprised, when you do this, at the reading speed you can reach *without* losing adequate comprehension. When you actually read too fast for adequate comprehension, the retention and comprehension questions will let you know.

Pre-reading: Read the concluding paragraphs thoroughly.

The speed level that is safe for comprehension with any piece of practical prose is *the top comfortable rate* at which you can read it. As your reading improves, you will find that if you always read practical prose at the top comfortable rate, you will automatically take account of variations in difficulty level from one piece of material to the next. Your own feeling for that top comfortable rate will come to be a much more accurate speedometer than any prescription of so-and-so many words per minute.

A third type of speed exercise, beginning in this chapter, is designed to help you carry your new speeds — and your awareness of how it feels to read at the top comfortable rate — over into your day-to-day reading. These Reading Speed Carry-over exercises ask you to choose material outside this book that you must read anyway, and to use it for concentrated speed-practice sessions. These sessions should be held not less than three times a week, ideally once a day, for about twenty minutes each time. For these integrated speed trials you will choose six to ten pages of difficult material that you want to read and comprehend fully. You will attack it in four steps. You will pre-read it quickly. Then — and here's the trick of it — you will read the material *twice*. On the first reading, you are to read as fast as you can push yourself, so that your speed feels dangerously above the comfortable rate. Then, before you read the second time, close the book and jot down in summary form all that pre-reading and high-speed reading have taught you about what the passage says. Then read the second time through, more slowly, to discover what you missed on the first reading.

Do you understand why this exercise is designed as it is? It combines pre-reading, very fast thorough reading, a pause to recapitulate to yourself what you have read, and a careful check to see how well you did. That final, slower reading is the equivalent of the comprehension questions after exercises in this book.

You will need repeated trials before you will get adequate comprehension on the first, very fast reading, but don't let that make you slow down too much. If you get full comprehension too consistently on the first reading in these practice sessions, you are missing the point of the test drive: remember, you can't crash, and the second reading will always provide the necessary comprehension check.

Stop pre-reading here. Your pre-reading alone should enable you to answer the following questions, without looking back.

1. What is the most important way to improve reading speed?

   ANSWER _____

   _____

2. What is the chief block to faster reading?

    ANSWER _____

    _____

3. You must learn to concentrate on your eye movements as you read.

    True _____   False _____

4. What is the best speed level for any piece of practical prose?

    ANSWER _____

5. What will be your precise purpose in reading this chapter thoroughly?

    ANSWER _____

    _____

6. The principal topics of this chapter are listed below, but not in the correct order. Number them to show the sequence in which they actually occur.

    _____ Subvocalizing: barrier to reading speed

    _____ The speed exercises in this book

    _____ How eye movements affect reading speed

    _____ Two eye-movement techniques to try in your daily reading

    _____ Speed practice in your daily reading

    _____ Peripheral vision

    _____ Two ways to break subvocalizing

    _____ Four exercises to improve eye movements

    _____ Caution: one danger to avoid

After answering these questions, read the chapter thoroughly.

EXERCISES FOR CHAPTER 4

Reading Journal

Phrase Flashing

Pre-reading
Introduction to *The Origin of Species,* by Charles Darwin

Summarizing, in Practice (a carry-over exercise)

Phrase Sense

Reading Speed Exercise: Difficult Level 2
"Aftermath," from *The Great Crash,* by John Kenneth Galbraith

Reading Speed Carry-over Exercise

Reading Journal

In the separate notebook you are keeping, bring the section on **current reading** up to date: list everything you have read since your last entry, including title, author, type of material or subject, length, and the time you spent on it. Add to each item your purpose in reading it.

Then add to each item a brief summary—one or two sentences—of the content of the piece, and your opinion of it.

Finally, try to note for each item *the reading techniques you used with it.*

Next, under the heading **future reading,** bring the list up to date with any additional material you now expect—or will be required—to read in the next several months: titles, authors, subject, and number of pages.

Then note next to each item, in detail (in at least a couple of sentences), exactly why you will be reading it, what your purpose is, what you expect the material to give you.

Then, for each item that you have already begun to read, note whether you have pre-read it and what the pre-reading disclosed about the *structure* and *content* of the piece.

You will return to your Reading Journal at the end of this chapter for the Reading Speed Carry-over Exercise.

Phrase Flashing

This exercise is designed to help you develop the quick and accurate perception of *phrases as units* upon which efficient reading speeds depend.

The materials for this practice are arranged so that you return to them repeatedly as you work through this book, progressing to longer phrases. For convenience and flexibility, therefore, the practice phrases and instructions have been grouped together beginning on page 476. Please turn to page 476 and follow the instructions.

Pre-reading

The following selection, a little more than half of Charles Darwin's introduction to *The Origin of Species,* presents the organization of the whole book. We have seen the important part that such introductory material will play in pre-reading nonfiction books. First, pre-read this selection and answer the *pre-reading questions* that follow. Second, return to the selection to read it thoroughly; then go on to the *thorough-reading questions* on page 105.

This is not a timed exercise. Please do *not* refer to the article when you answer the pre-reading questions. You *may* refer to the article for the thorough-reading questions.

Begin here.

From the Introduction
to *The Origin of Species*
by CHARLES DARWIN

A

In considering the Origin of Species, it is quite conceivable that a naturalist, reflecting on the mutual affinities of organic beings, on their embryological relations, their geographical distribution, geological succession, and other such facts, might come to the conclusion that species had not been independently created, but had descended, like varieties, from other species. Nevertheless, such a conclusion, even if well founded, would be unsatisfactory, until it could be shown how the innumerable species inhabiting this world have been modified, so as to acquire that perfection of structure and coadaptation which justly excites our admiration. Naturalists continually refer to external conditions, such as climate, food, &c., as the only possible cause of variation. In one limited sense, as we shall hereafter see, this may be true; but it is preposterous to attribute to mere external conditions, the structure, for instance, of the woodpecker, with its feet, tail, beak, and tongue, so admirably adapted to catch insects under the bark of trees. In the case of the mistletoe, which draws its nourishment from certain trees, which has seeds that must be transported by certain birds, and which has flowers with separate sexes absolutely requiring the agency of certain insects to bring pollen from one flower to the other, it is equally preposterous to account for the structure of this parasite, with its relations to several distinct organic beings, by the effects of external conditions, or of habit, or of the volition of the plant itself.

B

It is, therefore, of the highest importance to gain a clear insight into the means of modification and coadaptation. At the commencement of my observations it seemed to me probable that a careful study of domesticated animals and of cultivated plants would offer the best chance of making out this obscure problem. Nor have I been disappointed; in this and in all other perplexing cases I have invariably found that our knowledge, imperfect though it be, of variation under domestication, afforded the best and safest clue. I may venture to express my conviction of the high value of such studies, although they have been very commonly neglected by naturalists.

C

From these considerations, I shall devote the first chapter of this Abstract to Variation under Domestication. We shall thus see that a large amount of hereditary modification is at least possible; and, what is equally or more important, we shall see how great is the power of man in accumulating by his Selection successive slight variations. I will then pass on to the variability of species in a state of nature; but I shall, unfortunately, be compelled to treat this subject far too briefly, as it can be treated properly only by giving long catalogues of facts. We shall, however, be enabled to discuss what circumstances are most favourable to variation. In the next chapter the Struggle for Existence amongst all organic beings throughout the world, which inevitably follows from the high geometrical ratio of their increase, will be considered. This is the doctrine of Malthus, applied to the whole animal and vegetable kingdoms. As many more individuals of each species are born than can possibly survive; and as, consequently, there is a frequently recurring struggle for existence, it follows that any being, if it vary however slightly in any manner profitable to itself, under the complex and sometimes varying conditions of life, will have a better chance of surviving, and thus be *naturally selected*. From the strong principle of inheritance, any selected variety will tend to propagate its new and modified form.

D

This fundamental subject of Natural Selection will be treated at some length in the fourth chapter; and we shall then see how Natural Selection almost inevitably causes much Extinction of the less improved forms of life, and leads to what I have called Divergence of Character. In the next chapter I shall discuss the complex and little known laws of variation. In the five succeeding chapters, the most apparent and gravest difficulties in accepting the theory will be given: namely, first, the difficulties of transitions, or how a simple being or a simple organ can be changed and perfected into a highly developed being or into an elaborately constructed organ; secondly, the subject of Instinct, or the mental powers of animals; thirdly, Hybridism, or the infertility of species and the fertility of varieties when intercrossed; and fourthly, the imperfection of the Geological Record. In the next chapter I shall consider the geological succession of organic beings throughout time; in the twelfth and thirteenth, their geographical distribution throughout space; in the fourteenth, their classification or mutual affinities, both when mature and in an embryonic condition. In the last chapter I shall give a brief recapitulation of the whole work, and a few concluding remarks.

E

No one ought to feel surprise at much remaining as yet unexplained in regard to the origin of species and varieties, if he make due allowance for our profound ignorance in regard to the mutual relations of the many beings which live around us. Who can explain why one species ranges widely and is very numerous, and why another allied species has a narrow range and is rare? Yet these relations are of the highest importance, for they determine the present welfare and, as I believe, the future success and modification of every inhabitant of this world. Still less do we know of the mutual relations of the innumerable inhabitants of the world during the many past geological epochs in its history. Although much remains obscure, and will long remain obscure, I can entertain no doubt, after the most deliberate study and dispassionate judgment of which I am capable, that the view which most naturalists until recently entertained, and which I formerly entertained — namely, that each species has been independently created — is erroneous. I am fully convinced that species are not immutable; but that those belonging to what are called the same genera are lineal descendants of some other and generally extinct species, in the same manner as the acknowledged varieties of any one species are the descendants of that species. Furthermore, I am convinced that Natural Selection has been the most important, but not the exclusive, means of modification.

Now go on to the questions that follow.

They assume that you are examining the material because you intend eventually to read the book thoroughly. Enter the answer to each question in the appropriate space.

Pre-reading questions. (Do *not* refer to the material.)
1. Author's structure and purpose: What does Darwin do in this excerpt? (Choose the most complete answer that is still correct.) (a) He explains why he wrote the book, and what he hopes to prove; (b) he gives an annotated version of the table of contents, explaining what each chapter will contain; (c) he gives a brief explanation of some reasons for writing the book as he has, and explains what each chapter will contain and (briefly) why; (d) he analyzes a few examples of the problem of how species originate (such as the mistletoe); (e) he explains the importance to his work of the study of domesticated plants and animals.
ANSWER _____
2. Reading difficulty: The excerpt is certainly not "light reading." What ele-

ments seem to contribute to its difficulty? (Choose *all* correct answers.) (a) Highly technical vocabulary; (b) clumsy sentences; (c) sentences longer than usual in present-day writing; (d) paragraphs longer than usual in present-day writing; (e) content of the selection extremely difficult; (f) content of parts of the selection, at least, unfamiliar to the nonspecialist reader.

ANSWER _____

Now return to read the selection thoroughly.

Thorough-reading questions. (You *may* refer to the material.)
3. The examples of the woodpecker and the mistletoe are used to show (a) that a study of present species, by itself, seems to prove that they could not have been derived from different earlier species; (b) that any theory of species formation must explain — and not by reference to external conditions alone — how the many modifications occurred that have produced the perfection of structure we see; (c) why he begins his book with a chapter about plants and animals under domestication; (d) how his theory replaces all earlier ones on the subject; (e) none of the above.

ANSWER _____

4. A careful study of variation in plants and animals under domestication is required to understand "this obscure problem." "This obscure problem" is (a) the effect of external conditions on plant and animal structures; (b) the effect of external conditions, habit and "volition" on modification and coadaptation; (c) the means of modification and coadaptation, which must be understood before any conclusion about the descent of species can be satisfactory; (d) the fundamental subject of Natural Selection discussed in Chapter 4; (e) none of the above.

ANSWER _____

5. Darwin devotes Chapter 1 to "Variation under Domestication," Chapter 2 to "Variation in Nature," and Chapter 5 to "the Laws of Variation." Why all this stress on variation? (a) Because variation was denied by most previous naturalists; (b) because variation was thought by most previous naturalists to be only an *effect* of external conditions rather than something that permits the better-adapted individuals to survive; (c) because variation explains the imperfection of the geological record; (d) because Darwin desired to anticipate all objections; (e) none of the above.

ANSWER _____

6. Darwin spends three chapters building up to his central idea (in Chapter 4) that variations which are better fitted to survive are *naturally selected.* Chapter 5 again speaks of variation. But what is his next step? (a) Further demonstration of the correctness of his theories in many very specific cases; (b) discussion of the importance of what can be learned from geology about older species forms; (c) discussion of the flaws in the geological record of past species; (d) discussion of the major objections that may be raised against his theory of the origin of species; (e) none of the above.

ANSWER _____

7. Several times in this selection Darwin uses the term "coadaptation." What

does he seem to mean by it? (a) The gradual accumulation of varieties; (b) the complete adaptation of each part of the animal to its whole way of life, as with the beak and claws of the woodpecker; (c) the adjustment of a species to all the other species on which it depends for life; (d) the extinction of less improved forms of life; (e) none of the above.

ANSWER _____

Summarizing, in Practice (a carry-over exercise)

The excerpt from Charles Darwin's *The Origin of Species* that you have just read contains five paragraphs. Now reread each one and write a one-sentence summary of it.

A: _____

_____

_____

B: _____

_____

_____

C: _____

_____

_____

D: _____

_____

_____

E: _____

_____

_____

Phrase Sense

As you will remember, the purpose of this next exercise is to increase your understanding of which groups of several words within a sentence hang together as a meaningful unit. After you have completed the exercise above, go back to those same paragraphs and divide each sentence by circling the phrases or marking a "slash" (/) between them. Work as quickly as you can, without stopping to reason out or ponder over the phrases. You are to work for the *sense* of which words clump together. The first sentence of the article is reprinted again here, marked correctly.

In considering / the Origin of Species, / it is quite conceivable / that a naturalist, / reflecting on the mutual affinities / of organic beings, / on their embryological relations, / their geographical distribution, / geological succession, / and other such facts, / might come to the conclusion / that species / had not been / independently created, / but had descended, / like varieties, / from other species. /

Reading Speed Exercise: Difficult Level 2

1929—what, above all, does that year bring to mind? Panic in Wall Street and on Main Street, stock market prices tumbling and tumbling, the ticker tape hours late, millionaires and small-time speculators joined in ruin, financiers plunging from skyscraper window ledges—*The Great Crash.* And that is the title Harvard economist John Kenneth Galbraith chose for his fascinating history book from which the next article is drawn. In this passage he examines one odd aftermath of the financial panic. The content is on a difficult level, due largely to a somewhat technical vocabulary. The style is superbly readable, but its very elegance and wit invite the reader's pleased attention. For these reasons, skilled readers tend to read it at speeds somewhat lower than the maximum they would use with material of a factual nature, popularly written.

You are to read the selection against time. Follow your instructor's directions, or the Instructions for Timing on page 474.

Before reading, practice with the Eye Movements in Reading Exercise on pages 54–56.

Do not pre-read the selection; the timed reading exercises are designed to measure improvements in speed alone. After reading it and recording your time, go on to the ten multiple-choice questions beginning on page 110. There is no time limit for the questions, but it will invalidate the exercise if you refer to this passage while you answer them.

Begin reading here.

"Aftermath"
from *The Great Crash*[1]
by JOHN KENNETH GALBRAITH

In many ways the effect of the crash on embezzlement was more significant than on suicide. To the economist embezzlement is the most interesting of crimes. Alone among the various forms of larceny it has a time parameter. Weeks, months, or years may elapse between the commission of the crime and its discovery. (This is a period, incidentally, when the embezzler has his gain and the man who has been embezzled, oddly enough, feels no loss. There is a net increase in psychic wealth.) At any given time there exists an inventory of undiscovered embezzlement in — or more precisely not in — the country's businesses and banks. This inventory — it should perhaps be called the bezzle — amounts at any moment to many millions of dollars. It also varies in size with the business cycle. In good times people are relaxed, trusting, and money is plentiful. But even though money is plentiful, there are always many people who need more. Under these circumstances the rate of embezzlement grows, the rate of discovery falls off, and the bezzle increases rapidly. In depression all this is reversed. Money is watched with a narrow, suspicious eye. The man who handles it is assumed to be dishonest until he proves himself otherwise. Audits are penetrating and meticulous. Commercial morality is enormously improved. The bezzle shrinks.

The stock market boom and the ensuing crash caused a traumatic exaggeration of these normal relationships. To the normal needs for money, for home, family and dissipation, was added, during the boom, the new and overwhelming requirement for funds to play the market or to meet margin calls. Money was exceptionally plentiful. People were also exceptionally trusting. A bank president who was himself trusting Kreuger, Hopson, and Insull was obviously unlikely to suspect his lifelong friend the cashier. In the late twenties the bezzle grew apace.

Just as the boom accelerated the rate of growth, so the crash enormously advanced the rate of discovery. Within a few days, something close to universal trust turned into something akin to universal suspicion. Audits were ordered. Strained or preoccupied behavior was noticed. Most important, the collapse in stock values made irredeemable the position of the employee who had embezzled to play the market. He now confessed.

After the first week or so of the crash, reports of defaulting employees were a daily occurrence. They were far more common than the suicides. On some days comparatively brief accounts occupied a column or more in the *Times*. The amounts were large and small, and they were reported from far and wide.

The most spectacular embezzlement of the period — the counterpart of the Riordan suicide — was the looting of the Union Industrial Bank of Flint, Michigan. The gross take, estimates of which grew alarmingly as the investigation proceeded, was stated in *The Literary Digest* later in the year to be $3,592,000.

In the beginning this embezzlement was a matter of individual initiative. Unknown to each other, a number of the bank's officers began making away with funds. Gradually they became aware of each other's activities, and since they could scarcely expose each other, they co-operated. The enterprise eventually embraced about a dozen people, including virtually all of the principal officers of the bank. Operations were so well organized that even the arrival of bank examiners at the local hotels was made known promptly to members of the syndicate.

Most of the funds which were purloined had been deposited with the bank to be loaned in the New York call market. The money was duly dispatched to New York but promptly recalled while the records continued to show that it was there. The money was then returned once more to New York and put into stocks. In the spring of 1929 the group was about $100,000 ahead. Then, unfortunately, it went short just as the market soared into the blue yonder of the summer sky. This was so costly that the group was induced to return to a long position, which it did just before the crash. The crash, needless to say, was mortal.

Each week during the autumn more such unfortunates were revealed in their misery. Most of them were small men who had taken a flier in the market and then become more deeply involved. Later they had more impressive companions. It was the crash, and the subsequent ruthless contraction of values which, in the end, exposed the speculation by Kreuger, Hopson, and Insull with the money of other people. Should the American economy ever achieve permanent full employment and prosperity, firms should look well to their auditors. One of the uses of depression is the exposure of what auditors fail to find. Bagehot once observed: "Every great crisis reveals the excessive speculations of many houses which no one before suspected."

Now note your reading time. Record it below and go on to the questions.

YOUR READING TIME: _____MIN. _____SEC. _____W.P.M. COMPREHENSION SCORE: _____%
(WORDS PER MINUTE FROM THE TABLE ON PAGE 475.)

Please do not read these questions until you have read the selection itself against time. Do not refer to the selection as you answer the questions. Choose the *one best* answer to each question and enter the corresponding letter in the proper answer space.

1. To the economist, embezzlement is the most interesting of crimes, because (a) unlike other crimes, it increases as money is more plentiful, rather than the reverse; (b) unlike other crimes, it produces a net increase in psychic wealth; (c) it is the only form of larceny where time, often a long time, elapses between commission and discovery, a fact with curious consequences; (d) it is the most important form of larceny to fluctuate with the overall business cycle; (e) it is the most important form of larceny that fluctuates with the stock market.

ANSWER _____

2. The *bezzle* is defined in the article as (a) the man who does the embezzling; (b) the total of all embezzlements; (c) the total, at a given time, of undiscovered embezzlements in the nation's businesses and banks; (d) the total, at a given time, of undiscovered embezzlements *not* in the nation's businesses and banks; (e) the accounting methods and tricks by which embezzlement is concealed.

ANSWER _____

3. Which of the following was *not* listed as a cause or example of the reasons for the decrease of the bezzle during depressions? (a) Money is then watched with a narrow, suspicious eye; (b) less money is needed to play the stock market; (c) the man who handles money is presumed to be dishonest until he proves himself otherwise; (d) audits are penetrating and meticulous; (e) commercial morality is forced to improve.

ANSWER _____

4. In relation to the amount of embezzlement, the stock market boom caused (a) a decrease despite the good times, because employers were strongly aware of the temptations to play the market with embezzled funds; (b) a decrease, because the market provided an honest way to make money that otherwise might have been embezzled; (c) an increase in the bezzle, as usually happens in boom times; (d) an unusual increase, as the need for funds to play the market was added to the usual reasons for embezzling; (e) an unusual increase in the length of time embezzlements could remain undiscovered.

ANSWER _____

5. After the stock market crash, of all the influences that increased the rate of discovery of embezzlements the most important was (a) the many suicides; (b) the change of nearly universal trust into widespread suspicion; (c) penetrating audits; (d) the observation of strained or preoccupied behavior; (e) the irredeemable position, forcing confession, of anyone who had embezzled to play the market.

ANSWER _____

6. The most spectacular embezzlement of the period, the case of the Union Industrial Bank of Flint, Michigan, totaled (a) just over one million dollars; (b) just under two million; (c) nearly two and one-half million; (d) over three and one-half million; (e) close to five million.

ANSWER _____

7. Which of the following was *not* mentioned by the author as one of the sequence of events in the case of the Union Industrial Bank? (a) The embezzlement began when a number of the bank's officers each independently began making away with funds; (b) the embezzlers then became aware of each other's activities, and co-operated; (c) at one point the group had actually made money on the stock market, but then they made serious mistakes in their speculations; (d) the crash forced the group to confess; (e) the group was found to include about a dozen people, including most of the principal officers of the bank.

ANSWER _____

8. The "tone" of the article is (a) completely serious, as is appropriate to the major crimes the author discusses; (b) serious but heavily ironic, as is appropriate to the extraordinary human behavior the author describes; (c) witty, almost light, as is appropriate to the tale of human folly the author recounts, and also effective in driving home a basically serious lesson; (d) witty and light, to a degree that is not appropriate to the subject matter or the lesson to be drawn from it; (e) flippant, to a degree that spoils even the real humor in some of the things the author describes.

ANSWER _____

9. The "moral"—the lesson for the present day—to be drawn from the history of embezzlement before and after the crash, is that (a) the smaller men, operating on a small scale, account for the largest portion of the bezzle; (b) it takes a major crash to reveal the large-scale operators working with the funds of others; (c) accounting and auditing procedures should be used with especial care and thoroughness when the nation experiences high prosperity and employment; (d) those in positions of trust should not be permitted to trade in the stock market except under severe restrictions; (e) the bezzle is probably higher right now than even in 1929 just before the crash.

ANSWER _____

10. How is the article organized? From the following list, pick out the *three* major parts that make up the article and arrange them in the *correct order* that best describes the organizational sequence from beginning to end.

    a. Statement of the lessons to be learned from the history of embezzlement at the time of the 1929 crash;
    b. analysis of the motives of embezzlers;
    c. details and examples showing the effects of the 1929 crash on embezzlement;
    d. comparison of small-scale with large-scale cases of embezzlement and misuse of the funds of others;
    e. brief, but central, description of the detailed technical methods the author recommends to fight embezzlement;
    f. a general description of the nature of embezzlement and of the effect on it of good times and bad.

ANSWER _____

Now check your answers, and enter your score on your Progress Profile, page vii.

Reading Speed Carry-over Exercise

With this exercise you will carry new habits of speed and reading efficiency into your day-to-day reading of practical prose. Please choose, from the lists in your Reading Journal of books that you will be reading over the next month, one book that it is important for you to read thoroughly, and that is fairly difficult. You will return to that book repeatedly for these Speed Carry-over Exercises. Your speed practice has four steps:

Pick a passage you have not yet read—a chapter or a piece of a chapter that makes a sensible single unit, six to ten pages long. Pre-read it quickly.

Then read the passage very fast, pushing your speed to the point where it feels distinctly dangerous.

Close the book; in your Reading Journal, jot down in summary form all that pre-reading and fast thorough reading of this passage have taught you.

Then return to the passage and read it a second time, more slowly, checking your comprehension and adding to it.

The aim of that first, very fast reading, is to push your speed to the top possible limit without loss of comprehension: but that limit is, for most people, higher than at first feels safe. Therefore, in these exercises it is better to err by going somewhat too fast than too slowly. The second reading is your safeguard. Repeated practice will establish that top speed with some accuracy—which is one reason you should continue with the same book in future practice sessions until you finish it.

CHAPTER 5

Paragraph Analysis

Pre-read this chapter as your first step in reading.

Read normally the first several paragraphs;

then read the first sentence only of each remaining paragraph;

but when you reach the concluding paragraphs, read them thoroughly.

Begin pre-reading here.

Get the author on your side: use the techniques he puts into his writing to make your reading easier. Above all, as we have repeated, the organization of the reading matter is the key you must seek. So far we have discussed primarily the overall organization of the largest units of writing: books, book chapters, and articles. And we have introduced pre-reading as the most effective technique for opening your attack on them. You should by this time have a lively awareness of the power of pre-reading. This chapter treats a second approach to organization: *paragraph analysis.*

Pre-reading is the strategy, but paragraph analysis the tactics, of your attack on practical prose. Pre-reading shows you how the large units are put together; paragraph analysis will show you how smaller units are put together. Understanding this smaller-scale organization will develop your ability to comprehend, retain, and relate to each other the *details* of what you read. After all, detailed understanding is often your purpose in reading—and it is, for most readers, exactly the purpose they find most difficult to achieve. This is the first reason why paragraph analysis is an indispensable addition to your techniques of reading. The second reason is that paragraph analysis is itself the basis for other techniques: methods for improving concentration, for taking notes, for reading with questions in mind, and for critical reading.

Paragraph analysis has two aspects: structure, and rhetorical development. Structure, which this chapter treats, has to do with the way the author has put the paragraph together: where he has located its principal statement or point, and how, around that statement, he has clustered the details. Developmental analysis is also introduced in this chapter: it gets at the functions to which an author puts his paragraphs, the kinds and categories of statements he makes in them. In particular, this chapter discusses two of the most important paragraph functions: definition and summary/transition.

Paragraph Structure

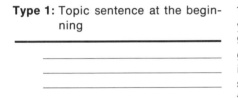

Why this blank space? Without thinking, most people recognize the indentation at the beginning of each paragraph as a signal that the author is about to begin a new thought. Even so slight an awareness of paragraphs helps us to read. But just as the author uses the indentation at the beginning as a signal, so he uses the sequence of sentences within as the framework on which his details are organized. Most paragraphs are built around a principal statement, which, you will recall from elementary grammar, is called the *topic sentence:* this principal statement is developed by the other sentences in a paragraph. The position of topic sentences within them primarily determines how paragraphs are organized. There are four basic positions topic sentences may take; in addition, it is possible for a paragraph to have no topic sentence. Therefore, five basic types of paragraph organization occur. We will discuss them in turn.

Type 1: Topic sentence at the beginning

_____
_____
_____
_____

(In the diagrams, the longer, heavier lines show the position of the topic sentence relative to the details of the paragraph.)

Type 1 is the paragraph organization you will find most frequently: 60 to 90 per cent of practical prose paragraphs are Type 1. The topic sentence is developed—that is, explained or supported—by the succeeding sentences of the paragraph. A writer who works with an outline from which the headings can be converted into topic sentences is especially prone to use Type 1 paragraphs.

Occasionally if the topic sentence is ambiguous, or seriously qualified by the second sentence, it is necessary in pre-reading and skimming to read the second sentence also, in order to grasp the principal statement. In such cases, we may say that the first two sentences make up the topic statement.

Here is an example of Type 1, with analysis:

The softwoods, which in the main are obtained from needle-leaved evergreen, cone-bearing trees, are graded to meet fairly definite building requirements. The pines, firs, and hemlocks are familiar examples of softwood species. The select grades of softwoods are based on suitability for natural and paint finishes; A Select and B Select primarily on the basis of require-

Topic sentence,

followed by examples clarifying *softwoods,* followed by a detailed listing of the grades of softwoods and how they relate to *building requirements.*

ments for natural finishes, and C Select and D Select for paint finishes. The utility-board grades are based primarily on their suitability purposes as influenced by the size, tightness, and soundness of knots.[1]

Type 2: Topic sentences at beginning and end

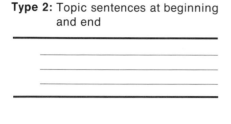

Type 2 has two topic sentences. It is similar to Type 1 in that the first sentence is a principal statement that is developed by succeeding sentences. The second topic sentence, at the end of the paragraph, is usually a restatement of the first, or a summary of the paragraph. Occasionally, however, the second topic sentence is more than a restatement or summary, if it states conclusions drawn from the paragraph, or if it states the significance or application of details set forth in the paragraph.

Here, in one passage, drawn from a current college text in psychology, are paragraphs of Type 1 and Type 2.

Although the impetus for the founding of laboratories and suggestions for problems to be dealt with at first came largely from Germany, especially from Wundt, other influences soon began to be felt. One set of influences came from England, especially from Sir Francis Galton (1822–1911). Galton pioneered in a measurement psychology in Great Britain which was devoted mainly to a study of the problem of individual differences, including inherited abilities. Hence he had an important influence on the development of intelligence tests and other kinds of tests that have become prominent in American psychology. He also had his influence upon the laboratory. It was he who invented the statistical technique of correlation and developed the index later to be named the *coefficient of correlation.* We shall meet that coefficient often in the pages of this book.

Also from England came the influence of the theory of evolution, as propounded

Topic sentence,

narrowed and made specific,

then followed by details about Galton's work,

and his influence.

The paragraph is Type 1.

Topic sentence,

by Charles Darwin (1809–82). Because Darwin's theory established the continuity between animal and man, it made *comparative psychology* important. American psychologists have closely studied lower animals, especially white rats, monkeys, and chimpanzees, not only in order to understand their behavior but also to learn principles important in the understanding of man. The notion of adaptation to environment, inherent in the evolutionary theory, led also to a psychology of adjustment. *That is, following Darwin, some psychologists believed that we could understand consciousness, emotions, and other psychological processes if we knew how they served the adjustment of man to his environment.*

followed by reasons for Darwin's influence, pointing out one result of that influence,

and a second result.

Because the last sentence summarizes the paragraph in part, and shows its significance, the paragraph is Type 2.

Another body of influence upon psychology came from medicine and psychiatry, especially from the treatment of the mentally ill. We need think only of the long history of hypnotism, dating especially from Anton Mesmer (1734–1815). And at every turn today we meet the influence of another Viennese physician, Sigmund Freud (1856–1939), the founder of that branch of psychology known as *psychoanalysis.*[2]

Topic sentence,

followed by one detail,

and a second.

The paragraph is Type 1.

Type 3: Topic sentences at beginning and middle

Type 3 contains two topic sentences. It consists of two paragraphs of Type 1, closely enough related to be printed as a single paragraph. Since the trend in modern practical prose is toward short paragraphs, Type 3 is now employed fairly rarely, though it will be found commonly in earlier writing, particularly that written before World War I.

Here, nonetheless, is a straightforward example of Type 3, taken once again from a current college text.

The plains Indians were generally superior in physique to the Indians of other regions. Although their culture varied from that of the peaceful tribes of the pueblos to that of fierce nomadic tribes, all the plains Indians shared the culture of neolithic man,

Topic sentence,

followed by details.

using stone knives, stone scrapers, and bone awls as tools. The warriors carried bows and arrows and fourteen-foot, stone-tipped lances for hunting and warfare. *Yet in combat the stone-age man asked no quarter of early industrial man.* With his short three-foot bow and a quiver of two-score arrows or more, the Comanche would ride three hundred yards and get off twenty arrows with startling force and accuracy while the Texan was firing one shot and reloading his long and cumbersome rifle. Even the Colt six-shooter, with which the white man began arming himself in the 1840's, did not entirely overcome the Indian's advantage. As armor he carried a loosely slung shield made of buffalo hide so tough that it could deflect a bullet. The arrows he used against an enemy, unlike those he used in the hunt, were fitted with heads that came off in the wound when the shaft was withdrawn.[3]

Second topic sentence begins a new subject, related to the first but different enough so that many authors would have begun a new paragraph. Details follow.

This example is from a history book; more often today, however, you will find Type 3 in closely reasoned writing, where one statement is explained, and then a contradictory statement is presented and explained.

Type 4: Topic sentence at end

_____
_____
_____
_____
━━━━━━━━━━━━━━━━━━━━━━━━━━━━━━━━━

Type 4, like Type 1, has only one topic sentence—but this time at the end. Type 4 is easy to spot: a series of details is given, and the topic sentence serves as a conclusion that draws the details together. Type 4 is employed infrequently in modern practical prose, but like Type 3, it was common before World War I.

Here is an example of Type 4:

Is Latin America just another name for South America? No, for Cuba and Mexico are in Latin America, but they are not parts of South America. Does "Latin America" refer to that part of the Western Hemisphere where Spanish is officially the language? No, because Portuguese is the official language of Brazil, and a variety of French is spoken in parts of the West Indies. Spanish, Portuguese, and French are all derived from Latin. But to define our term accurately, we must first take account of the French spoken in

The author is raising and elaborating questions that he will answer later. Here, a second question follows the first,

and details are given,

Quebec. *Then we may say that Latin America includes those parts of the Western Hemisphere, south of any part of Canada, where a Latin language (Spanish, Portuguese, or French) is the official language.*[4]

all capped by the topic sentence which states the definition finally arrived at.

Type 5: No topic sentence

Type 5 has no topic sentence—no principal statement that the rest of the paragraph develops by details. On the contrary, Type 5 does not *develop;* it may *catalogue* or *list details,* or it may *narrate* or *describe.* The sequence of statements is usually controlled by some simple, logical relationship, such as a progression of sizes, an order of events in time, or an arrangement of objects.

Here is an example of Type 5:

For many years Malaya has led in the mining of tin ore, producing about a quarter of the world supply. Other major producers are Bolivia, Indonesia, mainland China, the U.S.S.R., and the Republic of the Congo (Léopoldville). Malay ore is smelted at Singapore and Penang and then sent to the United Kingdom for refining; Indonesian ore is smelted locally and shipped to refineries in the United States. The major tin-smelting nations are Malaya, the United Kingdom, mainland China, the U.S.S.R., the United States, and the Netherlands. The United States, the world's major consumer of metallic tin, has virtually no tin ores. It must obtain foreign ores to smelt, and also buy smelted tin ores from Malaya and western Europe.[5]

General statement.

General statement.

Particular statements following out the course of the metal from the previous two general statements.
Other general statements,

followed by a particular consequence.

Note that no one sentence is a principal statement developed by the rest of the paragraph.

Paragraph Functions: Two Types of Development

So far we have discussed the organizational framework that topic sentences supply in the paragraph. As you practice spotting topic sentences, you will become vividly aware that authors use paragraphs of similar organization for widely different purposes. These purposes—the functions an author calls on his paragraphs to perform as he develops his subject—can also be analyzed; such analyses can be very helpful to your reading. We take up these detailed analyses in Chapter 14, "Introduction to Critical Reading: Development Analysis." Two special purposes, however, are so important that you should begin immediately to watch for them. These are *definition* and *summary/transition.*

How does one define *definition?* A proper definition is a statement with a precise logical form: it says about its subject just what kind of thing it is, and then how it differs from anything else with which you might confuse it. Sometimes a definition will tell you how a thing works or is done (a *process* or *operational* definition). Often the definition is clarified by examples.

A word or concept that is easy to define may be handled in a sentence or brief paragraph—as, for example, many words such as *cow* or *osmosis* are defined in a dictionary. Often in a defining paragraph the author will tell you how he proposes to use a term in an unusual or restricted sense. A difficult term may take many paragraphs, perhaps a whole chapter, to define adequately. And occasionally—though this is certainly an extreme example for our present purpose—an entire book may serve as an extended definition. One example is the pioneering work in semantics, *The Meaning of Meaning,* by C. K. Ogden and I. A. Richards: the authors' purpose, indicated by their title, is to investigate precisely what is involved when we say this or that "means" something. The book is a definition of *definition.*

Look back now at those last two paragraphs: they are themselves a definition. Can you find the various elements of a precise definition in those paragraphs? What sentence states what kind of thing a definition is? Where does the definition function by explaining *process?* Where does it give examples?

Can you find, earlier in this chapter, among the paragraphs given as examples of structure, one which functions as a definition?

Clearly, definitions are among the most important statements an author makes: note them to yourself when you come to them, catch them even while pre-reading if you can, read them carefully, for everything that follows a definition may depend on it.

Transitional/summary paragraphs are important in a quite different way. They are the author's structural signposts—the pauses that he provides to help you follow his thoughts. They serve to tell you that *we have been here,* and *now we go there.* Transitional paragraphs are easy to identify. You will find, for instance, that most of them contain key phrases like: *as we have seen . . . , we shall now discuss . . . , to this point we have been concerned with . . . ,* and other variations of these. Examples of transition in this book are the last paragraph on page 119 and the first paragraph on page 163. Like definitions, transitional paragraphs should be read thoroughly when pre-reading.

Here is another example, from an American history text, of a paragraph which performs its transitional function by summarizing what lies ahead.

The central theme of American history during the quarter-century following Reconstruction was laissez faire—"let alone." In this period control over public policy was surrendered very largely to private interest. The six chapters that follow will reveal this philosophy at work in all sections of the country, in the city as in the countryside, in economics as in politics. Laissez faire profoundly affected the lot of Negro freedmen and Indians, the fate of buffaloes, natural resources, and public lands, the course of railroad operations, industrial management, and labor relations. After 1877 the center of historical forces and the focus of historical interest shift away from Washington. The federal government and the major political parties retreated from responsibility for public policy and fixed their attention narrowly on political maneuvers and trade in public offices.[3]

Marginal Notes to Show Paragraph Structures

In your daily reading you will find it helpful to comprehension to mark in the margins the author's most important statements. These marginal notes are also useful when you review your reading. A system of marginal notes should be simple—easy to use and remember. Try this one:

|| A double vertical line—two quick strokes of your pencil—next to a topic sentence

| A single line next to an important detail or illustration

?   A question mark next to a statement you disagree with, or want to look up later

\"/   Quotation marks (shown here the way proofreaders mark them) next to a passage you might want to quote in a paper you are writing yourself

√   A check mark next to a line of print that contains a word to look up as part of your continuing vocabulary extension (see Chapter 8, page 194).

You will use the double vertical line most often. To help later review, you may want to write a *key word* or two next to your marginal mark. These key words can be a brief phrase about the content of the paragraph. They can also note paragraph functions, such as: *introductory statement of problem,* or *definition of* . . . . Underlining of sentences or phrases, by the way, is not a good note-taking device. Underlining is, in fact, harmful to good reading: it takes too much time to do, and it slows down rereading.

The purpose of any notation system such as the one above is to emphasize key concepts. This purpose is realized if you use the system but do not overuse it. Careful analysis of several beginning paragraphs of a selection, as you begin to read, will help reinforce the ideas you noted as you pre-read. From that point on, a flick of your pencil from time to time will hammer the author's ideas home and sort them out for later reference.

Stop pre-reading here. Your pre-reading alone should enable you to answer the following questions without looking back.

1. Pre-reading is concerned with overall organization of a selection. What is the main purpose of the new technique introduced in this chapter?

ANSWER _____

_____

2. What is a *topic sentence?*

ANSWER _____

_____

3. What are the types of paragraph organization? List all of them, in the *same order* that the chapter discusses them.

ANSWER _____

_____

_____

_____

4. Define a *definition.*

ANSWER _____

_____

5. What will be your purpose in reading this chapter thoroughly?

ANSWER _____

_____

_____

EXERCISES FOR CHAPTER 5

Reading Journal

Eye Span

Paragraph Analysis (a carry-over exercise)

Pre-reading
> Preface and Table of Contents from *The Invasion from Mars,* by Hadley Cantril, *et al.*

Summarizing
> "The Judiciary in America," from *Democracy in America,* by Alexis de Tocqueville

Phrase Sense

Reading Speed Exercise: Average Level 4
> "The Execution of Mary, Queen of Scots," from *The Armada,* by Garrett Mattingly

Reading Journal

In the separate notebook you are keeping, bring the section on **current reading** up to date: list everything you have read since your last entry, including title, author, type of material or subject, length, and how much time you have spent on it. Then summarize each new item briefly, its content and your opinion of it.

Under this same heading, set down your own comments on your reading development so far. Which of the techniques of reading have you found most difficult? Which kinds of exercises in this book have you found troublesome? Which have been most helpful? What techniques have you been applying in your daily reading? How well have they worked, and why? Which have you failed to apply, and why?

Then bring the **future reading** list up to date, with any additional titles you expect to read in the next several months: titles, authors, subjects, number of pages, your purpose in reading each item.

Eye Span

The following material is designed to extend your use of peripheral vision. Use a 3 x 5 card to cover the column you are working with. Move the card rapidly down the column, one line at a time. As each line is exposed, read it, looking at it only once and approximately at the center as shown by the dots between the words. Try to take in the entire width of the line. At first you may have to focus for several seconds on each set of dots before you are able to perceive all the words on the line.

We	. . . .	continued	end of	. . . .	the crypt
our	. . . .	route	there	. . . .	appeared
in	. . . .	search	another	. . . .	less
of the	. . . .	Amontillado.	spacious.	. . . .	Its
We	. . . .	passed	walls	. . . .	had been
through	. . . .	a range	lined	. . . .	with
of	. . . .	low arches,	human	. . . .	remains,
descended,	. . . .	passed on,	piled	. . . .	to the vault
and	. . . .	descending	overhead,	. . . .	in
again,	. . . .	arrived	the	. . . .	fashion
at a	. . . .	deep crypt,	of	. . . .	the
in	. . . .	which	great	. . . .	catacombs
the	. . . .	foulness	of	. . . .	Paris.
of	. . . .	the air	Three	. . . .	sides
caused	. . . .	our	of	. . . .	this
flambeaux	. . . .	rather	interior	. . . .	crypt
to glow	. . . .	than flame.	were	. . . .	still
At	. . . .	the	ornamented	. . . .	in
most	. . . .	remote	this	. . . .	manner.

From	....	the fourth	interior	....	recess,
the	....	bones	in depth	....	about
had	....	been	four	....	feet,
thrown	....	down,	in width	....	three,
and	....	lay	in	....	height
promiscuously	....	upon	six	....	or seven.
the	....	earth,	It	....	seemed
forming	....	at one point	to have	....	been
a mound	....	of some	constructed	....	for
size.	....	Within	no	....	especial
the wall	....	thus	use within	....	itself,
exposed	....	by	but	....	formed
the	....	displacing	merely	....	the interval
of the	....	bones,	between	....	two
we	....	perceived	of the	....	colossal
a	....	still	supports	....	of the roof.

Paragraph Analysis (a carry-over exercise)

To make your understanding of paragraph structures an effective tool for reading, you must acquire the habit of noting such structures as you read; and to acquire that habit takes conscious practice, at first, in your day-to-day reading. This exercise, therefore, is designed to help you carry over an awareness of paragraph structures into your daily reading.

1. Look through the pages of this book, and identify the paragraph type—Type 1, 2, 3, 4, or 5, depending on presence and position of the topic sentence or principal statement—of each of the following paragraphs:

    A. Page 91, paragraph 2—Paragraph Type _____

    B. Page 98, second from bottom—Paragraph Type _____

    C. Page 104, paragraph D—Paragraph Type _____

    D. Page 145, paragraph 3—Paragraph Type _____

    E. Page 181, paragraph L (Look carefully!)—Paragraph Type _____

    F. Page 210, paragraph I—Paragraph Type _____

    G. Page 423, last paragraph 9—Paragraph Type _____

    H. Page 348, paragraph E—Paragraph Type _____

2. By browsing through books you have listed as **current reading** in your Read-

ing Journal, find and copy out into that notebook, marking the principal statement in each:

   A. Three examples of Type 1, topic sentence at beginning;
   B. One example of Type 2, topic sentences at beginning and end;
   C. One example of Type 3, topic sentences at beginning and at middle;
   D. One example of Type 4, topic sentence at end;
   E. One example of Type 5, no topic sentence.

Pre-reading

You may have heard of the famous "Invasion from Mars" panic precipitated along the east coast of the United States, one evening in 1938, by Orson Welles' too-realistic radio dramatization of H. G. Wells' science fiction novel, *The War of the Worlds*. A team of social scientists seized this bizarre opportunity to study mass behavior; almost immediately after the broadcast and the panic, Hadley Cantril and his associates were able to launch an investigation of the reasons why listeners behaved as they did. Their research findings were later published.

From their book we reprint below the table of contents and a major part of the preface. Previous pre-reading exercises—and by now your independent application of the method—have shown the way careful examination of such "front of the book" materials can reveal a great deal about the organization and subject of the book. This next exercise is designed to give you further practice with pre-reading—and specifically, to demonstrate how a preface and a table of contents, pre-read together, can give you maximum understanding.

Please take this exercise in the following sequence. First, pre-read the preface itself, as you would any article or book chapter; then turn to page 129 and answer the pre-reading questions, without looking back. Second, return to the preface and read it thoroughly. Then go on to the table of contents and see what you can discover there about the organization of the book. Last, answer the rest of the questions beginning on page 130; for these you may of course refer to the material. This is not a timed exercise.

Begin here.

Preface and Table of Contents
from *The Invasion from Mars*[6]
by HADLEY CANTRIL, *et al.*

On the evening of October 30, 1938, thousands of Americans became panic-stricken by a broadcast purported to describe an invasion of Martians which threatened our whole civilization. Probably never before have so many people in all walks of life and in all parts of the country become so suddenly and so intensely disturbed as they did on this night. Yet what justification is there for conducting an elaborate investigation of a panic which was, after all, ephemeral and not sufficiently important to be recorded by historians?

There are essentially two ways to rationalize this study: one is hopefully scientific, the other frankly didactic.

Such rare occurrences are opportunities for the social scientist to study mass behavior. They must be exploited when they come. Although the social scientist unfortunately cannot usually predict such situations and have his tools of investigation ready to analyze the phenomenon while it is still on the wing, he can begin his work before the effects of the crisis are over and memories are blurred. As far as the writer is aware, this is the first panic that has been carefully studied with the research tools now available. A complete description of this panic should, in itself, be of value to anyone interested in social problems.

Furthermore, the attempts to determine the underlying psychological causes for a widespread panic in 1938 should give us insight into the psychology of the common man and, more especially, the psychology of the man of our times. From this point of view the investigation may be regarded as more than a study of panic. For the situation created by the broadcast was one which shows us how the common man reacts in a time of stress and strain. It gives us insights into his intelligence, his anxieties and his needs, which we could never get by tests or strictly experimental studies. The panic situation we have investigated had all the flavor of everyday life and, at the same time, provided a semi-experimental condition for research. Students of social psychology should find here some useful research tools. They will see shortcomings in the methods employed and should be able to profit from mistakes which have been pointed out wherever the writer has detected them.

A more practical justification for such a study concerns the educational implications which an understanding of this panic may have. Although citizens are not confronted every day with potentially panic-producing situations, they do face social or personal crises where their good judgement is taxed to the limit. If they can see why some people reacted unintelligently in this instance, they may be able to build up their resistance to similar occurrences. And if they are ever caught in a really critical situation, the information recorded here may help them make a more satisfactory adjustment. At least it will be discovered how superficial and misleading is the account of one prominent social scientist who said that "as good an explanation as any for the panic is that all the intelligent people were listening to Charlie McCarthy." In spite of the unique conditions giving rise to this particular panic, the writer has attempted to indicate throughout the study the pattern of circumstances which, from a psychological point of view, might make this the prototype of any panic.

Localized panics are frequently reported on shipboard, in congested buildings that have caught fire, or in specific areas suffering some natural catastrophe. More widespread panics are comparatively rare. Nevertheless, panics such as that occurring in the United States on the evening of October 30, 1938, are by no means confined to our own country or our own times.

The most similar predecessor to the panic resulting from the *War of the Worlds* broadcast occurred on January 16, 1926, in England during a period of unusual labor strife and shortly before the general strike. On that day the traditionally complacent English listener was startled by a description given by Father Ronald Knox (in the customary news broadcast) of an unruly unemployed mob. The mob was said to have attempted demolition of the Houses of Parliament, its trench mortars had brought Big Ben to the ground, it had hanged the Minister of Traffic to a tramway post. The London broadcast ended with the "destruction" of the British Broadcasting Corporation's station. After the broadcast, the newspapers, police and radio stations were besieged with calls from frantic citizens. However, the panic created by Father Knox's broadcast did not cause either as widespread or as intense a fear as the Orson Welles program.

The fact that this panic was created as a result of a radio broadcast is today no mere circumstance. The importance of radio's rôle in current national and international affairs is too well known to be recounted here. By its very nature radio is the medium par excellence for informing all segments of a population of current happenings, for arousing in them a common sense of fear or joy and for inciting them to similar reactions directed toward a single objective. It is estimated that of the 32,000,000 families in the United States 27,500,000 have radios—a greater proportion than have telephones, automobiles, plumbing, electricity, newspapers or magazines. Radio has inherently the characteristics of contemporaneousness, availability, personal appeal and ubiquity. Hence, when we analyze this panic, we are able to deal with the most modern type of social group—the radio audience—which differs from the congregate group of the moving picture theatre and the consociate group reading the daily paper. The radio audience consists essentially of thousands of small, congregate groups united in time and experiencing a common stimulus—altogether making possible the largest grouping of people ever known.

Because the social phenomenon in question was so complex, several methods were employed to seek out different answers and to compare results obtained by one method with those obtained by another. Such an approach seems advisable in analyzing any problem in social psychology. Otherwise, the investigator has difficulty in demonstrating that his assumption has not been "proved" merely because his method would give him no contradictory evidence. Furthermore, should the investigator reach no positive conclusions, he is unable to tell whether his presuppositions and theories are wrong or whether the fault lies in his method. The use of a pluralistic approach in a study such as this is particularly urgent since the phenomenon under consideration was of so transient a nature. Also, so far as was known, no other extensive investigation was being independently conducted on the problem, thus making it impossible to check one set of data and interpretations against another.

Much of our information was derived from detailed interviews of 135 persons. Over 100 of these persons were selected because they were known to have been upset by the broadcast. The names of the persons who were frightened were obtained almost entirely by the personal inquiry and initiative of the interviewers. The names of persons who were listed in the newspapers as having been frightened failed to produce more than a half-dozen interviews. Many more names were finally obtained than could possibly be interviewed with the limited funds available. Every attempt was made to keep the group fairly representative of the population at large. However, no pretense is made that the group *is* a proper sample of the total population, and the results and interpretations of the complete study do not depend on such a sample since these cases can be studied against the background of two extensive statistical surveys made prior to the intensive personal interviews. Twenty-eight persons who were not frightened but who tuned in late to the broadcast were included in the group interviewed.

The interviews were limited to the New Jersey area for reasons of finance and supervision. All names of respondents used in the text are fictitious and identifying characteristics are disguised, but the true flavor of the case studies is preserved. The interviewing began one week after the broadcast and was completed in about three weeks. The regrettable delay in getting to the respondents was unavoidable for two reasons: funds were not immediately available to begin the study; highly trained interviewers are difficult to obtain, and the danger of delaying the interval between such an experience and an interview is probably less than the danger of obtaining an inadequate or unreliable report from an unskilled interviewer.

Quotations have been freely used to illustrate psychological processes which are implied in the statistical figures. They have also been included at times wherever language failed and meaning could be better conveyed by the impression gained from a quotation.

After pre-reading the preface, go on to the pre-reading questions.

Table of Contents

After reading thoroughly, go on to the questions.

The questions assume that you are examining the material because you intend to read the book thoroughly. After pre-reading the preface, answer the pre-reading questions below. Then read both the preface and table of contents thoroughly, and answer the rest of the questions. For the thorough-reading questions, you should refer to the material.

Pre-reading questions on the preface. (Do *not* refer to the material.)
1. As is true for the introductory material in many books, the preface you have just pre-read has the general purpose of explaining why and how the book itself was written. But more particularly, *this* preface performs two main jobs. Of the following list, which is the *first* of the two major functions of this preface?

   a. To show (at the time the book was published, in 1940) the growing importance of radio as a fast and widespread means of communication;
   b. to show how (at the time the book was published, in 1940) its results gave valuable new understanding of the ways mass psychology can be manipulated in wartime;
   c. to justify conducting an elaborate investigation of a panic which was, after all, not in itself of great historical importance;
   d. to show how this particular panic is psychologically similar to other panics, perhaps to any and all panics;

     e. to explain why quotations were used in the text;

     f. to explain why several different methods were used in the research, and something of what they were;

     g. to justify the validity of the new research tools created by the researchers for this study.

ANSWER _____

2. From the same list, what was the *second* major purpose of this preface?

ANSWER _____

3. What does pre-reading of the preface reveal about the organization of the *complete book?* (a) Little or nothing; (b) only that it states a problem and then proposes a solution; (c) that it analyzes first cause and then effect; (d) that its organization is strictly chronological; (e) that it is essentially a fictional re-creation, one for one, of the two or three detailed case histories that the researchers were able to obtain.

ANSWER _____

4. Reading difficulty: what does pre-reading of the preface reveal about the probable level of difficulty of the complete book? (a) Little or nothing; (b) that it is clearly a highly technical scientific work; (c) that it is highly technical in subject, with this difficulty compounded by a dense and involved style; (d) that it is simple enough in writing style, though perhaps the subject itself will prove fairly technical; (e) that it is highly popular in style and subject.

ANSWER _____

Now return to read the preface and table of contents thoroughly, pages 125–29.

Thorough-reading questions. (You *may* refer to the material.)

5. In your further pre-reading of the complete book, before reading thoroughly, which chapter would you read to find the conclusions arrived at by the research? (Give a *chapter number* from the table of contents for your answer.)

ANSWER _____

6. From the preface and table of contents together, which *two* of the following should be included in your pre-reading of the complete book? (a) Chapter I, because it contains the script of the original Orson Welles broadcast; (b) Chapter IV, because it contains the first description of how people behaved in the panic; (c) Chapter VIII, because it contains all the individual case studies mentioned in the preface; (d) Appendix A, because it contains the chief discussion of the limitations of the study; (e) Appendix B, because it contains the actual text of the interview questionnaire, the results of which were the major basis of the study.

ANSWER _____

7. Which of the following best summarizes the first of the two main divisions of the preface? (a) The unusual opportunity presented by the panic was seized by the investigators, who applied several scientific techniques to

discover the psychological forces that had been at work; (b) the investigation is justifiable scientifically as a unique study of mass behavior in times of stress, and in more immediately practical ways by how it may teach people to behave more intelligently in the crises of the modern world; (c) the investigation was undertaken not only for scientific reasons, but also because we must learn how to deal with and control mass reactions in a world of instant communications and total war; (d) because the panic was silly and of small importance, at least in most commentators' views, investigation of it requires considerable and careful defending.

ANSWER _____

8. The table of contents for *The Invasion from Mars* is not, by itself, as informative as might be desired for pre-reading purposes. (Indeed, it was chosen for this exercise because it does require you to think and speculate about it.) But in the light of what you learn from the preface, close reading of the table of contents will lay bare the main organizational plan of the book. Included in the list below are all the main topics of the book. Please assign the chapter numbers, I through IX, all to their correct topics. Warning: the topics are not in their correct order; *one* topic may be dealt with by *several* chapters; and some of the topics listed will *not* be found in the table of contents. So in each answer space insert one or more chapter numbers, or write "none."

Topics   *Chapters*

Conclusion   _____

What particular listeners did about what they thought they heard.   _____

What was actually broadcast by Orson Welles, and what, in general, the public reaction was.   _____

General conditions or problems in the modern world that help explain why some people reacted with panic.   _____

The true role of intelligence and/or education in preparing people for stress.   _____

Why the panic was not foreseen and the broadcast prevented.   _____

Specific situations or problems in people's lives that help explain their panic.   _____

The essential differences between those who avoided panic and those who succumbed.   _____

What individual listeners thought they heard that prompted them to react as they did.   _____

The role of neurosis or extreme psychological maladjustment in predisposing the individual to panic.   _____

9. We can also come to a rough overall idea of the authors' general conclusions. Without the essential details and supporting evidence, to be sure, it appears likely that Chapter IX will explain the panic as the result (a) simply of an over-realistic treatment of the radio dramatization; (b) of the tense and worrisome times we live in; (c) of troublesome times plus the private worries

of individuals who led the panic; (d) of the effect of worries and tensions, both public and personal, that inhibited the critical ability of those who panicked; (e) of the neuroses and personal psychological tensions that led certain individuals to exaggerate world tensions, and so to be prone to believe what less disturbed individuals could tell was simply a radio play of some sort.

ANSWER _____

Summarizing

The passage below is taken from what many people hold to be the best analysis of American government and politics ever written: *Democracy in America,* by Alexis de Tocqueville. The book was first published a century and a quarter ago; it is still indispensable for the student of American political institutions and processes; and it is still a cause for remark and rueful respect that the author was not an American, but a Frenchman.

Here, Tocqueville outlines certain principles of judicial power and explains how they work in the United States. You will note as you read that his statements apply to today's headlines. Your purpose in reading the passage is to identify the principal statement (topic sentence or sentences) in each paragraph, and then to summarize each paragraph and the entire passage. As you read, mark the principal statements with lines in the margin. The questions follow the passage.

This is not a timed exercise. You may refer to the article as you answer the questions.

"The Judiciary in America"[7]
from *Democracy in America*
by ALEXIS DE TOCQUEVILLE

A

1   The first characteristic of judicial power in all nations is the duty of
2 arbitration. But rights must be contested in order to warrant the interference of a tribunal; and an action must be brought before the decision
3 of a judge can be had. As long, therefore, as a law is uncontested, the judicial authority is not called upon to discuss it, and it may exist without
4 being perceived. When a judge in a given case attacks a law relating to that case, he extends the circle of his customary duties, without, however, stepping beyond it, since he is in some measure obliged to decide
5 upon the law in order to decide the case. But if he pronounces upon a law without proceeding from a case, he clearly steps beyond his sphere and invades that of the legislative authority.

B

1   The second characteristic of judicial power is that it pronounces on
2 special cases, and not upon general principles. If a judge, in deciding a particular point, destroys a general principle by passing a judgment which

tends to reject all the inferences from that principle, and consequently
3 to annul it, he remains within the ordinary limits of his functions. But if he
directly attacks a general principle without having a particular case in
view, he leaves the circle in which all nations have agreed to confine
his authority; he assumes a more important and perhaps a more useful
influence than that of the magistrate, but he ceases to represent the judicial power.

C

1   The third characteristic of the judicial power is that it can act only
when it is called upon, or when, in legal phrase, it has taken cognizance
2 of an affair. This characteristic is less general than the other two; but,
notwithstanding the exceptions, I think it may be regarded as essential.
3 The judicial power is, by its nature, devoid of action; it must be put in
4 motion in order to produce a result. When it is called upon to repress
a crime, it punishes the criminal; when a wrong is to be redressed, it is
ready to redress it; when an act requires interpretation, it is prepared
to interpret it; but it does not pursue criminals, hunt out wrongs, or
5 examine evidence of its own accord. A judicial functionary who should
take the initiative and usurp the censureship of the laws would in some
measure do violence to the passive nature of his authority.

D

1   The Americans have retained these three distinguishing characteristics of the judicial power: an American judge can pronounce a decision
only when litigation has arisen, he is conversant only with special cases,
and he cannot act until the cause has been duly brought before the court.
2 His position is therefore exactly the same as that of the magistrates of
3 other nations; and yet he is invested with immense political power. How
4 does this come about? If the sphere of his authority and his means of
action are the same as those of other judges, whence does he derive a
5 power which they do not possess? The cause of this difference lies in the
simple fact that the Americans have acknowledged the right of judges to
6 found their decisions on the *Constitution* rather than on the *laws*. In
other words, they have permitted them not to apply such laws as may
appear to them to be unconstitutional.

E

1   I am aware that a similar right has been sometimes claimed, but
claimed in vain, by courts of justice in other countries; but in America
it is recognized by all the authorities; and not a party, not so much as an
2 individual, is found to contest it. This fact can be explained only by the
3 principles of the American constitutions. In France the constitution is, or
at least is supposed to be, immutable; and the received theory is that no
4 power has the right of changing any part of it. In England the constitution
may change continually, or rather it does not in reality exist; the Parlia-
5 ment is at once a legislative and a constituent assembly. The political

6   theories of America are more simple and more rational. An American
constitution is not supposed to be immutable, as in France; nor is it
susceptible of modification by the ordinary powers of society, as in
7   England. It constitutes a detached whole, which, as it represents the will
of the whole people, is no less binding on the legislator than on the
private citizen, but which may be altered by the will of the people in
8   predetermined cases, according to established rules. In America the
Constitution may therefore vary; but as long as it exists, it is the origin
of all authority, and the sole vehicle of the predominating force.

F

1   It is easy to perceive how these differences must act upon the position and the rights of the judicial bodies in the three countries I have
2   cited. If in France the tribunals were authorized to disobey the laws on
the ground of their being opposed to the constitution, the constituent
power would in fact be placed in their hands, since they alone would
have the right of interpreting a constitution of which no authority could
3   change the terms. They would therefore take the place of the nation and
exercise as absolute a sway over society as the inherent weakness of
4   judicial power would allow them to do. Undoubtedly, as the French
judges are incompetent to declare a law to be unconstitutional, the power
of changing the constitution is indirectly given to the legislative body,
since no legal barrier would oppose the alterations that it might prescribe.
5   But it is still better to grant the power of changing the constitution of
the people to men who represent (however imperfectly) the will of the
people than to men who represent no one but themselves.

G

1   It would be still more unreasonable to invest the English judges
with the right of resisting the decisions of the legislative body, since the
Parliament which makes the laws also makes the constitution; and consequently a law emanating from the three estates of the realm can in no
2   case be unconstitutional. But neither of these remarks is applicable to
America.

For each of the seven paragraphs in the passage, pick out below the best
summary. Enter the number of this summary in the answer space for that
paragraph; put down also the number of the topic sentence. Remember that
some paragraphs may have the principal statement expressed in *two* sentences,
or *none:* in such cases put down both sentence numbers, or write "none."
The last question below asks you to choose a summary statement for the complete passage. You may refer to the material.

A

1. To arbitrate effectively, judges must decide what the law is, as well as what
   the facts are; from this arises their power to attack laws.
2. The duty to arbitrate—to decide cases—is primary to judicial power, and this

may include decisions attacking particular laws; but the process can start only when a contest is brought before the judicial authority.

3. The first characteristic of judicial power is the duty of arbitration, which logically carries with it the power to attack laws as long as the judge does not himself enact new legislation by his decrees.

ANSWER _____ SENTENCE _____

B

1. Because judges are not legislators, they may decide only specific cases and may not modify general principles of law.
2. To annul a general principle or law, a judge must find a case where the general principle is relevant.
3. Judges pronounce on particular cases; any attack on a general principle can only arise as a particular case requires it.

ANSWER _____ SENTENCE _____

C

1. Finally, with important exceptions, it is true that the judicial power is passive, not active, in its ability to modify law.
2. Thirdly, the judicial power in most instances may not itself go out and find the cases on which it decides, but can act only when called upon.
3. In addition, in the author's view it is essential that judicial power wait for action until set in motion by other powers of the state.

ANSWER _____ SENTENCE _____

D

1. The judge in America too is limited by these three characteristics of judicial power, but he also has the right to decide whether or not a law is constitutional; this gives him immense political power.
2. Despite the fact that the three essential characteristics apply to the judicial power in America, the judge has immense political power over the laws.
3. The application of these three essential characteristics of judicial power is warped in America by the right of judges to decide for themselves whether a law is unconstitutional and so not to be applied; this gives them dangerous political power.

ANSWER _____ SENTENCE _____

E

1. In no other land has the right of the courts to judge the laws themselves been successfully enforced; but this is due to the fact that the constitutions of other lands go to one extreme or the other.
2. The American constitution differs from the British in that it is not just ordinary legislation; and from the French in that it may be changed.
3. The right of judges to determine the constitutionality of laws is recognized in America because the American constitution is unlike others: it can be changed, but at the same time it is set above, and rules, ordinary legislation.

ANSWER _____ SENTENCE _____

F

1. The lesser powers of the judiciary in France and England result from the failure of those countries to put their constitutions in the proper balance, both theoretical and practical.

2. The unique position of the American judiciary can be explained further by pursuing the comparison with other countries: in France, for example, to give judges such powers would make them masters of the state, since their judgment could never be changed.
3. In France, judges are not given the American power to make and unmake the laws, because the French know the dangers of judicial tyranny and prefer to keep legislation in the hands of legislators responsible to the people.

ANSWER _____ SENTENCE _____

G
1. In England, since there is no distinction between the constitution and other legislation, there is no basis for a judge to strike down a law.
2. What the French have done by implication (as explained earlier), the English have done openly: they have made the legislative body the supreme interpreter of the law.
3. In England, because there is no specific constitution as distinct from other legislation, the courts must find more limited, and more subtle, grounds for interpreting the laws as they wish.

ANSWER _____ SENTENCE _____

Now choose, from the following, the best summary of the entire passage.

1. Three characteristics of judicial power are: that it acts only when there is a particular case, that it cannot act on principles beyond the particular case, and that it cannot itself seek out the cases. The unique power of the American judges compared with those of France and England cannot be explained as a violation of these essential characteristics; it comes rather from a constitution that provides a separate basis from which to strike down legislation while, at the same time, the people have the right to modify the constitution.
2. Judicial power has the same essential characteristics in America, France, and England, except for differences in the degree to which their constitutions permit judges to attack laws: in this respect, the immutability of its constitution puts France at one extreme, America in a balanced middle position, and England at the other extreme.
3. Since the essential characteristics of judicial power are apparently the same in America, France, and England, it is the differences in their constitutions that provide the only basis for understanding how American judges have such immense political power while this development has been successfully avoided (despite occasional claims to the contrary) in the other two countries.

ANSWER _____

Phrase Sense

After you have completed the exercise above, go back to those same paragraphs and divide each sentence into phrases by circling them or marking a "slash" (/) between them. Work as quickly as you can, relying as far as possible on your "phrase sense" to group the words into meaningful units.

Reading Speed Exercise: Average Level 4

The life of Mary, Queen of Scots, runs as an erratic scarlet thread of romance through the tapestry of the sixteenth century; with her death, executed for treason by command of her cousin, Elizabeth I of England, the romance ended — only to launch a new drama of history on the grand scale, as the powers of Europe realigned themselves, and the threat of Spanish, Roman Catholic invasion of Protestant England became real in the launching, the extraordinary voyage, and the defeat of the Spanish fleet, the Armada. The distinguished historian Garrett Mattingly spent a lifetime studying those years. He untangled their political, dynastic, religious, and military events with scholarly care and cinematic color and excitement, in his brilliant book, *The Armada*. He began the book with the account that follows of the last hours of Mary.

You are to read the selection against time. Follow your instructor's directions in class, or the Instructions for Timing on page 474.

Before reading, practice with the *Eye Movements in Reading* exercise on pages 54–56.

Do not pre-read the selection; the timed reading exercises are designed to measure improvements in speed alone.

After reading the selection and recording your time, go on to the ten true-false and multiple-choice questions beginning on page 140. There is no time limit for the questions, but it will invalidate the exercise if you refer to this passage while you answer them.

Begin reading and timing here.

"The Execution of Mary, Queen of Scots"[8]
from *The Armada*
by GARRETT MATTINGLY

Fotheringhay,
February 18, 1587

Mr. Beale had not brought the warrant until Sunday evening but by Wednesday morning, before dawn outlined its high windows, the great hall at Fotheringhay was ready. Though the earl of Shrewsbury had returned only the day before, nobody wanted any more delay. Nobody knew what messenger might be riding on the London road. Nobody knew which of the others might not weaken if they waited another day.

The hall had been cleared of all its ordinary furniture. Halfway along its length a huge fire of logs blazing in the chimney battled against the creeping chill. Towards the upper end of the hall they had set up a small platform, like a miniature stage for traveling actors, jutting twelve feet into the hall, eight or nine feet wide, and less than three feet high. At one side a pair of stairs led up to it, and the fresh wood of the scaffolding had been everywhere decently covered in black velvet. On the platform, in line with the stairs, stood a single high-backed chair, also draped in black, and three or four feet in front of it a black cushion. Next to the cushion and rising above it something like a little low bench showed where the velvet imperfectly concealed an ordinary wooden chopping block. By seven in the morning the stage managers were satisfied, the sheriff's men trying to look soldierly in morion and breastplate and to hold their halberds stiffly had taken their places, and the chosen audience, two hundred or more knights and gentlemen of the neighborhood peremptorily summoned for that early hour, had filed into the lower end of the hall.

The star kept them waiting more than three hours. In the almost thirty years since she had wedded a future king of France in the glittering, devious court beside the Loire she had failed repeatedly to learn some of the more important lessons of politics, but she had learned how to dominate a scene. She entered through a little door at the side, and before they saw her she was already in the great hall, walking towards the dais, six of her own people, two by two, behind her, oblivious of the stir and rustle as her audience craned forward, oblivious, apparently, of the officer on whose sleeve her hand rested, walking as quietly, thought one pious soul, as if she were going to her prayers. Only for a moment, as she mounted the steps and before she sank back into the black-draped chair, did she seem to need the supporting arm, and if her hands trembled before she locked them in her lap, no one saw. Then, as if acknowledging the plaudits of a multitude (though the hall was very still), she turned for the first time to face her audience and, some thought, she smiled.

Against the black velvet of the chair and dais her figure, clad in black velvet, was almost lost. The gray winter daylight dulled the gleam of white hands, the glint of yellow gold in her kerchief and of red gold in the piled masses of auburn hair beneath. But the audience could see clearly enough the delicate frill of white lace at her throat and above it, a white, heart-shaped petal against the blackness, the face with its great dark eyes and tiny, wistful mouth. This was she for whom Rizzio had died, and Darnley, the young fool, and Huntly, and Norfolk, and Babington and a thousand nameless men on the moors and gallows of the north. This was she whose legend had hung over England like a sword ever since she had galloped across its borders with her subjects in pursuit. This was the last captive princess of romance, the dowager queen of France, the exiled queen of Scotland, the heir to the English throne and (there must have been some among the silent witnesses who thought so), at this very moment, if she had her rights, England's lawful queen. This was Mary Stuart, Queen of Scots. For a moment she held all their eyes, then she sank back into the darkness of her chair and turned her grave inattention to her judges. She was satisfied that her audience would look at no one else.

The earls of Kent and Shrewsbury who had entered with her, almost unobserved, had seated themselves opposite, and Mr. Beale was standing, clearing his throat and crackling the parchment of the warrant he had to read. He need not have been nervous. One doubts whether anyone was listening. "Stubborn disobedience . . . incitement to insurrection . . . against the life and person of her sacred Majesty . . . high treason . . . death." Nothing in the phrases could have mattered to Mary Stuart or to any person in the hall. Everyone knew that this was not the sentence for a crime. This was another stroke in a political duel which had been going on as long as most of them could remember, which had begun, indeed, before either of the enemy queens was born. Sixty years ago the parties had begun to form, the party of the old religion, the party of the new, and always, by some trick of fate, one party or the other, and usually both, had been rallied and led by a woman. Catherine of Aragon against Anne Boleyn, Mary Tudor against Elizabeth Tudor, Elizabeth Tudor against Mary of Lorraine, and now, for nearly thirty years, Elizabeth Tudor against Mary Stuart, the prisoner on the scaffold. The shrewdest politicians might wonder how for almost two decades England had managed to contain both these predestinate enemies and keep them both alive.

Whatever Elizabeth had done, Mary Stuart had, of course, sought by every means in her power to destroy her cousin and bring her low. In a duel to the death like theirs there were no foul strokes. When the arms of strength had fallen from her hands she had used whatever weapons weakness could grasp: lies, tears, evasions, threats and pleadings, and the hands and lives of whatever men her crowns, her beauty or her faith could win to her cause. They had proved two-edged weapons at last; but if they cut her now, she had dealt wounds with them, and kept her cousin's realm in greater turmoil from her English prison than ever she had been able to do from her Scottish throne. And she meant to strike one blow more. She turned a bored chin on Mr. Beale's concluding phrases.

The dean of Peterborough was even more nervous than Mr. Beale. She let him repeat his stumbling exordium three times before she cut him contemptuously short. "Mr. Dean," she told him, "I shall die as I have lived, in the true and holy Catholic faith. All you can say to me on that score is but vain, and all your prayers, I think, can avail me but little."

This, she was sure, was the one weapon which would not turn in her hand. She had been closely watched at Fotheringhay, but not so closely that she could have no word from the daring, subtle men who slipped in and out of the Channel ports in disguise. The north was Catholic, they said, and the west, and even here in the heretic's own strongholds, even in the midlands, even in London, more and more turned daily to the ancient faith. While the heir to the throne was a Catholic, likely to succeed without a struggle on her heretic cousin's death, those thousands had been quiet, but now, should the heretic slay her orthodox successor, surely they would rise in their wrath to sweep away all this iniquity. And there were Catholic kings beyond the seas who would be more eager to avenge the Queen of Scots dead than ever they had been to keep her alive.

That Mary herself was a devout Catholic is one of the few things about her not open to dispute, but it was not enough for her simply to die in her faith. The duel would go on. All men must know that she had died not only in her faith, but for it. Perhaps she had not always been its steadiest pillar. Perhaps her dubious intrigues had sometimes harmed her cause more than her devotion had helped it. Now the glittering sweep of the axe would cut off forever the burden of old mistakes, silence the whispered slanders, and her blood would cry out for vengeance on her enemies more unmistakably than her living voice could ever have done again. For years she had favored an ambiguous motto, "My end is my beginning." Martyrdom might make good both the promise and the threat. She had only to play this last scene well.

So she held the crucifix high, visible all down the long hall as she flung defiance at her judges, and her voice rose with a kind of triumph above the voice of the dean of Peterborough, always higher and clearer than his rising tones, arching over the vehement English prayers the mysterious, dominating invocations of the ancient faith. The queen's voice held on for a minute after the clergyman had finished. Her words were in English now; she was praying for the people of England and for the soul of her royal cousin Elizabeth; she was forgiving all her enemies. Then for a moment her ladies were busy about her. The black velvet gown fell below her knees revealing underbodice and petticoat of crimson silk and she stepped forward, suddenly, shockingly, in the color of martyrdom, blood red from top to toe against the somber background. Quietly she knelt and bowed herself low over the little chopping block. "In manus tuas, domine . . ." and they heard twice the dull chunk of the axe.

There was one more ceremony to accomplish. The executioner must exhibit the head and speak the customary words. The masked black figure stooped and rose, crying in a loud voice, "Long live the queen!" But all he held in his hand that had belonged to the rival queen of hearts was a kerchief, and pinned to it an elaborate auburn wig. Rolled nearer the edge of the platform, shrunken and withered and gray, with a sparse silver stubble on the small, shiny skull was the head of the martyr. Mary Stuart had always known how to embarrass her enemies.

Now note your reading time. Record it below and go on to the questions.

YOUR READING TIME: ____MIN. ____SEC. ____W.P.M. COMPREHENSION SCORE: ____% (WORDS PER MINUTE FROM THE TABLE ON PAGE 475.)

Please do not read these questions until you have read the selection itself against time. Do not refer to the selection as you answer the questions. Choose the *one best* answer to each question and enter the corresponding letter in the proper answer space.

1. Mary was Elizabeth's prisoner because she had fled Scotland pursued by her own subjects.   (T) True; (F) False

ANSWER _____

2. Some Englishmen, perhaps even some of those who watched her execution, thought Mary was rightfully queen of England. (T) True; (F) False

ANSWER _____

3. The enmity between Mary and Elizabeth had grown for nearly a decade before Mary's execution. (T) True; (F) False

ANSWER _____

4. Though both Mary and Elizabeth were Roman Catholic, most of England was Protestant. (T) True; (F) False

ANSWER _____

5. The author presents Mary's last hours as (a) a melodramatic gamble for time, in the hope of rescue by her Roman Catholic supporters in England; (b) a brilliant personal and political performance by a consummate actress; (c) a drama, but one of personal tragedy and anticlimax for the heroine; (d) a grim farce with a black-humor ending; (e) a movie-screen romanticization full of imagined details beyond what an historian could verify.

ANSWER _____

6. Mary dressed for the scaffold (a) as a nun, to emphasize her Roman Catholic faith even to those who might not be able to hear her; (b) in sober, but regal, black; (c) in the prison uniform of the period; (d) in dramatic black, but beneath that a scarlet petticoat which was revealed at the last moment; (e) in scarlet, the color of martyrdom.

ANSWER _____

7. When the warrant reached Fotheringhay, Mary's execution was carried out (a) promptly, because nobody wanted to allow time for the order to be rescinded from London, or for themselves to weaken in their resolve; (b) speedily, because everybody wanted to put an end to the danger to the realm, and to the Protestant faith, that Mary represented; (c) only after a delay to allow time for the order to be rescinded from London; (d) reluctantly, because many there believed, secretly, that Mary was rightfully queen; (e) in the greatest haste, to forestall the rescue plans that were under way in the Catholic north.

ANSWER _____

8. Mary was executed (a) for treason; (b) ostensibly for the murder of Darnley; (c) ostensibly for treason, but in fact because she was the leader of the party of the old religion; (d) ostensibly for the murder of Darnley, but in fact because she represented the power of France and Spain allied against England; (e) ostensibly for treason, but in fact because of the danger that she might escape back to Scotland.

ANSWER _____

9. Mary went to the block with a prominent display of her Catholicism, because (a) she was devout, and these were her last moments; (b) she was devout, but also a woman who would fully exploit the drama of her last moments; (c) she was devout, but also hoped to exploit the last weapon that might save her before this audience drawn from a part of England which was deeply divided in religion; (d) she was devout, but also hoped her piety and martyrdom would promote the Roman Catholic cause after her death, and so bring her revenge; (e) she was willing to use faith as she had

used men, armies, allies, power, and money when she had had them: as weapons.

ANSWER _____

10. The author's opinion of Mary, as it emerges, is complex, but essentially that she was (a) an opportunist with a pious streak; (b) a politician who hid her talents beneath a romantic mask; (c) a willful, wayward woman who had lost a political duel in large part through her own weaknesses; (d) a woman of great talent, and great weakness, whose defeat was tinged with tragedy; (e) a dangerous charlatan and adventuress.

ANSWER _____

Now check your answers, and enter your score on your Progress Profile, page vii.

CHAPTER 6

"Reading with Your Fingers": Skipping and Skimming

Pre-read this chapter as your first step in reading. After pre-reading, but before reading thoroughly, answer the questions at the end of the chapter.

Begin pre-reading here.

Skipping and *skimming* are the two most highly selective techniques of reading. Indeed, they might best be described as techniques for *not* reading — and the fundamental skill in each lies in knowing when and how to do it without missing what you need. As with so many reading skills, the selectivity is founded on your clear consciousness of your purpose in reading. To skip, of course, means to leave something unread altogether. You skip when you realize at any level of reading thoroughness (pre-reading, skimming, or reading thoroughly) that the material should be read no further. The skilled reader can tell accurately when it is safe and desirable to skip. Skimming, on the other hand, is a kind of disciplined, focussed, partial reading. You skim when your purpose is to extract certain particular facts from a large mass of material, or to test whether a passage can safely be skipped, or to locate material that needs to be read thoroughly, or to obtain a general, bird's-eye view of a work without the mastery of detail that thorough reading provides. For this last purpose, you are already using one form of skimming as part of pre-reading, when after reading the first paragraphs of a chapter thoroughly, you then read only the first sentence of each remaining paragraph until you approach the end. Skimming used that way yields an understanding of the main ideas and some significant details of a passage. Skimming is thus a technique that can be tuned with great accuracy, from the extreme speed with which you glance across the page of a dictionary to find one word, to the other extreme when it approaches thorough reading.

For three reasons, few people skip or skim effectively. First, most people do not pre-read. Second, few people bother to state to themselves, clearly and consciously, their purpose in reading. Third, few know how to skip or skim without risk or fear of missing material that they need to understand. This chapter will show you how. Used for the right purposes, skipping and skimming are precision tools with which you can save time on a large scale by avoiding reading that is not necessary to your purpose, while locating the materials that are necessary.

Skimming

Skimming is used for several different purposes:

To find a particular piece of information in a passage, a fact, a quotation, a reference.

To grasp quickly the main ideas and most significant details of a selection.

To test whether material can safely be skipped, or on the other hand to pick out, from a passage that seems otherwise irrelevant, any part that must be read thoroughly.

These different purposes call for different methods.

To skim with the purpose of finding a particular fact, or the answer to a specific question, let your eyes travel down the page without actually reading, stopping only twice on each line of print. The bars in this paragraph show where you would look when skimming this way. To practice this, place a pencil down the center of the page from top to bottom. Let your eyes make two fixations per line of print, one to the left of the pencil and one to the right. Your skimming for this purpose will be more accurate if you look at the white space between the lines rather than at the lines themselves. Your attention will then be spread more evenly throughout your field of vision, and not be concentrated on single words.

Two pauses are needed on each line for relatively wide columns of print. With a narrow column (like this one) in a newspaper or in a book with two columns to the page, place the pencil down the center of the column of print you are skimming. Pause only *once* on each line. Look to the left of the pencil for line one, to the right for line two, and continue zigzagging down the column in this manner. If you go on to another column, move the pencil to the center of the new column and repeat the process.

Once you begin to get the trick of skimming with just two fixations per line, stop using the pencil. The pencil is a help to the untrained reader learning to skim for a fact because it reminds him not to slip into normal reading; but for the skilled reader it is an extra prop that actually impedes accurate skimming.

When skimming for particular information, either a fact or the answer to a question, *keep in mind exactly what it is you are looking for.* As you become practiced in the technique, you will notice that the number, name, or phrase you are looking for seems **to stand out on the page** almost as if printed in heavier type.

The second purpose for which you skim is to find main ideas and significant details. Skimming for this purpose proceeds differently. You read the first sentence of each paragraph; occasionally, if you feel the first sentence is unhelpful, you may add a phrase or two from the second sentence. This reading of first sentences gives you main ideas because, as we established in Chapter 5, in practical prose that first sentence in the paragraph usually carries the principal statement. After you have read the first sentence, let your eyes swing quickly down the rest of that paragraph: names, dates, and numbers will catch your eye, as will other details that relate to your conscious purpose in reading. Sometimes, if the first sentence, plus those details, has not given you a sufficient notion of what the paragraph contains, you may find yourself reading the last sentence also, because as we also saw in Chapter 5, the last sentence may have a topic or summarizing role. Now go on to the first sentence of the next paragraph, repeating the process. The whole technique takes more time to describe than to do; you must keep it fast and flexible so that it feels like sprinting on tiptoe down an obstacle course.

When you are skimming to assess whether material can be skipped altogether, or on the other hand to find particular passages that demand thorough reading, the technique borrows a little from each of the approaches so far described. You will sample first sentences as when skimming for main ideas, but even faster and more cursorily; at the same time you must proceed with a very clear idea of what you are looking for, almost like when you skim for a fact. It is against this clear idea of purpose that you judge whether a book, an article, or a chapter may be skipped; and it is the clear purpose that trips the alarm bell when you stumble across a portion of a work that must be read thoroughly.

Skimming for particular facts is a specialized technique that you will probably use less often than skimming for main ideas and most significant details. You will skim for main ideas and details, or to assess material for skipping or thorough reading, principally on three occasions:

When pre-reading indicates that a selection deserves further perusal, but not thorough reading.

When you are too pressed for time to read thoroughly.

When you encounter material that apparently contains nothing new, but that may be too important to your purpose to risk skipping.

Skipping

On a large or small scale, material should be skipped when a complete reading would be unprofitable for any of these three reasons:

When the material contains *nothing new.*

When the material contains *nothing you need.*

When the material is *too difficult* for you to read without advance preparation.

Obviously, in all three cases, your decision to skip must be based on your clear awareness of your purpose in reading, plus a reliable judgment of what the skipped passage has to say. For this reason skipping as a reading technique is dependent on pre-reading and sometimes also on skimming or even thorough reading. The decision to skip an *entire* article, book chapter, or book is based upon pre-reading. The decision to skip *portions* of an article or chapter is a result of skimming or thorough reading of what goes immediately before the section skipped. Here is how skipping works in each of the three cases listed above.

When you discover through pre-reading or thorough reading that you are learning *nothing new*, you skip. However, if the material does not seem entirely familiar, *skim*, do not skip. If the material you skip is only a portion of the work you are reading, you will *skim* to find the place where you should begin again to read thoroughly.

Pre-reading or a start at thorough reading may show you that a selection has *nothing you need.* Be cautious here: you cannot always be sure something you don't know won't help you.

The point about skipping, for these reasons, is in what you do read, not what you leave out: once again, skipping is a way to be selective. Often, you will be faced with a superabundance of material that could be relevant to your purpose. Clearly some of it must be skipped: how do you choose? This could happen in last-minute studying for an examination, or when trying to solve a business or professional problem with a short deadline. Furthermore, beyond the required reading for a course or a job there is always more reading for general background than you will possibly have time to cover. The best solution is to pre-read as much useful material as you can, making a short summary of each selection. Then skip the least useful items on the list, concentrating your time and energy on the most useful material. Within each item that you read thoroughly, skip sections that deviate from your needs.

The third reason for skipping is when material is *too difficult*, over your head, when you lack the background to understand it. It is pre-reading that reveals this. And what pre-reading discloses in this case is that you must find help. If you are forced to skip only a part of a book or article because it is too difficult, the context of the difficult section may help you. Pre-read the book a second time, perhaps taking notes of your pre-reading: analyze thoroughly the table of contents and prefatory material, read introductory and concluding material again. This should relate the difficult passage to the rest of the book, so that you can apply the parts you do understand to help your comprehension in the difficult area. The second pre-reading will also locate, both before and after the difficult passage, material that may give you the explanations or insight you need.

A search for background or preparation beyond the level of a second pre-reading becomes a minor research project. You will want to begin by finding other works that relate to the one that stops you, but on a more elementary level. You will often find such material listed in the bibliography of the difficult book; the bibliography is thus the first place to turn. For further suggestions about how to find the help you need, turn to Chapter 11, on research.

Pre-reading, skipping, and skimming can be used together profitably. Lawyers, publishers, editors, reviewers, business executives, and others who work constantly with the printed word, have discovered that with practice they can use these skills together to get through and comprehend the essential items in great masses of practical prose every day. Skilled readers pre-read, skip, and skim when browsing in a bookstore. You yourself will find on your next visit to a library that you can save time by pre-reading, skipping, and skimming — by "reading with your fingers."

Stop pre-reading here. Your pre-reading alone should enable you to answer the following questions, without looking back.

1. For what three reasons do people fail to skip or skim successfully?

   ANSWER   a. _____

              b. _____

              c. _____

2. What are the grounds on which you must base a decision to skip either all or part of a work?

   ANSWER _____

   _____

3. What are the different *purposes* for which you skim?

   ANSWER _____

   _____

4. The most important topics of this chapter are listed below, but not in the correct order. Number them to show the sequence in which they actually occur.

   _____Why few people skip or skim well.

   _____Purposes for which you skim.

_____Three occasions when you should skip.

_____How pre-reading, skipping, and skimming can be combined.

_____Definition of skipping and skimming.

_____Three occasions when you should skim for main ideas and details.

_____How to skim for a particular fact.

_____How to skim for main ideas and details.

5. What will be your purpose in reading this chapter thoroughly?

ANSWER _____

_____

_____

EXERCISES FOR CHAPTER 6

Reading Journal

Skimming for a Fact—in the Physical Sciences

Phrase Flashing

Paragraph Analysis (a carry-over exercise)

Pre-reading
Table of Contents from *Character and Social Structure,* by Hans Gerth and C. Wright Mills

Summarizing
"The Arts of the Machine," from *Art Through the Ages,* by Helen Gardner

Reading Speed Carry-over Exercise

Reading Journal

In the separate notebook you are keeping, bring the section on **current reading** up to date: list everything you have read since your last entry, including title, author, type of material or subject, length, and time spent on it. Then summarize each new item briefly, its content and your opinion of it.

Then bring the **future reading** list up to date, with any additional titles you expect to read in the next several months: titles, authors, subject, number of pages, your purpose in reading each item.

You will return to your Reading Journal increasingly as this book continues, with carry-over exercises for many of the techniques you have learned. This chapter has two carry-over exercises, one in Paragraph Analysis, the other in Reading Speed.

Skimming for a Fact

Just before each of the following paragraphs, a particular piece of factual information is called for. You are to skim each paragraph to find the one fact. Try to break away completely from thorough reading. Instead, glance left and right very rapidly, stopping as little as twice on each line of print. *Keep clearly in mind the fact, stated at the beginning of the paragraph, for which you are skimming.*

As soon as you find the fact, put a pencil check in the margin next to it. Then go *immediately* to the next paragraph. When you have skimmed and checked all the paragraphs, record your time in the space provided on page 151, and then fill in the sentence number of each fact in the proper space there.

Work for speed. In class follow your instructor's directions for timing. On your own, follow the Instructions for Timing on page 474.

Begin timing here.

A

LOOK FOR: the temperature at which water ceases to contract as it cools

1 There are some liquids which do not expand uniformly like mer-
2 cury and alcohol. Water, as shown by the two graphs in Fig. 11H, is an
3 example of this. Starting at its freezing temperature of 0° C, and being
   slowly heated, water contracts until it reaches a temperature of 4° C and
4 then expands. At 4° C where it reaches its minimum volume it has its
5 maximum density. It might be considered fortunate that water expands
6 on being cooled from 4° to 0° C. If this were not the case and it contracted the way most liquids do, ice would form at the bottom of lakes
   instead of at the top.[1]

B

LOOK FOR: the material used to protect the cylinders of uranium

1   The Clinton pile consists of a cube of graphite containing horizontal
2 channels filled with uranium. The uranium is in the form of metal cylin-
3 ders protected by gas-tight casings of aluminum. The uranium cylinders
   or slugs may be slid into the channels in the graphite; space is left to
   permit cooling air to flow past, and to permit pushing the slugs out at
4 the back of the pile when they are ready for processing. Besides the
   channels for slugs there are various other holes through the pile for
   control rods, instruments, etc.[2]

C

LOOK FOR: the radial velocity of the base surge at one minute after the
            explosion

1   As the falling suspension of water in air from the outer part of the
   column reached the sea surface, it billowed outward and upward as the
2 base surge. This was first evident between 10 and 12 seconds after the
3 burst. At first the front of the base surge moved outward in all directions
   with a very high velocity, in excess of 100 feet per second, but this
4 velocity rapidly diminished. Thus, one minute after the explosion, the
   radial velocity in the cross wind direction was only 47 feet per second;
   between 2 and 3 minutes after the outward motion had ceased, and the
   whole mass of the surge was moving slowly down wind at about 10 feet
   per second, i.e., about 7 miles per hour.[3]

D

LOOK FOR: the date when micro-chemical analysis of plutonium was possible

1   The first evidence of the actual existence of plutonium and nep-
   tunium (ruling out the original erroneous interpretation of the splitting
   of uranium as evidence for their existence) was obtained by E. Mc-
   Millan and P. H. Abelson who isolated 93-239 from uranium bom-
2 barded with neutrons in the Berkeley cyclotron. This new element was
   identified as a beta emitter but the sample was too small for isolation
3 of the daughter product 94-239. The first isotope of plutonium studied
   chemically was not the 239 isotope but the 238 isotope, which is an
4 alpha-ray emitter with a half-life of about 50 years. U-238 bombarded
   with deuterons gives Np which disintegrates to Pu by beta emission.
5 Enough Pu-238 was prepared to permit Seaborg, Kennedy and Wahl
   to begin the study of its chemical properties in the winter of 1940–1941
   by using tracer chemistry with carriers according to practice usual in
6 radiochemistry. By such studies many chemical properties of plutonium
   were determined, and several possible chemical processes were evolved

7 by which Pu-239 might be removed from the chain-reacting pile. The success of experiments on a tracer scale led to plans to produce enough Pu-239 to be treated as an ordinary substance on the ultra-microchem-
8 ical scale. Such quantities were produced by prolonged bombardment of several hundred pounds of uranyl nitrate with neutrons obtained with the aid of cyclotrons, first at Berkeley and later at Washington
9 University in St. Louis. By the end of 1942, something over 500 micro-
10 grams had been obtained in the form of pure plutonium salts. Although this amount is less than would be needed to make the head of a pin, for the micro-chemists it was sufficient to yield considerable informa-tion; for one microgram is considered sufficient to carry out weighing experiments, titrations, solubility studies, etc.[2]

E

LOOK FOR: the angle between *compass* north and *true* north at San Francisco

1   The angle that a compass needle deviates from true north is called
2 the angle of declination. A map showing the angle of declination for the
3 United States during the year 1930 is shown in Fig. 18L. The more or less vertical set of irregular lines are lines of equal declination and are
4 called isogonic lines. At every point along the line marked 20° E, for
5 example, a compass needle actually points 20° east of true north. In the region of San Francisco the declination is seen to be about 18° E, while
6 in the region of New York it is about 11° W. The line through points where a compass points true *north,* 0°, is especially named the agonic line.[1]

Stop timing here.

     For each paragraph, enter the number of the sentence that contains the fact you were to find. (The sentences are numbered in the left margin.)

Skimming time in seconds for all items: _____

A: _____   B: _____   C: _____   D: _____   E: _____

Phrase Flashing

     This exercise is designed to help you develop the quick and accurate perception of *phrases as units* upon which efficient reading speeds depend. The materials for this practice have been grouped together at the back of the book so that you can return to them repeatedly as you work through the chapters, progressing to longer and longer phrases. Please turn to Page 476 and follow the instructions.

Paragraph Analysis (a carry-over exercise)

This exercise is designed to help you develop the habit of applying your knowledge of paragraph structures and functions in your daily reading.

1. Look through the pages of this book and identify the paragraph *function* — introductory, concluding, transition, or definition — of each of the following paragraphs. Some may have more than one function:

   A. Page 97, paragraphs 3, 4 — Paragraph function _____

   B. Page 114, paragraphs 1, 2 — Paragraph function _____

   C. Page 143, paragraph 1 — Paragraph function _____

   D. Page 147, paragraph 3 — Paragraph function _____

   E. Page 164, para. 5 ("We will . . .") — Paragraph function _____

   F. Pages 243–44, paragraphs 1–4 — Paragraph function _____

2. Browse through the books listed as current reading in your Reading Journal to find and copy out into that notebook:
   A. Two examples of paragraphs that give definitions.
   B. Two examples of transitional paragraphs.
   Then go back and mark the principal statement in each of those paragraphs.

Pre-reading

As an example of a book that is somewhat more difficult to pre-read, we reprint below the table of contents from an advanced college-level text. The field covered by the book is usually labeled *social psychology.* The reader who is not trained in this subject is likely to find the terminology somewhat specialized. This particular book, besides, offers the additional complication that it is written from a point of view which is distinctive, strongly held by its authors, and perhaps controversial within its field. Finally, the table of contents itself, while not intended to mystify or "tease" your interest (compare this with the previous pre-reading table of contents in Chapter 5), does use short labels rather than detailed descriptions of parts and chapters, to outline the book.

Compensating somewhat for these difficulties, the table of contents presents a very detailed breakdown of a book which is itself organized in an unusually neat and systematic pattern. Your experience in pre-reading should enable you to discover this pattern, together with a number of other characteristics of the book, implied by this table of contents. Examine it with care. Note that the outline has *three* levels: the Parts (One, Two, etc.), the Chapters (I through XVI), and a subsidiary breakdown we can call the Sections (in Chapter III, for example, these are 1 through 6).

The questions begin on page 156. You may refer to this material while answering them. This is not a timed exercise.

Table of Contents
from *Character and Social Structure*[4]
by HANS GERTH and C. WRIGHT MILLS

These questions assume that you are examining the material because you intend to read the book thoroughly. You may refer to the material while answering the questions.

1. Which chapters would you examine, as part of your pre-reading of the book, because their titles or positions in the book tell you that they may contain introductory or concluding matter? (Enter the *chapter numbers* as your answer.)

   ANSWER _____

2. Which single chapter is most likely to be transitional in nature, and should therefore be examined in pre-reading the book? (a) Chapter III, because it begins the first important part; (b) Chapter VI, because it sums up Part Two, as one can see from its section titles; (c) Chapter VII, because it begins Part Three, and judging from its section titles also relates back to the general subject of Part Two; (d) Chapter XIII, because it begins Part Four, and also relates back to Parts Two and Three; (e) Chapter XV, because it precedes the concluding chapter.

   ANSWER _____

3. Judging from the title of the book, Parts Two and Three would seem to complete the discussion of the subject matter. Relating Part Four to the rest of the book, how can we best explain its function? (a) Part Four is a much shorter, additional section, primarily concerned with furnishing additional examples of the mechanisms described in Parts Two and Three; (b) Part Four is a series of case studies showing how the principles of Parts Two and Three can be applied to understand and control the real world; (c) Parts Two and Three are essentially descriptive, while Part Four gets down to the basic analysis of mechanisms, which is the purpose of the book; (d) Parts Two and Three analyze the elements of Character and Social Structure, respectively, while Part Four shows how the elements work together in the real world.

   ANSWER _____

4. Your answer to the last question was in schematic, organizational terms. In what other major way is Part Four different from Parts Two and Three? (a) It leaves the analysis of contemporary problems and applies the method of the book to history; (b) it is concerned with the understanding of major problems of society and history, rather than with detailed analysis of social mechanisms; (c) it is concerned with major problems of society and history, applying to them the tools for understanding developed in the preceding detailed analysis of mechanisms; (d) it supplies proof of the highly theoretical analysis that preceded it.

   ANSWER _____

5. The introductory portion of the book is interesting because its organization parallels the entire book. Judging from this parallel structure, which section in Part One probably bears the closest relation to all of Part Two? (a) Chapter I, Section 1; (b) Chapter I, Section 2; (c) Chapter II, Section 1; (d) Chapter II, Section 2; (e) Chapter II, Section 3.

   ANSWER _____

6. Similarly, which section in Part One probably bears the closest relation to all of Part Three? (a) Chapter I, Section 1; (b) Chapter I, Section 2; (c) Chapter II, Section 1; (d) Chapter II, Section 2; (e) Chapter II, Section 3.

ANSWER _____

7. Again, which section in Part One probably bears the closest relation to Chapter III? (a) Chapter I, Section 1; (b) Chapter I, Section 2; (c) Chapter II, Section 1; (d) Chapter II, Section 2; (e) Chapter II, Section 3.

ANSWER _____

8. Now project the parallel construction further for a possibly revealing speculation about the nature of this book. See the title of Section 3, Chapter II. What *are* the "tasks of social psychology"? (a) Understanding and correcting individual character defects, through therapy, by applying the insights of Parts Two and Three, which are parallel to Chapter II, Section 3; (b) understanding the mechanisms of history, as in Chapter XIII, which is the only portion of the book parallel to Chapter II, Section 3; (c) understanding the processes of modern politics, by the analysis in Chapter XVI, which is the only portion of the book parallel to Chapter II, Section 3; (d) understanding, and controlling if possible, the kinds of major problems discussed throughout Part Four, which is probably the parallel to Chapter II, Section 3.

ANSWER _____

9. Chapters VIII and IX have similar titles. How are they most likely to be different from each other? (a) IX is not different from VIII, but simply a continuation; (b) VIII seems to analyze areas we might call "legal" or "public," while IX seems concerned with areas most of us consider "private"; (c) VIII considers the institutions of major, central importance, while IX deals briefly with a number of secondary matters; (d) VIII is introductory and descriptive, while IX carries on the main analysis of the mechanisms behind the descriptions.

ANSWER _____

10. Based on your examination of the table of contents alone, it is possible to say something about the overall viewpoint of this book—in very general terms, to be sure. Which of the following descriptions or "pre-reading summaries" best fits what the table of contents tells you? (a) History and the problems of the contemporary world are best explained in terms of the ceaseless conflict between individual character and the elaborate devices by which society controls the individual; (b) the nature, development, and present problems of our civilization can be understood in important ways as the result of the interaction between individuals—as they are shaped by a variety of social institutions and by biological inheritance—and the institutions themselves; (c) it is the task of social psychology to provide the means by which the major problems of the present day can be understood and promptly acted upon.

ANSWER _____

Summarizing

The passage below is from a history of the visual arts. After having traced the history of art from the earliest times, the author considers, toward the end of the book, an important new aspect of art today; the passage reprinted here is a central part of that discussion. For this exercise, your purpose in reading the passage is to identify the principal statement (topic sentence or sentences) in each paragraph, and then to summarize each paragraph and the entire passage. As you read, mark the principal statements with lines in the margin. The questions follow the passage.

This is not a timed exercise. You may refer to this passage as you answer the questions.

"The Arts of the Machine"[5]
from *Art Through the Ages*
by HELEN GARDNER

A

1   Consider for a moment what is perhaps the dominating factor of this
2 century—the machine. We who have become so accustomed to the machine find it difficult to realize that for thousands of years man had been making what he needed for daily living by hand; and that only in the last century has he opened the door upon the new world of technology, with its unbelievable potentialities, which is already initiating not only vast social and economic changes but is originating new trends and
3 traditions in the arts. Already we have seen that the machine, with the co-operation of the artist, can produce objects which not only function effectively, but which are as satisfying in their own way as the handmade
4 objects of premachine days. "Whenever the final product of the machine is designed or determined by anyone sensitive to formal values, that product can and does become an abstract work of art in the subtler
5 sense of the term."* Even mass production is not an unmitigated evil, for it gives the creative faculty wide scope for combining shapes, textures, and colors, which individually might seem commonplace, into novel arrangements.

B

1   In its early days, the machine was looked upon merely as a labor-saving device to reproduce quickly and in quantity handmade articles.
2,3 Unfortunately that conception has not been entirely outgrown. For we are still making electric candles and machine-made hand-wrought silver

* Herbert Read, *Art and Industry,* Harcourt Brace Jovanovich, Inc., 1935, p. 37.

4 and iron. The true product of the machine, on the other hand, has an
5 entirely different character from the product made by hand. There can
6 be no translation of the one into the other. In the handmade object appear the warmth of personality, the marks of tools, irregularity of shape,
7 and subtle variations of hue or texture. The machine, by contrast, is cold
  and precise, and in its products requires of the observer a response to
8 the beauty of geometry. To be sure, geometry is basically present in all
  art of all times, though it may not be discernible to the untrained eye.

C

1   Just what, then, is the character of machine art, and what is the func-
2 tion of the artist in its creation? Machine art we meet at every turn.
3 Almost imperceptibly this new art has permeated our everyday world
  from chain-store products to jet planes—our advertising, window dis-
  plays, automobiles, kitchens, packaging, household furnishings, and
4 utensils, to mention but a few. The materials of machine art include not
  only the old materials, often used in new ways—glass, for example—but
5 an ever increasing number of new ones, notably plastics. Each has its
  own potentiality for color and texture and, technologically, for machine
6 production. The forms of machine-made articles seem to bear a relation
  to the machine itself in their clean lines, often long and unbroken; in
  their unbroken surfaces made effective by texture; and in their lack of
7 ornament. This form, however, is dependent upon the "equilibrium of
  lines, proportions, masses," in fact upon all the elements used in the
  construction of any organic structure; and also upon function—to do
8 efficiently what it is made to do. The word "streamlined" is frequently
9 used in connection with machine art. The term has two connotations,
10 one technological, the other esthetic. As applied technologically to airplanes, locomotives and trains, automobiles, and ships, where movement
  is in question, the term is based upon the fact that smooth unbroken
  surfaces and rounding corners offer least resistance to air currents and
11 thus assure the greatest potentiality for power and speed. By extension
  of meaning, the term is being applied to static articles which have similar
  characteristics and in whose simplicity, clean unbroken lines, and smooth
  surfaces we take intuitive delight.

D

1   This machine art, though made in mass production, originates, after
  all, with the artist who collaborates with business and with the con-
2 sumer. He must be a technologist, just as the Gothic and the modern
3 builders were and are engineers. For he must know the potentialities
4 of his materials. Does this or that material lend itself to manufacture
5,6 by a machine? Does the product function adequately? Will it sell? How
7,8 will people react to it? It is at this point that artist and people come into
9 closest contact. And where the artist can win popular acceptance—and
  to a large extent he has done so—he is breaking down that present segre-

gation of the arts from life that has plagued the world for at least a hun-
10 dred and fifty years. Most people thrill at the sight of our airplanes and
"streamliners," the superlative curves of our highways, and the sweep of
our bridges, which seem to spring so lightly across rivers and canyons.
11,12 All these combine scientific skill and esthetic quality. Yet people seldom
consider them in the same category as buildings, paintings, and sculpture.
13 The reason for their delight, however, is essentially the same.

E

1   Basically, the machine arts are in total harmony with modern build-
2 ings and abstract or nonobjective painting and sculpture. And to bring
them into conformity with all buildings, painting, and sculpture of all
ages, which are as fundamentally geometric as they, may not be too dif-
3 ficult a step to take. Above and beyond the character of the form, how-
4 ever, lies its *quality*. And just as a painting, a building, a statue, or a
textile is judged in the last analysis by a *quality* that is as indefinable
as the nature of art itself and yet is felt intuitively by the artist and the
spectator, just so any machine-made article is to be judged on the basis
of whether the artist, after he has met all the demands of the machine,
of function, and of economics, has been able to infuse his original de-
5 sign with that *quality* which distinguishes art. It is the same problem that
6 faced the Paleolithic maker of flints. That many of our designers have met
7 this test seems inescapable. They have produced a dynamic art, definitely
expressive of contemporary living.

For each of the five paragraphs, choose the best summary; also note the topic sentence or sentences. Then choose the summary for the complete passage. You may refer to the passage as you answer the questions.

A

1. The machine—familiar, dominant, but only a recent development—has opened great social and economic opportunities—and great opportunities for the creative artist as well.
2. We are accustomed to the machine, so that we do not realize immediately how it has replaced the handmade in products for daily living—and in the arts as well.
3. Mass production does not necessarily mean the destruction of artistic and creative values.

ANSWER _____ SENTENCE _____

B

1. It is not the purpose of the machine simply to replace handmade items, but to go beyond them to purer, less accidental forms.
2. The geometry, and therefore the art, of machine-made articles differs from that of handmade objects.
3. The characteristics of handmade articles are warm, individual, and irregular; those of machine products are colder, more precise and geometric; neither should be translated into the other.

ANSWER _____ SENTENCE _____

C

1. The new arts of the machine have invaded almost every aspect of modern life with new materials and artistic rules.
2. Machine art is everywhere, applying a clean, sweeping, and unornamented simplicity to new materials and old.
3. Machine art, though it can delight us intuitively, has almost imperceptibly eliminated the traditional artistic values, replacing them with objects that are all basically similar in their coldly streamlined technological relation to the machine itself.

ANSWER _____ SENTENCE _____

D

1. The new economics and technologies of the machine and mass production give the willing artist a new opportunity to relate esthetic quality to many aspects of everyday life from which the arts have too long been separated.
2. The arts of the machine are a matter of popular acceptance not in the same category as the traditional visual arts.
3. The new and strict technological requirements of machine art oblige the artist to develop new forms in relation to production and sales possibilities, and to work for popular acceptance.

ANSWER _____ SENTENCE _____

E

1. The machine arts are in harmony with the fundamental geometric *quality* of modern architecture, painting, and sculpture, just as the arts of even the earliest ages have been in harmony with each other.
2. The products of the machine can be related, in terms of high artistic quality, to the most dynamic artistic forms of all ages.
3. Machine arts meet two tests: they are in harmony with modern architecture, painting, and sculpture (and can be harmonized with earlier forms); but more important, they can reach that indefinable *quality* that marks true art.

ANSWER _____ SENTENCE _____

Now choose the best summary for the entire passage.

1. The revolutionary arts of the machine, though at first sight destructive of earlier values, can and often do restate those values in dynamic contemporary terms.
2. Machine arts are new in the requirements and opportunities for popular acceptance that they impose on the artist, and in their new emphasis on streamlined simplicity; but they are not incompatible with the fundamental characteristics of art through the ages and they can show genuine artistic quality.
3. In a century dominated by mass production, the artist who would have dynamic popular effect must abandon the handmade, collaborate with the machine arts, master the technological and sales requirements, and produce in the forms (streamlined and geometric) that are in harmony with the economies of contemporary living.

ANSWER _____

Reading Speed Carry-over Exercise

With this exercise you will carry new habits of speed and reading efficiency into your day-to-day reading of practical prose. In the book you chose from your Reading Journal, and have been practicing with, pick a passage you have not yet read, a chapter or piece of a chapter that seems to form a sensible unit, six to ten pages long.

Pre-read the passage quickly.

Read it very fast, pushing your speed to the point where it feels distinctly dangerous.

Close the book; in your Reading Journal, jot down in summary form all that pre-reading and fast thorough reading of the passage have taught you.

Return to the passage and read it a second time, more slowly, to check and add to your comprehension. Remember, this second reading is your safeguard, allowing you to experiment with speed on your first reading, even though the material is important to you.

CHAPTER 7

The Questioning Reader

Pre-read this chapter as your first step in reading. After pre-reading, but before reading thoroughly, answer the questions at the end of the chapter.

Begin pre-reading here.

All the techniques of reading so far introduced — pre-reading, consciously controlled variations in speed, even skipping and skimming — have one aim in common: to make you a reader who is active, not passive, to put you into a constructive tension with your book. The most powerful, flexible technique of all for producing this constructive tension between you and whatever you are reading is the next to be introduced: reading with questions in mind.

Think back to the last time you took an important, difficult examination, at the end of a semester's work in a subject. How well could you have done on that examination, do you suppose, if from the *beginning* of the semester you had known what half of the test questions were to be? Imagine further that the test questions were well designed to examine not just your memory for facts, but your ability to use concepts, methods, and facts as well, within the subject matter of the course.

How would such advance knowledge of the questions affect your studying? You would still need to read the course materials thoroughly because you would not know the other half of the examination questions. But your reading would be considerably more purposeful and more accurately directed. Your speeds could be somewhat higher. Your comprehension and retention of the things you need to know would be improved markedly.

The technique of reading with questions actively in mind can produce precisely similar effects in your daily reading. You can best formulate these questions at two points in the reading process. First, with every piece of practical prose, the point between pre-reading and thorough reading is the time to ask yourself a series of general questions that will greatly enlarge your grasp of the entire work. Second, during thorough reading there is a more specialized question technique you can use to improve your mastery of details, to make difficult material clearer, and particularly to improve concentration.

The Four Master Questions After Pre-reading, Before Thorough Reading

You pre-read to discover the subject and organizational skeleton of a selection, and how these relate to your purpose in reading it. Your pre-reading prepares you to formulate questions that will fix the subject, organization, and purpose in your mind, so that you can associate the details within this frame-work, relate them to each other, and remember them. Indeed, as we shall see, these questions can become your most important memory aid, as well as a tool for improving your understanding.

After pre-reading you may want to ask many different questions of practical prose. You are already familiar with some of them. Your purpose in reading thoroughly is one question emphasized from the very beginning of this book. Structural, organizational questions are brought out by pre-reading itself; pre-reading also assesses the difficulty of a work's subject and style. The importance of spotting definitions and transitions was emphasized in the chapter on paragraphs.

Possible questions can be multiplied: one reason for the great power of reading with questions in mind is the method's adaptability. But fortunately, for speed and flexibility the important questions you will want to bear in mind while reading most practical prose can be brought together under four basic questions—a four-step check list.

What is the thesis or problem here?

What is your purpose in reading this particular work?

What is the main sequence of ideas?

What particular information or ideas can you now say you will be hunting for as you read thoroughly?

We will take up these four questions now. In addition, for some of your most important and difficult reading you will ask other questions between pre-reading and thorough reading. You will find these questions explained in Chapter 15, "Introduction to Critical Reading: Four Critical Questions."

What is the thesis or problem here?

What is the author's subject? What point of view does he seem to have about that subject? Is he trying to prove something?

At first thought, these questions may seem obvious; pre-reading of prefatory material—or a glance at the work's title alone—may already have given you provisional answers. But the answers you get from pre-reading, though they may be an excellent and indispensable guide to thorough reading, are too general for thorough understanding. You will quickly discover the remarkable sharpening of your mind that comes when you keep the author's thesis or problem suspensefully in question while reading thoroughly. At the very least you will pick out more clearly the most significant statements. You will be more alert to those places where the author tells you what he intends to prove, and beyond that to the facts and reasons that support the thesis. Similarly, and even more important, you will be quicker to note irrelevant material or possible weaknesses in the author's position. Furthermore, in some writing—in much history and social science, perhaps most political writing and current affairs, and surely much criticism of writing and the arts—the author's actual thesis or intention may be somewhat different from what he claims.

For example, although it is no slur to a historian or economist to say that he writes about the past with an eye to the effect of his writing on the present, it is certainly true that if you fail to understand such a purpose, you will miss half the point of many important American works of the past thirty years. A book like *A Monetary History of the United States, 1867–1960,* by Milton Friedman and Anna J. Schwartz, appeared, when it first came out in 1963, to be a massive, highly technical economic analysis of the workings of governmental monetary policy. Readers noted, however, that Friedman was also arguing that the record proved that the methods of the Federal Reserve Board went exactly counter, time and again, to what was needed to save the country from recessions or to slow down inflationary periods. And in the years since that book came out, Friedman's beliefs about the changed policies the government should pursue, the beliefs that once seemed so specialized and technical, have been winning increasing support in actual governmental practice. Only when you read with the conscious intention of determining what an author is up to, can you reliably detect what a passage really aims to demonstrate.

What is your purpose in reading this particular work?

What do you want out of it? Why is it important to you? How does your purpose in reading it compare to the author's purpose in writing it?

By now in your acquisition of the techniques of reading, you should find yourself, when you pick up any reading matter, rather more aware of what you intend to do with it. But it is after pre-reading that you formulate your purpose clearly and consciously. Pre-reading gives you information you need in order to state your purpose with precision. For example, or your first look at *Marcuse,* by Alasdair MacIntyre, you would note that the author is an English philosopher and sociologist, and that the book is about the writings of Herbert Marcuse, an American philosopher widely known for his criticisms of modern society. But at that point you could hardly formulate your purpose more precisely than to ask, "What has the one professor got to say about the other?" If you had heard something about MacIntyre's book or had read reviews of it, you might be able to state your purpose more specifically, perhaps "to determine what MacIntyre says are Marcuse's theories, and why and how he opposes them." But after pre-reading the book you would state your purpose far more precisely, for example: "to discover the sequence of development of Marcuse's ideas, as MacIntyre presents them; to see what the intellectual—and social or political—consequences of Marcuse's ideas may be; and to see whether MacIntyre's virtual demolition of Marcuse's philosophy seems to be justified and well argued."

For a further example, after pre-reading this chapter on questions you should have formulated your purpose in reading thoroughly much like this: "to discover whether this question technique can be useful, and if so, exactly how to use it."

Clearly, awareness of your purpose after pre-reading adds point and accuracy to your thorough reading. It does more than that. Precise statement of purpose enables you to know, as you read, how well each successive passage meets your purpose. It also puts the author's statements "in perspective" — tells you which of his points are most important for you to remember. And finally, awareness of your precise purpose *lets you know when you have mastered what you need.* This may sometimes mean that you will skip or skim large segments of the book, or, at the other extreme, it may mean that you will realize that you must read additional related books and articles before you can accomplish your purpose.

What is the main sequence of ideas?

Just how does the author organize the development of his subject, his thesis, his attack on his problem?

Here again, pre-reading provides the general framework that you correct and fill in as your read thoroughly with this question in mind. We cannot stress too often the importance of being always aware of the organization of what you are reading. The strength of this question is that it carries your awareness of organization from pre-reading into thorough reading. For this reason, when material is difficult or your reading purpose is complete mastery, it is very useful to outline the author's organization with pencil and paper as completely as you can from what you learn by pre-reading. You then answer the question, *What is the main sequence of ideas?* by correcting and expanding your outline as you read thoroughly.

What particular information or ideas can you now say you will be hunting for as you read thoroughly?

In other words, after pre-reading, what more specific questions of fact or theory do you expect to find answers to?

This master question, of course, usually demands not just one particular question but often a list of several items you are after. The question is closely related to the earlier one of purpose. In practice, this question usually gets you closer to the author's facts and details than a statement of purpose alone. Sometimes you will read without having an advance idea of exactly what questions you expect the selection to answer — you "don't know what you don't know." Wherever possible, however, you should bear in mind detailed questions you expect the selection to answer. You may be looking for just a few facts. (Would you then read thoroughly or skim?) At the other extreme, you may wish to learn all that the author has to tell you, in which case your several specific questions serve as bridges or points of attack, leading you from areas where you are now able to ask detailed questions, into more unfamiliar subjects.

In reading a history of the Dutch Republic, for instance, you might be concerned with the role of William the Silent. You would thus ask how the history treats that figure and what new information it gives you about him. In reading a scientific report you might be familiar with the conclusion, but want to know what experimental evidence the scientist gathered. You would then ask questions designed to help you discover that evidence.

The questioning reader has his own yardstick for comprehension.

These questions you ask between pre-reading and thorough reading act in the ways we have described to sharpen your comprehension and to allow full use of your best speeds. You will discover one thing more as you develop the new habit of reading with questions in mind. The question technique gives you a continual awareness of whether or not you are getting what you need from the material; and when you have read the material through, you will have a measure of whether or not you have understood it sufficiently for your purpose. Without such a measure of the adequacy of their work, many readers suffer from a constant, nagging sense of confusion: "Did I really understand? Did I master all the details I may need? Maybe I should have paid closer attention to that passage where . . ." Troubled with doubts like these, serious and otherwise skilled readers are often unable to use all their speed and comprehension skills to full advantage. For many readers, therefore, this new sense of sureness of what they are doing is the most important benefit from using the question technique. In effect, the questioning reader provides himself with a much improved version of the comprehension questions that follow the timed reading exercises in this book.

To make sure that you learn this new skill effectively and fully, we urge that for the next several weeks, at least, you regularly put your questions in writing. The blank half-page at the beginning of an article or chapter is a strategic place to write them down. If the book or article is not your own, write your questions on slips of paper and keep them between the pages. By adding the answers as you come to them, you will convert the question technique into a quick and useful form of note-taking. Indeed, you should find the habit of writing down your questions and answers so valuable that you will want to continue using it for all your most important thorough reading.

Questions Formulated During Thorough Reading

The second point where you ask questions is during thorough reading. Unlike the type of questions you ask *before* thorough reading, here you will use a method that is not applicable to all the reading you do, but is an emergency technique for first aid when you have one of the following problems:

When the material is very difficult or unfamiliar;

When you must master every fact and detail;

When you have trouble concentrating.

The technique is easy to use and to remember: *you turn the first sentence of each paragraph into a question.*

As Chapter 5 pointed out, the principal statement or topic sentence is usually the *first* sentence of a practical prose paragraph. When you rephrase the topic sentence to turn it into a question, you are asking how the author develops the principal statement.

Demonstration: Topic Sentences into Questions

Take this topic sentence:

Meanwhile in the Senate Chamber at Washington opposition to Wilson's League and Wilson's Fourteen Points increased in volume.

Turn it into a question:

How did Senate opposition to Wilson's program increase?

And here is the complete paragraph:

Meanwhile in the Senate Chamber at Washington opposition to Wilson's League and Wilson's Fourteen Points increased in volume. As early as December 21, 1918, Henry Cabot Lodge, intellectual leader of the Republicans in the Senate, announced that the Senate had equal power with the President in treaty-making and should make its wishes known in advance of the negotiations. He said that there would be quite enough to do at Paris without raising the issue of the League. And he set forth his idea of the sort of peace which ought to be made—an idea radically different from President Wilson's. Lodge and a group of his associates wanted Germany to be disarmed, saddled with a terrific bill for reparations, and if possible dismembered. They were ready to give to the Allies large concessions in territory. And above all they wanted nothing to be included in the peace settlement which would commit the United States to further intervention in European affairs. They prepared to examine carefully any plan for a League of Nations which might come out of the Conference and to resist it if it involved "entangling alliances." Thus to opposition from the diplomats of Europe was added opposition of another sort from the Senate and public opinion at home. Wilson was between two fires. He might not realize how they threatened him, but they were spreading.[1]

As you see, the question is answered. Now another topic sentence:

As compared with the striking increases in July, consumer goods rose relatively little in August.

As a question, it becomes:

Why did consumer goods increase less in August than in July?

And the paragraph answers the question:

As compared with the striking increases in July, consumer goods rose relatively little in August. Unquestionably, the figures on textile and clothing, for example, do not give a correct picture of the increase since monetary reform, because the release of hoarded stocks inflated the figures reported for July. The group increase shows a 23-per cent rise in July and a 1-per cent increase in August, but the rate of improvement has actually been very much smoother. Similarly, vehicles reported an 18-per cent gain in

July and only 3-per cent in August. The figures on producer goods and the extractive industries contain less striking examples, but the same phenomenon occurred in these categories to a lesser extent.[2]

In other words, the question of what happened in August is answered by a reevaluation of what happened in July.

Both methods of formulating questions—before thorough reading and during thorough reading—take longer to describe than to use. The time you take to ask yourself a few questions, after pre-reading but before reading thoroughly, will be more than made up by the rapidity with which you will comprehend and the ease with which you will retain the material. Turning first sentences into questions will retard your reading speed, but it is an effective method for attacking difficult material and for bringing your concentration back into focus. (You will find more about concentration in Chapter 9.)

Stop pre-reading here. Your pre-reading alone should enable you to answer the following questions without looking back.

1. What is the thesis or problem of this chapter?

   ANSWER _____

   _____

   _____

   _____

2. What is your precise purpose in reading it?

   ANSWER _____

   _____

3. The most important topics of this chapter are listed below, but not in the correct order. Number them to show the sequence in which they actually occur.

   _____ Four questions to ask before thorough reading of all practical prose.

   _____ The exact method for formulating questions during thorough reading.

   _____ How questions asked before thorough reading help you check your comprehension.

   _____ How the two question techniques can, in general, help comprehension.

   _____ The three "emergencies" that call for questions to be formulated during thorough reading.

4. What are the four main questions you are to ask about practical prose after pre-reading?

ANSWER　a. _____

b. _____

c. _____

d. _____

5. Exactly how do you formulate questions during thorough reading?

ANSWER _____

_____

EXERCISES FOR CHAPTER 7

Reading Journal

Pre-reading Application (a carry-over exercise)

Skimming for a Fact — in International Relations

Eye Span

Question Technique
　　"In Defense of Contemporary Fiction," from *How We Live*, edited by Penney Chapin Hills and L. Rust Hills

Reading Speed Exercise: Average Level 5
　　"The Morning After," by Otto Friedrich

Reading Journal

In your separate notebook, bring the section on **current reading** up to date, including for each item a brief summary of the content, and your thoughts about it. Then bring the **future reading** list up to date. At this point you should read through the **future reading** list from the beginning, to see which items you have already read or begun, and to note next to each of the others when you expect to get to it.

Turn now to the next exercise in this chapter, Pre-reading Application. This is a carry-over exercise, and you will use your Reading Journal.

Pre-reading Application (a carry-over exercise)

Which three books in your current or future reading lists are now the most important for you to master? Turn to your Reading Journal notebook and pick those out; then get the three volumes together.

Examine, briefly, the table of contents of each. Which book strikes you as the most fruitful for applying pre-reading?

Put the other two books aside. Take the one you have chosen and conduct a complete pre-reading examination of it—writing out in your Journal the results of each step as you go.

List title, author, publisher, date of publication.

Table of contents: read it thoroughly. Describe the structure of the book in a detailed paragraph. Why is each part where it is, and not earlier or later? Which chapters appear to be introductory? concluding? transitional or summarizing? What function does each chapter have in relation to the sequence of subjects in the book? Can you spot any important terms, locate any major definitions? what and where? Are there any repeated patterns to show that one section of the book resembles another?

Purpose: now analyze, again in a detailed paragraph, your own purpose in reading the book. What do you want from it? What particular questions do you expect the book to answer? Which parts or chapters are most relevant to what you want? least relevant?

Prefatory material: now read that and analyze it in writing in similar fashion. What can you now say of the author's aims, thesis, or problem?

Introduction, transitions, conclusion: then read (first pre-reading) each introductory, concluding, and summary/transitional chapter, writing out a full paragraph of analysis of each, as you go.

Don't be surprised if this entire process takes you an hour or more. But then, complete this final step.

Summarizing: close the book, write out in your own words a one-paragraph statement of what the book is, what it intends to do, how it is put together, the point of view it takes about its subject, and your opinion of it at this preliminary point.

Skimming for a Fact

Just before each of the following paragraphs, a particular piece of factual information is called for. You are to skim each paragraph to find the one fact. Try to break away completely from thorough reading. Instead, glance left and right very rapidly, stopping as little as twice on each line of print. *Keep clearly in mind the fact, stated at the beginning of the paragraph, for which you are skimming.*

As soon as you find the fact, put a pencil check in the margin next to it. Then go immediately to the next paragraph. When you have skimmed and checked all the paragraphs, record your time in the space provided on page 174, and then fill in the sentence number of each fact in the proper space.

Work for speed. In class follow your instructor's directions for timing. On your own, follow the Instructions for Timing on page 474.

Begin timing here.

A

LOOK FOR: the date of the Treaty of Paris

1   The Congress of Vienna, meeting from September 1814 to June 1815, assumed, like the congresses of Osnabrück and Münster, what
2 was practically the role of a great law-making body. It formed new states by the union of Sweden and Norway and of Holland and Belgium, and it confirmed the action of Napoleon in consolidating the numerous German states and formed them into a loose confederation of thirty-nine
3 members. Its chief object, however, was the restoration of the balance of
4 power in Europe which had been so greatly unsettled. The leading powers had announced in the Treaty of Paris of May 30, 1814, that it was their desire "to put an end to the long disturbance of Europe and to the suffering of the people by a stable peace based upon a just division of forces between the powers and carrying with it a guarantee of its
5 permanence." But the purpose thus announced was completely frustrated
6 by the reactionary principles which dominated the congress. The decisions taken by it proved to be the occasion throughout the nineteenth
7 century of new wars to undo the plans so carefully made. Domestic revolution followed in the wake of the restoration of the deposed monarchs, and wars of liberation followed the suppression of aspirations for national union.[3]

B

LOOK FOR: distance of the ship from shore at time of seizure

1   The next day the revenue cutter *Tampa* was ordered to find the
2 *Grace and Ruby* and bring her into port. Two days later, on February 23d, she discovered the schooner, and after some show of resistance on her part, which was overcome by a display of force by the cutter, the schooner was seized and brought into the port of Boston by the *Tampa*.
3 At the time of the seizure the *Grace and Ruby* was about four miles from
4 the nearest land. She had on board the balance of her cargo of liquor.
5,6 Her master in no way assented to the seizure. After the schooner was brought into Boston the present libels were filed, a warrant for her arrest issued, and she was taken into custody by the United States marshal.[4]

C

LOOK FOR: the date of the *Navemar*'s arrival at Buenos Aires

1   The shippers agreed to make arrangements to deliver the rest of the linseed cargo to the *Navemar* when she arrived at Buenos Aires, and the representative of the Linea Sud-Americana, Inc., the charterer of the steamship *Navemar,* informed him that he would call at the consul's office at Rosario when it opened the next morning, to obtain the ship's roll and would send it by mail to Martinez, c/o Linea Sud-Americana,
2   Inc., at Buenos Aires. Accordingly, the *Navemar* sailed at 5 P.M.,
3   October 23, 1936, without her ship's roll. After the *Navemar*'s return to Buenos Aires, arriving there at 2 P.M., October 24, 1936, he was informed that the Spanish Consul at Rosario had declined to deliver the ship's roll to the agent of the Linea Sud-Americana, Inc., and would
4   deliver it only to the master of the *Navemar.* Subsequently the Spanish Consul General at Buenos Aires obtained the ship's register from the
5   master and returned both it and the ship's roll to him. The master noted the indorsement thereon made by the Consul at Rosario and on the
6   register by the Consul General at Buenos Aires. The latter said he had no instructions to make with respect to the *Navemar* and that she should
7,8 continue her voyage. Nothing was said about taking possession. The Spanish Consul General at Buenos Aires, however, did tell Martinez to notify Madrid that he was sailing, and accordingly Martinez did cable the General Director of Merchant Marine at Madrid, on October 29,
9   1936: "Authorized by Consul General here sail for New York. Greet-
10   ings. (Signed) Master Navemar."[5]

D

LOOK FOR: names of islands leased by the United States from Nicaragua

1   The term "lease" is not mentioned in the treaty of 1903 by which "the Republic of Panama grants to the United States in perpetuity the use, occupation and control" of the zone of land and adjacent territory
2   for the construction of an interoceanic canal. Technically, Panama retained sovereignty over the territory, although it was expressly provided that the United States should be allowed to exercise over the territory "all the rights, power, and authority" which it would possess if it were
3   sovereign. In compensation for the rights acquired, the United States agreed to make both a cash payment and a smaller annual payment dur-
4   ing the life of the convention. The lease of Guantánamo and Bahia Honda
5   from Cuba presented fewer administrative complications. The treaty of 1903 defining the relations between the United States and Cuba provided that, in order to enable the United States to maintain the independence of Cuba and to protect the people of the island, as well as to further the island's own defense, Cuba should sell or lease to the United
6   States lands necessary for coaling or naval stations. The lease of the two areas was thereupon effected by means of an executive agreement

defining the territory leased, followed by a second agreement fixing
7 the conditions of the lease. In 1914 the United States, by the Bryan-
Chamorro Treaty, leased the Great Corn and Little Corn Islands in the
8 Caribbean Sea from Nicaragua for ninety-nine years. The validity of the
lease was contested by Costa Rica and Salvador in suits against Nicaragua before the Central American Court of Justice, which pronounced
against Nicaragua but found itself unable to declare the treaty void in
view of the fact that the United States was not a party to the suits.[3]

E
LOOK FOR: the court which made decision in the case of the *David J. Adams*
1   A diplomatic correspondence ensued with the United States Government protesting against what it contended to be a misinterpretation
of the Treaty of 1818 by the Canadian Government and His Britannic
Majesty's Government contending that, as the case of the *David J.
Adams* was still *sub judice*, diplomatic action was to be suspended for the
2 time being. After having been somewhat delayed, by reason of certain
negotiations which took place in 1886–1888 between the two Governments concerning fisheries, the action for forfeiture of the *David J. Adams*
and her cargo was decided on October 28, 1889, by the Vice-Admiralty
3 Court at Halifax. The ship and her cargo were condemned as forfeited to
Her Britannic Majesty for breach and violation of the Convention and the
various Acts in relation thereto, and ordered to be sold at public auction.[6]

Stop timing here.

For each paragraph enter the number of the sentence that contains the
fact you were to find. (The sentences are numbered in the left margin of the
page.)

Skimming time in seconds for all items: _____

A: _____   B: _____   C: _____   D: _____   E: _____

Eye Span

The following material is designed to extend your use of peripheral vision.
Use a 3 x 5 card to cover the column you are working with. Move the card
rapidly down the column, one line at a time. As each line is exposed, read it,
looking at it only once and approximately at the center, as shown by the dots
between the words. Try to take in the entire width of the line. At first you may
have to focus for several seconds on each set of dots before you are able to
perceive all the words on the line.

By the end . . . . of August, all the . . . . bread grains, with . . . . only a few . . . . exceptions, had been . . . . brought under . . . . cover. Rye . . . . has been harvested . . . . with only minor . . . . losses due to . . . . weather, and yields . . . . should be substantially . . . . better than . . . . last year. Even though . . . . wheat suffered . . . . slightly more . . . . than rye from . . . . having to remain . . . . in shocks too long . . . . the yield is expected . . . . to show an even . . . . greater improvement . . . . over that of . . . . last year. Owing . . . . to rains during the . . . . last week in June . . . . and during the early . . . . part of July . . . . there was some loss . . . . in winter barley . . . . that was cut early . . . . but yields are well . . . . above those of . . . . last year. Oats have . . . . suffered the most . . . . of any crop . . . . because of the . . . . bad weather during . . . . the harvest. There was . . . . still a quantity . . . . remaining to be cut . . . . in the north of the . . . . British Zone and in . . . . the high land of the . . . . extreme south of . . . . the U. S. Zone.

Much of the . . . . oat crop that was . . . . cut during the . . . . wet weather had to . . . . remain in shocks . . . . for an extended . . . . period, and a . . . . considerable loss must . . . . be expected. It is . . . . estimated, however, ... that the yield . . . . will be better . . . . this year than last. . . . . Sugar beet . . . . crops appear . . . . excellent and the . . . . actual yield from . . . . cutting the beets . . . . may fall only . . . . a little short of . . . . the prewar average. . . . . Due to lack of . . . . sunshine, the sugar . . . . content is estimated . . . . to be two per cent . . . . lower than for . . . . last year. The sugar . . . . content may be . . . . increased, however, ... provided the weather . . . . before harvest time . . . . in early October . . . . continues to be . . . . favorable. Early . . . . potatoes produced . . . . a good yield and . . . . the prospects for later . . . . potatoes are excellent. . . . . There is some risk . . . . that blight may affect . . . . the late crop but provided . . . . the weather continues . . . . to be dry and sunny . . . . the present estimates of . . . . a high yield should be . . . . realized.

Question Technique

As you start to read *each paragraph* of the following selection, turn the first sentence into a question. Does the rest of the paragraph answer that question? When you finish reading the selection, turn to the answer space on page 182. There, for each paragraph, write out the question you formulated, and then indicate which sentence in that paragraph contributes most to the answer. *In addition,* if you decide that a paragraph does *not* answer the question you derive from its first sentence, write out a new question that does fit the information given by the paragraph.

This is not a timed exercise. Of course you will need to refer to the selection while you work out the questions.

"In Defense of Contemporary Fiction"[7]

from *How We Live*

edited by PENNEY CHAPIN HILLS and L. RUST HILLS

A

The idea is very current and widespread that nonfiction rather than fiction is the characteristic form of literary expression of our time, the form that tells us most about ourselves and the way we live now. The view that fiction is in some sort of "decline" is stated virtually every day and five times on Sunday by those who review books for *The New York Times*. The National Book Council reports that the ratio of nonfiction books to fiction books published each year has dropped from about 4.5 to 1 in 1936 to 9 to 1 in 1966. One of the biggest successes of recent publishing seasons was Truman Capote's factual account of a Kansas murder, *In Cold Blood*; and this book was so detailed and so suspenseful and so well written that when the author started the silly business of calling it a "nonfiction novel," many who reviewed the book took the opportunity to launch into another round of laments about the fatigue of contemporary fiction and make proclamations about the vitality of the "new" nonfiction.

B

The worst of it is that the conviction that fiction is finished, repeated so often and in so many ways, not only convinces, it *causes*. The magazines that once featured fiction either have gone out of business or now publish more articles than short stories on a 10-to-1 basis, and most of the new magazines that start up never publish fiction at all. A magazine editor hearing over and over again that fiction has lost its vitality may decide to drop it entirely. Novelists who find short stories difficult to write are already too fond of the excuse that there's no good short fiction being written because "the market's gone." Book publishers, who always prefer riding trends to bucking them, regretfully turn down novels and enterprisingly think up nonfiction book ideas of their own and give authors big advances to write them—and it may be that they give the big advance and the idea to a *fiction* writer. Good-bye novelist. Enterprising magazines (*Holiday, Esquire,* etc.)

are always commissioning our best novelists to do articles (on politics or travel or on one another), and the between-novel energy that used to go into craft-sharpening short stories in the good old days that everyone now misses so (when Scribner's would publish a book of short stories by Hemingway or Fitzgerald or Wolfe alternately with their novels), all goes now into nonfiction that blunts the fiction technique. The short story is now, as a result, thought of as form only for beginners. The readership for a new novelist is scarcely larger than that for a new poet. What is described as already true — that fiction is in some sort of decline — may actually become true as a result of the conviction.

C

But any "decline" in fiction which may now exist is a decline in popularity rather than a decline in quality. Critics of contemporary fiction, when they aren't simply confusing the two, tend to try to put them into a cause-and-effect relationship. Sometimes the argument is that if contemporary fiction isn't much read, that must be because it isn't much good. Sometimes the causal factor is reversed: fiction is losing its vitality because it lacks a regular responsive readership. The decrease in the amount of fiction run in national commercial magazines is sometimes seen as the result, sometimes the cause, of the "fact" that the short story is a dying form in America today. And, if the short story is a dying form, it is a simple further misstep to the conclusion that the nonfiction article that has replaced it in our magazines must be "the characteristic literary form of our era" — a view actually put forward by Norman Podhoretz and John Fischer in *Commentary* and *Harper's* a number of years ago, and much repeated by others since.

D

But the fact is that most magazine articles are cliché structured from opening anecdote through supporting statistics to hope-for-the-future ending. Most of them are written to order by professional journalists from ideas thought up in editorial committee — thus not only from the ideas of others but from those whose job depends on conceiving ideas that will increase either the magazine's circulation or its advertising linage. Virtually always, a fiction writer writes better than a nonfiction writer, has at his command more language and style as well as profoundly more insight and conviction and integrity to bring alive his vision of the way things are now. He is more economical, his eye and ear are better, his observations more accurate and acute. He is infinitely more original. The best magazine articles, in fact, are those that are done by fiction writers, or by those who use fiction-like techniques. When a fiction writer like Mailer or Baldwin or Capote does a personal essay or a job of reportage, it is demonstrably far better written and intrinsically far more interesting than the work of journalists and critics who do nonfiction routinely. Those who attack contemporary fiction point to the excellence of such nonfiction by fiction writers to prove that the magazine article is the characteristic literary form now, but in fact it proves just the opposite. What it proves is *not* that fiction is on the decline but rather that modern fiction is so vital and its practitioners so skillful that when they apply their techniques and insights to nonfiction they are conspicuously successful. Everyone misses the irony that it is *fiction* methods — direct dialogue, scene setting, use of a participant point-of-view narrator, and so forth — that are being used to make these *fact* pieces seem more "real" and "true."

E

No one wants to belabor the meager thing that is the average magazine article, but neither does one like to see it puffed up in importance so as to justify not running fiction in magazines. Book publishers similarly overpraise nonfiction books to justify not publishing novels and collections of stories, but most of them know that the real reason they don't publish much fiction is because it doesn't sell. A good deal of the disparagement of modern fiction occurs as a result of the rationalizations and justifications of magazine editors and book editors for not publishing more of it. That their convictions rest on the hard economic facts of modern publishing as a big business with all the problems of mass distribution and competitive shelf space associated with marketing laundry soap or shaving cream is immaterial here, since we are supposing that even if editors and publishers aren't capable of dealing with the economics of their business in order to follow their convictions, they still ought to be able to separate the two in their minds. At any rate, there has come to be a kind of cumulative, accelerating, snow-balling, band-wagon quality to this misconception that modern fiction is "in decline." And unfortunately, it is a misconception that threatens to lead to a situation in which a whole generation of fine fiction writers will have virtually no readership in their own time.

F

We have said that any decline in fiction which exists today is a decline in popularity, not a decline in quality. But what has caused the decline in popularity, if the quality is good? There are many factors, some having to do with the nature of modern life, some with the nature of modern readers, some with the nature of modern fiction. It seems to us that far more of the fault can be found with modern readers than with modern writers.

It is often said that television has stolen fiction's audience, and if the average American family's set is on for eight hours a day (as we are told it is), that might have something to do with it; but so just as much might the boom in boating or bowling, for the sort of fiction reader who now goes to TV for his weekly quota of entertainment and escape never was much of a reader of literature anyway. Those who talk about a decline in fiction reading usually fail to make the distinction between the old "popular" "slick" magazine fiction (which is now indeed pretty much gone, and probably over to TV, both the reader of it and the writer of it) and the "serious" "literary" fiction (which perhaps never was read by many but is now read by proportionately even fewer). What has happened is that as a supposedly literate, college-educated population has grown in the United States, literary fiction has failed to keep its share of readers. Again, it should be clear that the serious reader of serious fiction has been lost not to TV but to nonfiction, especially to nonfiction books. One is constantly encountering well-informed, well-educated men and women who feel no reluctance admitting that they haven't read (or finished) a modern novel in years. In fact, it might be safe to say that the most serious and literate segment of modern American readers, those who read most and most intelligently, virtually never read fiction—unless it be an occasional mystery novel for entertainment and escape.

G

As the stories in this anthology have shown, our times are unsettled and complex, and our people are troubled and anxious. It is natural that the most educated and concerned Americans would turn to books that directly describe themselves and their society, books that will expose to them the lives of others, whether it be their neighbors or their leaders; books in recent history, in popular psychology, in the social sciences; books like *The Exurbanities, The Lonely Crowd, The American Way of Death, Games People Play, The Affluent Society,* and so on; books that are presented as offering them some new understanding of how they and others live now. They want *facts*—or at least they think that is what they want. What is really wanted is not so much facts, or at any rate not just more facts, but rather the truth, or at any rate more truth. It is inevitable that in the search for facts they will turn first to nonfiction. And virtually no one seeks for the truth about ourselves and our times where it is most certainly and most logically to be found—in our literary art, our contemporary fiction.

H

The way Americans now read has a good deal to do with the problem. Any sort of speed reading, quick scanning of pages solely for content, finds little of value in literature, where the meaning resides as much in the form as the content. The majority of book readers are too hurried, too pragmatic, too impatient to submit to the experience of an imagined reality required by fiction. And then too often they turn to the experts, the specialists, the professionals, to be told what their literature says. Unfortunately, professional criticism today seems to consist in one or both of two "approaches" to literature—that of the cultural critic and that of the literary critic—both of whom tend, in entirely different ways, to obscure from the general reader how much our best fiction could tell us about ourselves and our times.

I

The cultural critic's approach—similar to what is sometimes called "the sociology of literature"—when it is directed to contemporary writing, finds at least as much significance in the analysis of popular "slick" writing as it does in the study of serious "literary" fiction, in which the underlying ideas and assumptions are usually much less apparent. There is undoubtedly much to learn about our times from a study of our popular culture: from comic books, popular songs, films, TV series dramas and domestic comedies, advertising campaigns, and so forth. Critical reading of the "true confessions" magazines, of the more sensational men's magazines, and of the slick romantic magazines for women reveals a great deal about the falsity and fantasy implicit in the fiction and hence in the society: it exposes the nation's daydreams, so to speak. And such stories also depict, often quite accurately, the superficial manners and mores of our time—revealing a good deal about the norms of the society. In a mass society the mass culture disseminated through mass media has certainly got to be significant, and none of the serious study given it is in any way wasted.

J

But in such critical readings and in every analysis of popular culture, the truth lies in the analysis rather than in the material. Bad art inadvertently reveals more to such reading than real art purposefully will. By this approach, one attempts to understand the author's purpose in order to mock him, not to learn from him. So pervasive is this kind of approach to culture today that cults grow up for that which is worst. The so-called "camp" sensibility most admires the most false and the most vulgar. Sometimes it seems that there are more serious readers for the books and the magazine features that analyze and interpret our popular culture than there are for the literature that is our real culture, which truly (not falsely) depicts and expresses our times. Popular literature (like the advertising that usually supports it) is deliberately designed accurately to reflect readers' (consumers') expectations and hopes (secret or otherwise), and in that sense is not "false." But what is revealed is how widespread are certain misconceptions, how pervasive are certain daydreams and delusions and vulgarities. As an expression of the reader-audience-consumer rather than of the writer's own vision, popular literature truly reflects the false values of our culture. But always we are depending on the acuteness and insight and accuracy of the interpreter rather than on the vision and perception and accuracy of the creator for the truth of what this kind of fiction reveals about our times. And because this "approach" gets most from what is bad, it tends to separate us further from what is good.

K

The literary critic's approach has the opposite effect: the emphasis is so completely on finding the esthetic excellence of the work that everything else in the work is overlooked. The way students are now taught to read literature in our colleges and universities obscures from them what literature can tell us about ourselves and the way we live. In their famous first "Letter to the Teacher" (1938) in *Understanding Poetry*, Cleanth Brooks and Robert Penn Warren stressed that "though one may consider a poem as an instance of historical or ethical documentation, the poem in itself, if literature is to be studied as literature, remains the final object of study," and that "a poem should always be treated as an organic system of relationships." As everyone knows, this textbook had a tremendous influence: it introduced to the undergraduate teaching of all literature (not just poetry) the meticulous critical methods of the so-called New Criticism, methods based in the ultimate of esthetic theory, that Art should be considered as Art and not as anything else. The art object (the poem or story) should be judged neither as *expression* of the artist nor as *communication* to the reader but as an independent *object* — and its worth calculated through an internal analysis of its "organic" system of relationships. The introduction of these principles into the classroom was a great corrective to much foolishness in the way literature had been taught; but what began as a system of critical technique has now become the pervasive manner of teaching and studying literature, and the exercise of the technique has become an art in itself.

L

The question of evaluation is clearly what has been allowed to fog the issue here, for while literature should be *judged* as literature, it can be *read* in many ways. A critic evaluating a literary work of art is surely correct to consider the work *as art* and not as anything else. But not all undergraduates are training to be critics. When a student is taught to read literature as literature and *not as anything else,* then whatever else literature might have been to him is denied him. Contemporary literature may offer inspired insights into our times and troubles, but these insights are considered irrelevant. And so they may be — to a literary critic. What is unfortunate in this otherwise salutary revolution in teaching is the side effect: students are taught to read literature "correctly" — that is, as literature — but more or less exclusively so; and few professors seem able to go on and show them that there is another great kind of value in reading literature "incorrectly" — that is, as some kind of "historical or ethical documentation." A short story is not to be considered simply as a piece of sociology, but neither should it be the precious, exclusive province of the literary *cognoscenti* and critics. The importance of "understanding" fiction (as well as poetry) has had the effect of making the nonspecialized reader obsolete. While increasing the understanding of the literary specialist, it has alienated the general student from all except a few more or less underground "bibles" — *The Catcher in the Rye, Catch-22, Lord of the Flies,* the Tolkien series, and so forth — that to successive student generations become secret talismans of belonging. Right from his freshman English class it is obscured from the student that literature, even when read "incorrectly" as something it isn't even supposed to be, has as much of the truth to reveal about a civilization (our own, for instance) as have his textbooks in social science and history, which set out to describe that culture directly.

For each paragraph of the selection, write out here the question you formulated from the first sentence. After each question, write the number of the sentence in the paragraph that contributed most to the answer. You may refer to the material.

A _____

_____

_____

_____ Sentence number _____ No one sentence can be chosen _____
If the paragraph does not answer the question, what question *does* it answer?

_____

_____

_____

B _____

_____

_____

_____ Sentence number _____ No one sentence can be chosen _____
If the paragraph does not answer the question, what question *does* it answer?

_____

_____

_____

C _____

_____

_____

_____ Sentence number _____ No one sentence can be chosen _____
If the paragraph does not answer the question, what question *does* it answer?

_____

_____

_____

D _____

_____

_____

_____ Sentence number _____ No one sentence can be chosen _____
If the paragraph does not answer the question, what question *does* it answer?

_____

_____

_____

E _____

_____

_____

_____ Sentence number _____ No one sentence can be chosen _____
If the paragraph does not answer the question, what question *does* it answer?

_____

_____

_____

F _____

_____

_____

_____ Sentence number _____ No one sentence can be chosen _____
If the paragraph does not answer the question, what question *does* it answer?

_____

_____

_____

G _____

_____

_____

_____ Sentence number _____ No one sentence can be chosen _____

If the paragraph does not answer the question, what question *does* it answer?

_____

_____

_____

H _____

_____

_____

_____ Sentence number _____ No one sentence can be chosen _____
If the paragraph does not answer the question, what question *does* it answer?

_____

_____

_____

I _____

_____

_____

_____ Sentence number _____ No one sentence can be chosen _____
If the paragraph does not answer the question, what question *does* it answer?

_____

_____

_____

J _____

_____

_____

_____ Sentence number _____ No one sentence can be chosen _____
If the paragraph does not answer the question, what question *does* it answer?

_____

_____

K _____

_____ Sentence number _____ No one sentence can be chosen _____
If the paragraph does not answer the question, what question *does* it answer?

L _____

_____ Sentence number _____ No one sentence can be chosen _____
If the paragraph does not answer the question, what question *does* it answer?

Reading Speed Exercise: Average Level 5

For most people, the most casual, least questioning form of reading they do is in their daily newspaper. Beyond the headline, beyond the apparent importance of the subject matter, does a newspaper article carry any signs or labels that alert you to its importance, or betray its speciousness? Indeed it may—or so the next reading selection suggests. The essay reprinted below takes you into the world of reporting to show you some of the influences, outside of the news itself, that shape the writing of the news. Its wry view of the practice of journalism points out some simple truths about the ways that stories can be blown up or reduced in importance, and how you can detect the signs of this.

The selection is reprinted from a general magazine, and its difficulty of content and style is about average. That is, skilled readers read it at the same speed they use for materials of a factual nature, popularly written.

You are to read the selection against time. Follow your instructor's directions, or the Instructions for Timing on page 474.

Before reading, practice with the Eye Movements in Reading exercise on pages 54–56.

Do not pre-read the selection; the timed reading exercises are designed to measure improvements in speed alone.

After reading the selection and recording your time, go on to the ten true-false and multiple-choice questions. There is no time limit for the questions, but it will invalidate the exercise if you refer to this passage while you answer them.

Begin reading here.

"The Morning After"[8]
by OTTO FRIEDRICH

Journalism, as every student knows, deals with the who, the where, the when. But in answer to such questions as who, where, and when, there are not only the absolute facts but the *desirable* facts, which turn data into something interesting and therefore salable as news. Who? A celebrity. Where? Right here. When? Now.

Part of any newspaperman's job is to assemble what facts he can find and turn them into a story that will help sell the newspaper. Part of his pleasure in his work, moreover, is to "build up" his story and get it onto the front page. That is why a bricklayer sometimes gets described as a "contracting executive." Faraway events can be brought closer by concentrating on a New Yorker caught in a Baghdad riot, or by putting all foreign political news in terms of some supposedly "pro-American" faction. But the most curious and least appreciated journalistic technique goes into making the real time that something happened—whether it be yesterday or even last week—sound like the desired time: today.

The search for a "today angle" leads newspapermen into many strange maneuvers. Few are so desperate as the classic obituary that began: "John Smith was dead today. He died yesterday." Yet a recent UPI story about a man who had fallen off a building started: "Marvin R. Harber, thirty-five, was alive today. . . ." In theory, the newspaperman tries to find out what *is* happening in the aftermath of the event that didn't get into his paper the previous day; but often nothing new is happening at all. Since most afternoon newspapers are put together in the early hours of the morning, the new developments are largely verbal: An airplane crashed yesterday, so "investigators today probed the wreckage of . . ." A child disappeared yesterday, so "police broadcast a thirteen-state alarm today for the blonde blue-eyed . . ." After yesterday's sex murder, "police today began investigating all known sex deviates in a search for the killer who . . ."

There are certain words that a veteran newspaper reader should recognize immediately as signs of disguise, like the crease at the edge of an actor's wig. "After" is obviously telltale—"John Jones read his Bible in his jail cell today after confessing the triple murder of . . ." "Amid" is becoming fairly transparent, too — "Abdul A Bulbul Amir was named caretaker premier of Arabia today amid mounting anti-American riots that left twenty dead." Obviously the twenty were killed yesterday or the day before, but they were still "left dead" today. And there is another significant word there: "mounting." Although the same situation often continues from day to day, it is a rule of thumb that editors die of boredom at the sight of the word "continuing," and the only way to bring them back to life is to change it to "mounting" ("rising" or "spreading" will do too). In what tabloids call "pre-dawn darkness," the rewrite man also draws conclusions with words like "appeared": "Governor Rockefeller appeared today to have won his tax battle . . ." (i.e., he won it yesterday). But the perennial favorite is "told" or "talked," as in a recent UPI dispatch from Iola, Wisconsin: "Dr. Frank Wiley received patients as usual today and talked of how he robbed their homes to satisfy his passion for antiques."

Occasionally a newspaperman gets sick of all this hocus-pocus and decides to write a "timeless" drama of human interest (which one news service refers to as "the old H. I."). Here's a recent beginning from the Associated Press: " 'Grandma, would you do anything in the world for me?' asked 8-year-old Janice Wilberg." The idea, implicitly, is not only to obscure what day it is, but what the story is, until the reader has been lured into curiosity about what Grandma will tell Janice Wilberg.

I don't want to sound hostile toward such poetic devices. I once had to write a story about a ten-year-old who had butchered four or five members of his family after our last edition went to press the day before. After interviewing schoolteachers, neighbors, and police, I was quite pleased with myself for thinking up what I considered a boldly original "second-day lead" that began: "Why? That was the question that . . ." But the news editor had other things on his mind, didn't care about the case, and wanted it cut down to "what actually happened today," which I did in three dull paragraphs. Was it a vindication or merely a proof of banality to see the first edition of the rival tabloid with a long story on the same case that began: "Why? That was the question that . . ."?

There are various names for the process of making news seem newer than it is — "freshening it," "retopping it," "putting a second-day lead on it," etc. But the problems remain the same, whether the news was old before it was announced (like the New York *Times* report that "The State Department was still hopeful today" that Iraq would not go Communist), or whether the news was fully reported by some other newspaper published earlier in the day (news services refer to the "morningers" and "afternooners" as representing two different "cycles" of news). It is primarily this competitiveness that makes editors insist on putting newness ahead of importance in the "today angle." They seem unable to realize that newspaper readers, unlike editors, do not buy all the papers and compare them to see who's ahead on every story. In fact, most readers probably choose their papers because of the comics and features, and never notice whether there is a "today" in the lead of a story at all.

Finally, there is another important time element in the question of what news gets published. That is the day of the week, which roughly governs the amount of advertising, and consequently the size of the whole newspaper. Anything that happens on a Friday, for example, has to be pretty important to get printed at all, for the simple reason that few advertisers either can or want to reach anyone on a Saturday. The day after the thin, feeble Saturday papers wither on the stands, Sunday editions roll forth with so much space available that nobody can fill it all with news.

Days in advance, wire services and feature writers have been aiming for that fat target, with a complete inversion of the usual "today" approach. Instead of trying to make aging news sound as though it had just happened, they write about future events as though they were *about* to happen. The verbal techniques are familiar — officials prepared today, they mapped today, they charted today, they were set today to do something, they put the finishing touches on it — all of which is considered part of a "forward-looking" story.

The need for before-the-fact stories also accounts for H.F.R. (Hold for Release). A variation on the standard obit, which is prepared for the anticipated death of some octogenarian statesman, the H.F.R. is a story written in the past tense about an event that is expected to follow a preordained pattern but has not actually happened. The original idea was to save cable tolls by sending a story through the mails and then "releasing" it by a short cabled message, but today the H.F.R. is aimed at getting into a newspaper office before the rush hours. One fine example occurred during Queen Elizabeth's coronation, when my news agency sent out "colorful" descriptions of the event the night before it took place. A series of stories ran: "Queen Elizabeth began her coronation drive through London . . . ," "Queen Elizabeth entered Westminster Abbey today . . . ," "Queen Elizabeth was crowned today . . ." We watched it on television and periodically "released" the latest day-old account.

Another story that can be planned in advance is the "reaction" that editors consider mandatory on any major news. The UPI got into print on the tail of the Tibetan upheaval with a story from Tokyo that began: "Red China's image as a friendly model for neutral Asian nations was crumbling today under withering criticism of its bloody tactics in Tibet."

Even with such efforts, however, there simply isn't enough legitimate news on Saturdays to fill the holes among the giant sheaves of Sunday advertisements. To avoid having completely white spaces, newspapers rely on "timeless" dispatches like this one from a recent Sunday edition of the New York *Times*: "Mexico appears puzzled about declarations by President Ydigoras Fuentes of Guatemala that an invasion of his country is being planned here." Some editors call it "eight point" — meaning simply any old words or sentences that can be turned into print in the standard eight-point type. More generally, since the "facts" in such stories are insubstantial to the point of being ectoplasmic, they are known as "moonlight."

Now note your reading time. Record it below and go on to the questions.

YOUR READING TIME: _____MIN. _____SEC. _____W.P.M. COMPREHENSION SCORE: _____%
(WORDS PER MINUTE FROM THE TABLE ON PAGE 475.)

Please do not read these questions until you have read the article itself against time. Do not refer to the article as you answer the questions. Choose the *one best* answer to each question, and enter the corresponding letter in the proper answer space.

1. The "today angle" always refers to news events of previous days which are made to seem newer than they really are.   (T) True; (F) False

ANSWER _____

2. Events on Friday have to be unusually important to get into the next day's papers at all.   (T) True; (F) False

ANSWER _____

3. A "Hold for Release" story is written in the past tense, in advance of a predictable news event.   (T) True; (F) False

ANSWER _____

4. "Moonlight" is the term used for articles with a substantial factual basis, that are used for space-filling purposes.   (T) True; (F) False

ANSWER _____

5. The cause of the journalist's search for the "today angle" is (a) editorial competitiveness among the news services and syndicates; (b) editorial blindness of the papers themselves; (c) the belief that fresh-sounding news stories sell more papers; (d) the fact that most readers choose their papers for the comics or the features; (e) the need to fill space in the Sunday issues.

ANSWER _____

6. Which of the following was *not* mentioned as a variation on the "today angle"? (a) The "Hold for Release" article; (b) the obituary ("obit") all prepared and ready before the death of a person of importance; (c) the "timeless" human interest story, as a case where the "today angle" is reversed; (d) the publicity release, planted in advance of a staged event by a press agent or public relations firm; (e) the "forward looking" story that tells how some yet-to-happen event is "today" being led up to or prepared.

ANSWER _____

7. In your own pre-reading of newspaper articles, the reporters' tricks and devices that the author points out would be (a) helpful to you, since most of the telltale phrases are to be found in the first sentence of the story; (b) helpful to you, since they establish the subject matter of the story quickly and clearly; (c) sometimes useful, sometimes not, depending on where they appear in the newspaper story; (d) largely useless, since they are concerned with writing technique and not with subject-matter nor with

importance; (e) largely useless, since they rarely occur in those parts of the story you examine while pre-reading.

ANSWER _____

8. For someone who had not yet read the selection, which of the following descriptive subtitles would best tell him what it is about? (a) "The 'Today Angle' and How It Grew"; (b) "How to Tell Real Time from Fake Time in Newspapers"; (c) "The Influence of Advertising on the News We Read"; (d) "A Call for the Reform of the American Press"; (e) "Hidden Forms of Censorship at Work."

ANSWER _____

9. For the most part, the author uses humorous, even ludicrous, examples of the journalistic devices he is talking about. The principal effect of these examples is (a) to cast grave doubt on the author's seriousness about the problem; (b) to make us see more quickly and clearly just how silly the devices have become; (c) to get us "on his side" from the start; (d) to exaggerate the importance of the problem, since in more serious cases there would be more genuine substance to the stories written with these devices; (e) to sugar-coat the lesson he is teaching us.

ANSWER _____

10. Although it may not be explicitly stated, the overall purpose of the article is, most probably, (a) to state a growing problem and to call for a solution; (b) to protest, in the form of satire, against certain practices in newspaper writing; (c) to call the reader's attention to certain practices, so that he can read his newspaper with greater understanding; (d) to defend the working reporters against their editorial employers who cause the problems discussed; (e) to amuse the reader.

ANSWER _____

Now check your answers, and enter your score on your Progress Profile, page vii.

CHAPTER 8

Words, Phrases, Sentences

Pre-read this chapter as your first step in reading. As your second step, ask the questions you expect the chapter to answer. Before reading thoroughly, list those questions here:

_____

_____

_____

Words group into phrases, phrases into sentences. It is on these small units of meaning that your accurate comprehension of detail and efficient speed depend. Skillful reading demands a vocabulary of many thousands of words. It requires an accurate "feel" for which groups of words are meaningful units and which are not. It calls for effortless familiarity with standard sentence structures, and also for the ability to figure your way through the grammar of occasional passages that are more elaborate (or perhaps more badly written) than most.

If your native language is English, phrases and sentences probably will present no serious *reading* problem; vocabulary, however, may slow you down. This is because there are so many words; you keep meeting new ones as your reading becomes more advanced and varied. Nevertheless, words combine into groups and sentences in only a few ways, most of which you have practiced in speech and reading since childhood. This chapter, therefore, will go into some detail about vocabulary. Its discussion of word groups and sentences, however, will be devoted only to the points necessary to improve your ability to read by phrases and to help you get out of trouble when you meet an unusually difficult sentence.*

*Writing, of course, requires detailed understanding of how English grammar can be put to work to make phrases and sentences clear and apt. For this reason, the grammar taught, for example, in a composition text is much more extensive than we need here.

Words

Your present vocabulary may be adequate for most of your present reading, but it will require constant enlargement as your reading becomes more advanced within your field of specialization, and as you read more widely and seriously in fields other than your specialty. Your aim must be to add the words you need, as you come to them, extending your vocabulary over the years as a systematic part of the reading you do every day. The simplest, most effective method for doing this is presented here.

We are concerned with how your *reading* vocabulary can be developed. You use words on all sorts of occasions — in conversation and public speaking, in personal and business correspondence, in formal writing from essays and research papers to business reports and published works — and in reading. For these uses you have three distinct vocabularies. Your *speaking* vocabulary consists of all the words you use out loud, whether in informal conversation or on such careful, formal occasions as a debate or a conference. Your *writing* vocabulary is likely to be somewhat larger than your speaking vocabulary, for obvious reasons. Both speaking and writing vocabularies are *active*; your *passive, reading* vocabulary includes all those other words you recognize when reading, but which you would not think to use actively. Most people, whether highly educated or not, employ a relatively small group of words actively, unless speaking or writing about one of their special interests. Passive vocabularies are always larger than active ones, and they vary enormously in size; estimates range from a low of 10,000 "nodding acquaintances" for the average freshman entering college, to a high of over 150,000 words for a few exceptionally widely read adults.

The adequacy of your passive reading vocabulary can be measured by tests that ask you to define words selected to cover the full range of difficulty, from the fairly common to the very unusual. A series of 100 to 200 vocabulary questions, carefully chosen to represent words of increasing rarity, can indicate roughly the size of even quite large passive vocabularies. Tests of this type have been very widely used and refined. You may have been given a vocabulary test as a supplement to the Reading Skills Survey in this book. If you suspect that your vocabulary is deficient, you should arrange to take such a test: developmental reading centers and educational testing centers, found at many colleges and universities, offer vocabulary testing.

If you have a seriously deficient vocabulary, this will prove such a crippling obstacle to comprehension and will so frequently cause your speed to stumble, that you must make its improvement a continuing and first-ranking aim of your reading development. There is no single, simple method for correcting a serious deficiency. Many full-length books have been devoted to this objective; each good vocabulary improvement text attacks the problem with many different methods for grouping words by meaning, by linguistic history, and by specialized subject matter.

One of the most promising methods for vocabulary building at college level is thorough study of families of words that have entered English (and other modern Western languages) from Latin and Greek root words. This approach is especially helpful with the specialized vocabularies of modern science, where the beginning student is likely to find that he has many words to learn, and where a high proportion of the words have been created for scientific use by reference to the classic languages. The Greek and Latin numbers provide excellent examples of how this works:

three	Greek τρια *(tria)* produces words like triad, trimaran Latin *tres* appears in trefoil, trellis
four	Greek τεσσαρες, τετρα- *(tessares* or *tetra)* give tetrahedron, tetra- dactyl, tesseract Latin *quattuor* appears in quatrain
nine	Greek ἐννεα *(ennea)* yields ennead Latin *novem* is the basis for novena
thousand	Greek χιλιοι *(chilioi)* shows up in kilometer, chiliastic Latin *mille* appears in millenium, millenarian (which means the same as chiliastic)

There are hundreds of Greek-Latin pairs, for example, the words for *around* and *phrase:*

Greek περι *(peri)* + φρασις *(phrasis)* = English *periphrase*
Latin *circum* + *locutio* = English *circumlocution*

Periphrase and circumlocution are near synonyms.

But clearly, such a method for vocabulary improvement demands study of new words not just in English but in the ancestor languages as well; three languages or even more if you work with words that have come into English from Latin by way of French or Italian. The method is not quick. Instead, it is thorough and offers a system for relating the words and remembering them.

Indeed, all methods for vocabulary improvement have two aims: to relate new words to each other and to ones you already know, and then to give you practice in using them so you will remember them. But as the Greek and Latin examples suggest, the basic problem remains the same: the unique meaning (or several meanings) of each word must be learned; for a serious vocabulary deficiency this is a large job, though by no means hopeless. It also requires many more pages of practice materials than this book can give.

Fortunately, most readers have the easier task of learning to extend their vocabularies over the years as a regular part of the reading they do from day to day.

Activate Your Passive Vocabulary

You have had the experience—everybody has—of looking up a word in the dictionary only to find a few hours later that you have already forgotten the definition. You may also have realized that if you could find a place to *use* the new word, you would remember it more easily. This is exactly what you need to do: if you can make new words part of your active vocabulary, they will stay with you. But few people are professional speakers or writers with a natural opportunity to use many new words actively. How, then, can you make new words a permanent addition to your vocabulary? For the student who needs intensive vocabulary work, or who is curious about words, the Bibliography on page 473 lists several excellent books. For readers with adequate or nearly adequate vocabularies, the following discussion of methods for learning new words as you meet them presents the best-known approach to development.

Unfamiliar words are like some new species of wild animal. If you wish to master them you must do four things;

Hunt unknown words in context.

Cage them with the dictionary.

Tame them at once to your own uses.

Keep them under careful observation.

Hunt unknown words in context.

When you spot a new word in its native habitat, its natural context, you will learn far more about its habits, its strength, its relations with its neighbors, than you can ever tell when you see the same word tamed and caged in a dictionary. When you meet an unfamiliar word, don't interrupt your reading to spring for the dictionary. That will only impede your reading, breaking comprehension rather than adding to it. Instead:

Put a pencil check in the margin of the page next to the word.

Try to deduce the meaning of the word from its parts — prefix, suffix, and what you know of its linguistic ancestors.

When you reach the end of the article or chapter you are reading, collect all your pencil-checked words in context; that is, *write down each word, including the sentence or phrase in which it appears.*

Then write down next to each word your own guess of what it means.

Cage them with the dictionary.

When you look the word up in the dictionary, don't let it escape: instead, write down the dictionary definition. You will then have written out two statements of how to use the word: the sentence or phrase in which you originally found it, and the dictionary definition. Consider the word also in relation to other words, its synonyms and near-synonyms, and words of opposite meaning as well. Where should this word be used where no other word will do?

Tame them at once.

Use the word as your own, immediately. Write a sentence of your own invention, using the word correctly, just beneath the two examples you have already collected.

Keep them under observation.

During the next several days, it is especially important to come back to new words again and again in your mind, as you ride a bus, walk down the street, but even more importantly as you talk or write or read about any subject related to a word you want to master. Repeat the word to yourself, taste it and savor it, make up phrases using it, drop it into conversation, into letters. "Use a word three times and it's yours." The first three steps outlined here require you to put the new word down in three sentences; but the first three times you use that word spontaneously and appropriately, as part of your *active* vocabulary, you will make sure that it will stay permanently in your passive vocabulary.

Phrases and Sentences

Modern English is particularly fortunate in the uniformity of its phrase and sentence construction. Words combine into phrases, and phrases into sentences: *syntax* is that part of grammar that describes how these phrases are made. Uniform syntax and the trend toward short sentences in modern practical prose make English a language eminently suited to fast reading.

Words make meaningful groups only in a limited number of ways. For reading purposes this means that, although there are many ways you might break a line of print into groups of words, only a few of these take advantage of the language's natural division points so that each group is a self-contained unit of meaning within the sentence. Your progress from word-by-word to phrase reading is helped by a sense of what is and what is not a meaningful natural word group. Because phrases are fundamental building blocks of language which we have used since childhood, most of us have developed fairly well this sense for meaningful natural word groups. Your phrase sense should tell you, for instance, which of the following sentences is correctly divided.

Recent shortages / of technical and professional personnel / have drawn / nationwide attention / to the general problem / of trained manpower development / in the United States.

Recent shortages of / technical and professional / personnel have / drawn nationwide / attention to the / general problem of / trained manpower / development in the / United States.

If you will read these two versions of the sentence slowly aloud, *pausing* at each marked division, you will make an interesting discovery. In the first version your pauses before and after each word group will feel natural. Where the grouping is incorrect, however, as in the second version, you will feel a strong tendency when reading aloud to push past the *marked* division to include the words up to the next *natural* pause.

This discovery plus practice in identifying phrases is all that most readers need to sharpen their sense for word groups sufficiently for reading by phrases. Thus, if you are occasionally uncertain of the correct word groupings in the Phrase Sense exercises, by reading the troublesome sentence aloud you should be able to detect the natural pauses that define those groupings. As you practice further, this test will be necessary less often.

In modern English there are, in fact, less than a dozen major types of word groups that form natural units of meaning. Some of these occur much more frequently than others. The most important four are listed here, with examples.

1. Noun preceded by one or more modifiers

   dwarf *star*
   three French *hens*
   really ripe red *raspberries*

2. Verb preceded by one or more verbal auxiliaries

   was *whining*
   had been *warned*
   will have been *walloped*

3. Prepositional phrase

   from Hong Kong
   in a sampan
   over the surging sea

4. Conjunctional word group

   skull *and* crossbones
   poor *but* dishonest
   neither halberd *nor* pikestaff

If you have found it difficult to identify word groups correctly, study of these most frequent types will help you begin to build your awareness.

Modern English—unlike German, Russian, and many other languages—does not often require the reader to stop to untangle the various elements in a sentence in order to understand it. Why is English blessed this way? Primarily because the various main elements of English sentences almost always occur in the same standard sequence. This is what we meant by saying that English sentences have uniform syntax. What follows is a brief and practical reader's guide to the syntax of sentences.

There are three fundamental facts you should know about the construction of standard English sentences in modern practical prose. The first has to do with *the sequence of main elements* in the full sentence. The second is about *modifiers that take fixed positions.* The third is about *adverbial modifiers,* the only modifiers whose position in the sentence is not always fixed.

Overall, the normal sentence sequence is first subject, then verb, then any object or objects.

Modifiers within the sentence—
   a. if they are single words, usually *precede* the words they modify, but
   b. if they are group words, usually *follow* the words they modify.

Exception: most *adverbial* modifiers, both single words and word groups, are free to take several positions in the sentence — and a shift in this position will usually shift the meaning of the sentence.

The difference between *man bites dog* and *dog bites man* is obvious to you because you have followed the first of these rules automatically since childhood. But to refresh your memory for the terms, the subject answers the question you make by putting *who* or *what* before the verb. Thus we find the subject of each verb in the following sentence:

The President has lost support, as the Congressional elections will prove.

Who has lost?   *President*   *What* will prove?   *elections*

The objects (direct or indirect) answer the question you make by putting the subject before the verb, and *who* or *what* after the verb. With these questions we can find subject and objects in the following:

You should find your daughter a husband.

SUBJECT: *Who* should find? *You*

OBJECTS: You should find *what? husband*
You should find *whom* a husband? *daughter*

Fewer than about 10 per cent of the sentences in practical prose depart from this standard order of subject, verb, object. Inversions of subject and verb occur in emphatic statements:

Rarely will you find apples on peach trees

and in questions made from statements that contain an auxiliary verb:

Can you turn this question back into a plain statement?

Except where the statement has a helper verb, English questions retain the normal subject-verb-object sequence. So do sentences in which the verb is *passive:*

A special wall of selected bricks was built for Michelangelo's "Last Judgment."

What was built?   *wall*

Other types of sentence do occur in spoken English, but rarely in practical prose unless spoken dialogue is being reported. These other types include, for example: *Real chip off the old block, that boy; The bigger, the better; Get out of here!*

The main elements of standard sentences can be doubled up as follows:

Man bites dog.
The bulldog and the borzoi attacked and bit the burglar, the boy, and the bystander.

Observe that the standard sequence of subject, verb, object, is still maintained. Modifiers of these fixed position elements can be of two kinds: single word or word group. Modifiers also leave the standard sequence of main elements unchanged. In addition, they follow a sequence rule of their own, which is the second fact about the construction of standard English sentences.

Modifiers, if they are single words, usually *precede* the words they modify, for example:

> The *brown* bulldog and the *big, bounding* borzoi had attacked and were biting the *burly, over-burdened* burglar.

Modifiers, if they are word groups, usually *follow* the words they modify, for example:

> The borzoi *we had seen earlier* attacked *with great ferocity* the burglar *all burdened with the family silver.*

One class of modifier, however, is free of this second rule. This class includes single words and word groups that affect the meaning of the verb: as our third fact states, adverbial modifiers are free to take several positions in the sentence, though a shift in position will shift the meaning. Lancelot Hogben, the noted English scientist and philologist, offers an example that is an amusing piece of concrete poetry:[1]

> ONLY the bishop gave the baboon the bun
> The ONLY bishop gave the baboon the bun
> The bishop ONLY gave the baboon the bun
> The bishop gave ONLY the baboon the bun
> The bishop gave the ONLY baboon the bun
> The bishop gave the baboon ONLY the bun
> The bishop gave the baboon the ONLY bun

Adverbial phrases can move around the sentence, too, shifting emphasis:

> Among foreigners, English has apparently earned a bad reputation
>   1   2
> without deserving it.
>   3
>
> Apparently, English has earned, without deserving it, a bad reputation
>   2   3
> among foreigners.
>   1
>
> Without deserving it, English apparently has earned among foreigners a
>   3   2   1
> bad reputation.

In the hands of the skilled writer, these movable elements permit flexibility, precision, and variation of emphasis. Badly used, however—piled on too thick or allowed to wander too far from the verbs they refer to—adverbial modifiers can create confusion, ambiguity, awkwardness, and therefore difficult reading.

These three fundamental facts of English syntax are simply descriptions of basic patterns of writing; awareness of them should make it possible to figure out even the grammatical monstrosities that one writer has called "five-legged sheep"—for example:

The fat man ran down the stairs where the children played and slipped.

Or:

It may be interesting to leave completely alone part or all of a newly established wetland reserve if one wishes to improve the conditions for birds through an increase of woods or the other ground cover or the re-establishment of the climax flora balance, or if research is carried out into the progressive biological modifications under natural conditions. . . . Most wetlands gradually dry so that the bog becomes completely different either as a consequence of the elevation of the ground above the water-shed—a result of peat formation or sedimentation—or by sinking of the watershed after drainage in the neighboring region by deeper erosion of the water outlet. . . .

Knowing the three fundamentals also will help you understand certain sentence patterns, longer and more stylistically elaborate, that are not often found in modern practical prose but which are characteristic of many authors in earlier centuries. An example is this famous passage from Edward Gibbon's *The Decline and Fall of the Roman Empire*:

The policy of the emperors and the senate, as far as it concerned religion, was happily seconded by the reflections of the enlightened, and by the habits of the superstitious, part of their subjects. The various modes of worship, which prevailed in the Roman world, were all considered by the people, as equally true; by the philosophers, as equally false; and by the magistrate, as equally useful. And thus toleration produced not only mutual indulgence, but even religious concord.

Pre-reading almost automatically gives you the opportunity to assess vocabulary and sentence construction. While you are searching out the author's main sequence of ideas (examining introductory and concluding paragraphs and skimming those between) any major problems of words or sentences will call themselves to your attention. In justice to some excellent writers, however, you should realize that the use of short, plain sentences and simple words does not necessarily mark an author as a good writer, or his writing as easy to read. That is, a poor writer can make simple words and sentences hard reading for reasons of ambiguity, dullness, or inaccurate wording. On the other hand, a competent author uses the words and sentences he needs to express his meaning precisely. As a result, his work is clear and a joy to read. When it is not "easy," that is because his subject is not easy. This, too, you will learn to assess as you become practiced in pre-reading.

After reading this chapter thoroughly, go back to answer the questions you formulated after pre-reading.

EXERCISES FOR CHAPTER 8

Reading Journal

Pre-reading Application (a carry-over exercise)

Skimming for a Fact—in Business and Finance

Phrase Flashing

Summarizing
"How Dictionaries are Made,"
from *Language in Thought and Action,* by S. I. Hayakawa

Question Technique
"Aspects of Ceramic Technology in Archaeology," by
Frederick R. Matson

Reading Speed Exercise: Difficult Level 3
"The Culture Poverty," from *The Children of Sanchez,*
by Oscar Lewis

Reading Journal

In your separate notebook, bring the section on **current reading** up to date, including for each item a brief summary of the content and your thoughts about it. Then bring the **future reading** list up to date.

Turn now to the next exercise in this chapter, *Pre-reading Application.* This is a carry-over exercise and will use your Reading Journal.

Pre-reading Application (a carry-over exercise)

In the book you chose for thorough analysis in the pre-reading carry-over exercise in the last chapter, turn now to the next full chapter which you have not yet read. In your Reading Journal write out a detailed pre-reading analysis of that chapter.

List book title and chapter title.

Introduction: Read each of the first several paragraphs until you judge that you have finished the introductory part of the chapter; then write a one-sentence summary for each introductory paragraph.

Skimming the text: Write down the first sentence only of each remaining paragraph of that chapter; the process is somewhat laborious, but very instructive.

Conclusion: When you reach the last paragraphs, read them thoroughly; write a one-sentence summary for each concluding paragraph.

Then read through your summaries and first sentences again. See how the bone-structure of the chapter leaps out? Then, as a final step:

Summarizing and purpose: Close the book, write out *in your own words* a one-paragraph statement of what the chapter is about, how it is put together, the point of view it takes, its difficulty, your purpose in reading it, and your opinions about it at this preliminary point.

Then go back to read the chapter thoroughly.

Skimming for a Fact

Just before each of the following paragraphs, a particular piece of factual information is called for. You are to skim each paragraph to find the one fact. Try to break away completely from thorough reading. Instead, glance left and right very rapidly, stopping as little as twice on each line of print. *Keep clearly in mind the fact, stated at the beginning of the paragraph, for which you are skimming.*

As soon as you find the fact, put a pencil check in the margin next to it. Then go immediately to the next paragraph. When you have skimmed and checked all the paragraphs, record your time in the space provided on page 204, and then fill in the sentence number of each fact in the proper space.

Work for speed. In class follow your instructor's directions for timing. On your own, follow the Instructions for Timing on page 474.

A

LOOK FOR: the relative sizes of the two companies in the French takeover battle

1   For weeks the walls of Paris and the sides of its ancient buses had been plastered with huge red posters bearing the reassuring message: "Saint-Gobain . . .
2 a trustworthy trademark." Day after day, France's most aristocratic company, which was set up in 1665 by Louis XIV to make the glass for Versailles, blared its virtues in unheard-of fashion for French corporations—double-truck newspaper ads, regular radio and tele-
3 vision appearances. Since Christmas, France has experienced what in the business world is something like the student-worker upheaval of last May and June.
4 Compagnie de Saint-Gobain, Europe's largest—and by any measure its proudest —glass manufacturer, was fighting for
5 its corporate life. Still more astonishing, it was battling against an American-style takeover attempt by a much smaller competitor, Boussois Souchon Neu-
6 vesel. Last week the great glass battle ended with Saint-Gobain overpowering the upstart by sheer financial force.
7   **Frontal Attack.** Superficially, BSN's
8 attempt looked absurd. Saint-Gobain produces 22% of the world's plate glass, has extensive interests in chemicals, nu-
9 clear energy, cardboard and paper. The company has annual sales of glass and other products totaling $1 billion, al-

10 most five times BSN's. But Saint-Gobain's current reputation glitters less
11 than its history. Under the presidency of Count Arnaud de Vogüé, 64, the company lagged behind BSN in adopting the float-glass process that revolutionized
12 glassmaking a decade ago. On the other hand, BSN, which was formed when two firms merged in 1966, had eagerly adopted new management and production techniques under its wiry president, Antoine Riboud, 50, who advocates an aggressive French business policy to combat growing competition from the U.S. and elsewhere.[2]

B

LOOK FOR: the size of the first-quarter trade deficit

U.S. TRADE MOVES BACK TO SURPLUS

Influenced by Dock Strike, March's Figure Follows a Deficit in February

ECONOMIC INDEX SLIPS

Government Warns Against 'Reading Too Much' Into Leading-Indicator Drop

By **EDWIN L. DALE Jr.**
Special to The New York Times

WASHINGTON, April 28 —
1 United States foreign trade, still strongly influenced by the aftermath of the dock strike, moved back into surplus in March, the Commerce Department reported today.
2 The export surplus of $215.3-million contrasted with a $358.6-million deficit in February, largely because ships carrying imported goods had to be unloaded before they could be loaded again with American exports.

3 [The department also announced that its index of leading economic indicators declined slightly in March from February's record level.]
4 For the first quarter as a whole, the United States had a trade deficit of $68.1-million, the first quarterly deficit since
5 1950. It has become known that the over-all balance of payments, measured on the conventional "liquidity" basis, will also show a sizable deficit for the first quarter, partly because of the poor trade results.

Official Comments
6 William H. Chartener, Assistant Secretary of Commerce for Economic Affairs, said, "Overall, it is too early to derive any significant conclusions from the first-quarter trade developments.
7 "The effects of the dock
8 strike were enormous. However, extremely rough calculations suggest that the strike may have delayed exports by at least $500-million more than imports during January and February, only part of which was worked off in the March exports spurt."
9 The export total in March, seasonally adjusted, was $3,196,-000,000, up almost 40 per cent from February and only slightly below the record figure reached last September.[3]

C

LOOK FOR: Toyota Motor Company's share of the Philippine auto market

1   The system enables companies to use highly flexible
2 market penetration tactics. Two Japanese auto makers—
Nissan Motor Co. and Toyota Motor—established foot-
holds in the U.S. by offering dealers higher commissions
than were given on other imported cars, as well as unusually generous advertising support, according to the
3 Boston Consulting Group. In the Philippines, Toyota has
captured a quarter of all auto sales, after initially selling
to taxicab fleet owners on terms of nothing down and a
4 six-month holiday on installment payments. "They were
losing money on us outright for about two years just to
introduce Toyota vehicles in the Philippines," says Pablo
Carlos, executive vice president of Delta Motor Corp.,
Manila, which assembles and distributes Toyota cars.
5 Other Japanese companies readily acknowledge that they
6 forgo profits to break open new markets. "When there's
sharp competition and we want to introduce our products,
then in the initial sale we make a sort of sacrifice hit,"
declares Morihisa Emori, managing director of Mitsu-
bishi Shoji Kaisha, Ltd., the general trading company
7 with the largest total sales. There is a distinctively Japanese motive behind such tactics, he explains: "In America
top management people are big stockholders and are more
8 defensive about maintaining profits. For us, growth is
most important."[4]

D

LOOK FOR: the definition of "technically weak" as applied to the stock market

1   The phrases *technically strong* or *technically weak* do have fairly
2 precise meanings. Suppose stock prices have been moving more or less
3 steadily upward over a long period of time. Inevitably in such a bull
market movement, there are price advances and price reactions, ups and
4 downs in the market. If the volume of sales is heavy when stocks go up
and light when they go down during a bull movement, the market can be
5 described as technically strong. Conversely, in a long downward trend,
if volume is heavy on the down side and light on the rallies, the market
6 is technically weak. This interpretation is based on the theory that sales
volume always shows the dominant trend.[5]

E

LOOK FOR: the method used to set the value of manufacturers' inventories

1   Business sales and inventories as defined by the Office of Business
Economics are the sum of data for manufacturing, wholesale, and retail
2 trade. Sales are estimated aggregate values, and inventories are book

3 values at the end of the period. "Sales" signifies sales *or shipments* for retail and wholesale trade and billings or shipments for manufacturing.
4 Trade inventories are valued at cost of merchandise on hand, while manufacturers' inventories are valued at cost or market price, whichever
5 is lower. The data on sales and inventories for manufacturers (see tables 668 and 669) are based on annual data, published by the Internal Revenue Service in *Statistics of Income*.[6]

Stop timing here.

For each paragraph enter the number of the sentence that contains the fact you were to find. (The sentences are numbered in the left margin.)

Skimming time in seconds for all items: _____

A: _____   **B:** _____   **C:** _____   **D:** _____   **E:** _____

Phrase Flashing

This exercise is designed to help you develop the quick and accurate perception of *phrases as units* upon which efficient reading speeds depend. The materials for this practice have been grouped together at the back of the book so that you can return to them repeatedly as you work through the chapters, progressing to longer and longer phrases. Please turn to page 476 and follow the instructions.

Summarizing

The article below is taken from an excellent and widely read book about *semantics,* or how we use and misuse language to communicate different kinds of meanings. (For this exercise, your purpose in reading the article is to summarize each paragraph and then the entire passage.)

This is not a timed exercise. You may refer to this passage as you answer the questions.

"How Dictionaries Are Made"[7]

from *Language in Thought and Action*

by s. i. HAYAKAWA

A

It is an almost universal belief that every word has a correct meaning, that we learn these meanings principally from teachers and grammarians (except that most of the time we don't bother to, so that we ordinarily speak "sloppy English"), and that dictionaries and grammars are the supreme authority in matters of meaning and usage. Few people ask by what authority the writers of dictionaries and grammars say what they say. The docility with which most people bow down to the dictionary is amazing, and the person who says, "Well, the dictionary is wrong!" is looked upon as out of his mind.

B

Let us see how dictionaries are made and how the editors arrive at definitions. What follows applies, incidentally, only to those dictionary offices where first-hand, original research goes on — not those in which editors simply copy existing dictionaries. The task of writing a dictionary begins with the reading of vast amounts of the literature of the period or subject that it is intended to cover. As the editors read, they copy on cards every interesting or rare word, every unusual or peculiar occurrence of a common word, a large number of common words in their ordinary uses, and also the sentences in which each of these words appears, thus:

> pail
> The dairy *pails* bring home increase of milk
> Keats, *Endymion*
> I, 44–45

C

That is to say, the context of each word is collected, along with the word itself. For a really big job of dictionary writing, such as the *Oxford English Dictionary* (usually bound in about twenty-five volumes), millions of such cards are collected, and the task of editing occupies decades. As the cards are collected, they are alphabetized and sorted. When the sorting is completed, there will be for each word anywhere from two to three to several hundred illustrative quotations, each on its card.

D

To define a word, then, the dictionary editor places before him the stack of cards illustrating that word; each of the cards represents an actual use of the word by a writer of some literary or historical importance. He reads the cards carefully, discards some, rereads the rest, and divides up the stack according to what he thinks are the several senses of the word. Finally, he writes his definitions, following the hard-and-fast rule that each definition *must* be based on what the quotations in front of him reveal about the meaning of the word. The editor cannot be influenced by what *he* thinks a given word *ought* to mean. He must work according to the cards, or not at all.

E

The writing of a dictionary, therefore, is not a task of setting up authoritative statements about the "true meanings" of words, but a task of *recording,* to the best of one's ability, what various words *have meant* to authors in the distant or immediate past. *The writer of a dictionary is a historian, not a lawgiver.* If, for example, we had been writing a dictionary in 1890, or even as late as 1919, we could have said that the word "broadcast" means "to scatter" (seed and so on) but we could not have decreed that from 1921 on, the commonest meaning of the word should become "to disseminate audible messages, etc., by wireless telephony." To regard the dictionary as an "authority," therefore, is to credit the dictionary writer with gifts of prophecy which neither he nor anyone else possesses. In choosing our words when we speak or write, we can be *guided* by the historical record afforded us by the dictionary, but we cannot be *bound* by it, because new situations, new experiences, new inventions, new feelings, are always compelling us to give new uses to old words. Looking under a "hood," we should ordinarily have found, five hundred years ago, a monk; today, we find a motorcar engine.

For each of the five paragraphs in the article, pick out below the best summary. The last question asks you to choose a summary statement for the *complete* passage. You may refer to the article as you answer the questions.

A
1. Most words have correct meanings, and most people look on dictionaries as authorities on word meanings and usage.
2. Most people look on dictionaries as indisputable authorities on the correct meanings and uses of words; but should they?
3. Not enough people dare to say the dictionary might be wrong.

ANSWER _____

B
1. Dictionary research starts with extensive reading.
2. Dictionary research, at least in those offices where original research is done, starts by determining how words have been defined by others.
3. Dictionary research starts with extensive reading, during which notes are made showing exactly how words are actually used.

ANSWER _____

C
1. At the next step in preparing a dictionary, every word is represented by the collection of quotations that show how it has been used.
2. The accuracy of a dictionary depends primarily on the quantity of illustrations collected for each word.
3. It is only by its context that the exact meaning of a word is established by the dictionary researcher.

ANSWER _____

D
1. The purpose of this research procedure is to base the dictionary definitions on the way words have actually been used.
2. The purpose of this research procedure is to guide the dictionary editor in creating his definitions.

3. The purpose of this research procedure is to give the dictionary editor factual support for his authoritative opinions about the meanings of words.

ANSWER _____

E
1. Because dictionaries must always be at least a few years behind the times, they may not indicate the latest uses of some words.
2. Dictionaries provide a historical record of what words have meant in the past; but when new requirements necessitate new uses, we can ignore what the dictionary says.
3. Dictionaries may be helpful, as a historical record, in reading; but when we write we should not feel that the dictionary is a law to be followed.

ANSWER _____

Now choose, from the following, the best summary of the entire passage.
1. The authority of dictionaries is based on extensive research to establish the true definitions of words.
2. Many people look on dictionary definitions as the final authority; but a dictionary is, in fact, a history book that guides us, not a set of laws we must never break.
3. Many people look upon dictionaries as authoritative; actually, because of the cautious way they are researched, they are only the roughest guide to the history of what words have meant in the past.

ANSWER _____

Question Technique

The practice of turning topic sentences into questions, then reading the full paragraph to answer the question, is especially helpful when you need to concentrate on the details of a highly technical passage—such as the article below. As you start to read *each paragraph* of the article, turn its first sentence into a question. Does the rest of the paragraph answer that question? When you finish reading the article, turn to the answer space on page 211. There, for each paragraph, write out the question you formulated, and then indicate which sentence in the paragraph contributes most to the answer. *In addition,* if you decide that a paragraph does *not* answer the question you derive from its first sentence, write out a new question that does fit the information given by the paragraph.

This is not a timed exercise. Of course you will need to refer to the article while you work out the questions.

"Aspects of Ceramic Technology in Archaeology"[8]
by FREDERICK R. MATSON

A

The pottery found in most archaeological sites that were occupied by man after he began to farm and to settle on the land has changed very little in its appearance since it was fired and used. Although most excavated vessels are broken or exist only as remnants in the form of one or more potsherds, they serve as important evidences of the people who made and used them. Sherds are little affected by burial in the earth—they endure while metals corrode and disintegrate, and objects made of bark, wood or skin decay. Pottery preserves in its shape, decoration and physical properties a permanent though very fragmentary record of some of man's activities. Therefore, it must be studied intensively if the archaeologist is to reclaim from it all that is possible of the record remaining in such objects, and of their associations with other materials, in his excavations of ancient villages and towns.

B

If the mineralogical, physical and chemical properties of pottery are selectively determined in the light of the archaeological problem being studied, information can be obtained about the raw materials selected and used by the potter, their treatment before being formed into pots, the manner of fashioning the vessels and of firing them, and perhaps the uses to which they were put. The role of the potter as the active and controlling agent in these procedures must be kept in mind, and the function of his products in his community cannot be overlooked. We are concerned with the analytical data of products made by man, data which will help us better to understand this man's culture. Each study increases our historical knowledge of technological developments in areas of the world where ceramic products have been manufactured through long periods of time.

C

It is not necessary to have available expensive equipment in well-arranged laboratories in order to undertake the basic technological examination of pottery and other ceramic objects. Careful observations by one understanding the ceramic processes of pottery forming and firing can produce valuable information of direct use in the archaeological study of the wares. In this paper simple procedures requiring little laboratory equipment will be discussed first, followed by examples of the spectacular results obtained with special analytical equipment. Although technological pottery studies are the subject of this discussion, it should be recognized that similar approaches can be used in the examination of other important ceramic materials used by man such as brick, glass, glaze, enamel, faience, pigments, cement and plaster.

D

A close examination of the interior and exterior surfaces of sherds and of freshly fractured cross-sections through body walls can tell much about the ware and its production if one has some understanding of the properties of clays and the changes that occur as the surface of a semi-dried vessel is worked to its final condition by the potter, and as the well-dried ware is fired. A hand lens or a low-power binocular microscope helps one see the details sought, especially if oblique lighting can be arranged so that shadows are cast which emphasize the surface striations and textural variations. It is desirable to examine all of the sherds excavated at a site in this manner, if possible, after they have been washed, catalogued and assembled as parts of restorable vessels. When the latter is not possible, they should be sorted as to wares and then grouped according to the vessel area from which they came — rims, bases, shoulders, handles, body pieces, etc. By examining the entire ceramic production in groupings one can most effectively evaluate the materials and select characteristic as well as unique items for more intensive study. It is misleading to choose a sample for further analysis unless the selection is made with a background knowledge of the variations within the site's ceramic spectrum. In this connexion an appreciation of elementary statistical procedures and methods of sampling are useful.

E

One further step is desirable for the ceramic examiner. He should have a practical knowledge of the local clays available to the potters, and in his off hours of relaxation at the dig he should have sought such clays, tempered them with water, considered their textural variations, and attempted to make simple pots from them. I have done this with some success in Iraq, Iran and the eastern United States, and have found that this experience helped me to understand the ancient potter at work as I studied his sherds.

F

In the first sortings it is helpful to check the broken edges for fracture patterns transverse and parallel to the body walls that might indicate how the vessels were formed. In a large collection of sherds it is usually possible to find a few whose fractures show evidence of the junction of the body walls and the base, the joining of coils of clay while building the walls, or the addition of a rim to the formed vessels. The absence of such breaks in the fabric does not necessarily show more than that the potter was skilful, yet it could, with small pots, indicate that each was formed from one lump of clay.

G

If a paddle and anvil technique was used in the final shaping of the vessel to compact its walls, round out its base and prevent serious cracks from forming as the pot dried, its use can sometimes be recognized by the slight depressions on the interior surface that were caused by the rounded anvil, and by paddle marks on the exterior. When a wooden paddle has a carved design on its surface or a piece of coarse textile has been wrapped around it as in some parts of North America and the Far East, to mention but two areas of the world, it is easy to recognize this technique. If a smooth paddle is used, however, the surface must be carefully examined. I have seen the walls of olive jars in the Lebanon thinned and the bases of water jugs in Afghanistan rounded by the use of the paddle and anvil, and have been impressed by the force of the blows given as well as by the tough resiliency of the clay. This technique has probably been used far more frequently in the past than has been recognized.

H

Ridgings and striations on the exterior and interior surfaces of body sherds and the finishing marks on both faces of basal sherds can indicate whether or not the vessel was formed on a potter's wheel. This is not a simple matter to determine when examining sherds from the time period when the wheel was first being used as in the Uruk period in the ancient Near East — very roughly about 3,000 B.C. It is possible to fashion a pot by hand and then add a wheel-turned rim as has been done in Upper Egypt in recent times. It is also possible to rework the surface of a partly dried vessel on a simple wheel or lathe, scraping off the surface irregularities. This treatment leaves parallel striations on the smoothed surface, scratch marks caused by the dragging of mineral inclusions along under the scraping tool as it moves across the slightly moist clay surface. Usually the interior of narrow-mouthed vessels is not as well finished as the exterior, and the basic techniques of forming the piece can often be seen there.

I

A slip is sometimes applied to the surface of jars and to one or both surfaces of bowls. If this is a red slip on a clay body that fires to a brown or yellow colour there is no trouble in recognizing it. Such slips appear on pottery in the Near East from the very earliest ceramic strata of simple agricultural villages that were occupied well before 4,000 B.C. They were also common on pottery made in Europe and the Americas in later times. The red burning clay was available in the Near East on the mountain slopes, but it may have been enriched with abraded powder from soft ferruginous rocks, for well-worn fragments of such rocks are found in some of the excavations. Often, however, a yellow, tan or red surfacing is termed a slip when in reality its colour is due to a concentration of salts on the surface of the vessel or is caused by the wet hand of the potter as she smooths the surface of the piece she is fashioning. Wet smoothing concentrates the finest clay particles in a thin layer at the surface where they may develop a more intense colour when fired because the diluting effect of the coarser ingredients is masked by this fine-textured layer. Such a film, termed by Childe a 'self-slip,' may be described by a hasty observer as an intentionally applied slip. If it cannot be determined whether or not a slip is present from the careful examination of a significant series of sherds and this information would be useful, then a thin section of a characteristic sherd, should be prepared. When it is examined under a petrographic microscope it will usually show whether or not there is a layer of foreign material on the surface.

J

Freshly fractured edges of sherds uncontaminated by adhering clay or lime deposits will show clearly the textural variations in the ware and the degree to which it has been fired. When sherds are sorted under a binocular microscope with respect to texture, one quickly learns to recognize major variations in the quantity and size of the mineral grains present and is able to classify the sherds into one or more fabrics. If the core of the sherds is black or grey in colour, care is necessary so that one is not misled by the colour contrast between the mineral grains in the dark core and those in the tan to red oxidized clay zones near the surfaces. Whether the mineral inclusions were intentionally added as tempering material or occur naturally in the clay is a question of some interest that can be answered when one is familiar with the local clays and the possible variations from gravel admixtures through sandy to very fine that occur in them. The local deposits of sandy clays used for pottery in glaciated regions can often be traced to river banks of flood plains. Some such clays must be washed to remove the coarsest inclusions before they can be used successfully. If shell has been added to the clay as was done by some North American Indians, or straw was included as in many agricultural areas of the world, there is no difficulty in recognizing the intentional admixture.

For each paragraph of the selection, write out here the question you formulated from the first sentence. After each question, write the number of the sentence in the paragraph that contributed most to the answer. You may refer to the material.

A _____

_____

_____

_____ Sentence number _____ No one sentence can be chosen _____
If the paragraph does not answer the question, what question *does* it answer?

_____

_____

_____

B _____

_____

_____

_____ Sentence number _____ No one sentence can be chosen _____

If the paragraph does not answer the question, what question *does* it answer?

_____

_____

_____

C _____

_____

_____

_____ Sentence number _____ No one sentence can be chosen _____
If the paragraph does not answer the question, what question *does* it answer?

_____

_____

_____

D _____

_____

_____

_____ Sentence number _____ No one sentence can be chosen _____
If the paragraph does not answer the question, what question *does* it answer?

_____

_____

_____

E _____

_____

_____

_____ Sentence number _____ No one sentence can be chosen _____
If the paragraph does not answer the question, what question *does* it answer?

_____

_____

_____

F _____

_____

_____

_____ Sentence number _____ No one sentence can be chosen _____
If the paragraph does not answer the question, what question *does* it answer?

_____

_____

_____

G _____

_____

_____

_____ Sentence number _____ No one sentence can be chosen _____
If the paragraph does not answer the question, what question *does* it answer?

_____

_____

_____

H _____

_____

_____

_____ Sentence number _____ No one sentence can be chosen _____
If the paragraph does not answer the question, what question *does* it answer?

_____

_____

_____

I _____

_____

_____

_____ Sentence number _____ No one sentence can be chosen _____
If the paragraph does not answer the question, what question *does* it answer?

_____

_____

_____

J _____

_____

_____

_____ Sentence number _____ No one sentence can be chosen _____
If the paragraph does not answer the question, what question *does* it answer?

_____

_____

_____

Reading Speed Exercise: Difficult Level 3

As we said in Chapter 5, one of the fundamental strategies by which an author develops his subject is the extended definition. Extended definitions are particularly useful in serious, expository nonfiction; you will find them in scholarly writing and often in textbooks. The article below is an extended definition. It is taken from the introduction to a pioneering work of research in social anthropology, *The Children of Sanchez.* The book itself is a minutely detailed examination of the biographies and ways of life of five members of an extremely poor family in Mexico City, told in their own words from hundreds of hours of tape-recorded interviews. In the introduction, the author discusses some of the general implications of his research, and offers the idea that there is such a thing as the culture of poverty. The article is difficult in content and style, which means that skilled readers read it at speeds somewhat lower than they would use with material of a factual nature, popularly written.

You are to read the selection against time. Follow your instructor's directions, or the Instructions for Timing on page 474.

Do not pre-read the selection; the timed reading exercises are designed to measure improvements in speed alone.

After reading it and recording your time, answer the ten multiple-choice questions beginning on page 218. There is no time limit for the questions, but it will invalidate the exercise if you refer to this passage while you answer them.

Begin reading here.

"The Culture of Poverty"[9]
from *The Children of Sanchez*
by OSCAR LEWIS

It is the anthropologists, traditionally the spokesmen for primitive people in the remote corners of the world, who are increasingly turning their energies to the great peasant and urban masses of the less-developed countries. These masses are still desperately poor in spite of the social and economic progress of the world in the past century. Over a billion people in seventy-five nations of Asia, Africa, Latin America, and the Near East have an average per capita income of less than $200 a year as compared with over $2,000 a year for the United States. The anthropologist who studies the way of life in these countries has become, in effect, the student and spokesman of what I call the culture of poverty.

To those who think that the poor have no culture, the concept of a culture of poverty may seem like a contradiction in terms. It would also seem to give to poverty a certain dignity and status. This is not my intention. In anthropological usage the term culture implies, essentially, a design for living which is passed down from generation to generation. In applying this concept of culture to the understanding of poverty, I want to draw attention to the fact that poverty in modern nations is not only a state of economic deprivation, of disorganization, or of the absence of something. It is also something positive in the sense that it has a structure, a rationale, and defense mechanisms without which the poor could hardly carry on. In short, it is a way of life, remarkably stable and persistent, passed down from generation to generation along family lines. The culture of poverty has its own modalities and distinctive social and psychological consequences for its members. It is a dynamic factor which affects participation in the larger national culture and becomes a subculture of its own.

The culture of poverty, as here defined, does not include primitive peoples whose backwardness is the result of their isolation and undeveloped technology and whose society for the most part is not class stratified. Such peoples have a relatively integrated, satisfying, and self-sufficient culture. Nor is the culture of poverty synonymous with the working class, the proletariat, or the peasantry, all three of which vary a good deal in economic status throughout the world. In the United States, for example, the working class lives like an elite compared to the lower class of the less developed countries. The culture of poverty would apply only to those people who are at the very bottom of the socio-economic scale, the poorest workers, the poorest peasants, plantation laborers, and that large heterogeneous mass of small artisans and tradesmen usually referred to as the lumpen proletariat.

The culture or subculture of poverty comes into being in a variety of historical contexts. Most commonly it develops when a stratified social and economic system is breaking down or is being replaced by another, as in the case of the transition from feudalism to capitalism or during the industrial revolution. Sometimes it results from imperial conquest in which the conquered are maintained in a servile status which may continue for many generations. It can also occur in the process of detribalization such as is now going on in Africa where, for example, the tribal migrants to the cities are developing "courtyard cultures" remarkably similar to the Mexico City *vecindades*. We are prone to view such slum conditions as transitional or temporary phases of drastic culture change. But this is not necessarily the case, for the culture of poverty is often a persisting condition even in stable social systems. Certainly in Mexico it has been a more or less permanent phenomenon since the Spanish conquest of 1519, when the process of detribalization and the movement of peasants to the cities began. Only the size, location, and composition of the slums have been in flux. I suspect that similar processes have been going on in many other countries of the world.

In Mexico, the culture of poverty includes at least the lower third of the rural and urban population. This population is characterized by a relatively higher death rate, a lower life expectancy, a higher proportion of individuals in the younger age groups, and, because of child labor and working women, a higher proportion of gainfully employed. Some of these indices are higher in the poor *colonias* or sections of Mexico City than in rural Mexico as a whole.

The culture of poverty in Mexico is a provincial and locally oriented culture. Its members are only partially integrated into national institutions and are marginal people even when they live in the heart of a great city. In Mexico City, for example, most of the poor have a very low level of education and literacy, do not belong to labor unions, are not members of a political party, do not participate in the medical care, maternity, and old-age benefits of the national welfare agency known as *Seguro Social*, and make very little use of the city's banks, hospitals, department stores, museums, art galleries, and airports.

The economic traits which are most characteristic of the culture of poverty include the constant struggle for survival, unemployment and underemployment, low wages, a miscellany of unskilled occupations, child labor, the absence of savings, a chronic shortage of cash, the absence of food reserves in the home, the pattern of frequent buying of small quantities of food many times a day as the need arises, the pawning of personal goods, borrowing from local money lenders at usurious rates of interest, spontaneous informal credit devices (*tandas*) organized by neighbors, and the use of second-hand clothing and furniture.

Some of the social and psychological characteristics include living in crowded quarters, a lack of privacy, gregariousness, a high incidence of alcoholism, frequent resort to violence in the settlement of quarrels, frequent use of physical violence in the training of children, wife beating, early initiation into sex, free unions or consensual marriages, a relatively high incidence of the abandonment of mothers and children, a trend toward mother-centered families and a much greater knowledge of maternal relatives, the predominance of the nuclear family, a strong predisposition to authoritarianism, and a great emphasis upon family solidarity—an ideal only rarely achieved. Other traits include a strong present time orientation with relatively little ability to defer gratification and plan for the future, a sense of resignation and fatalism based upon the realities of their difficult life situation, a belief in male superiority which reaches its crystallization in *machismo* or the cult of masculinity, a corresponding martyr complex among women, and finally, a high tolerance for psychological pathology of all sorts.

Some of the above traits are not limited to the culture of poverty in Mexico but are also found in the middle and upper classes. However, it is the peculiar patterning of these traits which defines the culture of poverty. For example, in the middle class, *machismo* is expressed in terms of sexual exploits and the Don Juan complex whereas in the lower class it is expressed in terms of heroism and lack of physical fear. Similarly, drinking in the middle class is a social amenity whereas in the lower class getting drunk has different and multiple functions—to forget one's troubles, to prove one's ability to drink, and to build up sufficient confidence to meet difficult life situations.

Many of the traits of the subculture of poverty can be viewed as attempts at local solutions for problems not met by existing institutions and agencies because the people are not eligible for them, cannot afford them, or are suspicious of them. For example, unable to obtain credit from banks, they are thrown upon their own resources and organize informal credit devices without interest. Unable to afford doctors, who are used only in dire emergencies, and suspicious of hospitals "where one goes only to die," they rely upon herbs or other home remedies and upon local curers and midwives. Critical of priests "who are human and therefore sinners like all of us," they rarely go to confession or Mass and rely upon prayer to the images of saints in their own homes and upon pilgrimages to popular shrines.

A critical attitude toward some of the values and institutions of the dominant classes, hatred of the police, mistrust of government and those in high position, and a cynicism which extends even to the church gives the culture of poverty a counter quality and a potential for being used in political movements aimed against the existing social order. Finally, the sub-culture of poverty also has a residual quality in the sense that its members are attempting to utilize and integrate into a workable way of life the remnants of beliefs and customs of diverse origins.

Now note your reading time. Record it below and go on to the questions.

YOUR READING TIME: _____MIN. _____SEC. _____W.P.M. COMPREHENSION SCORE: _____%
(WORDS PER MINUTE FROM THE TABLE ON PAGE 475.)

    Please do not read these questions until you have read the selection itself against time. Do not refer to the selection as you answer the questions.

1. The author's name is (a) Lyman Hunt; (b) Ely Chinoy; (c) Garrett Mattingly; (d) Oscar Lewis; (e) David Mercer.

                                 ANSWER _____

2. Within this extended definition, the author sets out his basic or most central definition of *the culture of poverty* as (a) only apparently a contradiction in terms; (b) a design for living passed down from generation to generation; (c) a remarkably stable, persistent way of life, handed down the generations, without which the poor could hardly carry on; (d) a dynamic factor which affects participation in the larger national culture and which gives poverty a certain dignity or status; (e) a state of economic deprivation and disorganization.

                                 ANSWER _____

3. After giving that central definition, the author next lists certain groups that are *not* included in his idea of the culture of poverty. Which *two* of the following are the groups he rules out that way? (a) A group synonymous with the working class, the proletariat, the peasantry; (b) primitive people whose backwardness is the result of their isolation and undeveloped technology; (c) provincial or locally oriented cultures; (d) those people at the very bottom of the socio-economic scale; (e) that large, heterogeneous mass of tradesmen and artisans called the *lumpen proletariat.*

                                 ANSWER _____

4. The author mentions several ways that the culture of poverty can come into being, historically, in different places. Which *two* of the following does he explicitly apply to the Mexican version? (a) The breakdown of a stratified social or economic system; (b) imperial conquest after which the conquered are maintained in a servile status; (c) the industrial revolution; (d) detribalization and movement of the peasants to the cities; (e) increased upward mobility among those immediately above the extremes of poverty.

                                 ANSWER _____

5. In Mexico, the culture of poverty includes (a) at least the lower third of the rural and urban population; (b) those with an average per capita income of

less than $200 a year as compared with over $2,000 a year in the United States; (c) some who, despite the contrast with the United States, live like an elite compared to the lowest class of less developed countries; (d) those thrown upon their own resources in opposition to the usual institutions of society; (e) those whose ideas and behavior identify them more readily than their economic status, for example, by their attitudes toward sex, manliness, and drink.

ANSWER _____

6. The author, in building his extended definition, itemizes a number of general characteristics of the culture of poverty. Some of them are listed here, but not in the correct order. Reconstruct the author's own organization by listing all five items in correct order.
   (a) A critical attitude towards some of the institutions of the dominant classes
   (b) Social and psychological characteristics of the culture of poverty, such as overcrowding, lack of privacy, etc.
   (c) The peculiar patterning of the traits as characteristic of the poor
   (d) Economic traits, such as unemployment, child labor, etc.
   (e) Lack of integration into the national institutions.

ANSWER _____

7. Which *one* of the following was *not* listed as a characteristic of the culture of poverty in Mexico? (a) Frequent resort to violence; (b) the absence of food reserves in the home, and a pattern of buying small quantities of food many times a day; (c) widespread drinking as a social amenity; (d) relatively little ability to defer gratification and to plan ahead; (e) a trend toward mother-centered families.

ANSWER _____

8. As the author points out, some of the characteristic traits are also found in the middle or upper classes; what defines the culture of poverty, then, is (a), in particular, its peculiar brand of *machismo,* or sex and courage; (b) the presence of virtually all the traits together; (c) the use of these traits in opposition to the established culture; (d) the peculiar patterning of the traits; (e) the peculiar patterning of the traits, and by implication the presence of many of them together.

ANSWER _____

9. The critical attitude of the culture of poverty towards dominant values and institutions, the author says, (a) gives the culture of poverty a potential for being used in political movements against the existing social order; (b) is characterized by suspicion and avoidance; (c) is demonstrated most typically by hatred of the police; (d) makes them extremely suspicious of anthropologists; (e) includes remnants of beliefs and customs of diverse and ancient origins.

ANSWER _____

10. The author's overall attitude toward the culture of poverty, perhaps not explicitly stated in this passage, seems to be (a) one of clinical detachment; (b) one of detachment tinged with disapproval of feckless and improvident habits; (c) one of balanced admiration; (d) that of the student and spokes-

man, based on respect and understanding; (e) that of considerable admiration leading him by implication to defend the culture of poverty.

ANSWER _____

Now check your answers, and enter your score on your Progress Profile, page vii.

2

Special Reading Problems

CHAPTER 9

Concentration and Memory

Pre-read this chapter as your first step in reading. As your
second step, before reading thoroughly, list here the questions you expect the chapter to answer.

_____

_____

_____

_____

_____

Concentration and memory, both, are like health: qualities one only
notices when they are poor, yet so important that the prudent man takes precautions to keep them good. Poor concentration is the most vexatious problem
in reading—and certainly so when it is accompanied by difficulty in remembering. You undoubtedly have trouble with concentration at least occasionally,
when noise, other outside distractions, or something else on your mind seems
to make it impossible to keep your attention on the page for more than a sentence or two at a time. Sometimes it even seems that you can read a whole
chapter, then reread it without recognizing more than three or four familiar
statements. Whenever it happens, inability to concentrate is a barrier to enjoyment, speed, comprehension, and retention. A few readers report that for
them the problem is almost continual: in such cases individual psychological
counseling may even be needed to find and correct the causes. For most
readers, fortunately, poor concentration is only occasionally a problem; when
it is, steps can be taken to make concentration generally easier. This chapter
discusses those steps, then goes on briefly to discuss the closely related question of memory in reading.

What makes concentration difficult? Distractions are usually blamed, or the dullness of the reading matter, or some supposed lack of will power on the part of the reader. Of course repetitive interruptions can take your attention from the reading. Indeed, dull reading is hard reading. True, a reader must sometimes be able to pull his wandering wits together and direct his attention by a conscious effort. But it is useless simply to blame distractions or dullness or lack of will power for concentration difficulties, because that provides little clue to what to do. Fortunately, the problem of concentration has a different formulation that proves more helpful.

For most people, the ability to concentrate depends on *the balance of interests at the moment.* The point about the balance of interests is that it has two sides. In reading, trouble with concentration occurs when the book is less interesting at that particular time than other things that compete for your attention. Think of some book you read recently which really riveted your interest—about bee-keeping, Benin bronzes, geodesic domes, or whatever is your own subject that hardly anybody else seems to have heard of. You had no trouble concentrating there, even if the author's writing was not the most sprightly, even if a pop group was playing next door. But when the subject is one that seems dull to you, particularly when that feeling is compounded by dull writing, then obviously you find it harder to concentrate. On the other side of the balance of interests, a book that ordinarily would compel your attention may prove difficult to concentrate on, when some more urgent interest—say a family crisis—has you preoccupied.

Thus, the solution to concentration problems is to readjust your balance of interests. That is, you will make conditions more favorable to concentration if you can *diminish* distracting claims on your attention and *increase* your interest in the material you are reading. The suggestions below follow from this principle.

On the one side of the scales there can be two types of distractions that upset your balance of interest and attention. The first is external: your reading environment and the temptations it offers to lure your mind away from the book. The external distractions can usually be controlled by a few simple precautions. The second type is "what's on your mind"—the competing thoughts that preempt the attention you should be giving to the work at hand. The latter are perhaps the most difficult to deal with of all the causes of poor concentration. Finally, on the other side of the balance of interests, many of the techniques you have been learning can be used to increase your interest in the material, and thus help overcome distractions you cannot otherwise eliminate.

Controlling Outside Distractions: Your Physical Environment

A good reading environment can contribute greatly to your efficiency, especially if you regularly read in that one setting. The reason a good reading environment helps is that it becomes part of the whole complex pattern of your efficient reading. The setting itself tells you, *this is where you read*: on those occasions when you have trouble settling down to it, that environment will actively help to start the rest of your efficient reading habits rolling again.

Obviously a good reading environment must be quiet, free from distractions, free from interruptions by other people. Libraries offer the silence, at least; but other less formal, less public, more accessible, and emotionally warmer places may prove to be more conducive to reading efficiency. Do your reading in a firm, upright chair. You learn better while experiencing some degree of bodily tension; in a too-comfortable chair you may relax or get just sleepy enough to impede concentration. Put the book on a desk or reading table before you, so that you can have pen and paper and a firm writing surface close at hand. Support the book with a slanted bookrest, or prop it against another book, so that the top of the page is no farther away from your eyes than the bottom; thus your eyes need not adjust from far to near as you read down the page.

Some even find it helpful to read standing up. Stand-up desks were fairly common a hundred years ago, especially for bookkeepers; they are not unknown today, for example, the large worktables used by some architects and draftsmen. You might experiment by propping the book on a mantelpiece, or by clearing a shelf of a tall bookcase. Many skillful readers who do most of their reading sitting down will occasionally stand to read for half an hour or so as a way of combatting fatigue or sleepiness.

Lighting is adequate if you can read without strain. Not only the book, but the rest of the room as well, should be lit. If the lighting is properly balanced, there will be no glare on the page, and no sense of marked contrast between the lighted area and the rest of the room.

A problem related to efficient reading environment is eyesight. Your eyes may be tired, strained, or even in need of glasses (or new glasses) without your being aware of it. But you will, in one way or another, suffer from the irritating sensation that reading is more unpleasant and more tiring than it should be. As part of the Reading Skills Survey (page 14), we asked questions about regular care of the eyes and about danger signs that may indicate eye trouble. If concentration or fatigue in reading is a problem for you, review those questions. If you have not paid him a visit recently, see your eye specialist.

Not all eye fatigue, however, is caused by poor sight or faulty glasses. Reading for several hours without a break can cause eye fatigue and discomfort. Therefore, remember to rest your eyes about once each half hour by closing them or looking at a distant object for a few minutes. You will then return to your reading refreshed, and your reading efficiency will rise.

Poor concentration is usually associated with a number of bad habits in reading. For some people, these bad habits are hard to shake off. If this is your problem, a little planning to outwit such habits is well worthwhile. For example, that favorite and "so-comfortable" easy chair may be precisely the place where you are used to letting your mind wander and daydream; better stick to the straight chair and desk. Another common problem is sleepiness while reading in early afternoon or in the evening; you may need to eat a light lunch or dinner when you know you have a lot of reading to do afterwards.

Poor concentration will seize any opportunity to get you away from reading—to putter, to sharpen pencils, to go out for a cup of coffee, or even to read something else more beguiling than the job of the moment. Conquering habits like these requires honesty with yourself; it also takes ingenuity and forethought to anticipate what you are likely to do when the fit is on. Breaking such habits is much like quitting smoking: some people seem to do it by will power, but most of us require a good deal of awareness of how we react, what things tempt us to stray, and how truly short-lived is that tempting impulse once we master it. If concentration is a problem this serious for you, you will find it helpful to organize your attack, listing on paper the details and symptoms of your version of the malady, followed by a check list of steps to take. The place for this analysis is your Reading Journal.

Finally, it is important to realize that even the best reading environment cannot become an active, helpful part of your pattern of efficient reading unless you indeed make it habitual to read there with your top efficiency.

One reading environment that is usually *not* conducive to reading efficiency is a moving vehicle. Subways, buses, or commuter trains, for example, have several drawbacks as places to read. First, the constant swaying and joggling increase the risk of eye strain because your eyes must make constant tiny corrections as the distance to the page changes. Second, regular reading in such circumstances, traveling to work for example, can often deteriorate into reading for escape or to kill time, rather than purposeful, alert, and sensitive reading. Too much reading just to fill time can seriously dull your reading skills and habits, and more specifically, can lead to concentration difficulties in more serious reading. Such reading is flabby, lazy reading; it encourages you to skip steps like pre-reading and other efficient measures you need when reading is more serious. Reading is a skill like tennis or chess: the really skillful player finds that too much play "just for fun" against opposition that doesn't stretch him will soon put him off his game.

Controlling Inside Distractions: Your Mental Environment

The most serious block to concentration is the interruption which comes not from outside but from within: something else on your mind that is more important at the moment than what you are reading. Some of the most extreme preoccupations—professional or personal crises, the emotional effects of the death of a friend or relative, for example—obviously admit no easy, immediate solutions; they are beyond the scope of this book.

But the more ordinary distracting problem can usually be made less of a hindrance to concentration in reading if you take time from your reading to do something, if only minor, about the problem. Your action should be directed toward the prompt resolution of the disturbing problem; or, when the problem cannot be settled promptly, your action should make definite and realistic provisions to deal with it in the future. When a problem interferes with reading, invest half an hour first toward getting started on the solution. This can save you several hours of rereading later. For example, the businessman with an important conference in the morning learns that making some notes on his objectives for the meeting and reviewing the relevant correspondence will settle his mind about tomorrow so that he can attend to today's affairs. Similarly, the student with a quiz tomorrow in one subject, who is also worried about an important paper due for a second subject next week, may find it well worthwhile to spend a few minutes outlining what he will say in the paper so that he can then read more efficiently in preparation for the quiz. Actions like these, realistically initiating solutions of the problems, result in freeing your mind, to a degree at least, for the reading before you.

How to Increase Your Interest in Reading

The balance of your interests at the moment: Returning to this formulation as the key to concentration problems, we can see that all the suggestions made so far act on the one side of the balance, working to reduce the competition for your attention. It is on the other side of the balance, by increasing your interest in the reading, that the skills you have been learning for better comprehension and speed can also help concentration.

Speed has a unique contribution to make to concentration. When you perform any mental work with a half-interested, lackadaisical attitude — dawdling through the job — concentration is naturally difficult. This is true for writing a letter, a report, or a paper; for working out a series of problems in mathematics; for analyzing the score of a Beethoven symphony; or for preparing a list of legal case-references. It is pre-eminently true for reading. Most people find that a fast pace of work, with a sense of urgency, transforms a dull task, making efficiency and concentration far easier. A sustained effort to read at your top rate has exactly this same effect on your concentration: it leaves you less time to respond to distractions; it obliges you to pay close and constant attention in order to comprehend; and it helps generate a feeling of urgency, importance, and greater interest. To use your most efficient speeds for generating this sense of urgency, apply the method of the Reading Speed Carry-over Exercises of this book: pre-reading followed by two thorough readings, the first at such a speed that it seems too fast, the second somewhat slower to see what you missed. A similar approach to speed and concentration on long reading jobs is to add up the total number of pages, then break them down into reasonable units of length and set yourself a tight limit for the completion of each unit.

Sometimes concentration is difficult because the material is objectively of low interest to you; in other words the material seems to offer little that you really need. In this case skimming is an obvious and effective remedy. However, when you are having trouble concentrating, it may not be easy to be sure that the material is, in this sense, *objectively* of low interest. The test is how well it meets your purpose in reading (as is discussed more fully below where we take up the question technique in relation to concentration). Pre-reading is another method that will increase your interest in the material, and thus your concentration. Here, recall two of the benefits of pre-reading: it gives you a general view of the author's intentions, conclusions, and organization; and it makes you aware of the relation of details to the overall plan of the work. These, you remember, are the main ways in which, from the time you first pick up a work, pre-reading helps direct your attention and interest so that concentration is much less likely to become a problem. For these same reasons, when concentration is difficult you should repeat the steps of pre-reading before continuing to read thoroughly.

Of all the techniques of reading, by far the most helpful for concentration is the *question technique.* You will remember from Chapter 7 that before thorough reading you are to remind yourself to aim for a clear understanding of the author's *thesis* and *organization*. The questions you ask will sharpen and direct your interest in the material. As another question before reading, you examined closely *your own purpose* in reading this particular material. This spelled out for you the importance of the reading; thus when concentration is troublesome, you should review carefully these reasons why the reading is important. Because you stated your purpose before you became mired down in concentration problems, this statement about the importance of the reading is more objective and trustworthy than your reaction at the particular time when you have trouble. Finally, the questions you formulate about specific details, before reading thoroughly, are instrumental in keeping your interest high.

Chapter 7 also introduced questioning *during* thorough reading, whereby you convert the first sentence of each paragraph into a question, then read thoroughly for the answer. This technique, admittedly laborious, is specifically designed as a last resort for times when concentration is not sufficiently improved by other methods. You should practice this technique during the next several weeks, not only with the exercises in this book, but also outside them in your daily reading, often enough so that if you do need the method you will remember it and know how to use it.

We have seen how speed and comprehension skills can be applied to cure concentration difficulties. These skills also work to prevent concentration problems from arising during thorough reading. Reading is, in this respect, just like most other activities: we are uncomfortable and uninterested when we are obliged to do something that we cannot do skillfully, while we enjoy and are interested in activities we can perform really well.

Memory in Reading

Most of us are somewhat forgetful, yet there is no question that we can, if we wish, train our memories to perform extraordinary tricks. The stage entertainer who can call off in any desired sequence the names of fifty people in the audience whom he has just met is only exploiting systems of short-term memorizing which have been known for centuries. What such memory-training stunts rely on is a rigid system of chaining together a pattern of associations so that each link in the chain hauls up the next to the surface of memory. Such systems typically convert each bit to be memorized into a number, then provide a vivid mental image for each fact-number combination; a more ancient system got the same result by training the individual to memorize the series of facts by visualizing each one as occupying a place within an imaginary theater building, so that the details could be "read" out by visualizing the sequence of locations and what they contained.

Such memory systems produce striking but oddly limited results. The reasons for the limitations as well as for the results seem to lie in the fundamental nature of memory itself. Psychologists are not yet sure how human memory functions, but they have discovered that we have at least two different kinds of memory, short term and long term. Short-term memory is what you use, for example, when you look up a telephone number in the directory, then hold it in mind while you dial it. By the time you hang up at the end of the conversation you have forgotten the number. How you transfer something from short-term to long-term memory is not fully understood, though evidence suggests that the transfer takes at least twenty minutes, while it is well known that memory is helped by both repetition and organized association. Thus, in the trick systems what has really been built into the long-term memory is the number sequence or the visual imagery to which the momentary associations are to be hooked; the memory for these momentary associations is short term. Yet the tricks of the memory systems work because they are based on one fundamental psychological insight, which is that memory functions by linking the new with the already known. The trick memory systems also offer a useful psychological gimmick, which is that associations are easier to recall if they are visualized as vividly as possible.

Take an example: modern Turkish is a far simpler language than modern French, because its grammar has much less variety and irregularity, its total vocabulary is minute by comparison, its spelling is completely predictable. Yet for English-speaking people, French is much easier to learn than Turkish, especially at first. Why? Because every element of Turkish is unfamiliar, while French has many relations to English in grammar and especially in vocabulary. The point is the same for other problems of learning and memory: we find it easiest to remember new things for which we have many associations already learned, and most difficult to remember things for which we can find no associations.

Thus the fundamental strategy for a good memory is to have the network, the structure, of related information into which new material fits. This fact about learning and memory is still another reason for the never-ending emphasis in this book on techniques for getting at structures. What you learn about the organization of a piece of reading — from the large scale of pre-reading an entire book, to the fine scale of analyzing the structure of a paragraph — is exactly the network required to begin not only effective understanding but also lasting memory. In brief, to remember something you must first understand it.

The emphasis on structures, associations, linkages — and the intimate relation of memory with understanding — continues throughout the process of reading. For example, from the point of view of good memory, the power of the question technique is that it sharpens the relations of what you are reading — its relation to your purpose, to the specifics you expect to find in it, to the author's aims and thesis, and so forth. Again, when in Chapter 10 we discuss the art of taking notes, you will learn that one aim of any thorough note-taking system is to get the organization of the work onto paper in almost diagrammatic form, and then to attach the details to their proper places in that structure.

Note-taking, study, review and repetition — all these aspects of the most thorough reading, treated in the next several chapters, also relate to the second basic and obvious requirement for good memory, which is repetition of the new material. You saw one application of this principle in Chapter 8, on vocabulary, where we said about new words that you must *use them three times and they're yours.* Someone who is good at learning foreign languages develops similar tricks of repetition — rehearsing phrases and sentences to himself, holding small subvocal dialogues with himself in the new language as he rides a bus or walks along the street. One authority has called this "fingering the small change in your pocket." In much the same way, politicians and others who must be good at remembering names can be observed to work at it, unobtrusively but steadily:

when they meet someone new they listen for the name, repeat it immediately — "Glad to meet you, *Mr. Wagner*" — then work the name into the conversation once or more in the next few minutes. The same principle, of course, applies on a broader scale, and in many variations, for remembering what you are reading and learning.

If you find that your memory is not what you want it to be, make a point of going back to a recently completed work in your mind, trying first of all to reconstruct the overall organization of the book as if you were pre-reading it again. (Just what was the sequence of ideas in the chapter? the relation of the several parts in the book?) Continue, when you can, with an imaginary dialogue with the author. Return to the work in your Reading Journal by jotting down your own questions or developments of the author's thought. Another device for strengthening your memory is to use your skill at summarizing in regular mental exercises: every few pages of a work you want to remember well, stop reading for a moment, close the book, and run through a quick summary of what you have just read. Further methods of review will be suggested in the next chapter, on study.

A final tip from the wizards who perform memory tricks: vivid visualization is often a great aid to memory. At the simplest level, the aim is to create quick, powerful associations. Mr. Burns is the man with the mustache and you want to remember his name? Imagine his mustache on fire: "mustache = burns" goes the association. At that level, it often helps if the association is comical. A case in point is the elaborate, usually obscene, comic rhymes by which medical students memorize anatomy lessons. Vivid visualization has many applications in reading. One gladly makes the effort to call up the scene a great novelist is describing. But visualization also means something as pedestrian, but effective, as learning a complicated set of directions not simply by memorizing the sequence of words but by visualizing what they will mean in practice; for example, a new driving route in terms not just of towns and left turns but actually of the road signs you will look for; or a new cooking recipe by imagining three cups each full of flour, two eggs lying broken on the floor, and so on.

Which brings us back to where this chapter started: memory and concentration are closely and naturally related; most things that help one will help the other. Vivid visualization, like other ways to improve memory, is in effect still another means to heighten your involvement with what you are reading, to adjust your balance of interests.

EXERCISES FOR CHAPTER 9

Reading Journal

Skimming for a Fact—in Political Science

Paragraph Analysis (a carry-over exercise)

Pre-reading
Table of Contents from *The Mediaeval Mind,* Vol. I, by
H. O. Taylor

Question Technique
Rereading of "Culture," by Ely Chinoy (pages 34–36)

Reading Speed Carry-over Exercise

Reading Journal

In your separate notebook, bring the sections on **current** and **future reading** up to date.

Next, write out a self-analysis of your own concentration and memory. Your analysis should be at least a page or so in length. Its purpose is to give you an understanding of whatever problem you have here; therefore, you should try to answer—in light of the chapter you have just read—questions like these:

How good is your concentration in reading? memory? What particular kinds of reading do you find least trouble in concentrating on? What kinds are hardest to concentrate on? to remember? why? What was the last occasion when you had real trouble concentrating? What happened exactly? What distractions or preoccupations are typically troublesome?

Conclude your analysis of your concentration and memory with a list of the steps you can take to improve them, beginning with changes in the environment where you do your reading.

Skimming for a Fact

Just before each of the following paragraphs, a particular piece of factual information is called for. You are to skim each paragraph to find the one fact. Try to break away completely from thorough reading. Instead, glance left and right very rapidly, stopping as little as twice on each line of print. *Keep clearly in mind the fact, stated at the beginning of the paragraph, for which you are skimming.*

As soon as you find the fact, put a pencil check in the margin next to it. Then go immediately to the next paragraph. When you have skimmed and checked all the paragraphs, record your time in the space provided on page 234, and then fill in the sentence number of each fact in the proper space there.

Work for speed. In class follow your instructor's directions for timing. On your own, follow the Instructions for Timing on page 474.

Begin timing here.

A

LOOK FOR: a description of the European type of parliamentary government

1   In the relations between executive, legislative and judiciary the con-
2 stitutions summarized in this paper present several variations. At the one extreme, the Soviet Union and Yugoslavia represent, in theory at least, the so-called "government by assembly," in which all political power is
3 lodged in the parliament. The cabinet may be overthrown by a withdrawal of confidence by the parliament but has no power to dissolve that body, and the judiciary may not declare unconstitutional a law
4 which has been passed in due form. Canada, South Africa, Australia, Weimar-Germany and France represent variations of the European type of parliamentary government in which the cabinet is responsible to the lower house of parliament but has the power to dissolve that body and
5 call for a general election. In addition, certain limited but specific powers are granted to a head of state (a feature not provided for in the Soviet or
6 Yugoslav Constitutions). In all these countries there are procedures for judicial review, that is for determining the constitutionality (and hence
7 validity) of laws passed by parliament. In Switzerland the executive is collegial in form and is elected by the two houses of parliament together
8 for a fixed term of office during which it may not be removed. In the United States there is, as is well known, complete institutional separation of the executive, legislative and judicial branches of government—the President is elected directly by the people and is not responsible to Congress, and the judiciary has the power to declare invalid laws or executive acts which in its opinion are unconstitutional.

B

LOOK FOR: a reference to the constitution of Canada

1   *Written and Unwritten Constitutions.*—In considering the constitutions of other countries and in planning the features of a new German constitution, particular attention must be paid to the fact that the written constitution is often only a part of the constitutional structure of a government, and that many basic points will be dealt with by the "unwritten
2 constitution" which develops around every document. For example, the principle of judicial review, which is perhaps the backbone of United

States constitutional theory, does not appear in the written constitution; similarly the powers of the Canadian Senate in practice are merely a shadow of its theoretical powers, and the most important governmental official of Canada, the prime minister, is not mentioned in the written

3 constitution. In planning a written constitution, therefore, attempt must be made to foresee what kind of an "unwritten constitution" will develop

4 around it. Specifically, what will be the actual powers of the various federal and state organs of government and how will these organs operate in relation to each other.

C

LOOK FOR: any mention of legislation by referendum

1 *General.* — The concept of legislation is a flexible one and may in-
2 clude anything from a formal constitution to a parking regulation. As the term is commonly used by political scientists and will be used here, legislation means that body of law which is of lesser stature than the formal constitutional documents, but of greater stature than administrative regulations promulgated by a cabinet or department for the purpose of carry-
3 ing out functions which it already legally possesses. One could define legislation as that body of law enacted by representative parliaments according to regular procedure, or as the general process of enacting such laws; however, such a definition would leave out of account the fact that the Swiss Confederation often enacts legislation directly by referendum and that the Third French Republic, without giving up its essential democratic structure, has on several occasions granted its President (actually
4 the Cabinet) substantial powers to legislate by decree. Nor is it practicable to define legislation by subject-matter, since the ideas as to the proper border-line between the formal constitution and ordinary legislation and between ordinary legislation and administrative regulations vary
5 from state to state. For instance, the Swiss Constitution includes principles for the operation of slaughter houses, a subject which would be in
6 the administrative regulations of most other countries. It must, therefore, be borne in mind that the legislative organs and processes, as they will be discussed in the following section, cover a quite flexible area depending on how much detail the state in question has written into its constitution and how much it relies upon administrative regulations to establish the framework for implementing general principles which are stated in the laws.

D

LOOK FOR: the size of a quorum in the Australian House of Representatives

1 The House of Representatives of the Commonwealth of Australia consists of 75 members elected by single-member districts, the number of
2 which is allotted to each state according to population. An act increasing the size of the House to 122 will become effective at the next election.
3 The districting (or treatment of a state as a district at large) is left to the
4 Parliament of the state in question. The Constitution is not specific on

the subject of suffrage, but does provide that aboriginals who have not qualified to vote under state law (less than 0.3% of the population) shall
5 not be counted in apportioning the electoral districts. In a provision similar to that in the U. S. Constitution, it is provided that members of the House shall be elected according to the state law applying to the
6 most numerous house of parliament in that state. Voting is compulsory.
7 The term of members of the House is three years unless the House
8 should sooner be dissolved. The House elects its own speaker and makes
9 its own rules. Measures are passed by a majority vote and one-third of the whole number of members constitutes a quorum.

E

LOOK FOR: the method of collecting taxes in Yugoslavia
1   In the United States, Canada, Australia and Switzerland, the fed-
2 eral and state government each collect their own taxes independently. In the Soviet Union and Yugoslavia, collection of taxes is administered on a decentralized basis but according to laws and regulations issued by the central government and under the supervision of the central ministry of
3 finance. In Germany, during the early days of the Weimar Constitution, the central government took over and organized into a consolidated fed-eral service the state finance offices with the result that only a few taxes of lesser importance were still collected by the state or local governments.
4 During the occupation the finance offices have in the U. S. Zone been returned to the state governments, who are now responsible for collect-ing federal as well as state taxes.

Stop timing here.

For each paragraph enter the number of the sentence that contains the fact you were to find. (The sentences are numbered in the left margin.)

Skimming time in seconds for all items: _____

A: _____   B: _____   C: _____   D: _____   E: _____

Paragraph Analysis (a carry-over exercise)

This exercise continues to drill you in the habit of noting paragraph structure and functions in your daily reading.

Taking one of the textbooks you are currently reading, and which you have pre-read for your Reading Journal, select the next complete chapter that you have not yet read.

Pre-read the chapter.

Read the chapter thoroughly. As you read, mark in the margin the principal statement in each paragraph. Do any of the paragraphs have their topic sentences elsewhere than at the beginning?

Also as you read thoroughly, mark in the margin each paragraph which contains a definition, and each paragraph that has either a summarizing or a transitional function.

When you finish reading the chapter thoroughly and marking the paragraphs, go back and reread the chapter, reading only the introductory, transitional, and summarizing paragraphs completely, and the marked topic sentences of each of the other paragraphs. How effective do you find this as a method of review?

Pre-reading

From the first volume of one of our great history books, we have reprinted below the table of contents. Here the organizational skeleton of the book is laid out, with a clarity and completeness that makes this table of contents a classic in its own right. For readers without previous background in the historical period covered, this book would be difficult reading. Thoughtful analysis of the table of contents during pre-reading would pay great dividends in your later understanding of the book itself.

Read this material carefully. You may find yourself put off at first by the vocabulary and the unfamiliar subject matter: we repeat, this is *not* easy reading. But try to push past these difficulties to discover all you can about the organization of the book and its parts. Then go on to the questions. This is not a timed exercise.

Table of Contents
from *The Mediaeval Mind*, Vol. I[1]
by HENRY O. TAYLOR

BOOK I   THE GROUNDWORK

BOOK IV   THE IDEAL AND THE ACTUAL: SOCIETY

These questions assume that you are examining the material because you intend eventually to read the book itself. You may refer to the material as you answer the questions.

1. Which chapters of the book would you read as part of the pre-reading process? For your answer to this question, enter the *chapter numbers* of all chapters that seem — by title or by position in the book — to have an introductory, transitional, or concluding function.
                            ANSWER _____

2. Compare Book I with the other three books. Compare its title with the other three titles, and its sequence of chapters with the sequence in the other three books. Judging from this comparison, what seems to be the function of Book I? (a) To narrate, by way of brief introduction, the early history of the Christian church; (b) to make clear the political history, which is the setting in which the Mediaeval mind developed; (c) to relate the intellectual history that preceded the Mediaeval period and contributed to the forma-

tion of the Mediaeval mind; (d) to explain the causes of the failure of the antique and patristic world to restrain the barbarian incursions.

ANSWER _____

3. Which of the following is the best descriptive subtitle for Book I? (a) Barbarian versus Pagan; (b) The Classical and Barbarian Influences That Helped Create the Mediaeval Mind; (c) The Consequences of the Disruption of the Roman Empire; (d) The Spread of Christianity in the West.

ANSWER _____

4. Book II seems to be concerned with (a) the preliminary stages of growth of the Mediaeval mind; (b) the integration of the subjects that Book I discusses, in the first stages of growth of the Mediaeval mind; (c) the first stages of the Italian influence that later came to dominate Europe, politically and intellectually, in the Middle Ages; (d) the conversion of the barbarians to Christianity.

ANSWER _____

5. Now compare the *method* of Book I with that of Book II. In a general way, Book I seems to proceed on the basis of historical time sequence — dominated by two major features, the "antique and patristic" on the one hand, and the barbarian incursions on the other. Book II (a) simply continues the historical narrative further into the Middle Ages; (b) shifts entirely from the historical time sequence in order to analyze specific elements of Mediaeval intellectual activity; (c) is dominated by a geographical, country-by-country analysis of the intellectual situations prevailing at one instant of time; (d) is dominated by a geographical, country-by-country analysis where historical time sequence is used within each country.

ANSWER _____

6. Continue your comparison of *methods:* move on to Books III and IV. These seem to proceed (a) in the narrative manner of Book I, rather than by the separation and analysis of specific areas of intellectual activity as in Book II; (b) by the geographic or area-by-area analysis that also dominates Book II; (c) by the separation and analysis of a number of different strands of the intellectual and emotional activity that characterize the Mediaeval mind; (d) simply by historical time sequence, as in the first two books, but disguised by the extreme difficulty of subject matter and terminology.

ANSWER _____

7. What are Books III and IV concerned with?

_____

_____

_____

_____

_____

8. Within Book I there is a major break or division of subject matter between which two chapters?

ANSWER _____

9. Within Book III there is a major break or division of subject matter between which two chapters?

ANSWER _____

10. The title of the entire book is *The Mediaeval Mind*. What would be the best descriptive subtitle?

_____

Question Technique

Turn back to the article "Culture," by Ely Chinoy, which you read as the speed exercise at the end of Chapter 1. The article begins on page 34. Read it again; as you start each paragraph, turn the first sentence into a question. Does the rest of the paragraph answer that question? When you finish reading, write out, in the space below, the question you have formulated for each paragraph; then indicate which sentence in that paragraph contributes most to the answer. If you decide that a paragraph does *not* answer the question you derive from its first sentence, write out below a new question that does fit the information given by the paragraph.

This is not a timed exercise. Of course you will need to refer to the article while you formulate the questions.

A _____

_____

_____

_____ Sentence number _____ No one sentence can be chosen _____
If the paragraph does not answer the question, what question *does* it answer?

_____

_____/_____

_____

B _____

_____

_____

_____ Sentence number _____ No one sentence can be chosen _____

If the paragraph does not answer the question, what question *does* it answer?

_____

_____

_____

C _____

_____

_____

_____ Sentence number _____ No one sentence can be chosen _____
If the paragraph does not answer the question, what question *does* it answer?

_____

_____

_____

D _____

_____

_____

_____ Sentence number _____ No one sentence can be chosen _____
If the paragraph does not answer the question, what question *does* it answer?

_____

_____

_____

E _____

_____

_____

_____ Sentence number _____ No one sentence can be chosen _____
If the paragraph does not answer the question, what question *does* it answer?

_____

F _____

_____

_____

_____ Sentence number _____ No one sentence can be chosen _____
If the paragraph does not answer the question, what question *does* it answer?

_____

_____

_____

G _____

_____

_____

_____ Sentence number _____ No one sentence can be chosen _____
If the paragraph does not answer the question, what question *does* it answer?

_____

_____

_____

H _____

_____

_____

_____ Sentence number _____ No one sentence can be chosen _____
If the paragraph does not answer the question, what question *does* it answer?

_____

_____

_____

Reading Speed Carry-over Exercise

The aim of this exercise is to carry your new habits of speed and reading efficiency into your day-to-day reading of practical prose. In one of the books you have chosen from your Reading Journal, and have been practicing with, pick a passage you have not yet read — a chapter or piece of a chapter that seems to form a sensible unit, six to ten pages long.

Pre-read it quickly.

Read the passage very fast, pushing your speed to the point where it feels distinctly dangerous.

Close the book; in your Reading Journal, jot down in summary form all that pre-reading and fast thorough reading of the selection have taught you.

Return to the passage and read it a second time, more slowly, to check and add to your comprehension. Remember, this second reading is your safeguard, allowing you to experiment with speed on your first reading, even though the material is important to you.

CHAPTER 10

Study and Note-taking, with a Word About Tests

Pre-read this chapter as your first step in reading it. As your second step, before reading thoroughly, list here the questions you expect the chapter to answer.

_____

_____

_____

_____

Study: the word calls to mind late nights spent plodding through piles of books and papers; reading to memorize detail after uninteresting detail; the slow labor of copying passages into a notebook or onto file cards; the last frantic rush to cram a mass of detail into your short-term, rote memory in order to be able to spew it forth on an examination. Drudgery, detail, boredom, haste, confusion. For so many readers study means these and little more. But what is study, really? If you recall in broad terms the viewpoint of this book, you will understand what our answer must be. Study is thorough reading in its most extreme form—extreme in purpose, in subject matter, typically in duration as well, and extreme in what it demands of your reading techniques. In study, your general purpose is to make the materials completely your own, part of your own thinking. The subjects one studies also mark this form of thorough reading off from others: they are serious, they are difficult, and, usually, they include a high proportion of material that is new to you. Further, when the material you are studying is practical prose, the seriousness and difficulty often bring with them an unfortunate heaviness of writing style. Then too, studying often differs from other serious reading in its scope: not just one book, but a whole subject, is what your study may well be aiming to encompass, which in reading terms means a series of related books, parts of books, articles and so on—in the useful if old-fashioned phrase, *a body of knowledge.* From that characteristic large scale springs the fact that study is normally something you do over weeks and months of repeatedly returning to the subject. For all these reasons, study is thus the form of thorough reading that demands the fullest exercise of your every reading skill.

Study is by no means confined to students. Consider the business executive preparing himself to take over as marketing director of a company he has not worked for before; the lawyer preparing a brief; even the tourist getting ready for Morocco with guidebooks, histories, and maps. Whether they stop to realize it or not, each is reading to understand completely, to make a body of knowledge his own. And each will do so the more successfully, the more he is able to apply a variety of reading skills in an organized way.

When we recognize that study is a widespread type of reading, we begin to wonder why the word brings boredom and drudgery to mind. There are two reasons. At its best, study requires hard work, a struggle with the material, and scrupulous attention to detail. Along this road lie the greatest pleasures of mastery and thorough understanding, but few of us have learned to enjoy work this way. Also, study is for most people the form of reading that brings out their worst habits of undirected plodding through words without lifting their heads to see the importance and overall organization of the ideas. Of course it is painful to read this way. And it is unnecessary, for it should be clear that such techniques as pre-reading and formulation of questions, helpful when your purpose is not so thorough, become indispensable when you study.

The fundamental problem in study is *ordering:* that is, getting your priorities straight, defining your specific purposes, defining the subject matter you are studying so that you can be clear about what is most relevant and what is less important; then allowing the natural structure of the subject itself to create the sequence in which you will attack the reading; and finally, organizing your pattern of work to break the subject into a sequence of manageable units, to maximize your retention.

Study has four basic steps: *Purpose; Selection; Thorough Reading; Review.* This chapter will show how, at each of those steps, you can apply your basic reading skills. In addition to those, however, study frequently makes use of a set of techniques we have not yet discussed: the art of taking notes. Note-taking, as we will demonstrate below, is a powerful aid when your purpose is complete mastery of the material; also, at each of the four steps of studying, note-taking can amplify the effectiveness of your other reading skills.

The four basic steps are always necessary in study. To be sure, for the student taking a course with a prescribed reading list some of the steps seem to be accounted for in advance. The first step, *purpose,* means the quizzes and exams you will take. The second step, *selection of materials,* is taken care of by the reading assignments. But even with such guideposts, study is not so simple. Even for the bare minimum of achievement on examinations, successful study demands distinguishing the most important materials and organizing your work around them. To get more than that bare minimum from a course, some of the most important reading will be outside the required list. Not only selection but also purpose must concern the student. Though it is not easy to bear this in mind when the books are unread and the exam two days off, still it is true that exams are only a measure of accomplishment, that the main objective of the accomplishment lies in its use and enjoyment later. Thus, even for the student whose work is most likely to be specified in advance, all four steps in studying are important. They must necessarily be even more so for every serious general reader who must study without the directives of an instructor or required-reading list.

Why Clear Purpose Is Important

The more clearly you bear your purpose in mind, the more accurately you will select your materials and the more easily you will master them. To show why, let us continue the example of our college student, taking a course in European history. If he is studying merely to pass an exam, how can he tell which details are important and which are not; which facts he is likely to be quizzed about and which not? By outguessing the instructor? by rote memorizing? But if he makes it his purpose to know the trends of development in each period he studies, and to organize the dates and persons around those, why then, by stating his purpose even as simply as this, he has set up a standard for selecting what he will read, what he should take notes about, and what he must memorize.

Once again, what is true for the college freshman is equally true for the graduate student, the scholar, the business or professional man. Lack of clear purpose in thorough reading always makes for confusion, extra work, misdirection of attention, and that *anxious uncertainty about detail* that brings out the worst reading habits.

For example, most executives believe their jobs require a great deal of reading. The worry that "this might be *important*" dominates the reading of many men, driving them to try to master completely almost everything they start to read. This is one instance of what we mean by anxious uncertainty about detail. We cannot repeat too often that the most important cause of this confusion — with the college student as with the executive — is lack of clearly understood *purpose* in reading.

Selecting and Ordering the Materials for Study

How can you determine which materials are the basic ones with which an extensive study project begins, and around which the other reading is organized? How can you plan ahead in study to break the work to be done into manageable units? How, when you come to the readings beyond the basic materials, can you know which ones are relevant? When the problems of selecting materials and then putting them in sequence are put that way, the answer by now should be obvious: to choose and order the materials for study, you pre-read and formulate questions. But in study, you apply pre-reading and questions with one important difference.

In study, you pre-read carefully, with detailed notes, and then formulate questions, again in writing, *not just for one work but for many, perhaps all, the works you will be studying, before you do any extensive thorough reading.*

In other words, when you plan to read thoroughly a whole series of related materials, what you do first is survey them all, map out the entire territory ahead of you. In fact you pre-read and formulate questions for the body of knowledge as if it were a single, large, multi-volume work.

Such an approach is important even in subjects like mathematics or foreign languages, which do not at first seem likely to yield much to normal reading techniques. When an adult begins study of a new foreign language, for example, he will find it invaluable to learn first of all the general features of the language, so that even before settling down to learn the present tense indicative mood of the first conjugation of verbs, he knows: how many conjugations the language has, all told; whether other moods than the indicative are going to be important; how verbs are used in the typical word-order patterns in the sentence; how the vocabulary of the new language relates, if at all, to English; and so on. The point here is the same as in other instances of pre-reading: to know the overall structure of something allows the details to be learned and remembered more easily.

In selecting and ordering works to be studied, then, careful pre-reading over much of the body of knowledge lets you know where to begin, which parts of the subject are most important and basic, which individual works are therefore most important, which are useful only in part, and which are irrelevant to your purpose. What you learn from pre-reading is sharpened by the questions you formulate, as discussed in Chapter 7. To review, these are the master questions (in addition to the question of purpose) you ask after pre-reading but before thorough reading:

What is the thesis or problem here?

What is the main sequence of ideas?

What particular information or ideas will you be hunting for as you read this work thoroughly?

What you learn from pre-reading allows you to sketch preliminary answers to these questions. You are then able to relate each work to the rest of your study, and to locate the parts you must master. For example, when you use the last of the above questions, you set up a list of particular things you expect the work to tell you; thus you measure what the work may contain that relates to your purpose. Further, pre-reading has given you a map of the work's organization; in effect you match your list of particular things to look for with this map to pinpoint the relevant passages.

To this point we have developed the ways that your reading skills can organize your attack on a whole body of knowledge, as well as on the individual works in a study project. A related question is how to discover additional works on your subject, whose titles and authors are not now known to you: this question is taken up in Chapter 11, on research.

Thorough Reading in Study

At the same time that pre-reading and formulation of questions help you order the materials you must master, they prepare you to read thoroughly the materials you *do* select. Indeed, this is still the most important function of these techniques. They prepare you for studying just as for any thorough reading: they sharpen your comprehension, allow full use of your best speeds, and give you a way to measure how well you are getting what you need. Because these benefits are perhaps more important in study than at any other time, you will want to use the techniques carefully and thoroughly. You should write out your pre-reading analysis and your questions; then when you come to read thoroughly you should add the answers. Used this way, these important techniques are built right into your note-taking.

What about reading speeds in study? The skilled reader, of course, takes more time to master material completely than he requires when less complete comprehension is adequate to his purpose. He is likely, however, to need less time for complete mastery than the average reader, because he uses flexibility of speed as one of his tools for comprehension. As we have pointed out from the beginning, the skilled reader is *in tension* with his book. His highest comfortable speed is one way he maintains this tension to keep in control of the reading process rather than submerging himself passively in the words.

Skimming is a case in point. At first it might seem to have little place in studying, once you have pre-read the material. Actually, however, it can be very useful, and serves as an excellent example of the way speed and flexibility should be applied to studying.

You skim during study in two different situations. First, when you have your purpose clearly in mind you will discover in almost every work an occasional passage that is less relevant than the rest, or one where the material is already completely familiar to you. Often such passages can be skimmed. This can be true even of an assigned text in a college course—though, of course, this example dramatizes how, when you skim in study, you must know very accurately what your purpose is, and must watch carefully for the point where thorough reading begins again.

Secondly—and here is a paradox—skimming is used in study when the material becomes unusually difficult. This is precisely when most readers feel they must slow down. In difficult passages, the skilled reader will sometimes skim through what he has already read to review it quickly and then pick up the thread. Again, he will skim ahead of himself to guide his thorough reading. Thus, the skilled reader studies difficult material the way a combat patrol moves through enemy territory: scouts stay out ahead of the main concentration, while a rear guard keeps watch on the terrain just crossed.

At the other extreme from skimming, when you study you will also be using, almost constantly, your ability to pick out the key or topic statements in paragraphs and longer passages. This is still another technique that grows in importance with every increase in the difficulty or unfamiliarity of your reading material. When a passage is really difficult, or when you must master its details completely, no insight is more valuable than seeing clearly the relation of the skeleton of key statements to the flesh and blood of details that develop the author's thought.

Review

What makes effective review? What you want is to replace confusion and uncertainty at this last stage of the process of study with a sure, simple set of steps that will meet two objectives:

To assess how well you have mastered and retained the material.

To reinforce your memory of any parts or points which you discover you have retained imperfectly.

There is such a procedure and it springs directly from the techniques you have already learned. When you come to review, the first question is how long ago you read the material thoroughly. Obviously, what you read last week will be fresher in your mind than what you read three months ago; and the thoroughness of your review should vary accordingly. Note, however, that this same point applies to your *first* reading of a book from start to finish: when you put it down, the first chapters are likely to be less clear in your mind than the last. For example, right now you should be able to give from memory an accurate outline of our Chapter 9, Concentration and Memory, but you would find it much more difficult to do so for Chapter 1, the introduction. This suggests that in study *your first review of a work should be made immediately after you have finished reading it thoroughly.* And how do you do this? Simple enough: *you pre-read it all over again.*

Later reviews of the material will also start with pre-reading. This sets up for you the general content and overall organization of the work. Then, as may seem necessary, you will perhaps formulate your questions again. This time, of course, your immediate answers based on pre-reading will be more accurate and more complete; you are using the questions to help you reconstruct the details of the work in your mind. And finally, you may select some passages to read thoroughly again. This thorough reading can be done at a higher speed than the first time.

The Art of Taking Notes

Note-taking, properly done and not overdone, can be so helpful at every step that study itself can be redefined as *thorough reading with pen in hand.*

Why take notes? There are three reasons: to learn, for reference, and to keep you thinking. First, *to learn*: notes, well taken, are marvelously effective when you wish to master material completely. On the simplest level, this is because you are calling in another set of skills—another set of trained muscles, another mode of thinking—when you write as well as read. But more important, note-taking obliges you to put new facts and ideas into your own words, which is a giant step toward making them into your facts and your ideas.

Second, notes are *for reference.* When you study a subject, you will usually find that from each source you will want to pull out certain essentials, and that no one source gives you every one of the essentials. (After all, you cannot expect that an author's purpose in writing will become a summary of those key ideas and facts that are most relevant to your purpose.) Further, notes stand ready to remind you of exactly which article or book provided which fact, and of where to look for more complete treatment of each aspect of your subject.

Third, note-taking *keeps you thinking.* Your notes are the place to maintain a running commentary on your reading. Here you collect comparisons between authors; here you raise questions and objections; here you seize and preserve your own thoughts, formulations, and flashes of insight, some of which will later prove invaluable. Here you hammer your own ideas into shape by arguing with the author or by adding your observations to his.

The Nine Rules of Note-taking

Those objectives dictate certain rules your notes must follow. First, to help you make what you read part of your own thinking, your notes must indeed be the product of your own thought, working with the author's facts and ideas. It will not do merely to transcribe or abbreviate the author's exact words. The person who takes notes in that automatic fashion is like those stenographers who can type out pages of dictation yet be unable, when finished, to tell you anything about what those pages say. You cannot simply regurgitate; you must process, put the material through your own mind. The foremost rule of note-taking is, therefore:

A note should capture the original author's point, but *in your words, not his.*

The one exception is where you transcribe into your notes a direct quotation from your author because it is so central to his thesis and so well phrased that you may want to quote it later (of course, attributing it to him), for example, when you come to write a paper or report based on your reading.

If your notes are to be convenient for reference, you must be able to find the note you are looking for, and all your others on the same subject, even a year or more after you made them. This means that:

You must keep your notes always in the same way.

The subject of each note must be clearly labeled.

The many ways to keep notes all reduce to variations of two basic systems: *file cards* and *notebooks.* Each system has its advantages. The user of file cards — 3 x 5, 4 x 6, even 5 x 8 — puts one note on each card. The corners of the card carry labels or indexing. Here is one example:

Paper?   Call number *BAR*
                                                 808.82

Baranger, M.S., and David B. Dodson, *Generations*: An Introduction to Drama. Harcourt Brace Jovanovich, 1971.

Anthology of seven plays, each with the theme of the interrelationships or conflicts between generations. Includes Hansberry's *A Raisin in the Sun*, Miller's *All My Sons*, Arrabal's *Picnic on the Battlefield* (Barbara Wright's trans.), also *Ghosts*, *Miser*, *Romeo and Juliet*, *Antigone* -- in that order.

Brief introductions; also questions on each play. Paperback.

Possible paper -- "Generation gap" -- contrast in dramatist's treatment.

The advantage of file cards is that you can sort your notes quickly into groups, each group dealing with one aspect of the subject. The disadvantage is that in any extensive study or research project the pile of cards quickly grows large and unwieldy. Cards make it easy to compare several authors' statements about one fact. On the other hand, they also tend to break down the connections within the series of statements any one author may make on a group of closely related matters.

Notebook users put their notes one after another right down the page. Labels and indexing go into a wide margin reserved for them at the side of each page. A notebook entry might read the same as the sample file card shown above; the only difference would be the placing of the labels in the margin, not in the corners. With a notebook, it is true that sorting out or pulling together all references to a single topic is not so quick and automatic as with file cards, though the job can be done just as accurately. The advantages of notebooks are several. They are considerably more compact and portable than file cards. They are in some ways more flexible, so that there is no physical limitation imposed on the length of your note on one fact or on a group of related topics; similarly, there is always space for your own analysis or commentary. Finally, if you are reading extensively in any one book, you can maintain in your notes the overall sequence and organization of the author's discussion.

Modern note-taking instruction often advocates the use of file cards rather than notebooks. From the last two paragraphs you will gather that this author dissents. The basic reason is that notebooks permit you to keep an eye on the organization of what you read; and it is from their organization that facts derive so much of their significance. But for the success of your note-taking, what is far more important than the system you choose is the consistency and skill with which you use it.

Several further rules follow from the second objective in taking notes, that they be an efficient reference tool. As we said, you take notes for reference because no one author is likely to give you all the essentials demanded by your purpose in studying, while every author gives you some information that is less than essential. Therefore:

> Your note-taking must be selective, choosing the points that are potentially relevant to your purpose.

Clearly, the accuracy with which you select relevant points springs from your purpose, and from what pre-reading has told you of the overall content and organization of the work you are reading. As your note-taking proceeds, the reading skills you will call on are the ability to distinguish main ideas and to summarize.

You must not only be able to find your note later, you must be able to understand it when you find it. A lone word, date, name, or single phrase may seem loaded with significance now when you make the note. But will it be able, six months from now, to remind you of the complete context from which you took it? You don't want to be caught like the man who writes down telephone numbers without putting names next to them because, of course, he *knows* his friends' *names*. So:

> Each note must be complete enough to be intelligible later.

Specifically, if notes are to be useful for reference, you must be able, from the note, to locate quickly its exact source. When you read the note later, you may decide you need a fuller discussion of the topic, or you may simply wish to check your accuracy. For most students, the most frequent single demand they make on their notes is to be able to cite from them in the footnotes or bibliography to a research paper. For these reasons, then:

> Every note must include *the author and title of the work, the place of publication, publisher and date, and the page number.* If you have made the note at the library, include the library call number as well.

There is no substitute for this orderly habit that will allow you to make full quick use of the note later; the extra time it takes at the moment of making the note will be saved many times over. Suppose you have jotted down in your notes a quotation about the sloppy habits of symphony orchestras in Paris in the nineteenth century, with no more than the reference:

Berlioz Memoirs

—then months later you want to use the quotation in a paper on the habits of Paris musicians today. You would need to return to the library, look up the book in the card catalogue, fill out the call slip, wait for the book, and skim through hundreds of pages to find the place. But if your note included the reference like this:

> Hector Berlioz, *The Memoirs of Hector Berlioz,*
> tr. and ed. by David Cairns. New York:
> Knopf, 1969. p. 82. Call number: B45-781

—then you would be fully prepared to cite the work in footnote or bibliography, or to get it from the library stacks for checking or amplification with the least work and delay.

Another rule, just as simple, just as indispensable:

> Always use ink; write on one side of the paper only.

Silly? Then wait until you must try to decipher the dull grey smudge that is all that remains when your penciled pages have pressed together for several months; or until you have fingered three times through a box of three hundred file cards, only to discover—at last—that the reference you want is on the back of the second card in the box.

The next rule for the mechanics of note-taking springs from two of the objectives we discussed above, namely that notes are both for reference and to keep you thinking. It is clearly important to:

> Distinguish in your notes between what the original author says in his own words, what you have put into your own summary and paraphrase, and what you add by way of comment or development of your own.

The direct quotations, of course, are set off by quotation marks. You will find it very useful for finding such quotes later to signal their presence in the margin of your note with a large \!!/ —the typesetter's sign for quotation marks, which you met in Chapter 5. To set off your own comments, you might want to use ⌜ square brackets so that it reads clearly as an editorial addition ⌝, or ✳ a pair of asterisks, at beginning and end ✳, or simply / slashes like this around your remarks /. Asterisks and slashes have the advantage that they are found on the standard typewriter keyboard.

From the need to use notes for ready reference and to deepen understanding comes the final rule:

> Use notes on your notes—signs and words in the margins to index your work.

Thus, if you are reading widely about the life and career of a modern statesman, you will find yourself putting single words or brief phrases in the margin of your notebook or at the corners of your cards: *education, early politics, U.N. peacekeeping mission, journalism,* and so on. These topical signals not only let you find your place quickly, they enable you to sort the material later. For example, if you are reading and taking notes for a research paper, you would sort the annotated cards, as you work, into the various topics within the paper; before writing, you would put each group of cards into sequence. Notebooks can be used just as effectively to sort ideas. With topical signal-words in the margins, you can find related materials quickly, while just before writing you run through the entries for each topic, numbering them in the margins to show the sequence in which you want to use them. For example, *early politics 1, early politics 2, early politics 3;* and if you left something out, then *early politics 2A, 2B,* and so on. Besides words and brief phrases, you will also use signs in the margins of your notes to indicate main ideas, details, questions, and so forth. The best system for this is the same you use for marginal notes in the books, suggested in Chapter 5 and reviewed below.

Taking Notes in the Four Steps of Study

Note-taking in study starts with the first step, the definition of your purpose. Because awareness of purpose is so important to study, perhaps the best way to start most study projects is to write out a description of what you believe your purpose should be. This becomes your first note in the project. It can be brief. It will certainly be no more than a first rough approximation of what that study project means to you. Therefore this first note will need expansion and revision from time to time. Nonetheless, this first note is valuable because it fixes your purpose clearly in mind.

As you study you will continue making notes about purpose. This happens as part of your formulation of questions, at least once for every book and article you pre-read. It also happens, for example, whenever you detect a new subsidiary purpose that you should chase down within the subject. For a college student taking a course in European history, such a subsidiary purpose might be to master in some detail the lives of certain key figures he becomes interested in. Or, on a simpler level, he might decide to pull out from his readings and set down in notes a chronology of the main events in each period. Such plans for action within areas of a subject can be extremely valuable. They organize your work and, when completed, help you measure your accomplishment and progress. Each such plan should be noted when it is conceived.

Note-taking becomes intensive during the second step of study, the selection and ordering of materials. Selection begins by pre-reading a whole series of related works before reading thoroughly to any extent. For each work, you will want to write out in full your basic pre-reading analysis. Beginning with author, title, and publication information, this account will summarize everything pre-reading tells you about the subject and organization of the work. Move from there right into the questions you formulate, and the preliminary answers you may be able to sketch in from your pre-reading. Here you will also record your assessment of the work's value to your purpose in studying.

By this process you take fairly extensive notes even before you begin to read thoroughly. The benefit of this is to make conscious and explicit the reasons for deciding whether or not the work merits thorough study. Thus there is far less chance for error, laziness, or half-formed impressions to drive you away from the material you need. At the same time, if you do decide to read thoroughly, you have laid the best possible foundation for maximum comprehension at an efficient speed.

Thorough Reading May Call for Outlining

The points you will need to observe when taking notes during thorough reading have been covered by the nine rules. One form of note-taking not yet discussed, however, is the *outline*. This is the most complex form of note-taking, and the most troublesome. Outlining, but for quite different purposes, is an essential step in writing; in reading, even in most studying, there is rarely reason for it. Only where you must learn every detail, without fail, is outlining worth the time it takes.

Your aim in outlining is to construct a diagrammatic skeleton of the organization of the selection; within this skeleton you place each topic and detail in its proper sequence and relative importance. Sequence is shown by letters and numbers before the headings. Relative importance is shown by position left or right on the page; that is, you indent one step to the right each time you come to an item that is subordinate to the heading immediately before. The pattern of sequence and relative importance might look like this:

I. _____
    A. _____
    B. _____
        1. _____
            a. _____
            b. _____
                (1) _____
                (2) _____
            c. _____
        2. _____
    C. _____
II. _____

... and so on.

In the diagram, indentations from the left margin show the relation between major and minor topics and details. The farther a topic is indented from the left, the more subordinate it is. Topics of equal importance have the same indentation. If you read just the headings of major rank (I, II; and A, B, above) you should get the broad organizational pattern of the work. As you move to the right you reach progressively finer details.

Outlining calls on two groups of reading skills. First, to outline efficiently you will need to use every possible means of detecting the organizational framework of the work. Before outlining a passage, always pre-read it with care. Be especially alert for summarizing and transitional paragraphs within the text. A few considerate authors indicate their organization clearly enough to make outlining easy. With most selections, however, you will have to dig for the general plan. Careful pre-reading avoids the frustration of having to revise an outline because the author organizes his work poorly or fails to signal his transitions clearly.

Then, as you get into the detailed statements of facts and ideas, your skill at identifying an author's topic statement will help you determine for each item its proper sequence and relative importance.

Notes Are Essential in Review

Obviously notes come into their own at the fourth stage in study, review. You can, of course, review by rereading your notes. More effective is a technique which in effect uses the notes as a simulated exam, so that you ask yourself questions on two levels. First, without rereading your notes, try to set down briefly the overall organization of the subject or of the particular book or article; its principal points, in the sequence that explains how they develop one from another. Then check your recall of the organization against your notes. Second, for the details, use each of those general points you have just reconstructed as the cue to see how much of the relevant detail you can remember, checking your accuracy and completeness against your notes as you go. Compared to simply rereading your notes, this approach converts your review from a matter of passive recognition to active recall, which is, as you know, a more powerful way to remember.

You not only refer to your notes when reviewing, but you make new ones: lists, skeleton outlines, new overall summaries of the subject. The most valuable final product of note-taking, and indeed of an entire study project, is a full written statement of the core of what you have learned, in which the organization, the selection of details, the comparisons between authors and works, and the language all are essentially your own even while they spring naturally from the works you have been reading. The most formal end product of your note-taking is the term paper or research project. Even where study and note-taking does not have such an end product, however, try pausing as you work, from time to time, to write out in your notebook your own brief essay summarizing what you have learned and what you have thought about it. These essays may be no longer than a paragraph, though sometimes they may stretch to a page or more. Their effect will be to deepen your understanding and improve your memory; as they accumulate over months and years they will become the journal or daybook of your reading.

Notes in the Book Itself

Children are taught never to mark up books; since the markings they would make are not likely to be worth preserving, and since their sense of who owns what is not too well developed, this prohibition is necessary. But for an adult, a well-marked book is a well-used book—when it is your own, and when your purpose does not require notes that must be extensive or that must be convenient for later reference and comparison with other works.

A simple system of marginal notations was suggested in Chapter 5, following our discussion of paragraph structures:

|| A double vertical line—two quick strokes of your pencil—next to a topic sentence

| A single line next to an important detail or illustration

? A question mark next to a statement you disagree with, or want to look up later

Quotation marks (shown here the way proofreaders mark them) next to a passage you might want to quote in a paper you are writing yourself

 A check mark next to a line of print that contains a word to look up as part of your continuing vocabulary extension (see Chapter 8, page 191).

To these marks of emphasis or special attention you will want to add an occasional key phrase or an explanation to yourself; a word of comment, question, or disagreement; or perhaps a comparison with another author. This last sort of notation can be particularly fruitful as a way to develop your own thinking on a subject.

In addition to notes in the margins, the blank pages at the front and back of a book often prove to be a handy place to put your detailed pre-reading analysis and the questions you formulate. Thus, it is convenient to write out these reading steps even though your purpose may not require a more thorough and formal note-taking procedure. Also, these notes are thus kept right with the work to which they pertain, ready for instant reference and review whenever you pick up the book again.

Two points of advice are pertinent here. Underlining of sentences or phrases is not a good practice: it takes too much time, and adds unnatural emphasis which can seriously impede your comprehension at any rereading. Also, whenever you find your notes in any book becoming unusually heavy — especially if you have many questions or comparisons with other authors — this is a signal that you have work to do in pursuing these thoughts, and you should transfer the notes into your regular notebook or file card system.

Cramming and Tests

For most users of this book, the subject most closely related to study is that immediate purpose for which you are studying — the quiz at the end of the week, the examination at the end of the course. Quizzes, tests, and exams are a perfectly respectable, though not a primary, aim of study. If a test is well designed — and some are, after all — it relates closely to the primary aim of study, because it assesses how well you have achieved that primary aim of mastering a given body of knowledge so that you have made it part of your own thinking. Thus, if you have applied your reading skills diligently, you should be well armed with the information and ideas the examination calls for. But what if you have not been so diligent: can your reading skills help during that last rush to prepare for the test? And what about the exam itself: can you read it more efficiently so that you will score better? To both questions, the answer is *yes.*

When lack of industry and foresight have left you half prepared and up against the deadline, the last thing you want to hear is: "Tsk, tsk — cramming is not a good way to study!" What you want is help; and you will get it from a combination of the fastest and the slowest reading techniques. Cramming calls for thorough pre-reading and careful skimming on the one hand. And on the other, it requires that you take the time to write out the most important facts and ideas, in order to fix them securely in your mind.

Clearly, however, cramming (tsk, tsk) is an ineffective substitute for true study spaced out over several months. It is a poor substitute even for the purpose of doing well on the exam next Friday, and is useless for retaining material longer than a week or two.

An essential technique in preparing for exams, one that helps cramming and helps even more when you are well prepared, is to anticipate the questions that will be asked. This is, in fact, a specialized application of the question technique. It suggests first that you find out what you can about the way the examination will be set up: How long will it be? Exactly what parts of the subject are you warned will be included? Will the test ask for essay answers, multiple-choice, or a combination? Then, a week or so before the day, from your knowledge of the subject and the way it has been taught, begin a review of the subject in which you imagine that you are the examiner preparing the questions. Set down in writing as many of these hypothetical examination questions as you can, together with answers. You will be startled to discover how this approach sharpens and concentrates your studying.

With exams of the long-essay type, where there will be only a few questions, for each of which you are expected to write extended answers, a variation of this question technique can be strikingly successful. If you know in advance that you will be asked long-essay questions, several days before the exam predict some of the questions that may be asked. For each of your *guess questions,* write out a complete outline of the answer; also write out fully the key sentences you would use, including any introductory or concluding statements. To be sure, when you come to the examination itself, you will not often find that it asks exactly the same questions you sketched out. But much of your preparation may be adaptable in part. As a result, your answers will be clearer, more thoughtful and complete, better organized, and better written — each of which counts heavily in the scoring of this type of test.

When it comes to the exam itself, your reading skills have a right and proper place. Reading an exam skillfully is like getting free points. This is because the most important requirement of test-taking technique is *to budget your time correctly.* You must put your effort first into the questions that count most toward the grade, and into those where you are most sure of the answers. You must also leave time at the end to review your work to eliminate obvious blunders. In order to budget your time correctly, before you answer any questions you must take a quick look through the entire examination.

In short, this is yet another application of pre-reading. You pre-read an exam to check for special instructions, to discover how many questions it contains, and to find the portions that will be easiest or most difficult for you. You should then estimate, quickly and roughly, the amount of time you will be able to allow for each section of the exam.

There are two main categories of tests: "objective," which usually means questions where multiple-choice answers are presented for you to pick the right one, and "essay," where you write out your own complete statement of the answer.

Essay exams may have many questions with relatively short answers, or just a few questions where longer answers are expected. All essay questions, however, require you to recall the correct answer from memory; therefore they are usually more difficult than most "objective" questions, where you are merely asked to recognize the correct answer among the stated alternatives. (Some examination-writing committees have developed ingenious devices for objective tests to make mere recognition or elimination of wrong answers more difficult. Making the last of five alternatives "(e) none of the above" is one such device.)

Clearly, your reading techniques will be least useful in an essay exam where there are few questions, each requiring a long written answer. Even here, however, it is vital to pace your work against an approximate schedule. For example, in a two-hour exam with four essay questions, you might allow yourself fifteen minutes for the first and second, and thirty-five minutes each for the last two. You would then have a fifteen minute safety margin for review and in case you ran overtime at some point.

With long-essay questions it is also smart, before you start writing, to jot down a brief outline of your answer. This helps to make sure you put first things first, and omit no major part of the answer. It also gives you a way to measure your progress within each essay. For example, if you have allowed half an hour for one essay, and find yourself by the ten-minute mark much less than one-third of the way through your outline, then you must start immediately to put your case more briefly than you had planned.

Essay exams where the answers are brief—a phrase, a name, or a sentence—can of course include many more questions in the same allowance of time. Objective tests, which almost eliminate writing on your part, can include still more—as many as 160 questions in one three-hour exam that the author remembers taking. When there are many questions, each to be answered quickly, pre-reading comes into its own. On the basis of pre-reading, you decide how far along you should be after each fifteen minutes, taking into account the easier and the more difficult stretches you have spotted.

With exams of the objective type, there are three further points to watch. First, never allow yourself to be stalled by one or a series of difficult questions. Mark the place, skip the questions, and return to them later.

Second, check the instructions to see whether there is a penalty for guessing—that is, whether points are subtracted for wrong answers (rather than blanks) as well as added for right answers. If there is no penalty for guessing, be sure to fill in some sort of answer for every question; you should pick up extra points. If there is a penalty, still, on a multiple-choice test you should do *some* guessing, but only when you are certain you have narrowed the original four or five alternatives down to two, one of which must be right.

Third, you will sometimes face the problem of the ambiguous question, where the wording is such that either of two answers could be right. Often a question may seem ambiguous simply because you do not know the answer. Sometimes, however, you will be right: there *are* two correct answers as the question is phrased. This happens because the pressure of the examination situation makes the alert, well-prepared student extremely sensitive to every word of the question. No matter how skillful the man who wrote the question may be, because *he* knows what he means he will sometimes not realize that there is a second, unintended meaning hiding in his words. For this, the student has only one remedy. From the question, from the rest of the exam, and from his preparation, he must try to gather a "feeling" for what is wanted: "What 'they' meant to ask here was . . ." or "This *could* be right, but I'll bet *that* is the answer 'they' want."

EXERCISES FOR CHAPTER 10

Reading Journal

Pre-reading Application (a carry-over exercise)

Outlining
"Origins of Japanese Literature," from the Introduction to *Anthology of Japanese Literature*, by Donald Keene

Summarizing Application (a carry-over exercise)

Question Technique
"Magic and Science in the Renaissance," from *The Scientific Renaissance,* by Marie Boas

Reading Speed Exercise: Average Level 6
"Taking Notes," from *How to Read a Book,* by Mortimer J. Adler

Reading Journal

In your separate notebook, bring the section on **current reading** up to date, including for each item a brief summary of the content, and your thoughts about it; then bring the **future reading** list up to date.

Next, write out a brief description of your own note-taking practice. When was the last time you took notes on something you had read? What was it, how long, and what sorts of notes did you take? What system do you usually use for taking notes on reading? How often do you do so? Do you ever use outlining? Do you make notes in your own books? Do you make a written record of pre-reading analyses? of your questions? Which methods of note-taking do you think will be most useful to you in the future? Those are some of the questions your description of your own note-taking should answer.

After you have done this, turn to the next exercise in this chapter, *Pre-reading Application.* This is a carry-over exercise, and you will use your Reading Journal.

Pre-reading Application (a carry-over exercise)

In the chapter on pre-reading, we mentioned that some books nowadays offer two tables of contents, the first a short skeleton of the parts and chapters only, the second much more detailed about the sections or other divisions within the chapters. Pre-reading such a book can be complicated, but fun, particularly when the rest of the prefatory material is equally elaborate. There are other kinds of tables of contents as well that are unusually interesting to pre-read because of their organization, or their content, or perhaps even their tone. A few examples of such exceptional books to pre-read are listed below. All are standard works; you should be able to find most or all of them in your library. Choose three, get them at the library, and write out pre-reading analyses for them.

Asian Drama: An Inquiry into the Poverty of Nations, 3 Vols., by Gunnar Myrdal. New York: Twentieth Century Fund, 1968. A study of the economics of developing countries in Asia, with a three-page "outline of the book" followed by three elaborate tables of contents, one for each volume. Read and analyze them, then pre-read and read the extensive introductory material in Volume I.

Science and Civilization in China, Vol. I, by Joseph Needham. New York: Cambridge University Press, 1954. A unique and famous work of scholarship; the table of contents for this first volume is followed by the plan, in full detail, for the next six volumes. The parts of the work and their logical growth from one to the next are fascinating to analyze.

The Mediaeval Mind, Vol. II, by Henry O. Taylor. Published in several different editions. You analyzed the table of contents of Volume I in the pre-reading exercise in the last chapter; the table of contents of the second volume carries the complex, subtle structure forward — with a couple of surprises.

The American Jury, by Harry Kalven, Jr. and Hans Zeisel. Boston: Little, Brown and Company, 1966. A beautifully organized piece of research; read the table of contents with care, for the sequence and grouping of chapters is not instantly obvious. Then read the useful transitional notes that the authors have inserted between groups of chapters (for example, p. 1, p. 83, p. 191).

The Rise of the West, by William H. McNeill. Chicago: The University of Chicago Press, 1963. Read the six-page table of contents with one question in mind: What makes this history book different in its approach and emphasis from any other you have seen?

Mankind Evolving, by Theodosius Dobzhansky. New Haven: Yale University Press, 1962. A work of science by an eminent researcher and theorist, this book about the evolution of our species also has a distinctive philosophical viewpoint. From the table of contents and prefatory material, what does that viewpoint seem to be, and how does the author develop it?

Outlining

You are to construct a close and detailed outline of the main topics and subsidiary details of the following selection. Read the selection, marking topic sentences with a double pencil line in the margin next to each. Then turn to the answer space on page 262. There you will find the skeleton of the outline, with some of the topics already filled in. You are to add the other topics and details in their proper places. Further outlining exercises in later chapters will require you to work more independently.

This is not a timed exercise. You may refer to this material as you complete the skeleton outline.

"Origins of Japanese Literature"[1]
from the Introduction to *Anthology of Japanese Literature*
by DONALD KEENE

The earliest surviving Japanese book is the *"Kojiki,"* or "Record of Ancient Matters," completed in 712 A.D. It is clear, however, that there were books before that date, as well as a considerable body of songs and legends such as are found in every country. Some of this oral literature is preserved in the *"Kojiki"* and elsewhere, but much of it must certainly have perished, in view of the failure of the Japanese to develop independently a means of recording their language. It is interesting, if essentially fruitless, to speculate what course Japanese literature might have taken if the Japanese had devised their own script or had first come in contact with a foreign nation which had an alphabet. It was in fact the widespread adoption of Chinese culture, including the wholly unsuitable Chinese method of writing, which was to determine the course of Japanese literature over the centuries.

In the Ancient Period, if so we may designate Japanese history up to the establishment of the capital at Kyoto in 794, the important works, such as the *"Kojiki"* and the *"Man'yōshū,"* or "Collection of Ten Thousand Leaves," still show comparatively little Chinese influence, and may with some justice be termed examples of "pure" Japanese literature. The *"Kojiki"* opens with the Creation and continues until the seventh century of our era, moving from a collection of sometimes engaging myths to an encomium of the Imperial family, particularly of the line of the ruling sovereign. In its early sections the *"Kojiki"* has something of the epic about it, but because it was a compilation of different sorts of material and not a single long story (however complex) known and recited by professional poets, it lacks the unity and artistic finish of a true epic and tends to break down into episodes of varying literary value.

The *"Man'yōshū,"* on the other hand, needs no apologies. It is one of the world's great collections of poetry. It can never cease to astonish us that Japanese literature produced within the same century the pre-Homeric pages of the *"Kojiki"* and the magnificent artistry of the *"Man'yōshū."* The latter owes its reputation mainly to the genius of a group of eighth-century poets, notably Hitomaro, Yakamochi, and Okura. The period when the majority of the poems were being written rather resembled the Meiji era, when the introduction of Western civilization led to a tremendous explosion of pent-up Japanese energies in every field. In the eighth century the gradual diffusion of Chinese civilization produced a similar result. Within the *"Man'yōshū"* itself there are traces of Chinese influence which become quite apparent in the later poems, but there can be no doubt of the book's essential Japaneseness: what inspired the poets were the mountains and the sea of the Japanese landscape, and their reactions were fresh, Japanese reactions, not echoes of Chinese example.* "Countless are the

---

*There are examples of direct Chinese influence on some of the poems, but their number is not very considerable.

mountains in Yamato"; "In the sea of Iwami, By the cape of Kara, There amid the stones under sea"; "And lived secure in my trust As one riding a great ship" — these are truly Japanese lines in their imagery and evocation.

If Chinese influence is relatively small in the *"Man'yōshū"* there is another eighth-century collection which is almost purely Chinese in its inspiration. This is the *"Kaifūsō,"* or "Fond Recollections of Poetry," an anthology of poetry written in Chinese by members of the Japanese court. It was to be expected that Japanese poets writing in Chinese should have adhered closely to Chinese models, and some of the verses of the *"Kaifūsō"* are no more like original Chinese poems than Latin verses written by schoolboys today are like Horace. Why, it may be wondered, did Japanese choose to write poetry in a foreign language which few of them could actually speak? The answer is to be found partly in the prestige lent by an ability to write poetry in the difficult classical Chinese language, but partly also in the Japanese belief that there were things which could not be expressed within their own poetic forms. This was less true in the age of the *"Man'yōshū,"* when the poets enjoyed greater liberty than was to be known again in Japan for more than a thousand years, but even from the seventh century there are examples of parallel poems written in Japanese and Chinese which show what the poets thought to be the essential differences between the two mediums.

This skeleton outline refers to the article you have just read. Some topics of the outline have been filled in. You are to fill in the others, including details called for in the skeleton. You may refer to the selection while outlining.

A. Earliest Japanese literature
   1. Earliest surviving book: the *"Kojiki"*

   2. Before that date: _____

   3. Early and important influence of Chinese

B. Ancient period

   1. The time up to: _____

   2. _____

   3. Example: _____

      a. Plot: _____

      b. _____

   4. Example: _____

      a. _____

      b. Influences: similar to the Meiji period because _____

_____

_____

c. But book essentially Japanese, as evidenced by: _____

_____

_____

5. Example: _____
   a. Heavy Chinese influence
   b. Reasons for Chinese influence, and comparison with the *"Man'yōshū"*

   (1) _____

   (2) _____

   (3) _____

Summarizing Application (a carry-over exercise)

In previous summarizing exercises you have chosen, from alternatives provided, the best short summary of each paragraph and of the entire passage. This next exercise will help you develop your skill in summarizing in two ways. It asks you to write your own brief summaries, and it works with material from your day-to-day reading.

Take one of the textbooks you are currently reading and that you have pre-read from your Reading Journal. Select the next complete chapter you have not yet read.

1. Pre-read the chapter; write out your pre-reading analysis.
2. Write out the questions you will keep in mind while reading the chapter thoroughly.
3. Read the chapter thoroughly. As you read, pause after each paragraph to write out a brief, one-sentence summary of it. (When paragraphs are very short you will sometimes want to treat two as one.)
4. When you come to the end of each section of the chapter, stop to write out a summary of it.
5. When you finish reading the chapter thoroughly, reread your set of summary sentences; then write out a one-paragraph summary of the *entire* chapter, being sure to include the answers to the questions you posed after pre-reading.

Question Technique

As you read *each paragraph* of the article that follows, turn its first sentence into a question. Does the rest of the paragraph answer that question? When you finish reading the article, turn to the answer space that follows it, page 267. There, for each paragraph, write out the question you formulated and then indicate which sentence contributes most to the answer. In addition, if you decide that a paragraph does *not* answer the question you derived from its first sentence, write out a new question that does fit the information given by the paragraph.

This is not a timed exercise. Of course you will need to refer to the article while you work out the questions.

"Magic and Science in the Renaissance"[2]
from *The Scientific Renaissance*
by MARIE BOAS

A

To the layman, the scientist has always seemed something of a magician, seeing further into the mysteries of nature than other men, and by means to be understood only by initiates. The line separating Copernicus or Vesalius, ordering the stars and planets in their courses and penetrating to the innermost secrets of construction of the human body, from Faust, selling his soul to the devil for the knowledge that is power, was narrow indeed to the popular mind of the sixteenth century. Physician, alchemist, professor all then wore the same long robe, which might mark either the scholar or the magician. And when so much of what was new in science was concerned with the very frontiers of knowledge, and dealt with almost unimaginable problems of the organisation, complexity and harmony of Nature, scientists themselves were puzzled to know certainly where natural philosophy stopped and mystic science began. When problems failed to yield to traditional methods they were tempted to cry with Faust,

> Philosophy is odious and obscure;
> Both Law and Physick are for petty wits;
> Divinity is basest of the three,
> Unpleasant, harsh, contemptible and vile:
> 'Tis magic, magic that hath ravished me.

B

The difficulty was not that there was no difference between natural philosophy and mystic science; but rather that men saw that each rational science had its magical, occult or supernatural counterpart. Applied astronomy might be either navigation or astrology; applied chemistry either metallurgy or the search for the philosophers' stone. Yet at the same time even the most ardent practitioners of the mystic branches knew that their form of science was not as intellectually or morally reputable as the more normal forms. Astrologers were better paid than instrument makers, but even non-scientists in the sixteenth century knew in their hearts that astrologers, like magicians, gazed on things forbidden, though they also knew that not many of them were really in league with the devil.

C

This aspect of the mystic sciences even lent them a certain glamour, because forbidden learning was almost certain to be more exciting and more important than mere licit knowledge. Certainly astrology flourished outrageously in the sixteenth century, along with alchemy, natural magic (the occult form of the not yet invented experimental physics), even spiritualism. As later in the nineteenth century, the natural philosopher was attracted to this last, the most occult of all the magical arts; yet John Dee, hiring a medium to gaze at a crystal ball, became thereby no less an enlightened applied mathematician than Sir Oliver Lodge, three centuries later, nullified his contributions to physics by his addiction to *séances* and table rappings of a not very different sort. In each case it was only essential for the scientist to be aware of the difference between his two fields of interest; for in each case he accepted mysticism as the road only to that knowledge inaccessible by ordinary scientific means of investigation. The area to which magic could be and was applied in the sixteenth century was still very great; it is fascinating to observe the way in which, out of the muddled mysticism of sixteenth-century thought and practice, the scientifically valid problems were gradually sifted out to leave only the dry chaff of superstition.

D

The attack on astrology by fifteenth-century humanists like Pico della Mirandola had appealed particularly to literary men, already developing that cool and rational scepticism so characteristic of Montaigne; it had far less influence on astronomers. Yet though there was no agonising reappraisal in the early sixteenth century, astrology was already noticeably on the defensive, and was to remain so throughout the century. Society, while it continued to pay the astrologer better than the astronomer, increasingly expressed its disapproval of the "mathematician" who dabbled in the occult wisdom of the stars. And "judicial astrology" (the casting of personal horoscopes, as distinct from general prognostication) was legally forbidden, though commonly practised. It was a most tempting pursuit, especially in its medical aspects, for what physician and what patient would not want to try all means to determine an accurate prognosis?

E

Indeed, many were introduced to astrology by medicine. Jean Fernel, educated as a physician, neglected to practise his profession for some years because he found astrology so much more interesting; as his sixteenth-century biographer explained,

> contemplation of the stars and heavenly bodies excites such wonder and charm in the human mind that, once fascinated by it, we are caught in the toils of an enduring and delighted slavery, which holds us in bondage and serfdom.

Fernel spent his own and his wife's fortune on the construction of "mathematical" (i.e. astrological) instruments, and only desisted under the stern admonitions of his father-in-law and the necessity of earning a living. This was about 1537, when the Paris medical faculty was enforcing the edict against the practice of astrology quite strictly. Indeed, only a year later the Parlement of Paris, at the request of the faculty, publicly condemned Michael Servetus (1509–53), then a pupil of Guinther von Andernach, later more famous as a radical theologian, for giving public lectures on judicial astrology; legal proceedings being slow, he managed to forestall more severe punishment by hastily publishing *A Discourse in Favour of Astrology*, a denunciation of Pico and others and a defence of astrology on the grounds that it had been accepted by both Plato and Galen. The Italian physician and mathematician Cardan (1501–76) was, about the same time, an ardent practitioner of astrology, who cast horoscopes of himself, his patients, and even, it was said, of Jesus Christ; his patients might approve, but his colleagues regarded this as so highly dubious a practice as almost to amount to malpractice.

F

Professional astronomers tended to take astrology for granted; there is no doubt that most of them agreed with the common people that it was a legitimate application of astronomical knowledge, as well as a useful way of gaining a livelihood. They tended to avoid judicial astrology in the ordinary way, preferring general prediction and calculation, though they all upon occasion cast horoscopes for men of importance whose personal fortunes might affect the well-being of nations. So Regiomontanus produced his *Ephemerides*, the astrological almanacs which allowed others to calculate horoscopes and to be aware of such significant events as eclipses and planetary conjunctions; a common form of publication in the sixteenth century. There were general, non-technical works, like the *Prognostication Everlasting*, of the English practical mathematician Leonard Digges, from which a literate man could derive useful predictions. Every eclipse and every comet produced its spate of ephemeral literature, asserting that these heavenly events foretold famine, war and pestilence for mankind; this omnipresent trio never failed to oblige. (The astronomer Kepler, in his first formal attempt at astrology, predicted famine, a peasant uprising and war with the Turks for the year 1595, three events which duly occured.) Even Galileo cast horoscopes for his patron, the Grand Duke of Tuscany, coolly rational as he might be on other occasions.

G

The greatest observational astronomer of the sixteenth century, Tycho Brahe, had begun his astronomical career from astrological interest, and he never lost either his preoccupation with astrology or his conviction that it was true applied astronomy. The nova of 1572 provided him with a splendid opportunity for prediction, of which he took full advantage whenever he wrote about its scientific significance. As, so he thought, this was only the second time in the history of the world that a nova had appeared, he was not hampered by precedent, and was able to offer, for once, a cheerful prognostication. The nova, he concluded after some years' consideration, predicted a New Age—because it followed the conjunction of Saturn and Jupiter by nine years and was reinforced five years later by a comet—and foretold the future for the whole world—because it lay in the eighth sphere. The New Age would be one of peace and plenty; it would begin in Russia in 1632, sixty years after the nova's appearance, and thence would spread all over the world. An enterprising London printer published an English version in 1632 (entitled *Learned Tico Brahe His Astronomicall Coniectur of the New and Much Admired * Which Appeared in the Year 1572*) quite undeterred by the fact that Tycho's original astronomical prediction was patently inexact. But as Tycho had said, "These Prognostic matters are grounded only upon conjectural probabilitie," for the matter was difficult; or, as he was to write later, "it will hardly be possible to find in this field a perfectly accurate theory that can come up to mathematical and astronomical truth." Yet it was always worth trying, for "we ought not to imagine that God and Nature doth vainly mock us, with such new formed bodies, which do presage nothing to the world." Indeed, after his study of planetary orbits, he

> took Astrology up again from time to time, and . . . arrived at the conclusion that this science, although it is considered idle and meaningless not only by laymen but also by most scholars, among whom are even several astronomers, is really more reliable than one would think; and this is true not only with regard to meteorological influences and predictions of the weather, but also concerning the predictions by nativities, provided that the times are determined correctly, and that the courses of the stars and their entrances into definite sections of the sky are utilized in accordance with the actual sky, and that their directions of motion and revolutions are correctly worked out.

But, though he was sure his astrological method was correct, he would not make it public. "For it is not given to everybody to know how to use it on his own, without superstition or excessive confidence, which it is not wise to show towards created things."

For each paragraph of the selection, write out here the question you formulated from the first sentence. After each question, write the number of the sentence, in the paragraph, that contributed most to the answer. You may refer to the material.

A _____

_____

_____ Sentence number _____ No one sentence can be chosen _____
If the paragraph does not answer the question, what question *does* it answer?

_____

_____

_____

B _____

_____

_____

_____ Sentence number _____ No one sentence can be chosen _____
If the paragraph does not answer the question, what question *does* it answer?

_____

_____

_____

C _____

_____

_____

_____ Sentence number _____ No one sentence can be chosen _____
If the paragraph does not answer the question, what question *does* it answer?

_____

_____

_____

D _____

_____

_____

_____ Sentence number _____ No one sentence can be chosen _____
If the paragraph does not answer the question, what question *does* it answer?

_____

_____

_____

E _____

_____

_____

_____ Sentence number _____ No one sentence can be chosen _____
If the paragraph does not answer the question, what question *does* it answer?

_____

_____

_____

F _____

_____

_____

_____ Sentence number _____ No one sentence can be chosen _____
If the paragraph does not answer the question, what question *does* it answer?

_____

_____

_____

G _____

_____

_____

_____ Sentence number _____ No one sentence can be chosen _____
If the paragraph does not answer the question, what question *does* it answer?

_____

_____

_____

Reading Speed Exercise: Average Level 6

"How to do it." The phrase stands for one of the great money-spinners of modern publishing: surely, by now, a how-to-do-it book has been published on every conceivable subject from memorial brass rubbing to home beer brewing. It is pleasant to recall that one of the first modern how-to-do-it best sellers — it was originally published in 1940 — was Mortimer J. Adler's *How to Read a Book.* The success of Adler's book was a sensation at the time, and stands today (the book still sells well) as a testimony to the importance we do, after all, attach to reading. For example, Adler's book is not concerned with reading speed, nor to any great extent with practical prose. Rather, he writes of that other and most important fraction of the reading we do, those few major works of thought, reasoning, investigation, and literature, which he was one of the first to call the "great books." Anyone writing today about reading is in Mortimer Adler's debt; and at many points his interests intersect with those of a book like this one.

Note-taking is one such concern we share with him. The next article is drawn from Adler's book, from the passage where he discusses how he takes notes. The difficulty of content is about average; the style is relaxed, almost conversational. Skilled readers read the selection at the speeds they use for material of a factual nature, popularly written.

You are to read the selection against time. Follow your instructor's directions in class, or the Instructions for Timing on page 474.

Before reading, practice with the Eye Movements in Reading exercise on pages 54–56.

Do not pre-read the selection; the timed exercises are designed to measure improvements in speed alone.

After reading the selection and recording your time, go on to the ten true-false and multiple-choice questions that follow. There is no time limit for the questions, but it will invalidate the exercise if you refer to the article while answering them.

Begin reading here.

"Taking Notes"[3]
from *How to Read a Book*
by MORTIMER J. ADLER

The most direct sign that you have done the work of reading is *fatigue.* Reading that is reading entails the most intense mental activity. If you are not tired out, you probably have not been doing the work. Far from being passive and relaxing, I have always found what little reading I have done the most arduous and active occupation. I often cannot read more than a few hours at a time, and I seldom read much in that time. I usually find it hard work and slow work. There may be people who can read quickly and well, but I am not one of them. The point about speed is irrelevant. I am sure that is a matter on which individuals differ. What is relevant is activity. To read books passively does not feed a mind. It makes blotting paper out of it.

By my own standards of good reading, I do not think I have read many books. I have, of course, obtained information from a large number. But I have not struggled for enlightenment with many. I have reread some of those quite often, but that is somewhat easier than the original reading. Perhaps you will get my point if I tell you that now I probably do not read to understand more than ten books a year—that is, books I have not read before. I haven't the time I once had. It always was and still is the hardest work I do. I seldom do it in the living room in an easy chair, largely for fear of being seduced into relaxation and eventually sleep. I do it sitting up at my desk, and almost always with a pencil in hand and a pad at the side.

That suggests another sign by which to tell whether you are doing the job of reading. Not only should it tire you, but there should be some discernible product of your mental activity. Thinking usually tends to express itself overtly in language. One tends to verbalize ideas, questions, difficulties, judgments that occur in the course of thinking. If you have been reading, you must have been thinking; you have something you can express in words. One of the reasons why I find reading a slow process is that I keep a record of the little thinking I do. I cannot go on reading the next page, if I do not make a memo of something which occurred to me in reading this one.

Some people are able to use their memory in such a way that they need not bother with notes. Again, this is a matter of individual differences. I find it more efficient not to burden my memory while reading and to use the margins of the book or a jot pad instead. The work of memory can be undertaken later and, of course, should be. But I find it easier not to let it interfere with the work of understanding which constitutes the main task of reading. If you are like me—rather than like those who can keep on reading and remembering at the same time—you will be able to tell whether you have been reading actively by your pencil and paper work.

Some people enjoy making notes on the back cover or the end papers of a book. They find, as I do, that this often saves them the trouble of an extra reading to rediscover the main points they had intended to remember. Marking a book or writing on its end papers may make you more reluctant to lend your books. They have become documents in your intellectual autobiography, and you may not wish to trust such records to any except the best of friends. I seldom feel like confessing so much about myself even to friends. But the business of making notes while reading is so important that you should not be deterred from writing in a book by the possible social consequences.

If for the reason mentioned, or some other, you have prejudices against marking up a book, use a pad. If you read a borrowed book, you have to use a pad. Then there is the problem of keeping your notes for future reference, on the assumption, of course, that you have made a significant record of your reading. I find writing in the book itself the most efficient and satisfying procedure during a first reading, although it is often necessary later to make more extensive notes on separate sheets of paper. The latter procedure is indispensable if you are organizing a fairly elaborate summary of the book.

Whatever procedure you choose, you can measure yourself as a reader by examining what you have produced in notes during the course of reading a book. Do not forget, here as elsewhere, that there is something more important than quantity. Just as there is reading and reading, so there is note taking and note taking. I am not recommending the kind of notes most students take during a lecture. There is no record of thought in them. At best, they are a sedulous transcript. They later become the occasion for what has been well described as "legalized cribbing and schoolboy plagiarism." When they are thrown away after examinations are over, nothing is lost. Intelligent note taking is probably as hard as intelligent reading. In fact, the one must be an aspect of the other, if the notes one makes while reading are a record of thought.

Every different operation in reading calls for a different step in thinking, and hence the notes one makes at various stages in the process should reflect the variety of intellectual acts one has performed. If one is trying to grasp the structure of a book, one may make several tentative outlines of its main parts in their order, before one is satisfied with one's apprehension of the whole. Schematic outlines and diagrams of all sorts are useful in disengaging the main points from supporting and tangential matters. If one can and will mark the book, it is helpful to underline the important words and sentences as they seem to occur. More than that, one should note the shifts in meanings by numbering the places at which important words are used successively in different senses. If the author appears to contradict himself, some notation should be made of the places at which the inconsistent statements occur, and the context should be marked for possible indications that the contradiction is only apparent.

There is no point in enumerating further the variety of notations or markings that can be made. There will obviously be as many as there are things to do in the course of reading. The point here is simply that you can discover whether you are doing what you should be doing by the note taking or markings which have accompanied your reading.

Now note your reading time. Record it below and go on to the questions.

YOUR READING TIME: _____MIN. _____SEC. _____W.P.M. COMPREHENSION SCORE: _____%
(WORDS PER MINUTE FROM TABLE ON PAGE 475.)

Please do not read these questions until you have read the article itself against time. Do not refer to the article as you answer them. Choose the *one best* answer to each question, and enter the corresponding letter in the proper answer space.

1. Fatigue is a sign your reading is not going well, because great books properly read will invigorate and refresh the mind. (T) True; (F) False

ANSWER _____

2. The kind and quantity of notes you take provide a measure of how well you are doing the work of reading. (T) True; (F) False

ANSWER _____

3. At least for better memory, everyone must take notes. (T) True; (F) False

ANSWER _____

4. There are several different ways people take notes, but only one system — complete thematic outlining — is of any real value in the reading of great books. (T) True; (F) False

ANSWER _____

5. What does Adler think about reading speed, and how does his belief compare with what you have learned about speed from *this* book (that is, *The Techniques of Reading*)? (a) Adler believes that speed is irrelevant to comprehension, being merely a matter of individual differences — and that belief contradicts this book; (b) he believes that speed is irrelevant to comprehension of great and serious reading, which does not directly contradict this book because we have dealt primarily with practical prose; (c) he *says* only that speed is irrelevant, but it is clear that he *thinks* speed is dangerous, and so he is in complete opposition to the viewpoint of this book; (d) he says that speed is irrelevant except when it produces an active kind of reading, and so he is really in agreement with the viewpoint of this book.

ANSWER _____

6. What does Adler think about the importance of understanding the structure of a book, and how does that compare with what you have learned from *this* book? (a) He does not mention structure; (b) he does not discuss structure in detail, because he clearly believes it to be unimportant — thus he is in agreement with this book; (c) he clearly believes structure to be unimportant — thus he is in *dis*agreement with this book; (d) his references to outlining indicate that he holds structural analysis to be of great importance — thus he is in agreement with this book; (e) his references to outlining indicate that he holds structural analysis to be of such great importance that he thus goes far beyond the viewpoint of this book.

ANSWER _____

7. When he says that by his own standards of good reading, he has not read many books, the author means to emphasize that (a) really good, really serious reading is a different thing from simply reading for information; (b) great books are hard to read; (c) passive reading may be acceptable for some great books, but not for many; (d) rereading is both necessary and easier than reading the first time; (e) good reading takes time.

ANSWER _____

8. Which of the following is *not* mentioned by the author as a form of note-taking? (a) Notes in the margins; (b) notes on the endpapers of a book; (c) underlining; (d) writing of précis or short summaries; (e) schematic outlining.

ANSWER _____

9. The author stresses that there are two characteristics by which you can recognize whether you are taking notes properly. These characteristics

of good note-taking are (a) quantity and quality; (b) aid to memory, and reasoned disagreement with the book; (c) recording of your thoughts, and adaptation of your note-taking method to changes in your purpose; (d) activity and hard work; (e) quality and hard work.

ANSWER _____

10. By implication from the entire passage, we can conclude that the author would most probably define note-taking as (a) a written record, simple or elaborate, that preserves one's thoughts while reading; (b) a written record of one's thoughts, to serve as an aid to memory and as evidence by which to discipline one's reading; (c) the only proof that one has been reading creatively, not passively; (d) a control over excessive reading speed; (e) a record of one's thoughts to provide a basis for disputing the author's conclusions.

ANSWER _____

Now check your answers, and enter your score on your Progress Profile, page vii.

CHAPTER 11

The Tools of Research

Pre-read this chapter as your first step in reading. As your second step, list here the questions you expect the chapter to answer.

_____

_____

_____

_____

_____

_____

The word *research* calls to mind a great range of activities: the astronomer at his telescope, the businessman surveying the opinions of consumers about his product, the historian investigating the rise of coal mining in England, the archaeologist digging, the mathematician doodling. But all the examples you could list fall into two categories: *library research* and *laboratory and field research.*

Library research, to which this chapter is an introduction, means in broad terms what we do when we find facts, opinions, or evidence for theories, in the written record of man's accumulated knowledge. Research in the laboratory or in the field means, just as broadly, what we do when we use experiments or original observations to determine facts or evidence for theories. Over the past centuries, the facts and theories of the laboratory have emerged to change the world, so that microscope and cyclotron symbolize for many people the most important and exciting kind of research. But think for a minute: however brilliant and original, the scientist in the laboratory or out in the field bases his work on an enormous foundation, built by others, which he learns first in school and then by repeated, almost constant, combing of the written record of other men's work—that is, by library research. The theory of relativity could not have been developed if Einstein had first had to originate the work of Newton, Huygens, Michelson and Morley, Lorentz, and dozens more. Einstein built on their knowledge, accessible to him through books and articles. Or take a case where knowledge is *not* accessible. With great effort we are now developing ways to translate foreign-language scientific periodicals quickly and completely. Some rough translations may even soon be done by machines. Scientists now in school are being trained more and more intensively to read foreign languages. Why? Because too often in recent years, the work of one laboratory has been hampered by lack of the information already developed elsewhere—but published in a foreign language.

So we see that the laboratory—even the laboratory—depends on the library.

Evidently, library research is closely related to study (Chapter 10). In fact, what we will now introduce are the tools you need, and how to use them, to carry out any extensive study or research project, and in particular that step in study and research where you find, select, and put in order the materials to be mastered. As does study or any other reading task, library research starts with your clear awareness of your purpose. In a research project your purpose may be quite general, at least at the start: you may want to know which are the most important books to read for an understanding of some topic. For example, what histories and biographies will give you a good knowledge of the reign of Henry VIII? Your purpose may be more specific: for example, what books and articles will tell you the essentials of what is known about Henry's naval policy? Or your purpose may be very specific indeed: for example, who was Henry's admiral, and what was the exact number of ships for the naval campaign in the English Channel against the French in the spring of 1513?

We can also say (which amounts to the same thing) that library research answers questions, and that therefore, to do a good job of it, you must first know what your questions are. As the preceding paragraph pointed out, at the start of a research project your questions may be quite general. As you proceed, however, they will tend to become more specific. To continue the example, perhaps your quest for books about Henry VIII brings you to read Chapters 8 through 13 of *The Earlier Tudors,* by J. D. Mackie, and the biography *Henry VIII,* by A. F. Pollard. Mackie's excellent survey will provide an outline of the main events of Henry's reign. But it may make you aware of a variety of more detailed questions. Henry's naval policy is not described in detail; you might therefore wish to pursue this topic through other books and historical articles. Again, Pollard's biography, though well written and the standard work, takes perhaps an uncritically favorable attitude toward Henry VIII. It may leave you with the desire to find out why Mackie seems to regard Henry's early foreign policy as disastrous. This question might in turn bring you to read Pollard's biography of Henry's first "prime minister," Cardinal Wolsey, who had a great deal to do with making that foreign policy; and it might take you to such a book as Garrett Mattingly's biography of Catherine of Aragon, Henry's first queen, who was also closely involved. At this point, you would have read four times through the events of the first part of Henry's reign, and you would begin to notice discrepancies in factual detail, emphasis, and interpretation. These differences would raise further questions — and so the process continues.

The broader your purpose and questions, the easier it is to find material in the library that will help you. It is not the big general survey books that are likely to prove difficult to find, but the ones containing the particular fact, isolated detail, date, or quotation. Indeed, once you have mastered the basic tools for finding material that may potentially be relevant to a large-scale project, your problem will often be one of too much material, and therefore of how to organize your examination of it. Now let us see how you use those tools of library research.

Naturally enough, libraries are organized to help researchers pursue their questions. The library contains three categories of research tools:

the card catalogue, which indexes all the books;

bibliographies, which are lists of books, usually related by subject; and

"quick reference" books — dictionaries, encyclopedias, atlases, biographical dictionaries, and so forth.

The Card Catalogue

Standard library practice is to list every nonfiction book in the card catalogue in three ways: by author, by title, by subject. See the typical cards illustrated on page 278, one a title entry, the other an author card.

Starting from the top, cards like these give you the following information:

1. Top right (or top left) is the *call number.* This number, or combination of letters and numbers, tells in what section of the library and on what shelf the book will be found. The call number may well be different for the same book in two different libraries. It is an essential number for you to note down when you first use the book. If you have access to the *stacks* (the library shelves not normally open to the public; stacks privileges are usually limited to graduate students only), the call number leads you through the tunnels of shelving to where you will find the book, placed with other books about the same or closely related subjects. Even if you do not have stacks privileges, the call number may tell you that the book is on the open shelves: most quick reference books, because they are so often in demand, are typically shelved along the wall of the library reference room where students can go directly to them. When a book is on the open shelves, the call number will be coded to show that fact at a glance. The most widely used code is the letter *R* prefixed to the call number, but you should check the code used at your library. When the book is not on shelves to which you have access, you need the call number to complete the *call slip* — the printed form you fill out and turn in (at the *call desk*) to get the book brought out for you.

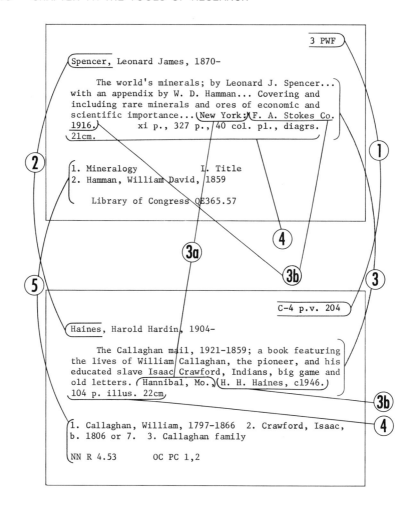

2. The first line of an author card gives you his name and the dates of his birth and death (if dead when the card was prepared). The first line of a subject entry is the name of the subject. A title card begins with the title of the book.
3. The main paragraph of the card copies the information shown on the title page of the book, normally without change or deletion. It will include the city of publication (3a), the publisher, and the date of publication or copyright of this edition (3b), even if the first and last of those three items are not actually shown on the title page. In special cases, certain facts may be added in this paragraph; for example, when the library's copy of the book is known to be a second or later edition, or when the author's name on the title page is a pseudonym (pen name). If the book's title page does not give full information of this sort, the catalogue card will signal the additions with square brackets.
4. The next line describes the physical details of the book: the number of pages of prefatory material, shown in roman numerals; the number of

pages in the main text in arabic numerals; and the number of pages of index and supplementary material in roman numerals. Next on the same line of the card you find details about illustrations in the book: frontispiece, photographs, maps, diagrams, and so on. Last on this line is the height of the book, always given in centimeters.

5. Then at the bottom of the card is a listing which can prove very useful at the start of a research project: it ticks off the other cards in the catalogue for the same book, including the subject headings. These subject headings will guide you to the places in the card catalogue where other books closely related to your interest are likely to be found. Beneath the subject headings, the card carries technical information for libraries, such as the Library of Congress Catalog card number of the book and other classification numbers.

Five Pointers for Using the Card Catalogue Most Efficiently

1. *Learn the alphabet.* Although of course you will say that you can recite the alphabet, our suggestion is not as ridiculous as it sounds. It is likely that you are *not* able to go backward as well as forward, fluently and automatically, starting with any one of the twenty-six letters. And librarians report that such lack of elementary fluency with the alphabet is one of the main reasons students come to them for help in using the card catalogue.

For card catalogues, bibliographies, and all other basic reference works, the rules of alphabetization are simple and uniform. If the first word of a title or classification is an article (*the* or *a*), the location of the entry is determined by the initial letters of the next word. (This applies to titles in other languages as well.) Where two entries begin with the same first letter, letters, or word, the order is determined by the earliest letter that is different. Thus, *Histories of Vanished Empires* comes before *A History of the English Language.* It is probably right here, when alphabetization proceeds beyond the first several letters of the words, that most of the difficulty that the librarians report occurs. Finally, when there is more than one title by an author, the set of cards for that author is arranged alphabetically by title. If the library has books of several categories that relate to a single author, they are catalogued in the following sequence: his collected works, his individual works, works he has edited though not himself written, works about the author but written by others, and (last, or sometimes first) bibliographies of his works. Knowing this sequence is part of knowing how the card catalogue alphabet works.

2. *Learn to remember books by their authors' names* as well as by titles. This habit makes finding books far easier. Some libraries do not make title entries for more routine titles. Even if the title card is there, a slight error of memory may take you to *The First Tudors,* when you wanted *The Earlier Tudors;* indeed, in a large library an error like *The Early Tudors* might leave you inches down the file drawer from the correct card. Remembering the author, J. D. Mackie, avoids the bothersome error.

3. A simple, time-saving practice is to finish each session of work in the library by filling out the call slips you will need to turn in at the beginning of your next session. For an extended project, keep a packet of call slips with your notes, so that whenever you know you will be needing a book, you can prepare the slip, or duplicate slips, saving a later trip to the card catalogue.

4. The subject headings in the card catalogue can provide a ready-made reading list (or rather, pre-reading list) if you know how to use them. The art is to find the right subject headings. Here, the librarians can help you get started. You will want to think up and search out possible variations of subject headings.

Your approach to your subject is based, after all, on your own previous reading and point of view, which makes certain headings seem logical for the books you seek. But the card catalogue is designed to be as useful as possible to all; you must learn to think of subject headings as they might be conceived by the librarian with this broader viewpoint. For example, the naval policy of Henry VIII might conceivably be found under "maritime history," under "naval history," under "British Admiralty," and elsewhere, as well as under "Henry VIII." The best single way to discover the right subject headings is to let one card in the catalogue lead you to others. Read those subject headings at the bottom of the card for each book you find. When you find a new subject heading, go to it in the catalogue. Careful reading of the cards under that new heading will speedily help you discover other material you must examine as you define the extent and sequence of your research.

5. Sometimes your research will lead you to a book that is not available at your library; for example, one of the bibliographies described below may produce a title that you cannot find in the card catalogue. If the book is important to your project, ask a librarian about how to use the *National Union Catalog* (see below). Through the Union Catalog you may find a nearby library that has a copy of the book you need. Alternatively, it is usually possible to arrange what is called an *inter-library loan*. If the item you want cannot be borrowed — as may be true with newspapers and journals — often it can be microfilmed. Microfilms are now so widely used that even these are catalogued and can be borrowed from other libraries by interlibrary loan.

Bibliographies

Bibliographies are lists of books; they are normally arranged according to subject matter, and then by title or author within subject categories. As we have seen, a basic form of bibliography is the card catalogue of a large library. Other forms include everything from the brief list of additional readings at the end of a textbook chapter, to complete multi-volume analyses of particular subjects (for example: the *Bibliography of British History* in four volumes published to date). When you consider all the book lists that have been published, you might reasonably think that what is needed is some sort of guide to the bibliographies available. Bibliographies to bibliographies have indeed been published. An invaluable tool for finding bibliographies and other reference works is:

Winchell, Constance M., *Guide to Reference Books,* 8th ed., Chicago: American Library Association, 1968.

Two other useful books about books:

Besterman, Theodore D. N., *A World Bibliography of Bibliographies, Bibliographical Catalogues, Calendars, Abstracts, etc.,* 4th ed., 5 Vols., Lausanne, Switzerland: Societas Bibliographica, 1965–66.

Shores, Louis, *Basic Reference Sources.* Chicago: American Library Association, 1954.

All of these are normally kept on the open shelves of the library. Five other general bibliographies are important; each has a different purpose, coverage, and origin.

The National Union Catalog, a Cumulative Author List. Washington: The Library of Congress. Issued monthly or bimonthly, cumulated into half-yearly and yearly volumes. Successor (since 1956) to *The Library of Congress Catalog – Books: Authors.*

Two copies of every book copyrighted in the United States must be given to the Library of Congress; the Library acquires many other titles; the total collection is one of the largest in the world. The *Catalog* lists all the books in the Library of Congress; and since 1956 it has also listed newly published books acquired by a number of major American libraries cooperating with the Library of Congress, with a note as to which library has the book. The books are listed by printing photographic miniatures of the index card prepared by the Library of Congress. They are listed by author only, however, with an entry under title or subject only if there is no author. Despite this limitation, the *Catalog* can prove essential for establishing whether a book exists, where it can be found, and the correct details about it.

General Catalogue of Printed Books. London: The British Museum, Department of Printed Books, in many volumes, with supplements every ten years. The British Museum library performs the copyright function for the United Kingdom; its collection too is one of the largest in the world.

Cumulative Book Index: a World List of Books in the English Language. New York: H. W. Wilson Company. Monthly, with yearly and five-yearly cumulations. An index by author, title, and subject, of all books published in English in the time period covered by the particular volume.

Books in Print: An Author-Title-Series Index to the Publishers' Trade List Annual. New York: R. R. Bowker Company. Compiled, as the subtitle suggests, from publishers' catalogues; because these sources are sometimes statements of intention rather than performance, you will sometimes need to verify that a listed title has in point of fact been issued on schedule. Books are listed very briefly, in separate author and title indexes, adding only publisher and price. Bowker also publishes, though not all libraries and booksellers buy it, a separate annual subject index to *Books in Print.*

Paperbound Books in Print. New York: R. R. Bowker Company. Monthly, with cumulative indexes three times a year.

For related research problems, you may also want to consult one of the indexes to periodicals listed with the quick-reference books, below.

Those are all *general* bibliographies. There are so many *specialized* bibliographies that no comprehensive list can be given here. They range from the five-volume *Cambridge Bibliography of English Literature* to monthly, quarterly,

---

268   *Discovery, Exploration, and Colonization*   [3170–

B. THE EARLY EXPLORERS

For Thomas Cavendish, the Circumnavigator, cf. his life in *D.N.B.* (9), for George, Earl of Cumberland, cf. 3501.

(1) THE CABOTS

(a) *Bibliography*

Winship's admirable bibliography (3170) obviates the necessity of any exhaustive list of the voluminous literature on this subject. The work of Williamson (3185) is most valuable; also Deane's essay on the Cabots in Winsor (3278b). Reference should also be made to the bibliographical note in Channing (3270), i, 55.

3170 WINSHIP, G. P. Cabot bibliography, with an introductory essay on the careers of the Cabots. New York, 1900.
An admirable guide to all sources of information on the subject.

(b) *Sources*

Harrisse (3179) prints nearly all the important evidence dealing with the Cabot voyages. Markham prints the documents relative to the 1497 voyage in his *Journal of Columbus (Hakluyt Soc.*, Lond. 1893). *Cal. S.P., Spanish* (867), i, and *Cal. S.P., Venetian* (992), i, contain something of value.

3171 THE NORTHMEN, COLUMBUS AND CABOT, 985–1503. By J. E. Olson and E. G. Bourne. *Original Narratives of Early American History*. New York, 1906.
Includes letters from Italian diplomats in London, 1497–8.

3172 NOTICES CONCERNING JOHN CABOT and his son Sebastian . . . from original manuscripts in the Macrian library at Venice. By Rawdon Brown and Edward Cheney. *Philobiblon Soc., Bibliographical and Historical Miscellanies*. Lond. 1854–6.

3173 AN EARLY GRANT TO SEBASTIAN CABOT, 1504. By A. P. Newton. *E.H.R.* xxxvii (1922), 564–5.

(c) *Later Works*

The work of Williamson (3185) is the standard account. Also valuable are the works of Harrisse (3179–81), Beazley (3174), Dawson (3176), and Weare (3184) are all good.

3174 BEAZLEY, C. R. John and Sebastian Cabot; the discovery of North America. New York, 1898.

3175 [BIDDLE, RICHARD.] A memoir of Sebastian Cabot with a review of the history of maritime discovery. Philadelphia, 1831.
One of the earliest of modern contributions to the subject of discovery, giving occasion for a large number of critical articles, for which see Winship (3170).

3176 DAWSON, S. E. The voyages of the Cabots in 1497 and 1498; with an attempt to determine their land-fall and to identify their island of St. John. *Proc. and Trans. Roy. Soc. of Canada*, xii (1894), 51–112; 2nd ser., ii (1896), 3–28; 2nd ser., iii (1897), 139–268.[1]

or yearly publications like *Art Index,* which set out to list by author and subject all the books and articles published in one specialized field in that period of time. The social sciences and especially the natural sciences are rich in *abstracts,* periodicals whose only function is to provide brief current summaries of all work of significance published in that science. The quickest way to find out if such a specialized bibliography exists that will help your research is to ask the librarian. You will find other useful guides to the literature in your subject in the bibliographies and "suggested reading" lists published at the ends of chapters or at the end of the entire volume in textbooks, in some biographical dictionaries, encyclopedia articles, and indeed in many general scholarly books.

It is important to remember that no two bibliographies, no two reference books of any sort, are organized in exactly the same way. Therefore, always stop to pre-read a work of this sort before searching out your particular reference. The prefatory material and table of contents will tell you how the book has been put together and how you should use it. Pre-reading of this type will make your research much faster and more accurate.

Many bibliographies are *selective*: that is, they list only those works the author considers most valuable for pursuit of your subject. The "suggested reading" list at the end of a textbook is the most familiar example; but you will discover as you pre-read them that even some of the multi-volume bibliographies to special subjects, with thousands of entries, are highly selective. A selective bibliography, especially if it discusses the contents and value of the works listed, is a tremendous help when a subject is new to you. As you become more expert, however, you may sometimes have cause to question whether a book *not* listed was left off because it is indeed not a good book, or simply because it was not known to the editor of the bibliography.

Remember also that *every* bibliography begins to be out of date as soon as published, for new works on the subjects continue to appear. Therefore, as you begin to use a bibliography, make special note of the date beyond which new works are not included.

Quick-reference Books

Collections of facts for ready reference are as familiar to you as a dictionary, almanac, or encyclopedia. But if you are not a professional researcher you will be astonished to discover what a tremendous variety of subjects is covered by all the various compilations. Books of this type—dictionaries, encyclopedias, atlases and gazetteers, language dictionaries, biographical dictionaries, and also the books of bibliography discussed in the previous section—are normally kept on the open shelves in the reference room of the library, for your ready access. Among the most essential quick-reference books, remember, is Constance Winchell's *Guide to Reference Books,* mentioned earlier. Among the most important of the thousands of other quick-reference books are the following:

General, unabridged dictionaries

Oxford English Dictionary ("the *O.E.D.,*" or sometimes from its original title, *The New English Dictionary*, "the *N.E.D.*"), 12 Vols. and supple-

ment. New York: Oxford University Press, 1933. The most exhaustive
and authoritative English dictionary through the time of publication,
citing the earliest appearances and meanings of words and charting
their historical development, with over 414,825 words supported and
illustrated by nearly two million quotations.

Webster's Third New International Dictionary. Springfield, Massachusetts:
G. and C. Merriam, 1961. Authoritative and complete for current American and British English, up to its time of issue.

Dictionary of American English on Historical Principles, 4 Vols., by
W. A. Craigie and J. R. Hulbert. Chicago: University of Chicago Press,
1938–1944, reissued 1959. Corresponds to the *O.E.D.*; covers American
usage up to the beginning of the nineteenth century.

Etymological Dictionary of the English Language, by Walter W. Skeat.
Oxford: The Clarendon Press, 1910. Gives the origin and history of
words.

Origins: A Short Etymological Dictionary of Modern English, by Eric
Partridge. New York: Macmillan & Co., 1959.

Random House, Funk and Wagnalls, and others have issued unabridged dictionaries of considerable merit, in the attempt to capture some of the lucrative
market dominated by *Webster's Third.* Many publishers issue the familiar
desk dictionaries, as well as thesauruses, dictionaries of synonyms and anto-
nyms, and the like. You should know, also, that there are dictionaries of slang,
of which perhaps the most important is:

A Dictionary of Slang and Unconventional English, 6th ed., by Eric
Partridge. New York: Macmillan & Co., 1967.

Dictionaries of quotations

Bartlett's Familiar Quotations, 14 eds. of which the latest is: Boston:
Little, Brown & Co., 1970. Copious and well arranged, but each edition
contains material not found in the others.

Oxford Dictionary of Quotations, 2nd ed. New York: Oxford University
Press, 1953.

General indexes to periodicals

These works can function as indexes to historical events and sources, and
as bibliographies to magazine, journal, and newspaper articles. Their functions
and arrangement vary considerably; careful pre-reading is essential.

The Reader's Guide to Periodical Literature, 1900 to the present. Issued
monthly, but accumulates into one-year indexes, listing authors, subjects, and titles of articles from a wide range of general periodicals.

Poole's Index, 1802–1906. Covers American and British magazines, unfortunately by subject only; essential reference tool for nineteenth-
century periodicals.

International Index to Periodicals, 1907 to the present. Lists more scholarly publications in the humanities, including some foreign-language periodicals.

Index to the Little Magazines, 1949 to the present. Indexes more than fifty of the smaller, serious, usually literary publications not covered by *The Reader's Guide.*

The New York Times Index, 1894–1904 and 1913 to the present. Gives date, page, and column number for the major news reported; invaluable in conjunction with the microfilmed complete sets of *The New York Times* which many libraries now own.

New York Tribune Index, 1876–1909

Official Index, The Times (London), 1906 to the present.

General encyclopedias

Encyclopedias are a problem. They can introduce you to a subject and to the literature about the subject: in effect, they can help you pre-read a body of knowledge. But even the best of them are "canned research," curt, cut, difficult to assess for accuracy and up-to-dateness. Independent investigation of one of the best-known encyclopedias has demonstrated that it is often entirely accurate, sometimes wrong about facts, sometimes sadly incomplete and obsolete; the worst problem is that unless you are yourself too much of an expert in a subject to need the encyclopedia, there is no way to tell which articles you can rely on and which are suspect. The only rule is to use an encyclopedia, if at all, at the beginning not the end of your research; everything you learn from it must be rechecked in sources closer to the original data.

Columbia Encyclopedia, 3rd ed. New York: Columbia University Press, 1963. One volume, comprehensive range of articles which make an advantage of their brevity; usually good bibliographies.

Encyclopedia Americana, 30 Vols., 1960.

Encyclopaedia Britannica, 24 Vols., 1947. Further revisions at later reprintings.

Those last two are the standard works; despite their names, both are now published in the United States. In years past, the *Britannica* was written by the outstanding authorities in each subject, so that wherever the subject itself does not make an earlier view automatically obsolete, you may want to consult an earlier edition, for example, the famous Eleventh Edition, 1911.

Biographical dictionaries

Who's Who. The original of this title; British, issued every year, short biographical sketches of all kinds of important people living at the time of issue, including some outside of Great Britain.

Who's Who in America. Same plan, published every two years. Similarly titled volumes of current biographical data are published for many other countries. If the most recent edition does not include the person you want, earlier editions may.

Who Was Who. Similar, but more selective treatment of notables now dead.

Dictionary of American Biography, Dictionary of National Biography. In many volumes and supplements, these standard and scrupulously researched reference tools give brief biographies of all the principal and many minor figures through the history of the United States and Great Britain, respectively.

Yearbooks, almanacs, current events

The Annual Register; 1758 to the present. A record of events, well indexed, published yearly in England, naturally with British priorities of interest.

American Year Book; 1910–1919; 1925–1950.

Britannica Book of the Year; 1944 to the present.

Information Please Almanac; 1947 to the present.

The World Almanac; 1868 to the present.

See also the listing above for *The New York Times Index.*

Atlases and gazeteers

The Times Atlas of the World, "Mid-century Edition," 5 vols., 1955–1960. For some areas, consult the 1922 edition also.

Rand McNally New Cosmopolitan World Atlas, rev. ed., 1968.

The Standard Reference Atlas. London: George Philip & Son Ltd., 1956.

Historical Atlas, 9th ed., by William R. Shepherd. New York: Barnes and Noble, 1964.

Columbia-Lippincott Gazeteer of the World. New York: Columbia University Press, 1952.

Webster's Geographical Dictionary, rev. ed. Springfield, Massachusetts: G. and C. Merriam Co., 1966.

The Times Index-Gazeteer of the World. London: Times Publishing Company Ltd., 1965.

What Kind of Reading Does Research Demand?

Thus far we have been describing the physical tools libraries offer. Obviously, you read every time you use one of these tools, and you apply many of your reading techniques. For example, you pre-read bibliographies, as we noted, and also every kind of quick-reference book, even a dictionary. The prefatory material, table of contents, and "back-of-the-book" apparatus in these reference works will show you how to avoid mistakes and confusion — how to get far more value from them. (If you have never pre-read your own desk dictionary, do so now; this will prove, faster than these exhortations, how much you may be missing that is useful in such a tool.) For every catalogue card or bibliography page you read thoroughly, there are many you skim; and what else but skimming is your hunt through the pages of any quick-reference book?

So you read as you use the tools of library research. As a result you discover books and articles: where you first thought there was nothing at all that might meet your purpose, you now find there is far too much! Here is where you call in the methods for selecting and ordering the materials, described in our discussion of study on pages 245–47, in particular the techniques for pre-reading an entire body of knowledge before doing much extended thorough reading.

It must be stressed that research reading is as highly selective as any other form of study. You will find that the process works something like this:

Of the hundreds of entries you have glanced at in the card catalogue and bibliographies, you may call for several dozen. Many of these you will return to the shelves after pre-reading and skimming, with perhaps one or two passages read thoroughly. A few of the best and most pertinent you will read thoroughly near the start. This hard core of books and articles should be selected to orient you to the full range of your subject. When you have mastered these you will have further questions to answer, new avenues to explore, until you are satisfied that your command of the subject is reasonably sufficient for your purpose.

Throughout the research process you must take notes. You will be helpless without them. On your first trip to the card catalogue, you should enter each book of potential interest in your notebook, complete with every detail you may need later, including, of course, the call number. Your bibliographer's annotations to his entries are noteworthy additions to your own growing list of material. So are the results of every pre-reading you undertake, even if you then decide not to read that book thoroughly for the time being. And by all means, note every question that comes to mind, every discrepancy or problem you perceive, no matter how trivial it seems. Reputations in scholarship and research are made by clues, followed up; many such clues start as no more than an itchy feeling that your author is somehow in error. Although you may note twenty questions for one that proves productive, if you have failed to note that one, then you are guilty of destroying the evidence.

This alertness to the promptings of your own intelligence, which you capture in notes and then hunt down with the tools the library offers, brings us back to what is for the researcher the most valuable of all reading skills. Awareness of purpose, continuing consciousness of the questions you have set out to answer — it is this above all that gives you control of your materials and accuracy in using them; it is this that keeps your work in perspective, so you can know when to stop pursuing a bypath, or when a newly discovered book is truly pertinent; it is this, finally, that tells you when you may in good conscience say that your research has reached a conclusion.

EXERCISES FOR CHAPTER 11

Reading Journal

Skimming for a Fact—in the Arts

Outlining
"The Need for Currency Reform in Post-war Germany," from *The Monthly Report of the Military Governor*, June 1948

Paragraph Analysis (a carry-over exercise)

Pre-reading
Introductory material and Table of Contents from *Social Class and Mental Illness*, by August B. Hollingshead and Frederick C. Redlich

Reading Speed Exercise—Difficult Level 4
"Whom Does the Learner Imitate?" from *Educational Psychology*, by Lee J. Cronbach

Reading Journal

In your separate notebook, bring the sections on **current** and **future reading** up to date.

At some time in the next three days, plan to spend two hours at the library. There, you will answer the following questions.

1. Where is the card catalogue located?
2. What system of cataloguing and call numbers does this library follow? Do the cards follow the same pattern as those illustrated on page 278?
3. How can you get stacks privileges?
4. Does your library have the *National Union Catalogue*? Where is it located?
5. Does your library have machines for reading microfilm, such as the microfilmed back issues of *The New York Times*? Where are they? How can you learn to use them?
6. In your separate notebook, take a full page to draw a diagram of the reference room of the library. On the diagram show the location of each of the following reference materials discussed in Chapter 11:
   a. *Guide to Reference Books,* Constance Winchell

   b. *Cumulative Book Index, Books in Print,* and *Paperbound Books in Print*

   c. Specialized bibliographies

   d. *The Oxford English Dictionary*

   e. Other dictionaries and etymologies

   f. *The Reader's Guide to Periodical Literature*

   g. *The New York Times Index*

   h. General encyclopedias

   i. *Who's Who*

   j. *The Dictionary of American Biography* and *The Dictionary of National Biography*

   k. Atlases and gazeteers

7. As you search out the items to complete your diagram, examine each one carefully by means of a quick pre-reading. Make notes of these pre-readings in your Reading Journal for dictionaries, bibliographies, and so on. Be sure to examine several entries so that you can note down what kinds of material you can expect to find in each reference source. For example, how does an entry in *The Oxford English Dictionary* differ for the entry for the same word in *Webster's Third New International Dictionary?* Again, how does the *Cumulative Book Index* differ from *Books in Print?*

Skimming for a Fact

Just before each of the following paragraphs, a particular piece of factual information is called for. You are to skim each paragraph to find the one fact. Try to break away completely from thorough reading. Instead, glance left and right very rapidly, stopping as little as twice on each line of print. *Keep clearly in mind the fact, stated at the beginning of the paragraph, for which you are skimming.*

As soon as you find the fact, put a pencil check in the margin next to it. Then go immediately to the next paragraph. When you have skimmed and checked all the paragraphs, record your time in the space provided on page 292, and then fill in the sentence number of each fact in the proper space.

Work for speed. In class follow your instructor's directions for timing. On your own, follow the Instructions for Timing on page 474.

Begin timing here.

A

LOOK FOR: the critical reaction to *Figaro* after its first performance

1   *Figaro* was Mozart's first venture with his most famous librettist, Lorenzo da Ponte (who incidentally provided the libretti for no less than four operas which had their first performance during 1786, the
2 year of *Figaro*'s debut). Although he had had no Italian comic opera produced since *La Finta Giardiniera* in 1775, Mozart had in the

meanwhile worked on *L'Oca del Cairo* and *Lo Sposo Deluso,* each of
3 which he abandoned. He had also composed the music for *Der Schau-
spieldirektor,* a slight piece but sufficient evidence of the continuing de-
4 velopment of his theatrical and musical craftsmanship. It is surprising in
retrospect to note that, in spite of the brilliant libretto and even more
brilliant music, *Figaro* made only a moderate success when it was produced in Vienna, where it had to wait until after the triumph in Prague
5 before being received into popular affection. It was incidentally the
success of *Figaro* in Prague which led to the commission to compose
Don Giovanni for that city.[2]

B

LOOK FOR: who originated the term "action painting"

1   In this climate the Surrealist ideas of the pictorial function of the
2 unconscious and of automatism acted as catalysts. The war years produced a new constellation, characterised chiefly by psychic improvisa-
3 tion and the dissolution of the Cubist pictorial structure. This was
4 the period of Matta's mythical "inscapes." With the help of Miró,
Kandinsky, and Matta, Gorky freed himself from Picasso and Cubism.
5 Hans Hofmann, already over sixty, tried out a number of automatic
methods, including drip-painting, and experimented with an Abstract
Expressionism which already had all the hallmarks of "Action
Painting", a term suggested in 1952 by the critic Harold Rosenberg.
6 Baziotes began to record his romantic legends of magical animals and
7 nature sprites. Gottlieb did his first "pictographs" — panels inspired by
the magical designs of the Indians — in which magical signs, eyes, hands,
heads, snakes, etc., are combined into a cryptic script in separate com-
8 partments of the surface. Rothko shrouded his picture surface in a dim
magical light, through which one discerns a fantastic submarine flora.
9 De Kooning slowly freed himself from Cubism and laid the groundwork
for his Abstract Expressionism.[3]

C

LOOK FOR: the date when French furniture prices advanced beyond the levels
of the 1920s

1   This recovery has been extremely recent because the boom in
French furniture of the 1920s was not repeated after the great financial
2 depression. Nor were prices in the seven post-war years any better than
3 in the later 1930s. In fact, by reason of the fall in money, they were not
4 half as good. Nothing that could be called an advance beyond the prices
of the 1920s occurred before the Cassel von Doorn sale in Paris in 1956,
when a Louis XV writing-table with the popular signature BVRB fetched
5 £20,245, including taxes. Since then the high limits have been set by the
Llangattock table of 1958 at £35,700 and the Powis Castle commode of
6 1962 at £33,000. Only the first was a really exceptional work; the second
would hardly have been a £5,000 piece in the 1920s or before the First
7 World War. We do not therefore know the present-day value of the

kinds of furniture that have been most esteemed in the past — for instance, the Riesener furniture from the Royal *Garde meuble* in the Hamilton Palace sale of 1882: certainly more than £35,700 apiece, but how much more?[4]

D

LOOK FOR: the place where cantatas would have been performed

1   The cantatas, which number over a hundred, about three-quarters of them for solo voice (generally soprano) and continuo only, have
2   seldom received the attention they deserve. Alessandro Scarlatti had treated the cantata as a dramatic fragment, the exposition of the state of
3   mind of a single character at some emotional crisis. It was the chamber equivalent of opera and probably differed little from it in performance; it would be sung by an opera-singer to an opera-loving audience in
4   a private house or palace. Handel used Scarlatti as a model, and although he rapidly assimilated the influence he never wholly threw it off; it can be detected in the many Siciliano movements throughout the ora-
5   torios. Again we find a partial affinity between the older and the younger man: neither was by inclination a reformer or an innovator, both were more adept at expressing the sufferings of humanity and the moods of nature than the consolations of religion, and both had a rich melodic gift and a keen ear for harmony as a means of dramatic expres-
6,7 sion. But there the resemblance ends. Handel's whole temper was far more robust and grandiloquent than Scarlatti's; in this respect his Italian counterpart was Giovanni Bononcini, whose strutting rhythms and extro-
8   vert flourishes also left their mark. Scarlatti's operas were of course subject to the same conventional restrictions as Handel's (discussed at the end of this chapter), but his dramatic impulse was less masterful.
9   Not until the very end of his life, in *Marco Attilio Regolo* (1719) and *Griselda* (1721), did he begin to break out of the narrow bonds which he
10 himself had done so much to forge. Scarlatti's was essentially a pliant,
11 lyrical muse. Historically his relationship to Handel may be compared with that of Bellini to Verdi: in each case the fusion of the intense energy of the younger composer with the lyrical legacy of the elder produced supreme dramatic genius.[5]

E

LOOK FOR: the initial public reaction to Millais' paintings

1   The Pre-Raphaelite phase of J. E. Millais is generally taken to extend from 1849, when he exhibited the remarkable 'Lorenzo and Isabella', till 1856, when he painted 'The Blind Girl' and 'Autumn
2   Leaves'. Pre-Raphaelitism in this context means the minute rendering
3   of detail and the study of important passages out of doors. In this period of seven years Millais, between the ages of twenty and twenty-seven, produced a series of paintings, each of which was of capital importance
4   in itself and a milestone in the progress of the movement. 'Christ in the House of his Parents (The Carpenter's Shop)' of 1850, when exhibited

at the Royal Academy, sparked off the storm which led to Dickens' denunciation and Ruskin's later defence, gaining notoriety for the group.
5 In the following year the Academy showed that they were unshaken by
criticism by their acceptance of three paintings by Millais: 'Mariana',
6 'The Woodman's Daughter' and 'The Return of the Dove to the Ark'.
Of these 'Mariana' represented for the first time a subject chosen from
Tennyson, and 'The Woodman's Daughter', based on a poem by Coventry Patmore, was the first theme by the leading P-R.B. taken from
7 contemporary life. In the following year, 1852, his two exhibits 'Ophelia'
and 'The Huguenot' met favour with the public, and marked the end of
the short battle for recognition which the Brethren had had to fight.[6]

Stop timing here.

For each paragraph enter the number of the sentence that contains the
fact you were to find. (The sentences are numbered in the left margin.)

Skimming time in seconds for all items: _____

A: _____   B: _____   C: _____   D: _____   E: _____

Outlining

You are to construct a close and detailed outline of the main topics and
subsidiary details of the following selection. Read the selection, marking topic
sentences with a pencil line in the margin next to each. Then turn to the answer
space, where you will find the skeleton of the outline with some of the topics
already filled in. You are to add the other topics and details in their proper
places.

This is not a timed exercise. You may refer to this material as you complete
the skeleton outline.

"The Need for Currency Reform in Post-war Germany"
from the *Monthly Report of the Military Governor,* June 1948

Currency reform in Germany was necessary in order to withdraw
excess money from circulation, to eliminate the black market, and to create
an incentive to produce.

The unstable currency situation in Germany was the result of Nazi
methods of finance during the war, which created in Germany an inflated
financial structure. At the same time, potentialities for production were
drastically reduced by wartime destruction. This disproportion between the

money in circulation and the actual output had undermined the economy to such an extent that, except for the purchase of basic food rations, the Reichsmark was almost valueless, resulting in large-scale barter transactions and in the payment of a part of the wages in kind.

Between 1935 and 1945 the currency in actual circulation increased from about RM 5 billion to over 50 billion, and bank deposits grew from about RM 30 billion to over 150 billion. During the same period the Reich debt expanded from RM 15 billion to 400 billion, excluding war damage and other war-connected claims of RM 300 to 400 billion. In contrast, the real wealth of Germany decreased by one-third from about RM 390 billion to 250 billion; her capacity to produce had been reduced to about one-half the prewar level; and by 1946 the national income had been reduced from RM 60 billion to about RM 25 to 30 billion in 1936 prices. This situation is expected to be a long-term phenomenon, as the destruction caused by war can hardly be expected to be overcome in the near future.

There are no reliable figures available on the volume of goods and services that pass through the black market, although it has been estimated at 50 to 60 per cent of production. Black-market prices have been so high, often 50 to several hundred times the official prices, that purchases could not be made with current income but were paid for out of hoarded money, from the sale of property, or out of black market operations. The fact that scarce essentials were readily available to a small minority has had demoralizing effect on the population as a whole.

The abundance of money in the hands of the population greatly reduced the incentive to work, as people have been reluctant to work merely in order to obtain more money with which nothing could be bought. In Germany the primary motive for working has not been the need to meet living expenses but the desire to obtain a ration card. As a result, there has been a scarcity of labor throughout the country despite the fact that at the same time there has been a large sector of hidden unemployment which currency reform will later force back into the labor market.

Similarly, the manufacturer's incentive to produce and sell commodities has been impaired by the inflated conditions and the resulting uncertainties about the stability of the currency and of the economy. There can be no doubt that this lack of incentive has had its share in preventing business from making an all-out effort to increase production and sale of vital commodities.

The spread of barter trade and a growing unwillingness to work and sell for Reichsmarks have threatened a further reduction in legitimate supplies and a disintegration of the labor force. The real danger was not that of a sudden collapse but of a creeping paralysis of the body economic. Currency reform was necessary not only to prevent a breakdown in price controls but also to protect production and prevent economic chaos. In a more fundamental way, currency reform is an essential factor in the reconstruction of Europe and in the participation of Germany in the European Recovery Program (ERP).

Note that some topics of the outline have been stated in the skeleton. You are to fill in the others. You may refer to the passage while outlining.

I. Currency reform necessary for three major reasons:

   A. _____

      1. Caused by:

         a. Nazi methods of finance

         b. _____

         c. _____

         _____

      2. These causes resulted in:

         a. _____

         b. _____

         c. _____

   B. _____

      1. Involves perhaps 50 to 60 per cent of production

      2. _____

      3. _____

   C. Abundance of money

      1. Reduced the incentive to work — new incentive needed because

         _____

      2. Reduced the incentive to _____

         _____

II. Other reasons for the importance of currency reform:

   A. _____

      _____

      _____

Paragraph Analysis (a carry-over exercise)

Take one of the books (*not* a textbook) you are currently reading, and which you have pre-read from your Reading Journal; select the next chapter you have not read.

1. Pre-read the chapter; write out your pre-reading analysis.
2. Write out the questions you expect the chapter to answer.
3. Read the chapter thoroughly. As you read, mark in the margin the principal statement in each paragraph. Do any of the paragraphs have their topic sentences elsewhere than at the beginning?
4. Also as you read thoroughly, mark in the margin each paragraph that contains a definition and each paragraph that has either a summarizing or a transitional function.
5. When you finish reading and marking the chapter, go back to reread the chapter, reading only the introductory, summarizing, and transitional paragraphs completely, and only the marked topic sentence of each of the rest.

How much difference in paragraph structures and functions do you find when you compare this book to textbooks you have previously analyzed in the same way?

How close is the topic sentence skeleton to being a complete outline of the chapter?

From the topic sentences and special-function paragraphs alone, how completely can you answer the questions you asked after pre-reading?

Pre-reading

Insanity — how it arises, the forms it takes, how it is treated — has always been one of the difficult problems in the relation of man to the society he lives in. To focus that problem more sharply for modern American society, to understand better how mental illness of all sorts should be seen as a social phenomenon, a team of researchers at Yale has investigated with great thoroughness just who gets treated for what, and how, in the city of New Haven. They have reported their research in a series of papers and books, whose impact on professional and general audiences has been startling and profound. From the first of these books, by the two senior members of the team, part of the preface, the complete table of contents, and part of the introductory chapter are reprinted below. You are to read these materials as if you were using them to pre-read the entire book. The questions, which are of the short-essay type, begin on page 304.

Preface, Table of Contents, and Introductory Chapter (abridged)
from *Social Class and Mental Illness*[7]
by AUGUST B. HOLLINGSHEAD and FREDERICK C. REDLICH

PREFACE

The research reported here focused upon two questions: Is mental illness related to social class? Does a mentally ill patient's position in the status system affect how he is treated for his illness? To answer these questions we studied the social structure of the community, the psychiatric patients in treatment, the institutions where they are cared for, and the psychiatrists treating them.

Stated briefly, we have found that the New Haven community is characterized by a distinct class structure. Each class exhibits definite types of mental illness. Moreover, each class reacts to the presence of mental illness in its members in different ways, and the treatment of psychiatric patients within the various classes differs accordingly. Successive chapters tell the story of how members of the community became patients, how they and their families responded to psychiatric intervention, and the effects of social class on patients and therapists. The book ends with some recommendations on what our society could do about improving socially determined shortcomings of psychiatric practice. The details of linkages between social class and mental illness can be seen only by reading the book.

Although it is a report of scientific research, the writing is directed toward both a professional and a lay audience. Nevertheless, the medical and social science content of the material has been retained. Its findings, conclusions, and recommendations should be of interest to psychiatrists, psychologists, sociologists, nurses, educators, social workers, public health administrators, lawyers, judges, and others who shape public policy in health and welfare. Persons interested in questions of vital concern to all of us, such as how our way of life affects our health and how we are treated when mental illness strikes, will want to read this book.

The two volumes that report the results of this research are the product of ten years of work. In the fall of 1948 the authors of this volume, who are the senior men, began to lay plans for the ensuing research. . . .

contents

part one • scope and methods

Chapters One and Two relate how a sociologist and a psychiatrist selected social class and mental illness as a problem for research and how the data were collected to test a series of hypotheses which assume that the class system of a metropolitan community in New England is connected, on the one hand, with the distribution of mental illness in its population, and, on the other, with the ways mentally ill persons are treated by psychiatrists.

A reader who wishes to gain an understanding of why we studied the social system and the practice of psychiatry should begin with Chapter One. Readers who are not interested in the necessary details of scientific procedures may wish to omit Chapter Two. However, such readers after studying subsequent materials may desire to return to the discussion of methodological procedures in Chapter Two to learn how we collected the data and our reasons for organizing and analyzing them as we did.

the research problem • chapter one

INTRODUCTION

Americans prefer to avoid the two facts of life studied in this book: social class and mental illness. The very idea of "social class" is inconsistent with the American ideal of a society composed of free and equal individuals, individuals living in a society where they have identical opportunities to realize their inborn potentialities. The acceptance of this facet of the "American Dream" is easy and popular. To suggest that it may be more myth than reality stimulates antagonistic reactions.

Although Americans, by choice, deny the existence of social classes, they are forced to admit the reality of mental illness. Nevertheless, merely the thought of such illness is abhorrent to them. They fear "mental illness," its victims, and those people who cope with them: psychiatrists, clinical psychologists, social workers, psychiatric nurses, and attendants. Even the institutions our society has developed to care for the mentally ill are designated by pejorative terms, such as "bug house," "booby hatch," and "loony bin," and psychiatrists are called "nutcrackers" and "head shrinkers."

Denial of the existence of social classes and derisive dismissal of the mentally ill may salve the consciences of some people. The suggestion that different social classes receive different treatment for mental illness may come as a shock, but to repress facts because they are distasteful and incongruent with cherished values may lead to consequences even more serious than those we are trying to escape by substituting fantasy for reality.

Social Class

American ideals relative to social status are premised upon the "self-evident truth" that "all men are created equal." If our ideals corresponded to reality, there would be no classes in our society. However, students of American society have pointed out on numerous occasions that American ideals and American reality are two different things. More than a half-century ago, Lord Bryce in his astute analysis of our society put the problem succinctly when he said:

> There is no rank in America, that is to say no external and recognized stamp marking a man as entitled to any special privileges or to deference or respect from others. No man is entitled to think himself better than his fellows. . . .
>
> The total absence of rank and universal acceptance of equality do not, however, prevent the existence of grades and distinctions which, though they find no tangible expression, are sometimes as sharply drawn as in Europe.

In more recent years, Myrdal summed up the disparity between what we profess publicly as members of a democratic society and how we act in private life as "an American dilemma." The observations of these discerning Europeans have been documented many times by the researches of American social scientists. Some 25 years ago, the Lynds in their widely acclaimed books on "Middletown" demonstrated the reality of social classes in the daily activities of Middle Western Americans. In the ensuing years a number of social scientists have published extensive evidence to support the fact that American society is stratified.

Nevertheless, the phrase "social class" is an emotionally provoking symbol to Americans. The idea that people are unequal socially is resisted strongly. Even when Americans privately "draw the line" between one another in subtle ways, they do not like to admit it in public. Our reluctance to admit that we discriminate among our fellow citizens is traceable to the doctrine of equality enunciated in the Declaration of Independence. Publicly we talk about equality; privately we practice inequality. A consequence of this conflict in values is that some of the most highly charged emotional issues facing our society revolve around the everyday practices of some members of our society who behave toward other members in invidious ways. The inconsistency between our public protestations and our private acts presents us with deep moral issues.

This is recognized officially in the area of race and ethnic relations. It is expressed by fair employment practice acts and the efforts of national, state, and local governments to end segregation in the schools and other areas of public life. The official efforts of men and women of good will, however, are resisted mightily by other members of the society. Such actions are based upon the traditional conviction that some men are socially superior to others.

Mental Illness

Our attitudes toward mental illness are also a product of our cultural heritage. Historical evidence indicates that mental "disturbances" have been known in all civilized societies. The severe disturbances of kings, generals, religious leaders, and other personages have been recorded since ancient times. Persons who were not important enough to have their mental aberrations written into the human record undoubtedly also were afflicted, even though their ailments and their numbers have been lost in the mists of time. Although man's mental and emotional maladjustments are not new, the public is more clearly aware of them now than in the past, and responsible leaders have become increasingly concerned with their alleviation.

In the last decade mental illness has been recognized as one of the most serious unsolved health problems facing our society. A few figures will indicate its magnitude. The approximately 750,000 persons who are currently hospitalized in mental institutions occupy some 55 percent of all hospital beds in the United States. Hundreds of thousands of other mentally ill persons are treated by psychiatrists in clinics and in private practice, but the number of hospitalized cases increases year by year. During World War II, 43 percent of all disability discharges (980,000) from the Armed Forces were granted on psychiatric grounds, and 865,000 young men were rejected for psychiatric reasons in Selective Service examinations. Moreover, some 16,000 to 17,000 persons commit suicide each year and, according to the best estimates, there are about 3,800,000 alcoholics in the adult population. We are certain that patients hospitalized in mental institutions in addition to those cared for by psychiatrists in private practice and in clinics represent only a portion of those who are mentally ill. Estimates indicate that there are from seven to eight million other Americans who are less seriously disturbed but who could benefit from psychiatric care if it were available.

Social Class and Mental Illness

Is the presence of mental illness in the population related to class status? Is the treatment received by a mentally ill member of our society an effect of his class position? These questions are crucial to the research reported here. They are even more important from the viewpoint of their scientific meaning and their implications for social policy.

Detailed evidence will be presented in this book to support the answers we have reached. If our answers support American ideals of equality, class status should have no effect upon the distribution of mental illness in the population. Neither should it influence the kind of psychiatric treatment mentally ill patients receive. However, the reader should remember that our ideals and our behavior are two different things.

Both social class and mental illness may be compared to an iceberg; 90 percent of it is concealed below the surface. The submerged portion, though unseen, is the dangerous part. This may be illustrated by recalling what happened when an "unsinkable" trans-Atlantic luxury liner, the *Titanic,* rammed an iceberg on her maiden voyage in 1912. In that crisis, a passenger's class status played a part in the determination of whether he survived or was drowned. The official casualty lists showed that only 4 first class female passengers (3 voluntarily chose to stay on the ship) of a total of 143 were lost. Among the second class passengers, 15 of 93 females drowned; and among the third class, 81 of 179 female passengers went down with the ship. The third class passengers were ordered to remain below deck, some kept there at the point of a gun.

The idea that stratification in our society has any bearing on the diagnosis and treatment of disease runs counter to our cherished beliefs about equality, especially when they are applied to the care of the sick. Physicians share deeply ingrained egalitarian ideals with their fellow citizens, yet they, too, may make subtle, perhaps unconscious, judgments of the differential worth of the members of our society. Physicians, among them psychiatrists, are sensitive to statements that patients may not be treated alike; in fact there is strong resistance in medical circles to the exploration of such questions. But closing our eyes to facts or denying them in anger will help patients no more than the belief that the *Titanic* was "unsinkable" kept the ship afloat after it collided with an iceberg.

•   •   •

In sum, our review of the literature indicated that social scientists and psychiatrists in the years before World War II carried on their researches and developed their theories in splendid isolation. When they traveled parallel paths they tended to ignore each other. If their interests took them along the same road, they were careful to take opposite sides. In view of this situation, we desired to bridge the gap between the theoretical positions represented by sociologists and psychiatrists.

Two Research Questions

After several months of preliminary work, the central questions of this research emerged, namely: (1) Is mental illness related to class in our society? (2) Does a psychiatric patient's position in the status system affect how he is treated for his illness?

The first query is related to the etiology of mental illnesses. The psychodynamic concept of unconscious conflict between instinctual forces and the demands of the environment is crucial for many attempts at explanation of most neurotic and psychotic illnesses. Knowing that the different social classes exhibit different ways of life, we conjectured that emotional problems of individuals might be related to the patterns of life characteristic of their class positions.

The second question is focused on treatment. Our observations and experiences with psychiatric treatment led us to think that the kind of treatment a patient receives is not a function solely of the state of medical knowledge which is embodied in the art and science of making a diagnosis and prescribing treatment. Subtle and powerful psychological and social processes appear to be important determinants in the choice of treatment and its implementation. We are interested particularly in finding out whether the various psychiatric treatments patients receive are affected by class status.

Working Hypotheses

The third major step in the formulation of our research plans was taken when we crystallized our thoughts on these questions around a series of tentative hypotheses. Eventually, five working hypotheses were written into the research design. Each hypothesis connected the two major concepts of the research, namely, social class and mental illness, in such a way that the resulting proposition could be tested empirically. The several hypotheses were phrased thus:

Hypothesis 1. The prevalence of treated mental illness is related significantly to an individual's position in the class structure.

Hypothesis 2. The types of diagnosed psychiatric disorders are connected significantly to the class structure.

Hypothesis 3. The kind of psychiatric treatment administered by psychiatrists is associated with the patient's position in the class structure.

Hypothesis 4. Social and psychodynamic factors in the development of psychiatric disorders are correlative to an individual's position in the class structure.

Hypothesis 5. Mobility in the class structure is associated with the development of psychiatric difficulties.

Assumptions

Several assumptions are implied in these hypotheses: First, the social structure of our society is characterized by a system of stratification. Second, individuals living in a given class are subjected to problems of living that are expressed in emotional and psychological reactions and disorders different in quantity and quality from those expressed by persons in other classes. Third, psychiatrists, who are responsible for diagnosing and treating mental illness, are controlled, as members of the society, by its value system. This presumption implies that psychiatrists work with phenomena that are essentially social in origin, and they cope with them in ways that are prescribed, on the one hand, by the professional subculture of psychiatry as a medical specialty and, on the other, by the expectancies, working rules, and values that impinge upon them in their day-to-day professional and lay activities. Fourth, the working rules of psychiatry are practiced in ways that arc connected implicitly with class status. Fifth, mental illness is defined socially; that is, whatever a psychiatrist treats or is expected to treat must be viewed as mental illness. This position is based upon the fact that in our society psychiatrists treat individuals whose behavior would be ignored in a second society, punished by the criminal courts in a third, and in still others given over to priests. We agree with Romano that "the conventional conceptual scheme of disease is not applicable to mental disease." Sixth, the class status of individuals in the society is viewed as the independent or *antecedent* variable; the diagnosis of a patient's illness and the treatment prescribed for him by a psychiatrist are considered to be dependent or *consequent* variables. Demonstration of the validity of these assumptions rests upon a systematic examination of the five hypotheses. . . .

After reading the table of contents and prefatory material, answer the following questions. You may, of course, look back at the material while answering the questions.

1. Though the preface is brief, it performs three essential functions: it tells you the subject of the book, it outlines the findings to be reported, and it defines the audience for whom the book was written.

   a. What is the subject? _____

   _____

   _____

   _____

   b. In one sentence, what is the central finding of the book, to be supported

   by the evidence the authors will offer? _____

   _____

   _____

   _____

   c. In the third paragraph of the preface, about the book's audience, the authors define and redefine those who they think will read their work. The definition grows from a type of *reader* to a type of *attitude* they expect the reader to have. Who are those readers; what is the attitude they are expected to have; and why are they expected to have it?

   _____

   _____

   _____

   _____

2. From the table of contents, which chapters would you read as part of pre-reading because they perform an introductory, summarizing, or conclud-

   ing function? _____

3. What appears to be the relation between Chapter One and Chapter Two?

   _____

4. For additional information about the subject treated in Chapter Two,

   where else in the book would you look? _____

5. What appears to be the relation between Part One and Part Two? (Specifically, if Part One is introductory, can Part Two be introductory as well, in a different way? What is the importance of the word "setting"?)

   _____

   _____

_____

_____

6. What seems to be the relation between Parts Three and Four? _____

_____

_____

_____

7. You will have noticed that the second paragraph of the preface relates closely to the organization of the book as shown in the table of contents. Which chapter:
   a. describes the "distinct class structure" the authors found in New

      Haven? _____

   b. shows how "each class exhibits definite types of mental illness"? _____

   c. describes how "the treatment of psychiatric patients within the various

      classes differs"? _____

   d. tells "how members of the community become patients"? _____

   e. describes "the effects of social class on patients and therapists"? _____

   f. contains the authors recommendations? _____

8. The authors expect their conclusions to run counter to the opinions of many readers—indeed, to be upsetting. Summarize how and why.

_____

_____

_____

_____

_____

_____

_____

9. How do the authors define *social class*? _____

_____

_____

_____

_____

10. How do they define *mental illness?* What do they say mental illness is *not?*

_____

_____

_____

_____

11. The authors clearly have not only research results to report but also a point of view about those results to urge on the reader. What does that

    point of view seem to be? _____

    _____

    _____

    _____

    _____

    Where would you look for extensive discussion of that point of view?

    _____

    Does that point of view seem justified? Why? _____

    _____

    _____

12. What questions would you pose to yourself before reading the book

    thoroughly? _____

    _____

    _____

    _____

    _____

    _____

Reading Speed Exercise: Difficult Level 4

The subject of the next article is the learning psychology of the child. The source is a well-regarded college-level text. The article is on a difficult level of content and style.

You are to read the selection against time. Follow your instructor's directions in class, or the Instructions for Timing on page 474.

Before reading, practice with the Eye Movements in Reading exercise on pages 54–56.

Do not pre-read the selection; the timed reading exercises are designed to measure improvements in speed alone.

After reading the selection and recording your time, go on to the ten multiple-choice questions beginning on page 309.

There is no time limit for the questions, but it will invalidate the exercise if you refer to the article while answering them.

Begin reading here.

"Whom Does the Learner Imitate?"[8]
from *Educational Psychology*
by LEE J. CRONBACH

To say that the child learns by imitation, and that the way to teach is to set a good example, oversimplifies. No child imitates every action he sees. Sometimes he ignores the example his parent wants him to follow and he takes over contrary patterns from some other example. Therefore we must turn to a more subtle theory than "Monkey see, monkey do."

Look at it from the child's point of view. He is in a new situation, lacking a ready response and seeking a response that will gain certain ends. If he cannot reason out what to do, he observes a model who seems able to get the right result. He looks for an authority or expert to imitate. The point is charmingly illustrated by Nevitt Sanford's story of the 2-year-old, initially terrified of a new puppy, who within a few hours was crawling about, barking, and threatening to bite people—and less charmingly illustrated by Bettelheim's description of concentration camp inmates adopting the mannerisms of the all-powerful guards. The child sees other persons attain goals or suffer penalties; the consequences they experience modify his subsequent tries much as the consequences of his own behavior do.

There is a second element at work in this situation. The child may attain his immediate goal only to find that his method brings criticism. "Hold your fork properly," he is told. When he shouts across the classroom to deliver a message, he is told emphatically that such a racket is unpleasant, that he should walk across the room and say what he has to say quietly. Thus, the desire to cope with a situation is overlaid with the desire to act properly. The child gets more affection and approval when his parents like his action. Other adults, and peers, reward some actions and criticize others.

Consequently the child eventually acquires a conscience, i.e., a desire to act in an approved manner, even when no one else is present to judge his actions.

A person who is repeatedly accepted as an example for conduct and interpretations is called an *identifying figure*. Identification is a complex way of perceiving another person, partly rational and partly emotional. The feeling about the identifying figure includes these ideas: "This person knows what to do and how to act in most situations." "If I do as he does, I will be more likely to attain my goals." "I want and expect him to like and approve of me." In short, you respect, admire, and like your identifying figures, and you model yourself on them.

Identification occurs from earliest childhood to adulthood. Even the most eminent adults take values and techniques from those they admire. A mark of maturity is a decrease in blind emotional loyalty — "my hero, right or wrong" — and an increased ability to criticize the hero's example. This objectivity depends upon the individual's sense of worth, upon his feeling that "I'm all right even if I disagree with this admirable person."

The child's first identification is normally with his parents. Parents minister to the child, increase his happiness, and take care of things that go wrong. The child's gratification broadens into respect for his parents' wisdom, desire to be like them, and desire for their love in return. . . . The success of the identification process depends upon the warmth of the home. By the age of 5, the child frequently picks playmates and older members of the family as models: "Johnny showed me how to ride the scooter," or, "Why don't we have the kind of cake I had at Johnny's house?"

Adults outside the home are also identifying figures. Most children see their first teacher as wonderful, the keeper of uncounted delightful surprises. So powerful is the teacher's hold that soon her views are quoted at home in arguments against the once-infallible parents. Children differ in the firmness of their loyalty to the teacher. Some pursue the teacher's example in all things, transferring that loyalty to later teachers so clingingly that they are estranged from their peers. Others come to feel that the teacher "isn't my kind of person."

As reading, television, and community contacts broaden his knowledge of people, the older child has a much wider choice of identifying figures. Some children in the range 8 to 12 seem to identify strongly with fictional characters (the Lone Ranger), historical personages (Lincoln), or famous athletes. Jesus becomes an identifying figure to many. Such identifications are one possible basis for vocational choice, for political attitudes, and for moral standards. Everyone the child encounters is a possible identifying figure, yet he identifies with only a few people. His choice reflects the sort of person he is and helps to determine the sort he will become. A teacher may set the best of examples, yet only a few of the students will take over his patterns. Each pupil selects among his teachers; some are his models to a far greater degree than others.

Psychologists do not have adequate methods of finding out who a child's chief models are. Sometimes the child himself does not know whose example he follows. Moreover, when he answers a direct question, he has a fairly good idea of what sort of person he will be praised for naming. In the research on children's ideals, no child names a contemporary criminal as his hero. The reflections of adult criminals, however, show clearly that they identified with unsavory models during childhood.

Each choice of an identifying figure is based on needs and attitudes already present. If Allen's parents have rewarded him for being quiet and passive, he cannot, on the school-ground, see himself becoming like tough and energetic Rudy. Rudy's conduct would be accepted as an ideal only if Allen were willing to reject everything he had been trying to be. This may happen where there has been such tension between child and parents that he is inclined to reject their standards, that is, when his identification with them has failed.

As the child grows into an adult, his identifying figures represent successive differentiations of his ideal. In his earlier years all adults seem glamorous and powerful to him. By school age some adults seem more "his type" than others. As a boy begins to take pride in his own physique and his ability to oppose others, he is ripe to idolize people who represent a high development of that asset: athletes, daredevil lawmen, stronger boys at school. The medical student rejects as a model the teacher he admires but whose research on animals he sees as inconsistent with his own ideal of serving the patient directly.

A boy who bases his self-respect less on physical attainment and more on intellectual interests is likely to find identifying figures in a field such as science. Clark, who gets from his father a feeling that carpentry is worth doing and is not too hard, is ready for further stimulation along that line. He can attach himself far more comfortably to an older boy whose hobby is telescope-making than he could if craftwork were foreign to him. Identifications overlap, some fading as others grow more intense.

Now note your reading time. Record it below and go on to the questions.

YOUR READING TIME: _____MIN. _____SEC. _____W.P.M. COMPREHENSION SCORE: _____%
(WORDS PER MINUTE FROM THE TABLE ON PAGE 475.)

Please do not read these questions until you have read the article itself against time. Do not refer to the article as you answer them. Choose the *one best* answer to each question, and enter the corresponding letter in the proper answer space.

1. To say that a child learns simply by imitation (a) is essentially correct; (b) is incomplete because it does not explain why the child imitates some actions but not others; (c) is wrong because it leaves out the process of identifica-

tion; (d) is wrong because it says only "Monkey see, monkey do"; (e) is wrong because it leaves out direct instruction, which can be as important as setting a good example.

ANSWER _____

2. When you look at it from the child's point of view, the *first* element in his learning a new response by imitation is (a) the need to find an authority or expert; (b) the need to find a way to achieve the desired result; (c) the need for more affection from his parents; (d) the desire to reach his ends properly, in a way that meets the standards of his social group; (e) the desire to maintain his own self-respect.

ANSWER _____

3. The *second* element in the child's learning of a new response is (a) the need to find an authority or expert; (b) the need to find a way to achieve the desired result; (c) the need for more affection from his parents; (d) the desire to reach his ends properly, in a way that meets the standards of his social group; (e) the desire to maintain his own self-respect.

ANSWER _____

4. An *identifying figure* is defined as a person (a) whom we repeatedly accept as an example for desirable conduct and attitudes; (b) whom we copy because imitating him leads to success in the field where he is expert; (c) whom we respect, admire, and like; (d) who proves to be a dependable model; (e) none of the above.

ANSWER _____

5. Adults, as well as children, identify; but a decrease in blind emotional loyalty is a mark of maturity, because (a) such objectivity depends upon your sense of your own worth; (b) the most eminent adults, though they may take values and techniques from those they admire, do so selectively; (c) it leaves you free to criticize; (d) it is more rational; (e) none of the above.

ANSWER _____

6. Which of the following is *not* specifically mentioned as *an example of an identifying figure?* (a) The child's parents; (b) concentration camp guards; (c) playmates and older members of the family; (d) leaders the community would not call respectable; (e) the baseball player with a good batting stance.

ANSWER _____

7. Why don't psychologists have adequate methods for discovering a child's identifying models? (a) The child may not know whose example he follows; (b) the child may not know who they are, or he may give answers he thinks will be approved; (c) the child has a fairly good idea what sort of person he will be approved for naming; (d) no child names a contemporary criminal as his hero; (e) none of the above.

ANSWER _____

8. At the beginning of the article, an important question about learning is raised when the author observes that "sometimes [the child] ignores the example his parents want him to follow and he takes over contrary patterns from some other example." Which of the following statements made later in the selection suggests one way this can happen? (a) "He [the child] is in

a new situation, lacking a ready response . . ."; (b) "He looks for an authority or expert to imitate"; (c) "the desire to cope with a situation is overlaid with the desire to act properly"; (d) "[The child may be] willing to reject everything he had been trying to be . . . where there has been such tension between child and parents that . . . his identification with them has failed"; (e) "the older child has a much wider choice of identifying figures . . . [which] represent successive differentiations of his ideal."

ANSWER _____

9. The article is taken from a textbook in educational psychology; what is its purpose? (a) To explain why children take the models they do; (b) to explain how children learn; (c) to explain why children don't always learn as they are expected to; (d) to provide an extended definition, with examples, of a process that is one of many that a teacher should watch for; (e) to show students who will become teachers why they cannot expect every child to be equally eager to follow his example.

ANSWER _____

10. Which of the following is the best description of the overall organization and sequence of the article? (a) Problem (whom does the learner imitate?) followed by solution (how the learner selects identifying figures); (b) analysis of how the child finds responses to imitate followed by definition of an identifying figure; (c) analysis of the psychological origins of identification, definition of an identifying figure, analysis of the sequence of such figures from childhood on; (d) identification described as it takes place with parents, with peers, with adult models outside the home, and finally with "heroes" who become life models; (e) a problem of learning, explained by the mechanism of identification, followed by the admission that the mechanism itself raises problems since the child's models can't be discovered.

ANSWER _____

Now check your answers, and enter your score on your Progress Profile, page vii.

CHAPTER 12

Newspapers and Magazines

Pre-read this chapter as your first step in reading. As your second step, list below the questions you expect the chapter to answer.

_____

_____

_____

_____

_____

_____

What newspaper do you read? Have you ever examined it closely, compared it with others? Have you ever stopped to consider just how you read it?

A good modern newspaper is an extraordinary piece of reading. It is remarkable first for what it contains: the range of news from local crime to international politics, from sports to business to fashion to science; and the range of comment and special features as well, from editorial page to feature articles and interviews to criticism of books, art, theater, and music. A newspaper is even more remarkable for the way one reads it: never completely, never straight through, but always by jumping from here to there, in and out, glancing at one piece, reading another article all the way through, reading just a few paragraphs of the next. A good modern newspaper offers a variety to attract many different readers, but far more than any one reader is interested in. What brings this variety together in one place is its topicality, its immediate relation to what is happening in your world and your locality now. But immediacy and the speed of production that goes with it means also that much of what appears in a newspaper has no more than transient value. For all these reasons, no two people really read the same paper: what each person does is to put together, out of the pages of that day's paper, his own selection and sequence, his own newspaper. For all these reasons, reading newspapers efficiently, which means getting what you want from them without missing things you need but without wasting time, demands skill and self-awareness as you modify and apply the techniques of reading.

So: what newspaper do you read? And first, with what paper do you begin that process of making your own selection and sequence? Is it one of the good modern papers? There are many, but by no means all newspapers are among that number. The greatest newspapers in the world are very few, but they doubtless include:

The New York Times,
The Washington Post,
Le Monde, Paris,
Die Neue Zürcher Zeitung, Switzerland,

and according to some, *The Times* of London, though that paper has declined in quality in recent years.

Have you ever taken a careful look at two or more of these? The first two, at least, ought to be available at a library, bookstore or newsdealer near you. Careful reading of several issues will demonstrate the qualities of thoroughness, completeness, balance, seriousness, independence, concern, vigor, and so on, that ought to be consistently present for a newspaper to be great; careful reading of several issues even of these world-class newspapers will doubtless show you examples where the standards are not entirely met. Other very good American newspapers include:

The Los Angeles Times
The St. Louis Post-Dispatch
The Chicago Daily News
The Christian Science Monitor, Boston
The Wall Street Journal

And strong cases could be argued for two or three more. Which of these have you examined and compared with your regular newspaper?

Or do you get your news from television? TV news and commentary has obvious values of immediacy and vividness. Its drawbacks are not so obvious, but are considerable. Broadcast news programs necessarily are highly simplified and condensed. They are also inflexible, giving you no choice to get less or more information than brief capsules about each item. No matter how vivid the pictures, the information that explains them is limited to the lock-step speed of speech: leaving out the commercials, a ten-minute broadcast can contain no more information than you should be able to read in about 90 seconds. Television news is essential and inescapable today; but its limitations are built into the way broadcasting works, and therefore make newspapers more important than ever.

As always, so with newspapers, the first question is your purpose in reading. With a ruthlessly clear idea of what you need, you will be able to select, to skip, to use to the full your ability to skim, to pre-read, and to question the value of everything your eye falls on. Indeed, nobody should *read* a newspaper. For example, the Sunday *New York Times* contains (excluding advertising) upwards of three quarters of a million words, equal to half a dozen sizable novels. You must skip in newspaper reading; you can do so easily and wisely if you remember several facts. First, since most newspapers appeal to a large, general readership, their coverage extends far beyond your particular interests. Second, most news stories follow a basic organizational pattern that is peculiar to newspaper journalism, which concentrates the most essential facts in the headline and the first several paragraphs of the article.

These special characteristics of newspaper writing require you to modify your techniques of pre-reading, skipping, and skimming. Let us consider first the *headline stories,* which make up the bulk of a paper's nonadvertising content. There are reasons why such stories are organized with the most important material at the top. (See pages 316–19 for an illustration and schematic analysis of an actual news story, reprinted from *The New York Times,* October 21, 1970.) Readers are impatient, and want to get the gist of the story quickly. Also, newspaper articles must be written so that they can be shortened quickly and easily by cutting off the end paragraphs. For example, an article on the United Nations may be placed on the first page in an early edition. Then the story of a murder trial may replace it that same day in the next edition, with the United Nations story appearing on page 3 with its last paragraphs chopped off to make it fit the space available.

Thus, you will find that newspaper headline stories are already set up for pre-reading. Usually the headline will tell you whether you want to read farther; if you do, you will then read the first several paragraphs thoroughly and skim the rest of the article until you are satisfied you have everything you need. As our example shows, much of the material after the first several paragraphs recapitulates in expanded form the topics of the opening paragraphs. The expansion is made by adding new details that the reporter and editor judge less important.

Newspapers try to increase circulation by attracting readers through the apparent urgency of their front page headline stories. Therefore, most stories are written from the point of view of what is happening right now—journalists call it the "today angle." (The speed-reading selection following this chapter discusses the strange results of this journalistic stress on immediacy.) But regardless of what the screaming headlines insist, you can often save time by remembering that what today's story adds to yesterday's information may be very little indeed. Some readers even claim they miss surprisingly little by reading the paper fairly thoroughly only every other day!

Other kinds of reporting in newspapers include editorials, feature articles, and syndicated articles and columns. In contrast to headline stories, these other types are not so much required to look like "new" news. Instead, they may furnish you with background analysis for understanding current news; they may present political opinion; or they may treat subjects of more lasting interest, and thus be similar to magazine articles. Because these three kinds of articles are not often cut to make room for later news, they are unlike headline stories and may be organized similarly to other practical prose. That is, they are likely

NAVY CONSIDERING PLAN TO MOTHBALL 6 OF 18 CARRIERS

Main headline: it leads with the most exciting news — topic *A* — of a story which you will see has other important ramifications as well.

Proposal Would Drop All 4 Antisubmarine Vessels and Reduce Fleet in Pacific

Series of secondary or subheadlines: first one develops *A* —

BUDGET CUTS A FACTOR

next one adds topic *B,* a cause or explanation —

New Study Calls for Use of Vertical Take-Off Jets and Big Copters on Ships

last subheadline introduces an entirely new, though related, topic, *C.*

By WILLIAM BEECHER
Special to The New York Times

WASHINGTON, Oct. 20—The United States Navy, facing the prospect of shrinking budgets and increasing costs, has a plan to mothball up to six of its 18 aircraft carriers, according to authoritative sources.

First four paragraphs develop topic *A,* with some reference to cause *B.*

The most novel feature of the plan, which is said to have the support of the new Chief of Naval Operations, Adm. Elmo R. Zumwalt Jr., would eliminate all four specialized antisubmarine warfare carriers from the active fleet, along with two additional attack carriers, the sources said.

(Note introduction of a person; many news stories give individual protagonists more prominence than this.)

If the plan is adopted—and ranking Defense Department officials say this is likely within the next few years—all aircraft carriers remaining and in the future will be dual purpose, having both jet fighters and antisubmarine patrol planes. The precise mix of fighters and patrol planes would depend on each carrier's mission and the threat at any given time and place.

Cut in Pacific Fleet

4 Another probable result of the projected carrier cutback, officials say, would be to reduce to two the minimum number of aircraft carriers maintained at any one time in the Western Pacific. For nearly two decades, the Navy has kept at least three attack carriers in the Far East, and during the height of the Vietnam war this number temporarily was five.

5 These are among the far-reaching changes being worked up for the Navy, with Navy planners taking the initiative.

Transitional paragraph, needed to organize the complex story.

6 Pentagon officials disclosed that shortly after Admiral Zumwalt took office in July he went to Defense Secretary Melvin R. Laird and Deputy Defense Secretary David Packard with an unusual request. It would scrap the traditional pattern of proposing what the Navy believed it would like to have in the way of forces and having defense budget officials and systems analysts chop away at the total. In its place, Admiral Zumwalt asked for—and got—60 days in which to come up with alternative Navy programs, each pegged to progressively lower budget levels.

Topic *B,* the budget, developed with background that turns out to be the most important longer-term point of the story.

7 It was not known how much money would be saved by the proposals expected to be approved.

8 The most radical idea emerging from the study was to perform surgery on the once sacrosanct carrier force, establishing a dual purpose role for those ships that remain.

Back to *A,* tying up the relation between *A* and *B.*

9 Other novel ideas being pressed by Admiral Zumwalt include the following:

Transition to *C.*

¶The placement of Harrier vertical-take-off jets, currently being purchased by the Marine
10 Corps from Britain, on amphibi-

Four paragraphs developing *C.*

ous and other ships to help protect convoys from attack by long-range antishipping missiles fired from Soviet submarines and fast missile boats.

¶The use of large helicopters carrying air-to-air missiles on a variety of Navy ships, possibly including destroyers, for additional stand-off protection. — 11

¶The use of very fast hydrofoil ships, equipped with surface-to-surface missiles that are now being developed on a crash basis, to "shadow" major Russian warships in places like the Mediterranean, where a political crisis might one day erupt suddenly into a battle between the fleets of the two nations. — 12

Still *C,* though not even hinted at in original subheadline.

¶Possible development of a radically new class of aircraft carriers that would be propelled just above the surface of the water on powerful air cushion engines at speeds of up to 130 knots, roughly four times the speed of current carriers. — 13

Officials close to this new line of Navy thinking say that a combination of factors is forcing one of the most far-reaching reassessments in the Navy's history. — 14

Back to *B,* as developed in paragraphs 6 and 7.

Big Cost for Deterrent

A large part of the Navy's budget is devoted to deterring a nuclear attack with the fleet of 41 Polaris missile submarines. The costs of this force will continue to rise as 31 Polaris submarines are reconfigured to take the multiple-warhead Poseidon missile. And if defense planners decide to build a fleet of follow-on missile submarines, carrying from 20 to 30 longer range missiles each, this will increase the cost of the strategic force substantially. — 15

But while these costs climb, Navy officials believe the prospect is for either a leveling off or a reduction in the Navy budget. Thus, whatever cuts are necessary must come from the Navy's conventional warfare forces. — 16

Complicating the situation is the size and increasing venturesomeness of the Soviet fleet, pushing out from its traditional coastal defense role to roam the seven seas. — 17

Further background to B, as developed.

---

18 Another complication stems from the Nixon Doctrine, which looks to placing increased reliance on the ground forces of Asian allies to carry the main burden of their self-defense but holds out the prospect of fast Navy and Air Force reinforcement in certain circumstances if the ground forces are in danger of being overrun, as in the case of South Korea.

19 Navy planners worry that unless they can come up with ways to protect the sea lanes from the United States to Asia, America's commitment to reinforce in a crisis may not have much credibility. Thus, the sudden interest in experimenting with increased sea control measures, including hydrofoils and vertical-take-off aircraft.

Senior Admirals Upset

20 In a Navy where the carrier task force has long been king, the idea of cutting back drastically is upsetting to many senior admirals.

21 But Admiral Zumwalt and some of his aides believe there is not much choice if the Navy is going to continue its functions of showing the flag around the world, keeping the sea lanes open during periods of crisis and bing able to project air strikes, naval gunfire and marines ashore in a limited war situation.

22 Customarily, as new attack aircraft carriers have been built, the older, smaller carriers have been assigned to special antisubmarine hunter-killer teams. These teams have included varying numbers of destroyers and have also worked with land-based patrol planes as well as carrier-based sub-hunting planes and helicopters.

23 These teams range usually some miles from America's Pacific and Mediterranean fleets to keep track of potentially hostile submarines. Others have played a similar role off the Atlantic and Pacific coasts of the United States.[1]

This news story is unusually long and complicated; thus it illustrates fully the way stories can be put together to give the most important information about each of several closely related topics, then return to add further details about each. *Note that the story could be shortened simply by cutting everything after the point marked here,*

or after any of the six other points marked above.

to show the familiar pattern of introduction, development, and conclusion. You should therefore pre-read and read them just as you would other practical prose. These articles, however, are also written at a level for general audiences; you read them at top speed.

Another newspaper category includes articles reviewing the theater, television, books, and music. Often these reviews are written regularly by the same critics; often, their approach to reviewing—within the limits of space, audience, and urgent deadlines—is highly individual. Regular reading of a reviewer, however, will quickly teach you both his habits and his quality, and therefore how you will read him. Does he habitually put his opinion in the first few paragraphs, or bury it at the end? How does he typically support his judgment with reasons? Are his judgment and his writing good enough so that you really want to read his thoroughly whenever he appears? Or can you skim most of his reviews?

A final category of newspaper article deserving separate consideration is the *national column,* the piece signed by the same author or team and appearing several times a week in perhaps hundreds of newspapers across the country. Some of these are humorous (like Art Buchwald), others are merely trivial (Hollywood or New York gossip, personal advice, and so on)—what you read of those is a matter of taste. The serious columnists range from James Reston of *The New York Times* (syndicated in many papers) to Joseph Alsop, Evans and Novak, William F. Buckley, Jr., and others. Almost all of these columns are about politics, which means first of all events, trends, and gossip in Washington, similar events of national importance elsewhere in the country, and international relations. The columnists sometimes offer a tidbit of inside information, but their chief claim is that they give you analysis and informed opinion about national and international affairs. Appropriately, they often appear on the editorial page of the papers that carry them. Acquaintance with such opinions and analyses is, arguably, an essential for responsible citizenship—but so is critical, highly selective reading of them. The views they offer are political, though in the best sense of the word, and indeed vary over a fairly wide political spectrum, so that an effective form of critical reading is simply to compare various columnists on the same topic. Beyond their differences, though, these columns share one bias which also makes critical and selective reading essential: the topics they treat are among the most important of the day, but their very topicality makes them liable to an exaggerated sense of urgency and a correspondingly short-term view.

Magazines

Magazines can be divided by type of content into two broad categories: *general* and *specialized.* Specialized magazines include *trade journals, business publications,* and *technical, scientific* and *scholarly periodicals.* We will discuss these below. General magazines include *pulps, slicks,* and *quality.* *Pulps* and *slicks* acquired their names from the paper on which they are printed. *Quality* magazines are so named because they are edited to attract, hopefully, a somewhat more educated, thoughtful audience.

Most pulps are devoted to light fiction in which every emotion and meaning is clearly labeled; subtlety and artistry are not commodities in this market.

Pulps are easy to read and pose no problems for the reader who has ever exercised his intelligence. We mention them at all because in recent years a few pulps have laid claim to better quality of content (notably the better science-fiction and detective-story collections), with the result that they are now read by a more discriminating audience than before. The general level of pulps, however, remains low.

Slick magazines, so called because they attract advertisers by printing on glossy-finish paper, are somewhat more adult in content. In the past decade general magazines have faced serious problems of readership, costs, and advertising revenues, problems which have been felt most acutely by the slicks because many of their most important advertisers have switched to television. A number of the most general magazines, notably *The Saturday Evening Post,* have folded; even the biggest of the slick weeklies, *Life,* has lost money in recent years. Casting about for ways to hold readers and attract advertisers, the slicks have experimented with editorial content. Their nonfiction can occasionally have lasting importance. For example, *Life* has published major parts of such books as Winston Churchill's history of World War II, and more recently can claim that its political exposés have led to the defeat of the appointment of at least one Supreme Court justice. Such magazines are frequently timely and informed. That, after all, is their sales appeal; but it is up to the reader to determine if they are *well* informed or *mis*informed. Nonfiction in slick magazines should be read quickly but critically. Thorough pre-reading will often be all you need for even the best articles in slicks, because they are written by highly professional writers and editors with the purpose of presenting a few facts, ideas, and opinions briefly and unmistakably.

The craftmanship that goes into the writing of the best articles makes critical awareness doubly imperative for the reader: "slick" can indeed apply to the argument as well as the paper it is printed on. Fiction in slick magazines has become rarer in recent years, particularly with the death of *The Saturday Evening Post.* The honorable tradition by which such magazines bought for good fees, and published, stories by major writers like William Faulkner and Ernest Hemingway, is now all but vanished. On the whole, these days the quality of what little fiction appears in slicks is thin.

A special category of general magazines comprises the news weeklies, notably *Time* and *Newsweek.* The original of the species, *Time,* was founded in the 1920s and was known for years for its brash assurance, its somewhat affected style, its deep conservatism; since World War II a succession of managing editors has sobered up its style, and more recently some of its arrogance as well as its die-hard conservatism has mellowed as well. *Newsweek,* started in imitation of *Time,* has made its reputation by being smaller (in resources as well as circulation), but quicker and livelier. Both magazines are written by their own staffs rather than outside contributors; indeed, to a surprising extent *Newsweek* is run by ex-*Time* editors; the result of their centralized writing and editing, as well as the extreme pressure for space, is a kind of writing that is highly condensed, somewhat simplified, bland, and overly tidy. Greater maturity, greater seriousness, and the competition of television news has meant that the news magazines have given up what claim they had to being a complete accounting of each week's most important events; nonetheless, they perform a useful function as a summary of the news, while some of their sections—one example: the law section of *Time*—are outstanding popular journalism about serious matters. News magazines should be read at high speed, and many of the articles no more than skimmed.

Quality magazines often demand thorough reading. Their fiction and their poetry may be representative of the best currently written. The nonfiction in a few quality magazines is devoted primarily to political questions; as the United States in the past decade has become more deeply disturbed by political and social problems, the quality magazines have become more concerned with such issues, and considerably more urgent in their tone. Most of them publish nonfiction of almost every variety—political, critical, philosophical, and historical. Among the leaders are *The New Yorker, Harper's, The Atlantic.* This is an area where, counter to the general trend, new publications have been successfully launched in the past few years; an interesting example is *The New York Review of Books,* which regularly uses the book reviews of its title to launch into extended and often heated commentary, usually from the political left, on current issues both political and intellectual.

Quality magazines thus present reading problems of considerable complexity. Their articles are not marked by any typical features of structure or style; however, the reading techniques that apply to them are those you would use with other practical prose of a somewhat difficult level, with particular attention to the need for careful critical reading.

In contrast to magazines aimed at the general (consumer) mass, specialized magazines are edited to meet the particular interests of a particular audience, a group of readers who do the same type of work or who share some other interest. Some specialized magazines, except for their narrow range of subjects and the absence of fiction, are no less popularly written than any slick. This is especially true of magazines in the hobby or business fields. The same rules for efficient reading apply to these as to slicks.

At the other extreme, in specialized magazines, are technical, scientific, and scholarly publications that may contain material of great difficulty—and of great importance. For example, it is in some of these publications that the most important day-to-day developments in scientific fields first reach their professional public. These articles, therefore, should be read just as you would read a chapter in a difficult book, and with careful consideration of your purpose in reading.

Fortunately, to overcome the sheer bulk of this kind of publication, many such journals print brief abstracts of the contents immediately before each article. (See the examples, pages 66 and 67.) Here, in effect, your pre-reading is set up for you by the editor. Nonetheless, extreme selectivity, sure use of skimming, and your best speeds are essential in reading publications of this sort if you are to have time left for your main work.

Finally, it is perhaps worthwhile to point out that the compulsion to read material that is actually a waste of time can be very great with some specialized magazines of professional interest. Many businessmen, for example, are unable *not* to read any business article that catches their attention: "It might contain something *important.*" However, though your job may demand a wide and thorough technical grasp, this is no reason to become less selective. In self-defense—if only to preserve the time and attention to *master* whatever you *do* decide to read thoroughly—you should prune out every article that contains nothing new, as shown by pre-reading, and everything that meets no purpose of yours, as shown by the questions you ask.

READING SKILLS RE-SURVEY

Skimming for a Fact—in Newspapers and Magazines

Pre-reading
Table of Contents and Preface from *The War for America, 1775–1783*, by Piers Mackesy

Outlining
"A Chemist's Look at the Bacterial Cell," from *Molecular Biology of the Gene*, by James D. Watson

Question Technique
rereading of "A Chemist's Look at the Bacterial Cell," by James D. Watson

Summarizing
"The Conservatism of American English," from *The Origins and Development of the English Language*, by Thomas Pyles

Reading Speed Exercise: Average Level 7
"Off to a Good Start," from *Kon-Tiki*, by Thor Heyerdahl

At the beginning of Part I, just after the introductory chapter, you surveyed your reading skills before training began. Now at the end of Part II, the following exercises repeat with some additions the types of exercises in the original Reading Skills Survey. The aim of this Re-Survey is to allow you to compare your reading now with what it was as you began this book. Then Part III will ask you to practice applying your developed skills in a coordinated way to longer and more difficult articles.

Skimming for a Fact

Just before each of the following paragraphs, a particular piece of factual information is called for. You are to skim each paragraph to find the one fact. Try to break away completely from thorough reading. Instead, glance left and right very rapidly, stopping as little as twice on each line of print. *Keep clearly in mind the fact, stated at the beginning of the paragraph, for which you are skimming.*

As soon as you find the fact, put a pencil check in the margin next to it. Then go immediately to the next paragraph. When you have skimmed and checked all the paragraphs, record your time in the space provided on page 326, and then fill in the sentence number of each fact in the proper space there.

Work for speed. In class follow your instructor's directions for timing. On your own, follow the Instructions for Timing on page 474.

Begin timing here.

A, B—from *Time*
LOOK FOR *TWO* FACTS AT THE SAME TIME:
   how long patients remain at Geel
   who now regulates the boarding system at Geel

MENTAL ILLNESS

A Town for Outpatients

1   On the surface, Geel looks like any other country town in northern Belgium.

2   Its cobbled marketplace is surrounded by 15th century homes and shops; its neat brick farmhouses look much, the same as they did in Brueghel's day.

3   What makes Geel different is the fact that 1,800 of its 30,000 inhabitants are mental patients—and that most of them are not confined to an asylum but cared for by normal families in the town.

4   While this kind of outpatient care is still relatively new to psychiatry, the good people of Geel have been sheltering the sick in their homes for more than 500 years.

5   In Geel, one in seven families is responsible for the care of one or two mental patients, and about 85% of the families who take in *malades* can truthfully say that their parents and grand-

6   parents did the same. "Here no one is afraid of mental patients," says Psychiatrist Herman Matheussen, 38, di-

7   rector of the program. When a schizophrenic plowing a field suddenly stops and begins gesticulating in a hallucinatory argument with an imaginary persecutor, his foster father may say calmly, "Joseph, why don't you finish that furrow?"

8   **Beheaded Virgin.** Geel's enlightened approach to mental care is the product

9   of a 1,300-year-old religious legend. According to the story, an Irish Christian princess named Dympna fled from her widowed pagan father when he ordered

10   her to marry him. He pursued her across the sea to Geel, where, insane with in-

11   cestuous lust, he beheaded her. He instantly recovered his sanity, thereby establishing Dympna's reputation as a virgin martyr with powers to cure the

12   mad. The date of her canonization is un-

certain, but in the 13th century a chap-

13   el in Geel was named for her. Mentally afflicted pilgrims to the chapel soon overflowed the small lodge built to house them, and the Geeloise peasants, cannily combining religious devotion with thrift, began to take the pilgrims as boarders.

14   Those who were not cured often

15   stayed on. They were treated as human beings by their foster families at a time when the mentally ill almost everywhere else were banished from society to asylums of appalling squalor

16   and cruelty. Originally, Geel's boarding system for the mentally ill was supervised by officials of the Roman Catholic Church: since 1860, the Belgian government has had the responsibility of screening the patients and administering the program.

17   **Carefully Screened.** Mental hospitals and clinics from all over Europe refer

18   patients to Geel. Two general practitioners and four psychiatrists observe new arrivals for two to three weeks in a small hospital: about half the ap-

19   plicants are rejected. Those who remain —some 50 a year—are the ones found suitable to Geel's way of life, mostly nonviolent psychotics and people with sub-

20   normal intelligence. The carefully screened families who take them in receive a practical compensation: extra hands for simple work, plus stipends

21   of 80¢ to $2 per day. "The first time they take a patient they are doing it for economic reasons," says Matheussen, "but after five or six years, it becomes an act of humanity."

22   A doctor visits each patient monthly, a nurse every other week. Though the program is geared to the long-term patient, about half of the patients newly placed in foster homes are able to go

23   home after about 16 months. Those who remain in Geel, some for as long

as 50 years, may make little if any progress, but at least they are exposed to normal human conversation and society and have the simple dignity of hon-
24 est work. Patients are treated like members of their foster families, eating with them, sleeping in their own rooms, helping with household and farm chores (or working outside the house in bakeries, dairies or shops), sharing in the up-bringing of the children or going out
25 to movies and clubhouses. Families learn to tolerate a certain amount of odd behavior, and Geel has been re-
26 markably free of mishaps. Thanks in part to the use of modern tranquilizers, there has been no serious outburst of violence by a patient for at least 15 years.
27 **Gentle Rhythm.** Patience, understanding and the gentle rhythm of life have been almost the only real treat-
28 ment at Geel. Now Matheussen is plan-

ning to set up several neighborhood treatment centers where patients will meet regularly for group therapy, school-
29 ing and vocational training. This additional therapy may be crucial to Geel's survival because modern life is at last changing the town's stable, close-knit
30 medieval patterns. Factory jobs are replacing the farm work that is suitable
31 for many patients. Trucks and cars thunder through the square, their drivers not accustomed to watching for dazed people who forget to look both ways at corners.
32 The use of these intensive-treatment neighborhood centers may mean that more patients will recover, so that families will be required to surrender their
33 charges. That will present Matheussen with a special problem of diplomacy, since many do not want to let their
34 boarders go. "Families adjust," he sighs. "They get attached to their patients."[2]

C—from *The Economist*
LOOK FOR: the effect of pop music on hearing

1 By far the most easily identi-
fiable noise hazard is that it can
2 cause deafness. Any continuous noise above 85 decibels can
3 cause deafness. Industrial noise was once the only sort of noise that was loud and persistent enough to make people deaf.
4 But now pop music is taking its
5 toll. A recent survey of American teenagers showed that many of them had hearing no better than the average for people aged 65.
6,7 This is not totally surprising. A "teeny bopper" standing near a pop group's amplifier is assailed by noise that matches that of a jet aircraft taking off: only it lasts longer.
8 But deafness is not the only
9 health hazard. Noise also produces a variety of other psycho-physical effects such as changes in muscle tension, in gastric

activity, in the electrical resistance of the skin and so on.
10 These are typical symptoms of
11 anxiety and stress changes. Experiments in various countries, though not in Britain, indicate that the anxiety caused by noise can adversely affect physical
12 and mental health. But the British Government still insists that the problem does not exist, and that no evidence in Britain indicates that noise contributes
13 to mental illness. Meanwhile it does precious little to encourage
14 research. What does seem clear is that the problem is not so much psychological harm (if any) caused by the physical sound, but the anxiety, stress and irritation caused by particular types of noise, plus the little-understood effects on the amount and quality of sleep.[3]

D—from *The New York Times*
LOOK FOR: the minimum wage for people who are not farm workers

THE NEW YORK TIMES,

ROCKEFELLER ASKS
$1.40 FARM WAGE

Minimum Would Increase to
$1.50 an Hour in 1971

By WILLIAM E. FARRELL
Special to The New York Times

1   ALBANY, Feb. 3 — Governor Rockefeller sent to the Legislature today a bill that would place most of the state's 49,000 farm workers under the state minimum wage law for the first time.

2   Mr. Rockefeller, in one of three bills affecting farm workers, proposed a minimum wage of $1.40 an hour effective Oct. 1, with an increase to $1.50
3   an hour in February, 1971. The measure would affect all workers on farms with an annual payroll of $1,200 or more.

4   In a statement, Mr. Rockefeller said that his proposal covered over 80 per cent of the state's farm workers.

5   "Farm workers are especially vulnerable to exploitation, and New York State must provide the protections necessary for them to earn a decent living and live in healthy surroundings," Mr. Rockefeller said.

6   "Our state has recognized and fulfilled a similar responsibility to its industrial work-
7   ers. The unique problems of agriculture make it impossible simply to extend wholesale the laws that have enabled our industrial workers to enjoy the highest standard of living in the world."

Competition Recognized

8   The state minimum for other than farm employment is currently $1.60 an hour.

9   The Governor's statement said "the provisions of the bill take into consideration the competitive position of New York State farmers and the cost differentials involved in varying types of farming activities in erecting a minimum wage structure."

10   Other recommendations covered in the three bills included:

11   ¶Giving the State Industrial Commissioner authority to regulate such farm practices as piecework pay and requirements for weekly or
12   monthly compensation. Employers now decide how and when farm workers are paid.

13   ¶Establishing an advisory council made up of representatives of growers, farm workers and the public to study and advise the Industrial Commissioner on wage rates.

14   ¶Strengthening procedures for enforcing the Public Health Law and sanitary code with regard to labor camps for migrant farm workers.

15   ¶Permitting farmers to volunteer coverage for farm workers under the State Unemployment
16   Insurance Law. Mr. Rockefeller said that farmers had complained about their inability to recruit workers because they were unable to provide such coverage.[4]

E—from *The Times,* London
LOOK FOR: the main student group behind the strike at the London School of Economics

Adams to meet LSE students

By BRIAN MacARTHUR.
Education Correspondent

1 Dr. Walter Adams, director of the London School of Economics, has agreed to attend a students' union meeting at the school next Wednesday to answer questions from students.

2 He will undoubtedly be questioned on the decision of the standing committee of the governors to dismiss two lecturers. Mr. Robin Blackburn and Mr. Nicholas Bateson, and the subsequent offer to establish an appellate tribunal to hear appeals from them.

3 Mr. Christopher Pryce, president of the students' union, said last night that the last time Dr. Adams had attended a union meeting he had been roughly handled and that the meeting had ended in chaos.

4 If Dr. Adams agreed to answer questions and did not go through the usual forms of disavowal he might get a hearing on this occasion. "It could do some good,"

5 he said. The idea to ask Dr. Adams was put by members of the union's Socialist Society, which has been the main focus of the student action initiated against school authorities.[5]

Stop timing here.

For each paragraph enter the number of the sentence that corresponds to the fact you were to find. (The sentences are numbered in the left margin.)

Skimming time in seconds for all items: _____

A:_____ **B:**_____ **C:**_____ **D:**_____ **E:**_____

Pre-reading

How does a great issue, or a great conflict, look from the other side? In *The War for America*, British historian Piers Mackesy writes of the American Revolution—but from the viewpoint of eighteenth-century London, of the ministers and generals of George III, and in the context of what was, for those protagonists, a world-wide struggle of twentieth-century scope. Seen from this view, the battles and names so familiar to American readers take on a sudden three-dimensional vitality, become more comprehensible and memorable as threads of a far larger fabric. What is the pattern of that fabric? What were the determining forces in the long struggle of which the American Revolution was a part? What is Mackesy's aim in writing a history from this viewpoint; what are his methods; what biases does he bring to it? These are the kinds of questions you would be asking as you picked up the book itself, and which you will bring to pre-reading the table of contents and preface which are reprinted here.

The chief difficulty you are likely to find is the relative unfamiliarity of many of the names and scenes of action. This is merely symptomatic of the wrench in one's usual perspective which the book imposes: the very unfamiliarities, pondered, should help you come to a preliminary understanding of what it is the author is trying to bring out. Read the table of contents; then turn to page 334 to list several questions your reading has suggested. After that, return to pre-read and read the preface. Then turn to the questions beginning on page 335. You may refer to the material as you answer the questions. This is not a timed exercise.

Table of Contents and Preface
from *The War for America, 1775–1783*[6]
by PIERS MACKESY

CONTENTS

Now turn to page 334, to formulate some questions about the book.

PREFACE

The Servants of Kronos

The Muses attend the births of gods and nations: Clio to record and Calliope to adorn the great event. They tell how the infant Zeus was snatched from the jaws of his father Kronos; and inevitably it is the infant who is sung, while old Kronos fades back into the mists of antiquity, the half-forgotten symbol of an outdated and regrettable past.

So it happened with the American Revolution. The triumph of the rebels was of overwhelming importance for the future of the world, and the struggle was recorded in terms of American battles on American soil. The red coats of old Kronos's hirelings are visible; but the mind that moved them, the Kronos of Whitehall and St James's, was thrust aside to be forgotten or turned into a background buffoon.

This treatment accentuated a characteristic feature of British historiography: the distortion of diplomacy and warfare by the elimination of strategy. Strategy falls between two kinds of history. For the political historian it is a marginal activity of government which occasionally erupts to disturb the course of diplomacy, debate and electioneering. For the military historian it is a background to operations in the field and on the seas; and the decisions of governments are too often seen through the eyes of distant and half-informed commanders. Sir John Fortescue, the historian of the British army, was a devoted operational historian; and the thirteen volumes of his history, magnificent in their energy, style and range of narrative, form a splendid monument to the vanishing regiments which made the British empire. Yet his devotion to the army narrowed and warped his judgment. In the sphere where strategy merged with policy, he was incapable of justice. For him the appalling problems of the government which waged the war for America were reduced to "the folly and ignorance of Germain."

Though strategy has emerged to take its rightful place in the history of the twentieth century, the direction of war before 1914 is a little known area of British history. In no war has less attempt been made to strike the balance between strategy and operations than in the War of American Independence. There is now much interest in Lord North's administration; yet though the war covered seven of its twelve years of life, the task of assessing its efforts to direct the war in the context of eighteenth-century warfare remains to be done. The neglect is largely due to the consequences of the war, which concentrated the interest and emotions of historians on the struggles of the new state and its embryo armies beyond the Atlantic. Yet the injustice which has been done in the past to Lord North and his colleagues has two other causes: that the war was lost, and that George III and his Ministers were blackguarded by domestic enemies.

The men who conduct a war are more intemperately and uncharitably criticised than those who run an administrative machine in peacetime. Statesmen and commanders are equally victims; for in war the results are swift, harsh and measurable, and censure readily precedes understanding. The vilification of the Ministry was perpetuated because the most accessible and digested source of information was the Parliamentary Debates. There one may read the half-informed and largely disingenuous criticisms of the Opposition, and the misleading and partial replies of the Ministers. The failure to blockade Brest will demonstrate the effect. The Ministry's enemies maintained that if it had been done the enemy would have been unable to seize the initiative: his overseas expeditions and his concentrations in home waters would have been prevented, and England would have maintained her maritime ascendancy. Yet Lord Howe, whose slow mind required time to choose its political stance, flatly declared in the House of Commons that Ushant was no station for a fleet. Though naval historians are aware how great a margin of superiority was necessary to maintain a close blockade, it is rarely asked whether the country had the necessary means, and whether the policy which had succeeded in the Seven Years War and was to succeed again in the struggles with revolutionary France could have been applied in the different circumstances of the American War.

The *Parliamentary History,* supplemented by the *Annual Register* and memoirs like Horace Walpole's, dominated the entire history of the reign for generations: they are riddled with lies, special pleading and gossip. Though the political history is being re-written from better sources, the major decisions of the war have not been reassessed. Yet better sources are freely available, and some of the most important have been in print for many years. It is not necessary to accept opinions as facts, or to mistake uninformed hindsight for wisdom.

The American War was Britain's only clear defeat in the long contest with France which began with the Revolution of 1688 and ended at Waterloo. Unique characteristics explain the uniqueness of the failure. England was maintaining nearly 60,000 soldiers beyond the Atlantic, most of them in a hostile country: a feat never paralleled in the past, and in relative terms never attempted again by any power until the twentieth century. The territory was vast, and the people were in arms. Even so the resistance of the Americans might have been worn down and a settlement (though probably a temporary one) achieved. But for the first time England faced what she had always dreaded and averted: a coalition of maritime enemies undistracted by war in Europe.

In simple terms of power the consequences are clear, and after a struggle of several years a momentary tilt of the naval balance brought the disaster at Yorktown which broke the country's will to fight on. The same factor made the strategic choices which faced the North Ministry infinitely more complicated than those which faced the two Pitts. With a general command of the sea it was possible to take as much or as little of the war as one desired: to feed the war fronts in Europe as much as one judged necessary, and to take the initiative in colonial warfare. In other words it was possible to a considerable degree to treat the theatres of war in isolation, and to neutralise one theatre in order to act in another. But for Lord North's government, whose enemies had free access to ocean communications, all problems of war were interrelated. An additional effort in North America might expose in the West Indies, a strong fleet in the Channel endanger India.

The Ministry which faced these problems was not a strong one. Its parliamentary majority was insecure, it was troubled by internal stresses, it lacked leadership, and it waged war without gusto. But weak leadership was not unique in English warfare. The Elder Pitt had been a brilliant exception—perhaps the only exception in two centuries. And he had everything in his favour: a European war which engaged the resources of the enemy, friendly colonies in America, Spanish intervention delayed till the French navy and empire had been broken. The country and Parliament were united behind the war, and Pitt's junction with the Newcastle system gave the government an unbreakable majority. One often hears how the North government alienated its generals and admirals; yet only one, Keppel, was court-martialled, and he through unhappy circumstances. The reason for the government's forbearance was timidity and fear of outcries. In the Seven Years War two successive commanders were recalled from America with no outcry; the general at Gibraltar was court-martialled, and a "revision" of his sentence was discussed when he was aquitted; Sackville was broken, and Byng was shot. What would have been the fate of Burgoyne under the régime of Pitt and Newcastle? How long would Clinton have held his command?

There was much administrative inefficiency in the American War. But North was using the machinery he had inherited; and the more one lifts the curtain of adulation from the Ministry of the Elder Pitt, the less does the scene appear to match the script, and the more one uncovers the characteristic inefficiencies of the age. One finds the same delays in despatching expeditions; vital reinforcements held up by contrary winds; time lost by naval commanders in securing prizes. There are the same shortages of shipping, the same departmental friction over transports, the same slow and piecemeal embarcations. Pitt and his friends planned distant offensives in the same manner as Germain, with no allowance for wastage from sickness and the same optimistic reliance on precise timing.

If one looks forward the same scene is revealed. In the American War much was made of the Ministers' summer habit of haymaking in the country; yet as the Helder expedition prepared to embark in the summer of 1799 the Younger Pitt was to write that in a few days he and many of his Cabinet would be out of London. His faults as a war minister were shrouded by the necessity of his leadership, to which almost all subscribed. The Ministry of All the Talents of 1806–7 were less fortunate: their failures were scrutinised under the microscope; and even their successes were harvested by their opponents, for the swift and secret Copenhagen expedition of 1807 sailed in transports which they had assembled. If one contemplates the arrangements for the Mediterranean in the autumn of the same year, one may wonder how far Castlereagh and Canning excelled Germain and Sandwich in overcoming the difficulties of slow communication and uncertain weather.

The first purpose of this book is to examine the making and execution of strategy in one of England's great eighteenth-century wars, and to create a detailed model of the machine at work; the second, to judge a war Ministry in the light of circumstances rather than results. This is how one at least of the Ministers wished to be judged. Defending the Admiralty after Yorktown against charges of operational mis-management, Lord Sandwich wrote: "These charges are not so easily answered, because there is no demonstrative evidence that the orders given have been right; the event certainly does not decide that question; but those who mean to find fault, wait the event, and then adopt whichever side of the question best suits their purpose." To under-stand the war, one must view it with sympathy for the Ministers in their difficulties, and not with the arrogant assumption that because they were defeated they were incompetent, and that all their actions proceeded from folly.

This, then, is not a history of the War of Independence, but a study of British strategy and leadership in a world war, the last in which the enemy were the Bourbons. I hope that American readers will not be disconcerted by the Whitehall perspective: that they will forgive my disregard of the great moral truths of the struggle, and bear with the habitual designation of the Patriots as rebels. The term is used with deliberation. It was the contemporary British usage, and any other would alter the perspective. "Patriots" is the language of opposition, not of those who fought the rebellion. "American" in many contexts is misleading. And rebels are conceded to be Revolutionaries only when they have succeeded, whereas the struggle was waged by men who believed that the rebellion could still be defeated.

After reading the table of contents, list here several questions you would expect the book to answer.

1. _____
_____
_____

2. _____
_____
_____

3. _____
_____
_____

Now return to pre-read and read the preface, starting on page 331, before going on to the questions below.

1. The overall organization of the book is, as you see, straightforward narrative; complexities in organization result from the fact that the story has many threads. To get at the organization of a history book like this one, it helps to read the table of contents with a great effort to *visualize* the movement of the story. Imagine you are a movie camera zooming in and out as necessary, swinging across wide areas when the script calls for it. Thus, the first part of the table of contents has a sweep of scenes like this:

    Introduction: *London, government offices*

    Part One, Chapter I: *America, London, America*

    Chapter II: *London, government offices*

    Chapter III: *England, possibly moving westward across the Atlantic*

    Chapter IV: *America — Quebec and Boston briefly, then New York*

    Chapter V: *London, then the camera pulls back to take in England*

Now continue establishing the scenes for the rest of the chapters, where possible.

Part Two, Chapter VI: _____

Chapter VII: London (why?) _____

Chapter VIII: _____

Chapter IX: _____

Chapter X: _____

Chapter XI: _____

Chapter XII: _____

Part Three, Chapter XIII: _____

Chapter XIV: _____

Chapter XV: _____

Chapter XVI: _____

Part Four, Chapter XVII: _____

Chapter XVIII: _____

Chapter XIX: _____

Chapter XX: (more specifically than the title of the chapter, or than

just "England," please) _____

Part Five, Chapter XXI: _____

Chapter XXII: _____

Chapter XXIII: _____

Chapter XXIV: _____

Part Six, Chapter XXV: _____

Chapter XXVI: _____

Chapter XXVII: _____

Chapter XXVIII: _____

Chapter XXIX: _____

Conclusion: _____

2. What does that analysis tell you about the *balance* of the book? Which

   Part title sums up the scope of the book most closely? _____

   _____

   _____

   _____

   _____

3. From the viewpoint of the British ministers (those "servants of Kronos"),
   the war presented certain problems that American histories of the Revolution often fail to emphasize. Reading through the table of contents again,
   and comparing it with the preface, you will see problems like these:
   Shipping and supplies (Chs. III, V, XI, XXI, XXV)
   Command of the seas and control of the English Channel (*Ch. X*)
   Which of the following other problems do you find? If in the table of contents, mark the chapter number; if in the preface, mark "P," if both, mark
   chapter number and "P," and if neither, mark "X."
   a. The strategic difficulty of waging world war in eighteenth-century

      conditions _____

   b. British governmental politics _____

   c. British public opinion _____
   d. The Far East, and India in particular (your answer to this may depend on

      how much history you know, but that's all right) _____

   _____

   e. British trade _____

   f. Problems with military commanders _____

   g. Defense of Gibraltar; the Mediterranean _____

   h. The quality of the American military commanders _____

4. *Where is Bunker Hill, or Lexington?* Which is to say that from an American point of view, many familiar elements in the Revolution are missing from the overall plan of this book, just as some elements are prominent that do not figure so large in most of our history books. What are some of the miss-

   ing items? _____

   _____

5. More importantly, for your understanding of this book, what less familiar

   elements are most emphasized? _____

   _____

6. What is the author's purpose in this book? _____

   _____

   _____

7. The preface breaks into three parts. What is the chief concern of each?

   a. _____

   b. _____

   c. _____

8. Who was Britain's enemy in the war? Which part or chapter of the book

   supports your answer? _____

9. As distinct from the author's stated purpose, he clearly has a thesis to prove about the British conduct of the war. What does the thesis seem to be?

   _____

   _____

10. Of the many elements that contributed to Britain's defeat, which ones does

   the author hold were the most important? _____

   _____

Outlining

For this exercise construct a close and detailed outline of the main topics and subsidiary details of the following article. Read the article, marking topic sentences with a double pencil line in the margin next to each. Then turn to the answer space where you will find a partial skeleton of the outline. You are to complete the skeleton with topics and details in their proper places. This is not a timed exercise. You may refer to the article as you complete the outline.

"A Chemist's Look at the Bacterial Cell"[7]
from *Molecular Biology of the Gene*
by JAMES D. WATSON

The most important aspect of living cells is their tendency to grow and divide. In this process, food molecules are absorbed from the external environment and transformed into cellular constituents. The rates of cell growth vary tremendously, but in general the smallest cells grow the fastest. Under optimal conditions some bacteria double their number every 20 minutes, whereas most larger mammalian cells can divide only once about every 24 hours. But, independent of the length of the time interval, growth and division necessarily demand that the number of cellular molecules double with each cell generation. One way, therefore, of asking the question, "What is life?" is to ask how a cell doubles its molecular content, that is, how biological molecules are replicated as a cell grows.

BACTERIA GROW UNDER SIMPLE, WELL-DEFINED CONDITIONS

Today most serious questions about cell growth and division are studied by using microorganisms, especially the bacteria. The tendency to concentrate on microorganisms does not arise from a belief that bacteria are fundamentally more important than higher organisms. The converse is obviously true to human beings, naturally curious to know about themselves and anxious to use information about their own chemical makeup to combat the various diseases threatening their existence. Nonetheless, upon even a superficial examination, the difficulties of thoroughly mastering the chemical events in a higher organism are staggering. There are about 5×10^{12} cells in a human being, each of whose existence is intimately related to the behavior of many other cells. It is therefore difficult to study the growth of a single cell within a multicellular organism without taking into consideration the influence of its surrounding cells.

Much effort has been devoted to learning how to grow the cells of multicellular organisms in an isolated system. In this work (often called *tissue culture*) small groups of cells, or sometimes single cells, are removed from a plant or animal and placed under controlled laboratory conditions in a solution containing a variety of food molecules. In the first experiments, the isolated cells almost invariably died, but now, partly because of a better understanding of the nutritional requirements of cells, they often grow and divide to form large numbers of new cells. Such freely growing plant and animal cells have been of much value in showing how cells aggregate to form organized groups of similar cells (tissues), and even more striking, how tissues unite in the test tube to form bodies morphologically identical to small regions of organs, such as the liver or the kidney. On the other hand, tissue culture cells are not ideal objects for studying cell growth and division. Even though many cells of higher organisms will grow in isolation, it must be remembered that this is not their normal way of existence, and, unless precautions are taken, they tend to aggregate quickly into multicellular groups. Thus even today the isolated growth of cells from higher organisms can be difficult and time consuming.

In contrast, the cells of many microorganisms normally grow free, as single cells, separating from each other as soon as cell division occurs. It is thus fairly easy to grow such single-celled organisms under well-defined laboratory conditions, since the conditions of growth in the scientist's test tube are not radically different from the conditions under which they normally grow outside the laboratory. In contrast to mammalian cells, which require a large variety of growth supplements, many bacteria will grow on a simple, well-defined diet or medium. For example, the bacteria *Escherichia coli* will grow on an aqueous solution containing just glucose and several inorganic ions (Table 3-1).

TABLE 3-1   *A simple synthetic growth medium for E. coli*[a]

NH_4Cl	1.0 g
$MgSO_4$	0.13 g
KH_2PO_4	3.0 g
Na_2HPO_4	6.0 g
Glucose	4.0 g
Water	1000 ml

[a] Traces of other ions (e.g., Fe^{2+}) are also required for growth. Usually these are not added separately, since they are normally present as contaminants in either the added inorganic salts or the water itself.

The growth of a specific bacterium is usually not dependent on the availability of a specific carbon source. Most bacteria are highly adaptable as to which organic molecules they can use as their carbon and energy sources. Glucose can be replaced by a variety of other organic molecules, and the greater the variety of food molecules supplied, the faster a cell generally grows. For example, if *E. coli* grows upon only glucose, about 60 minutes are required at 37°C to double the cell mass. But if glucose is supplemented by the various amino acids and purine and pyrimidine bases (the precursors of nucleic acids), then only 20 minutes are necessary for the doubling of cell mass. This effect is due to the direct incorporation of these components into proteins and nucleic acids, sparing the cell the task of carrying out the synthesis of the building blocks. There is a lower limit, however, to the time necessary to double the cell mass (often called the *generation time*): No matter how favorable the growth conditions, bacteria are unable to divide more than once every 20 minutes.

E. COLI IS THE BEST UNDERSTOOD ORGANISM
AT THE MOLECULAR LEVEL!

Over the past 20 years there has been an increasing polarization of effort toward work with the bacterium *E. coli* and evolutionarily related organisms. Because of its small size, normal lack of pathogenicity to any common organism, and ease of growth under laboratory conditions, *E. coli* is now the most intensively studied organism except for man. Many other bacteria besides *E. coli* possess the same favorable attributes, and the original reasons for choosing *E. coli* are essentially accidental. Once serious work had started on *E. coli,* however, it obviously made no sense to switch to another organism if *E. coli* could be used. Even now the tendency to concentrate on *E. coli* is increasing, because parallel with the chemical studies, extensive successful genetic analysis has also been carried out. Our knowledge of the genetics of *E. coli* is thus much more complete than our knowledge of that of any other bacterium or lower plant. As we shall see, the combined methods of genetics and biochemistry are so powerful that it is often just not sensible to use in biochemical studies an organism with which genetic analysis is not possible.

The average *E. coli* cell is rod-shaped and about 2μ in length and 1μ in diameter. It grows by increasing in length, followed by a fission process that generates two cells of equal length. Growth occurs best at temperatures about 37°C, perhaps to suit it for existence in the intestines of higher mammals, where it is frequently found as a harmless parasite. It will, however, regularly grow and divide at temperatures as low as 20°. Cell growth proceeds much more slowly at these low temperatures; the generation time under otherwise optimal conditions is about 120 minutes at 20°C.

Cell number and size are often measured by observation under the light microscope (and occasionally the electron microscope). Such observation, however, cannot reveal whether a visible cell is alive or dead. This can be determined only by seeing whether a given cell forms daughter cells. This determination is usually made by spreading a small number of cells on top of a solid agar surface (Figure 3–2), which has been supplemented with the nutrients necessary for cell growth. If a cell is alive, it will grow to form two daughter cells which in turn give rise to subsequent generations of daughter cells. The net result after 12 to 24 hours of incubation at 37°C is discrete masses (*colonies*) of bacterial cells. Provided that the colonies do not overlap, each must have arisen from the initial presence of a single bacterial cell.

The growth of bacteria may also be followed in liquid nutrient solutions. If a nutrient medium is inoculated with a small number of rapidly dividing bacteria from a similar medium, the bacteria will continue dividing with a constant division time, doubling the number of bacteria each generation time. Thus the number of bacteria increases in an exponential (logarithmic) fashion. *Exponential growth* continues until the number of cells reaches such a high level that the initial optimal nutritional conditions no longer exist. One of the first factors that usually limits growth is the supply of

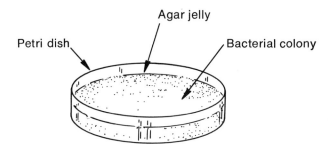

Agar jelly

Petri dish

Bacterial colony

FIGURE 3-2   The multiplication of single bacterial cells to form colonies. *E. coli* cells are usually not motile. Thus when a cell has divided on a solid surface, the two daughter cells and all their descendants will tend to remain next to each other. After 24 hours at 37° C, each initial living cell has given rise to a solid mass of cells.

oxygen. When the number of cells is low, the oxygen available by diffusion from the liquid interface is sufficient, but as the number of cells rises additional oxygen is needed. It is often supplied either by bubbling oxygen through the solution or by shaking the solution rapidly. Even with violent aeration, the growth rates begin to slow down after the cell density reaches about 10^9 cells per milliliter, and a tendency develops for the cells being produced to be shorter. Finally, at cell densities of about 5×10^9 cells per milliliter, cell growth is discontinued, for still unclear nutritional reasons. The term *growth curve* is frequently used to describe the increase of cell numbers as a function of time.

As guideposts, a few topics of the skeleton have been filled in; yet the skeleton has been left only partially complete. You are to complete it.

I. _____

   A. _____

     _____

     _____

II. Research today relies heavily on microorganisms, especially bacteria.

   A. Problems of using _____

     1. _____

     2. _____

       a. Uses: _____

       b. _____

B. _____

_____

_____

_____

_____

_____

C. *E. Coli* _____

1. _____

_____

_____

2. Growth _____

_____

_____

3. _____

a. _____

b. _____

(1) on agar _____

(2) _____

(a) _____

_____

_____

(b) _____

_____

_____

_____

Question Technique

Return to the article you have just outlined (page 338). Turn the first sentence of each paragraph into a question. Does the rest of the paragraph answer that question? When you finish rereading the article, write out (in the answer spaces below) the question you formulated for each paragraph, and then indicate which sentence contributes most to the answer. Or, if you decide that a paragraph does not answer the question you derive from its first sentence, write out a new question that does fit the information given by the paragraph.

When you have finished all the paragraphs, write out one master question that fits the information provided in the entire article.

This is not a timed exercise. Of course you will need to refer to the article while you work out the questions. Since the paragraphs have not been labeled *A, B, C,* etc., you will need to supply the labels.

A _____

_____

_____

_____ Sentence number _____ No one sentence can be chosen _____
If the paragraph does not answer the question, what question *does* it answer?

_____

_____

_____

B _____

_____

_____

_____ Sentence number _____ No one sentence can be chosen _____
If the paragraph does not answer the question, what question *does* it answer?

_____

_____

_____

C _____

_____

_____

_____ Sentence number _____ No one sentence can be chosen _____
If the paragraph does not answer the question, what question *does* it answer?

_____

_____

_____

D _____

_____

_____

_____ Sentence number _____ No one sentence can be chosen _____
If the paragraph does not answer the question, what question *does* it answer?

_____

_____

_____

E _____

_____

_____

_____ Sentence number _____ No one sentence can be chosen _____
If the paragraph does not answer the question, what question *does* it answer?

_____

_____

_____

F _____

_____

_____

_____ Sentence number _____ No one sentence can be chosen _____
If the paragraph does not answer the question, what question *does* it answer?

_____

_____

_____

G _____

_____

_____

_____ Sentence number _____ No one sentence can be chosen _____
If the paragraph does not answer the question, what question *does* it answer?

_____

_____

_____

H _____

_____

_____

_____ Sentence number _____ No one sentence can be chosen _____
If the paragraph does not answer the question, what question *does* it answer?

_____

_____

_____

I _____

_____

_____

_____ Sentence number _____ No one sentence can be chosen _____
If the paragraph does not answer the question, what question *does* it answer?

_____

_____

_____

Summarizing

The following article is from a history of the development of the English language. It treats the roots in history of the differences between present-day British Standard English and present-day American. For this exercise, your purpose in reading the article is to summarize each paragraph (the first labeled paragraph is actually two together) and then the entire passage. There are no multiple-choice questions. Instead, use the answer space, as you finish reading each paragraph, to write out your own one-sentence summary; when you come to the end of the article, use a couple of sentences to summarize it as a whole. This is not a timed exercise. You will need to refer to the article as you write your summaries.

"The Conservatism of American English"[8]
from *The Origins and Development of the English Language*
by THOMAS PYLES

A

Since language undergoes no changes as a result of crossing an ocean, the first English-speaking colonists in America continued to speak precisely as they had done in England. But people isolated from their mother country tend always to be conservative, linguistically as well as in other ways, and the English spoken in America at the present day has retained a good many characteristics of earlier British English which do not survive in present British English, much as Icelandic has retained characteristics of older Scandinavian which have been lost in the other Scandinavian languages.

Thus to regard American English as inferior to British English is to impugn earlier Standard British English as well, for there was doubtless little difference at the time of the Revolution. There is a strong likelihood, for instance, that George III and Lord Cornwallis pronounced *ask, after, path, glass, dance,* and the like exactly the same as did George Washington and John Hancock — that is, as the overwhelming majority of Americans do to this day. It was similar with the treatment of postvocalic *r*, whose loss under certain circumstances did not occur in the speech of the London area until about the time of the Revolution.

B

Other supposed characteristics of American English are also to be found in pre-Revolutionary British English, and there is very good reason indeed for the conclusion of the eminent Swedish Anglicist Eilert Ekwall that from the time of the Revolution on, "American pronunciation has been on the whole independent of British; the result has been that American pronunciation has not come to share the development undergone later by Standard British, but remains at about the stage it had reached by the time of the Revolution." Ekwall's concern is exclusively with pronunciation, but the principle implied holds good also for many lexical items, some morphological characteristics, and probably to some degree for intonation as well. American retention of *gotten* is an example of conservatism, though it was of course not consciously preserved. This form, the usual past participle of *get* in older British English, survives in present Standard British English mainly in the phrase "ill-gotten gains"; but it is very much alive in American English, being the usual past participial form of the verb except in the senses 'to have' and 'to be obliged to.'[a] Similarly, American English has kept *fall* for the season[b] and *deck* for a pack of cards (though American English also uses *pack*); and it has retained certain phonological characteristics of earlier British English to be discussed later in some detail.

C

It works both ways, however; for American English has lost certain features — mostly vocabulary items — which have survived in British English, for example *waistcoat* (the name for a garment which Americans call a *vest*, a word which in England usually means 'undershirt'), *fortnight*, a useful term completely lost to American English, and a number of topographical terms which Americans had no need for — words like *fen, wold, spinney, copse, dell, heath,* and *moor.* Americans, on the other hand, desperately needed terms to designate topographical features different from any known in the Old World. To remedy the deficiency, they used new compounds of English words like *backwoods, watergap,* and *underbrush*; they adapted English words to new uses, like *creek*, in British English 'a small arm of the sea,' which in American English may mean 'any small stream,' and they adopted foreign words like *prairie* (ultimately derived from Fr. *pré* 'field'), *canyon* (Sp. *cañón* 'tube'), and *mesa* (likewise Spanish). It was similar with the naming of flora and fauna strange to the colonists. When they saw a bird that somewhat resembled the English robin, they simply called it a robin, though it was not the same bird at all. When they saw an animal that was totally unlike anything that they had ever seen before, they might call it by its Indian name, if they could find out what this was, for example *raccoon* and *woodchuck.* It was similar with the names of plants: *catalpa* and its variant *catawba* are of Muskhogean origin; *Johnny-jump-up* was inspired by a crude kind of fancy; *sweet potato* might have originated just as well in England as in America except for the fact that this particular variety of potato did not exist in England.

---

[a] For instance "He has gotten permission to go" and "He would have gotten there sooner if he had left earlier" as contrasted with "He hasn't got the nerve to do it" and "He has got to do it."
[b] *Autumn* was first used in English by Geoffrey Chaucer, according to the *OED.*

D

American English is, as we have said, essentially a development of seventeenth-century British English. Except in vocabulary, there are probably few significant characteristics of American English which are not traceable to British English. There are also some American English characteristics which were doubtless dialectal British English in the seventeenth century, for there were certainly dialect speakers among the earliest settlers, though they would seem to have had little influence. A literary standard had arisen in London long before, as we have seen, which had greatly influenced the various regional types of common speech of England — the speech of the majority of those Englishmen to settle permanently in the New World, for these were not illiterate bumpkins but ambitious and industrious members of the upper-lower and lower-middle classes, with a sprinkling of educated men — clergymen, lawyers, and even a few younger sons of the aristocracy. It is likely that there was a cultured nucleus in all of the early American communities. Such facts as these explain why American English resembles present Standard British English more closely than it resembles any other British type of speech.

E

In American English there are three main regional types — Northern, Midland, and Southern — with a good many different blendings of these as one travels westward. There are also a number of subtypes on the Atlantic Coast, such as the speech of the New York and Boston areas in the North and the Charleston-Savannah area in the South. All types of American English have grown out of the regional modifications of the British Standard — with some coloring from the British dialects — as it existed in the seventeenth century, when it was much less rigid than it is today. Boston failed to maintain its early pre-eminence as the hub of American culture, such as it was. Had it not done so, America might well have had a geographical and ultimately a caste standard based upon the speech of Boston. As things have turned out, an American may use with complete social impunity any of the types of speech to which we have referred or practically any modifications thereof. So long as it is obvious from his bearing and from what he talks about that he is an educated man (in the American sense of the term), his speech will pass muster, that is, be socially acceptable in any part of the country despite occasional references to a "harsh Midwestern *r*" and a "lazy Southern drawl." It should be stressed at this point that, compared with British English, French, Italian, Spanish, German, and other European languages, American speech is quite homogeneous: there is no type of American English which is not readily understood — though regional prejudice may cause an occasional eyebrow to lift — in all parts of the country, with the exception of Gullah, spoken by about 100,000 Negroes who live along the coastal region of South Carolina and Georgia, and who have lived there in cultural isolation for many generations. A Texas oil magnate speaks in one way; a Back Bay Bostonian in a slightly different way; and a landed

Virginian in a yet slightly different way. But as long as they all speak like "educated" men, they all speak "good" American English. The Chicagoan is just as proud of pronouncing his *r*'s — provided that he ever gives a thought to the matter — as the Charlestonian is of losing them. Neither practice is ordinarily regarded as either superior or inferior; they are merely regarded as somewhat different, and the difference is not always noticed, though it usually is.

Write your summaries below.

A. _____

_____

_____

B. _____

_____

_____

C. _____

_____

_____

D. _____

_____

_____

E. _____

_____

_____

The entire article: _____

_____

_____

_____

_____

Reading Speed Exercise: Average Level 7

It has, of course, been the aim to have all the speed exercises of the same level about the same in difficulty. But one aspect of the difficulty you find in any passage is, naturally, what you bring to it by way of interest and familiarity. As we are now at the end of the series of speed exercises in this book, for the next "measured mile" we return to the same source as the first speed exercise you took. Because this is the final measurement you will make of your progress in developing your reading speeds, we want to come as close as possible to that first exercise, in general style of writing and familiarity of subject matter.

The next selection, then, is from *Kon-Tiki,* by Thor Heyerdahl. The difficulty of content and style is about average. That is, skilled readers read it at the speed they use for other material of a factual nature, popularly written.

You are to read the selection against time. Follow your instructor's directions in class, or the Instructions for Timing on page 474.

Before reading, practice with the Eye Movements in Reading exercise on pages 54–56.

Do not pre-read the selection; the timed reading exercises are designed to measure improvements in speed alone.

After reading the selection and recording your time, go on to the ten true-false and multiple-choice questions starting on page 353. There is no time limit for the questions, but it will invalidate the exercise if you refer to the passage while answering them.

Begin reading here.

"Off to a Good Start"[9]
from Kon-Tiki
by THOR HEYERDAHL

There was a bustle in Callao Harbor the day the *Kon-Tiki* was to be towed out to sea. The minister of marine had ordered the naval tug *Guardian Rios* to tow us out of the bay and cast us off clear of the coastal traffic, out where in times gone by the Indians used to lie fishing from their rafts. The papers had published the news under both red and black headlines, and there was a crowd of people down on the quays from early in the morning of April 28.

We six who were to assemble on board all had little things to do at the eleventh hour, and, when I came down to the quay, only Herman was there keeping guard over the raft. I intentionally stopped the car a long way off and walked the whole length of the mole to stretch my legs thoroughly for the last time for no one knew how long. I jumped on board the raft, which looked an utter chaos of banana clusters, fruit baskets, and sacks which had been hurled on board at the very last moment and were to be stowed and made fast. In the middle of the heap Herman sat resignedly holding on to a cage with a green parrot in it, a farewell present from a friendly soul in Lima.

"Look after the parrot a minute," said Herman. "I must go ashore and have a last glass of beer. The tug won't be here for hours."

He had hardly disappeared among the swarm on the quay when people began to point and wave. And round the point at full speed came the tug *Guardian Rios*. She dropped anchor on the farther side of a waving forest of masts which blocked the way in to the *Kon-Tiki* and sent in a large motor-boat to tow us out between the sailing craft. She was packed full of seamen, officers, and movie photographers, and, while orders rang out and cameras clicked, a stout towrope was made fast to the raft's bow.

"*Un momento*," I shouted in despair from where I sat with the parrot. "It's too early; we must wait for the others—*los expedicionarios*," I explained and pointed toward the city.

But nobody understood. The officers only smiled politely, and the knot at our bow was made fast in more than exemplary manner. I cast off the rope and flung it overboard with all manner of signs and gesticulations. The parrot utilized the opportunity afforded by all the confusion to stick its beak out of the cage and turn the knob of the door, and when I turned round it was strutting cheerfully about the bamboo deck. I tried to catch it, but it shrieked rudely in Spanish and fluttered away over the banana clusters. With one eye on the sailors who were trying to cast a rope over the bow I started a wild chase after the parrot. It fled shrieking into the bamboo cabin, where I got it into a corner and caught it by one leg as it tried to flutter over me. When I came out again and stuffed my flapping trophy into its cage, the sailors on land had cast off the raft's moorings, and we were dancing helplessly in and out with the backwash of the long swell that came rolling in over the mole. In despair I seized a paddle and vainly tried to parry a violent bump as the raft was flung against the wooden piles of the quay. Then the motorboat started, and with a jerk the *Kon-Tiki* began her long voyage.

My only companion was a Spanish-speaking parrot which sat glaring sulkily in a cage. People on shore cheered and waved, and the swarthy movie photographers in the motorboat almost jumped into the sea in their eagerness to catch every detail of the expedition's dramatic start from Peru. Despairing and alone I stood on the raft looking out for my lost companions, but none appeared. So we came out to the *Guardian Rios*, which was lying with steam up ready to lift anchor and start. I was up the rope ladder in a twinkling and made so much row on board that the start was postponed and a boat sent back to the quay. It was away a good while, and then it came back full of pretty *señoritas* but without a single one of the *Kon-Tiki's* missing men. This was all very well but it did not solve my problems, and, while the raft swarmed with charming *señoritas*, the boat went back on a fresh search for *los expedicionarios noruegos*.

Meanwhile Erik and Bengt came sauntering down to the quay with their arms full of reading matter and odds and ends. They met the whole stream of people on its way home and were finally stopped at a police barrier by a kindly official who told them there was nothing more to see. Bengt told the officer, with an airy gesture of his cigar, that they had not come to see anything; they themselves were going with the raft.

"It's no use," the officer said indulgently. "The *Kon-Tiki* sailed an hour ago."

"Impossible," said Erik, producing a parcel. "Here's the lantern!"

"And there's the navigator," said Bengt, "and I'm the steward."

They forced their way past, but the raft had gone. They trotted desperately to and fro along the mole where they met the rest of the party, who also were searching eagerly for the vanished raft. Then they caught sight of the boat coming in, and so we were all six finally united and the water was foaming round the raft as the *Guardian Rios* towed us out to sea.

It had been late in the afternoon when at last we started, and the *Guardian Rios* would not cast us off till we were clear of the coastal traffic next morning. Directly we were clear of the mole we met a bit of a head sea, and all the small boats which were accompanying us turned back one by one. Only a few big yachts came with us out to the entrance to the bay to see how things would go out there.

The *Kon-Tiki* followed the tug like an angry billy goat on a rope, and she butted her bow into the head sea so that the water rushed on board. This did not look very promising, for this was a calm sea compared with what we had to expect. In the middle of the bay the towrope broke, and our end of it sank peacefully to the bottom while the tug steamed ahead. We flung ourselves down along the side of the raft to fish for the end of the rope, while the yachts went on and tried to stop the tug. Stinging jellyfish as thick as washtubs splashed up and down with the seas alongside the raft and covered all the ropes with a slippery, stinging coating of jelly. When the raft rolled one way, we hung flat over the side waving our arms down toward the surface of the water, until our fingers just touched the slimy towrope. Then the raft rolled back again, and we all stuck our heads deep down into the sea, while salt water and giant jellyfish poured over our backs. We spat and cursed and pulled jellyfish fibers out of our hair, but when the tug came back the rope end was up and ready for splicing.

Now note your reading time. Record it below and go on to the questions.

YOUR READING TIME: _____MIN. _____SEC. _____W.P.M. COMPREHENSION SCORE: _____%
(WORDS PER MINUTE FROM THE TABLE ON PAGE 475.)

Please do not read these questions until you have read the article itself against time. Do not refer to the article as you answer them. Choose the *one best* answer to each question, and enter the corresponding letter in the proper answer space.

1. The raft *Kon-Tiki* left Callao Harbor early in May. (T) True; (F) False

   ANSWER _____

2. Newspaper reports had mentioned the expedition, but not many people came down to the quays to watch the *Kon-Tiki*'s departure. (T) True; (F) False

   ANSWER _____

3. The author was the only member of the expedition who could speak Spanish. (T) True; (F) False

   ANSWER _____

4. The raft did not finally get started until late afternoon. (T) True; (F) False

   ANSWER _____

5. The naval tug *Guardian Rios* was assigned to tow the raft (a) past the surf; (b) past the breakwater at the harbor entrance; (c) out of the bay and clear of coastal traffic; (d) out into the eastward-flowing currents; (e) out of sight of land.

   ANSWER _____

6. How did the parrot get out of its cage? (a) One of the movie cameramen let it out to add excitement to the scene; (b) the cage door had never been properly fastened; (c) the parrot turned the knob of the cage door with its beak; (d) the motion of the raft loosened the cage door; (e) it never did get out, but was prevented just in time.

   ANSWER _____

7. The parrot played an important role in the story because (a) while the author was chasing it, the sailors from the tug cast off the raft from the pier; (b) it attracted the attention of the sailors, and delayed them from casting off the raft; (c) it attracted the attention of one of the raft's crew, on shore, bringing him back to the raft just in time; (d) it caused one of the author's companions, while chasing it, to miss the raft; (e) while preventing its escape from the cage, one of the sailors let go the last rope to the pier.

   ANSWER _____

8. At the entrance to the bay, the towrope broke (a) because the raft met very heavy head seas; (b) because of the weight of the water rushing over the bow; (c) despite the fact that the sea was quite calm; (d) despite the fact that the tug could make little progress through the many small boats; (e) despite the fact that it had been made of the primitive materials the expedition was relying on to prove their theory of early crossings of the ocean.

   ANSWER _____

9. The breaking of the towrope is mentioned because (a) it was an ominous warning that the raft was having difficulty even in fairly calm weather; (b) it adds a further touch of comedy to the situation; (c) it shows that the raft was poorly equipped; (d) it was the crowning accident in a day full of mishaps; (e) it was the first incident to lead to the disproving of the expedition's theory about early crossings of the ocean.

   ANSWER _____

10. What is the best explanation of the lighthearted tone in which the author recounts these incidents? (a) He is clearly preparing the reader for further comic incidents that will occur throughout the book; (b) he is looking for "comic relief" to lighten what would otherwise be a dry scientific discussion; (c) without saying so directly, he is dramatizing the real danger and adventure they are undertaking, by the ironic device of contrast with the "comic-opera" mood of their start; (d) he is preparing the reader for a philosophic acceptance of the failure of the expedition; (e) he is preparing to shock the reader with a sudden change of tone to serious danger and even tragedy.

ANSWER _____

Now check your answers, and enter your score on your Progress Profile, page vii.

3

Integrated Application
of Basic Techniques

CHAPTER 13

Reading in Specialized Subjects

Pre-read this chapter as your first step in reading. As your second step, list below the questions you expect the chapter to answer.

_____

_____

_____

_____

_____

_____

The basic techniques of reading, from pre-reading a whole book, or even a whole subject for study, down to individual analysis of paragraphs, can be applied almost universally because as we have said they take advantage of basic and almost universal similarities in practical prose, patterns that writers tend to follow regardless of subject matter. But, of course, there are also differences between kinds of practical prose, between writers, and between subject matters. An everyday example is the newspaper headline story, whose typical structure, as we saw in Chapter 12, is unlike any other form of writing. The most striking differences from the usual reading patterns and problems, and the most striking difficulties in reading, are normally found in certain specialized subjects, like natural sciences, social sciences, history, law, and business. The reading problems of specialized subjects are the concern of this chapter. Its purpose is to show you how you can approach the mastery of even the most difficult subjects by the flexible and imaginative use of your basic techniques.

What is a *specialized subject?* We have listed some broad categories above. But why should these subjects present special reading problems?

We can discover part of the answer by contrasting two different reports of the same event, one report "specialized," the other not. Here are the opening paragraphs of a report in the scientific journal *Nature,* and of a newspaper story based on that report.

Demonstration: A Popular and a Specialized Report of the Same Research

Science Report
Physics: Energy waves undetected

One of the more imaginative theories in physics—that there are waves of energy associated with gravity—has received a setback. An attempt to detect these so-called gravitational waves from deep in space by searching for radio pulses, which would almost certainly be produced at the same time, has so far drawn a blank.

Gravitational waves were predicted many years ago in Einstein's general theory of relativity but experimental evidence which seemed to point to their existence came as recently as 1969 from Professor J. Weber's investigations at Maryland University and the Argonne National Laboratory in the United States. He claims that two large metal cylinders, spaced 1,000 km. apart at the two laboratories, are set vibrating several times each week by gravitational waves. The waves are recognized by the receipt of two simultaneous signals from the electronic instruments that detect the vibrations.

Scientists in Dublin and Cambridge have set up radio receivers at five different sites in an attempt to obtain supporting evidence for Professor Weber's discovery. They have looked out for radio pulses arriving at all the detecting stations at the same time and in this way claim to have eliminated spurious results caused by local radio disturbances.

So far their search has been unsuccessful, but Professor Weber has recently found that the centre of our galaxy may be a focal point for the production of these elusive waves. The collaborators on this side of the Atlantic have made sweeping changes to their experiment so that they can look for radio pulses coming from the same place.

All their new instruments, which include an extra station on Malta, are aimed at the centre of the galaxy. They hope to find radio pulses which can be directly related to the signals received from Professor Weber's apparatus.

If the new radio experiment produces positive results it will be excellent support for Professor Weber, but if it is' inconclusive it does not by any means spell the end for the theory of gravitational waves. Radio pulses associated with the waves could be absorbed on their way to Earth or they may not be produced at all. But this is unlikely because the rather violent conditions necessary to produce gravitational radiation would also certainly be ideal for the production of radio waves.

By Nature-Times News Service

Source: Nature. October 24 (228. 346 ; 1970).

Spaced Receiver Observations of Radio Pulses[1]

by

W. N. CHARMAN
J. V. JELLEY
J. H. FRUIN
Nuclear Physics Division,
Atomic Energy Research Establishment,
Harwell, Berkshire

E. R. HODGSON
P. F. SCOTT
J. R. SHAKESHAFT
Mullard Radio Astronomy Observatory,
Cavendish Laboratory,
University of Cambridge

G. A. BAIRD
T. DELANEY
B. G. LAWLESS
The Physics Department,
University College, Dublin

R. W. P. DREVER
W. P. S. MEIKLE
Department of Natural Philosophy,
University of Glasgow

R. A. PORTER
R. E. SPENCER
University of Manchester,
Nuffield Radio Astronomy Laboratories,
Jodrell Bank, Cheshire

Preliminary observations have been carried out to look for radio signals associated with gravitational waves. Although inconclusive, the observations from five receivers in the British Isles suggest the value of pressing on with further experiments.

Towards the end of last year, the evidence for the detection of pulses of gravitational waves had reached a significance sufficient to arouse interest in many areas of astronomy and physics. It occurred to one of us (J. V. J.) that if Weber's flux were $\sim 10^4$ erg cm^{-2} s^{-1} (ref. 1) at the Earth, an exceedingly small fraction ($\sim 10^{-19}$) of this energy, which might be radiated into ~ 1 MHz bandwidth of the radio spectrum, would be detectable with the very simplest of radio antennae (a single dipole for example) and a receiver of even modest performance. This suggestion, made casually at a meeting in Cambridge, was immediately taken up by the Mullard Radio Astronomy Observatory. It was realized that the detection of isolated radio pulses, of say a few per day, in the presence of man-made interference, lightning or other geophysical phenomena, required simultaneous observations at widely spaced sites. It was further realized that observations at two or more frequencies could in principle provide valuable evidence as to whether any events observed were galactic in origin, for the interstellar plasma would cause dispersion. Any such events need not, of course, necessarily be associated with gravitational pulses but could originate, for example, in supernovae explosions or in the rather energetic events which Scargle and Harlan suggest are responsible both for the wisp activity and the pulsar spin-up in the Crab nebula. It may be of relevance that coincident radio pulses have already been observed, on a baseline ~ 150 km and during hours of darkness, in the course of early work on scintillation phenomena; as far as we know, these events have not been explained and further events of this type might easily have been overlooked in the course of subsequent radio astronomical investigations.

We are here reporting some preliminary observations which have been carried out simultaneously with receivers sited at five locations distributed over England, Scotland and Ireland, covering a range of baselines between 110 and 500 km. These sites are shown in Fig. 1.

At 151 MHz all five sites were equipped with almost identical systems. Each station had two half-wave dipole antennae mounted on the ground, 5λ apart, approximately $(\lambda/4)$ above a metal ground plane on an EW-baseline; they operated as phase-switched interferometers. Bandwidths varied among the stations, between 200 kHz and 1·5 MHz, and integrating time constants of between 0·3 and 1·0 s were used. The central lobes of these five interferometers were aligned to account for the differences in geographical longitude. Recordings were made on chart paper at speeds ranging between 6 inch and 24 inch per hour, and time marks enabled an accuracy ranging from ±24 s to ±6 s to be attained for the times of the recorded events. Similar interferometers at lower frequencies also operated at certain stations as noted in Fig. 1. Most of the stations were operating by January 1, 1970, and the observations have been analysed until the end of May.

Many two-fold and multiple coincidences were obtained from the outset, but it soon became apparent that most of these were occurring during daylight hours and were attributable largely to Type III solar bursts. We therefore use in the analysis only events which occurred between sunset and sunrise. . . .

During five months of operation, some seventy-two "prompt" two-fold coincidences were observed within a 1 min resolving time, compared with forty-seven "delayed" coincidences. When the coincidence resolving time was reduced to 20 s, these numbers fell to thirty-five "prompt" and twenty-two "delayed" coincidences. The numbers of "prompt" two-fold coincidences are thus barely distinguishable from those expected by chance.

Five "prompt" coincidences occurred between three stations, however; these twice involved sequences of more than two pulses. Examples are shown in Fig. 2. Inspection of these three-fold events suggests that they are not attributable to a distant source, for (i) the precise pulse shapes differ at the individual stations and (ii) the polarity changes in the pulse sequence are inconsistent with the motion of a celestial source through the interferometer lobes. It is also significant that no four or five-fold coincidences have ever been observed. The 151 MHz data alone have therefore not so far yielded any evidence for radio pulses of extraterrestrial origin.

Recordings at the other frequencies have been scrutinized for evidence of delayed pulses. The technique used has been to assume a particular value of DM, compute the radio pulse delays expected at different frequencies and then, starting with event times recorded at the highest observing frequencies, look for corresponding events at the appropriate delay at lower frequencies. A computer program performs this analysis for successive increments of 25 in values of DM up to 2,000 electrons cm^{-3} pc. . . .

The newspaper article—true to the news formula that leads off with whatever seems most interest-arousing—begins with the significance of the findings: "One of the more imaginative theories . . . has received a setback." It then pauses to give background which the scientists themselves left out of their article, but which the general reader, even if interested in science, cannot be presumed to know: "Gravitational waves were predicted many years ago in Einstein's general theory of relativity . . . Professor J. Weber . . . claims that two large metal cylinders . . ." The language is nontechnical. Though space has been taken to supply background, much detail of the scientists' actual procedure and results has been left out. The difficulty of the article has been kept carefully within limits. Quick reading should give you a good grasp of the newspaper story, so far as it goes in explaining the subject.

When you then turn to the scientists' own report, it is immediately evident that it goes much farther. It is not so concerned with advertising the significance of the findings: indeed, from the first paragraph of the *Nature* report you could get almost the opposite impression from what the first paragraph of the newspaper article seems to mean. Another obvious fact about the scientists' own report is the highly technical vocabulary. Then when you look closer you see that a great deal of space is given to the procedures which obtained the reported results. All these differences that set off the scientific report from the journalistic one relate to a single general problem of specialist literature: it is characteristically written with the assumption that the reader is also a specialist. Thus, the reader is expected not only to know the words, but to be familiar with the recent developments, to be interested in the subject without needing a neon-lit lead paragraph to entice him into reading, and to see the significance of conclusions without trumpet fanfare. Then too, specialized writing is often clumsy, sometimes jargon-laden. More importantly, it is constructed with different aims—for, to a scientist, the significance of his results cannot by the very nature of science be more important than the validity of the procedures that obtained those results.

The contrast between these two reports of the same research points out the kinds of difficulties you must anticipate when you read in specialized subjects. To recapitulate, these difficulties begin with the author's sense of his audience, his assumption, except in the most elementary texts, that the reader will come to him prepared. Therefore vocabulary is technical, background clues are scanty, procedure and detail relentless and essential. And finally, the author cannot be expected to write with the skill of a professional journalist.

Yet often it would be fooling yourself to blame the difficulty of specialized material on bad writing. Writing is at most only one cause of difficulty. Many scientists and professional men are competent reporters. The best scientists often demonstrate an extraordinary talent for lucid explanation of their work, while among historians, for example, a clear or even an elegant style has traditionally been prized. Yet the best specialized writing suffers by comparison with the high craftsmanship of the popularizers, journalists, and editors of freshman textbooks, who have conditioned most readers to expect ideas, hard words, and tough concepts to be introduced carefully and cautiously. But, after all, there are still some subjects that are difficult by their very nature. Even if all scientists were writers of the quality of Charles Darwin or Julian Huxley, much scientific literature would be difficult to understand. And when the genuine difficulties are compounded by vocabulary, multiplied again by stiff or awkward style, and then squared and cubed by the need to master detail as well as general concept and conclusions—then your best reading skills are essential.

Natural Sciences

Vocabulary.   The Nobel Prize in Physics, one recent year, was shared by a Swede who worked in plasma physics and a Frenchman who first elaborated the distinctions between ferromagnetism, antiferromagnetism, and ferrimagnetism. Which demonstrates that even the names of world-famous scientific specialties may be words of highly technical meaning: can you state the difference between a physicist's plasma and a physician's? between ferro- and ferri-magnetism? Does it have to be said that accurate understanding of the technical terms is absolutely necessary for the reader in the natural sciences? Learning of terms continues throughout a scientific career. To illustrate the importance of technical vocabulary among a scientist's most basic skills, we need only point to studies that have discovered that it is precisely the leading scientists in every field who have the most complete mastery of the vocabularies of their fields. Yet, one of the first complaints of every teacher of graduate students in the sciences is the inadequacy and fuzziness of students' technical vocabularies.

Not many years ago, a beginning student had to learn as many new words in a science class as he had to learn in a foreign language class. Today, however, editors of elementary science textbooks are aware of the vocabulary problem, and work to ration new words where possible. Still, in a beginning science course, the student is hard put to learn even the carefully controlled vocabularies—perhaps as many as a thousand new words in a year's study. And when he comes to read original sources—the papers and books addressed by scientists to an audience of equals, the materials on which the textbooks are based—a far more extensive technical vocabulary is demanded.

You must learn the words. This is the obvious and only solution. It is imperative that you work intensively with your vocabulary whenever a selection in science contains more than two or three new words; unless you master them, your comprehension will suffer grievously. But you have two advantages working for you. First, you may call to your aid the methods for day-to-day extension of vocabulary that were presented in Chapter 8. Second, scientific words usually have a single, precisely defined meaning, or at most a small group of closely related usages. This makes the vocabulary of a science considerably easier to acquire than, for example, the basic vocabulary of a foreign language, where some of the simplest but most widely used words may have a dozen or more distinguishable meanings.

But even when you look up a technical word in the dictionary, the definition may be so abstruse that it helps you little. For example, consider the Merriam-Webster definition of *osmosis,* reprinted on the next page, which only a person who already has some training in biology would understand. In texts, at least, you will often find glossaries. The newest standard desk dictionaries are as up-to-date with scientific terms as their compilers can make them. But if you are reading widely in one specialized subject, you should buy one of the specialized dictionaries for that subject. Some, such as a good medical dictionary, are expensive; many are quite cheap, like the excellent paperback Penguin series (*Dictionary of Music, Dictionary of Geography,* and so on). When these most accurate tools are not available—say, in a midnight cramming session when the library is closed—you may find first aid by skimming farther ahead in the book you are reading, to discover other contexts for the puzzling terms, or by consulting the glossary of another text.

Pre-reading is simpler in the natural sciences than in most other subjects, yet even more essential. It is simpler because structural patterns are highly regular; for example, a scientific paper is put together something like the following:

os·mo·sis \äz'mōsəs, ä'sm-\ *n, pl* **osmo·ses** \-ō,sēz\ [alter. (influenced by Gk -*sis*) of ¹*osmose*] **1 :** the flow or diffusion that takes place through a semipermeable membrane (as of a living cell) typically separating either a solvent (as water) and a solution or a dilute solution and a concentrated solution and thus bringing about conditions for equalizing the concentrations of the components on the two sides of the membrane because of the unequal rates of passage in the two directions until equilibrium is reached; *esp* **:** the passage of solvent in distinction from the passage of solute; compare ABSORPTION 1c, DIALYSIS, ELECTROOSMOSIS, ENDOSMOSIS, EXOSMOSIS, IMBIBITION 2 a, SAP, TURGOR   **2 :** a process of absorption, interaction, or diffusion suggestive of the flow of osmotic action ⟨owing to the usual mysterious news ∼, had already heard about it —Agnes S. Turnbull⟩: as   **a :** an interaction or interchange (as of cultural groups or traits) by mutual penetration esp. through a separating medium   **b :** a usu. effortless often unconscious absorption or assimilation (as of ideas or influences) by a seemingly general permeation ⟨absorbing democratic habits and ideals as by ∼ —H.G.Rickover⟩ ⟨working alongside pupils in higher grades, the bright student gets advanced learning practically by ∼ —Gertrude Samuels⟩ ⟨acquired his ideas through thought processes, not through social ∼ —Roscoe Drummond⟩ ⟨a kind of cultural ∼, the unconscious absorption of Oriental influences through seemingly trivial contacts —Edmond Taylor⟩²

By permission. From *Webster's Third New International Dictionary*, copyright 1961 by G. & C. Merriam Co., Publishers of the Merriam-Webster Dictionaries.

"Abstract," that is, a short overall summarizing paragraph (see example page 66);

Brief orienting statement of what the problem is, in the context of current research;

Approach to the problem: the idea to be examined and means (experiments, observations, significant facts) to test it;

With that, or following it, the findings;

Conclusions, possibly discussed in relation to further research needed.

The more difficult the material you are reading, the more pre-reading is needed, for just as the immediate context of an unfamiliar word can give you your first suggestions of its meaning, so the overall context of an idea or concept, or the overall structure of a line of experimental investigation, are essential to understand the details in perspective.

While pre-reading, you will get an idea of the sentence and paragraph habits of the writer. Scientific writing tends to be dry, precise, close-grained, logical in sequence, and these qualities produce a certain uniformity of sentence structure within an author's writing. Paragraphs, to an even greater extent than usual in practical prose, have topic sentence first, expanded and supported by what follows.

Questions. In the natural sciences, the answers to the questions you bear in mind while reading are fairly obvious. After pre-reading a selection you will usually have a clear idea of the author's thesis and the problem he is attacking. Responsible scientists, also, conscientiously state the limitations of their studies and indicate whenever their conclusions should be accepted as tentative rather than final. Finally, in the natural sciences you will find it especially helpful, to grasp the details and to concentrate on the material, to turn the first sentence of each paragraph into a question and then read for the answer.

Thorough reading, skipping, and skimming. Since, as we have said, your understanding of an experiment or analysis usually depends on grasping every detail of exposition and reasoning, you must usually read thoroughly in the natural sciences. Skipping and skimming (preceded, of course, by pre-reading) do have a place in reading science, however. You skip and skim as you begin your overall research into the information already available, that is at the initial survey of an entire subject to determine what must be read thoroughly. Then during thorough reading, when you lose your way, skim when necessary to pick up the thread of development. When skimming for this purpose, skim the pages immediately preceding your place, then skim ahead of your place as well, to remind yourself of the line of development, to get further clues and insight, and to anticipate the coming difficulties.

History and the Social Sciences

Vocabulary in historical writing can be extensive, difficult, and sometimes technical. History is, after all, in its largest sense concerned with *all* man's activities, so that there can be a history of mathematics that will require a mathematical vocabulary, a history of bookbinding that will require appropriate technical terms, and so on. But in most cases, history books present no problems of vocabulary you cannot meet with techniques already described. Vocabulary in the social sciences, however, is uniquely deceptive. Many terms have the appearance of everyday language when they are actually used in special senses. (You have already seen an example of such a term in the extended definition of *culture*, pages 34–36.) Furthermore, the precise meanings of some key terms are the subject of disagreement and debate among social scientists. For example, *ego, myth, structure, status, crowd*—each is variously defined. Economists are almost alone among social scientists in having been able to reach agreement on the precise meanings of many of their technical terms. Agreement is possible in economics, sometimes at least, because such phrases as *marginal utility, indifference curve,* or *elasticity of demand* can also be stated mathematically.

Problems of vocabulary are, of course, worst for the beginner. He can turn to his dictionary or to the glossary of his textbook; yet these can only furnish the beginnings of understanding. In the social sciences, just because the words often appear commonplace, it is a useful habit to note key terms that may require careful attention, then seek out contexts and definitions from a variety of sources. Extended definitions (like that of *culture*) are frequent in writing in the social sciences, and extremely useful; you can often find one in one of the books listed in the bibliography of the work you are reading at the moment. In the social sciences, and history, too, it is especially true that wide comparative reading is often necessary to elucidate key terms. Finally, you will find it an excellent practice to pause in your reading from time to time to write out your own extended definitions of the most important words and concepts. When you can do that, you are no longer a beginner in the subject.

Pre-reading and questions. We have pointed out how in the biological and physical sciences writing is usually organized according to the problem-solution nature of the subject. In history, of course, organization is fundamentally chronological — but when pre-reading a history book, you will want to note just how its particular chronology works. There is an obvious difference between a political and an economic history; an equally obvious difference between a book like William H. McNeill's *The Rise of the West,* which spans more than 6,000 years of the "history of the human community," and C. V. Wedgwood's *The King's Peace,* which deals with only five years of the reign of Charles I. Chronology can be sweeping or detailed; it can take the form of a single narrative or of an intricate tapestry of interwoven threads of development. Furthermore, the nature of the events selected, and so of the chronology, will vary greatly depending on the author's purpose and thesis. Thus when pre-reading you will want to look not only for the period spanned and the significant events, but also for the trends, the thesis, the clues as to the kind of history book it is.

In the social sciences, the problem-solution formula is widely used; sometimes organization will be chronological as well. The tight organization typical in the natural sciences is often lacking. Watch for the progression of development from one aspect of the problem to the next, and from simple to complex, small to large, particular to general, or the reverse of any of these. For instance, in a study of a group of mentally disturbed children in a home, the author may begin with a description of the typical day of a counselor at the home, and then describe the different kinds of emotional maladjustments among the children, together with details of treatment over a long period of time. The description of the counselor's day provides an immediate particular setting for his following theoretical study of emotional disturbance and its pathology; the closely focused chronology of one day gives way to the time span of months and years in individual case histories.

History and social sciences demand critical, questioning reading. (The next two chapters, on critical reading, will serve you well here.) Compared with the problems of the natural scientist, the problems of the historian or the social scientist are by their nature more complex and inconclusive. Single causes can rarely be isolated. History never has experiments, social science rarely. The facts can be hard to ascertain, which obviously conditions the interpretations based on them. And if there is more room for difference of opinion in these disciplines, so too there is more to engage an author's passions and convictions, dealing as he does with personalities, policies, emotions, and issues. In history and the social sciences, then, objectivity is harder to maintain; bias is harder to detect. Much history and most social science goes beyond fact to persuasion. A writer on the sociology of cities may urge, explicitly or implicitly, reform of the police, may oppose indiscriminate slum clearance, may advocate neighborhood control of schools. The economist who writes an extensive history of government monetary policy may aim to convert officials to his point of view about how to control inflation and secure growth. As we will explore in more detail in Chapters 14 and 15, there is nothing inherently wrong with a persuasive purpose — as long as you are able to discover it and judge its merits. That is one of the chief aims of critical, questioning reading in these subjects.

With these critical precautions in mind, history and the social sciences should present you with all the usual, but no unusual, problems in thorough reading. "Fast and flexible" is the watchword; pre-reading, your purpose and questions, and your developed feeling for your top comfortable rate will guide your application of speed and other techniques to each individual work.

Law

Most laymen (and some lawyers!) overestimate the difficulty of reading in law. There are two apparent obstacles that make reading of such material difficult: vocabulary and long, involved sentences. Once these are overcome, reading in this subject is no more difficult than reading in any other field.

The special vocabulary of law seems formidable because it is a strange mixture of Latin and archaic English words. Obviously this vocabulary must be fully mastered before you can read efficiently in the legal field. Fortunately the terms in law, as in the natural sciences, usually have precise definitions. If you must learn legal vocabulary, apply all the techniques for vocabulary extension set forth in Chapter 8, with special emphasis on using the words in context for retention.

Even though sentences in legal documents and books are sometimes long and involved, legal phrasing has become so standard through centuries of growth that once a reader accustoms himself to it, the difficulty is largely banished. For instance, a series of words such as "sell, transfer, convey, assign, deed, give" refers at each occurrence to the idea of transfer of ownership, and the series is a standard form used to plug every possible loophole of a transfer. Similarly, many documents have standard forms. A real estate lease, for example, is standard in most details within each state; once the reader has familiarized himself with one California lease, he knows the main provisions of them all, and then he must pay extra attention only to special clauses.

The law student and the practicing lawyer face somewhat different reading problems. The student is setting out to master the totality of a subject. His is a study program in which early and thorough attention at two extremes of a scale — vocabulary and the overall organization of the subject and its parts — will pay great dividends of intellectual power. The student needs to apply zealously the techniques discussed in Chapter 10, on study. The practicing lawyer, depending on his speciality, finds that much of his reading is like a small-scale research project, where the aim is to locate, out of a mass of possible sources, some one relatively short passage — perhaps a few pages, even a few sentences — to be read thoroughly. Most law books and documents are therefore systematically designed to aid the search for any particular passage: page headings, indexes, tables of contents, printed marginal notes, and abstracts of sections of books — all these are elaborated much more than in other fields. Keep firmly in mind what you are searching for as you skim through legal references, so that you can take full advantage of these mechanics without having to retrace your steps.

The skilled lawyer is thus an expert at skimming; he reads thoroughly only at strategic spots. Even within the compass of a page or two, he will skim until he finds the exact passage he is looking for. Then he will read with care, though except when names and dates or new vocabulary crop up, a brisk rate will usually be possible. When a passage is more than ordinarily difficult, he skims the preceding pages to pick up anew the structure of the material, and skims forward to anticipate what is to come.

Demonstration: The 1, 2, 3 of a Business Letter

W H I R L I G I G   M A N U F A C T U R E R S,   I N C.

1 Windmill Street
Turner, California

WHIRL!

November 30, 1974

1. Glance at the letterhead to see where the letter originated. Then jump immediately to the signature.

Dear Sir:

The body of a business letter should be skimmed quickly before reading thoroughly. What is the letter about? Is it all on one subject, or more than one? Should you or somebody else deal with it?

Good letter writers will usually warn you in the first paragraph when the letter treats more than one subject. But not always--so if you fail to skim the entire letter before dealing with the details, you may miss some important point.

While skimming, check off in the margin the places where you will want to return.

3. The third step is to skim the entire body of the letter for the main point and key words and phrases.

A further point: modern business letters are often written with very short paragraphs. Businessmen and their secretaries often paragraph unnecessarily, dividing up topics that would be kept together in an article or book chapter. This means that your skimming must be for key words and phrases. If you skim the entire first sentence of each paragraph, often you will be reading virtually every word!

One more point: the last paragraph, or next-to-last, often contains the writer's main request or instructions.

Yours truly,

Horace Judson

2. The second place to look, when pre-reading, is the signature. Often this will tell you what the letter is about.

Business

Some practical prose can indeed be read for enjoyment as well as for information. There is good writing in history, sometimes in sciences, sometimes in law. Any pleasure that comes from reading in business, however, comes from reading efficiently. Efficiency is imperative in business reading because of its volume: the average executive reads from a quarter to half his working time, exclusive of the briefcase he takes home at night. A skilled reader has an advantage over his competitors, outside and inside his firm.

Business reading has few special characteristics. For the most part such reading is of average difficulty, made up of articles, memorandums, reports, correspondence, newspapers, and an occasional book. The subject matter of this reading will usually be familiar to the reader; only when a legal document or technical report crops up will he have to concern himself with acquiring a vocabulary or background for understanding. The sentence and paragraph habits of business writers are usually uniform.

Your paramount problem in business reading is to determine what you should read thoroughly. In the office of the average executive as little as one half of the reading matter that crosses his desk requires his direct attention and action. Pre-reading and skimming will suffice for much of the material, with but occasional paragraphs requiring thorough reading. Required reading should be noted as such in the margin during pre-reading, to be read thoroughly.

Business correspondence should always be pre-read. Because of the way most business letters are written, the standard sequence for pre-reading must be modified to fit. The steps in pre-reading business correspondence can best be shown by the example on page 367.

EXERCISES FOR CHAPTER 13

Reading Journal

Integrated Exercise 1: Five Historians State Their Aims and Methods

    From *The History of the Peloponnesian War*, Book I, by Thucydides

    From the Preface to *The Rise of the Dutch Republic*, by John Lothrop Motley

    From the Introduction to *The Outline of History*, by H. G. Wells

    From *The Whig Interpretation of History*, by Herbert Butterfield

    From *The Uses of the Past*, by Herbert J. Muller

Integrated Exercise 2: A Biologist Reports an Experiment

    "The Heart-beat in Limulus," by A. J. Carlson

The reading exercises in this and the next three chapters call for *integrated* application of your skills. Each exercise will ask you to practice not just one but many of the reading techniques you have learned. Because you are now more proficient in reading than when you began this course, the reading selections are somewhat more difficult, as well as longer. The questions on them are also more difficult, both in the things they call on you to do, and in the independence with which you are expected to do them. For example, the questions for the most part abandon the multiple-choice form, requiring you instead to write out short answers.

No two of these integrated exercises are alike. The reading selections themselves differ widely. Your purpose in reading should be appropriate to each, so that this, too, will vary from one exercise to the next. You will be asked to put together a different, appropriate tool bag of techniques for each exercise. Finally, reflecting all that, the instructions you are to follow, both for reading the selections and for answering the questions, also change from one exercise to the next.

Reading Journal

In your separate notebook, bring the sections on **current** and **future reading** up to date. You will now be calling on the future-reading list once more.

With your reading skills, you are now in the position of the amateur clock repairman sitting on the floor with the springs, cogs, wheels, and dials of the mechanism spread out in order all around you: you have all the pieces, each one is in working order, but you will have nothing functional until you put them all together. The most important integrated practice you can perform is to apply your entire battery of reading skills to an entire book — while making a careful, conscious record of every step as you go.

Check through your list of future reading to select one of the next books you have planned to read thoroughly. It should be nonfiction, perhaps 300 to 500 pages in length, and for your present purpose it should probably not include unusual difficulties like a great deal of mathematics or a foreign language. It should be a book you want to master completely. This book will be your practice material.

Read it.

Make notes of each step.

Begin, of course, by pre-reading the entire book, writing out a detailed pre-reading analysis. Go on to questions, including your purpose in reading it — a dual purpose, not only for this exercise, but also for the book itself. Pre-read each chapter as you come to it, making notes of that, too, as you go. Note and take care of any problems of vocabulary. Mark topic sentences, or at least all the main ideas, as you read; then summarize each section in a sentence, and each chapter in a paragraph. Decide which parts of the book are most important to your purpose, and make detailed outlines of those. And so on: deliberately apply everything you have learned about reading, including your top appropriate speeds. When you have read the book thoroughly, review it.

The project should take you several sessions of a couple of hours each, spread out over a week or more. As you work, you will also be going ahead with the rest of *this* book; therefore, by the time the project is complete, you will have certain further skills to try out—those of critical reading.

As the final step, write out your own analysis of your performance.

Integrated Exercise 1:
Five Historians State Their Aims and Methods

One of the most interesting and troubling of man's intellectual concerns is the question of *historical knowledge.* Is there value in knowing the past? *Can* we truly know the past? If yes, then *how?* Can we trust the historians who claim that in some sense they do tell us the past? Is history science, or art? or self-deception? And so the puzzling questions go—producing much good argument in a discussion that is never surely completed.

Most historians, in fact, either by direct statement or by implication, have a point of view in this discussion. You will now read statements pertaining to "aim and methods," written over a span of 2,400 years by five historians, and then try to determine what points of view they hold, and how these points of view can be compared. In doing this, you will be exercising your skills in pre-reading; in analyzing the organizational structure of relatively short passages; in thorough reading; in questioning; in summarizing; and, overall, in critical reading.

Pre-read the entire exercise by looking over the reading selections *and the questions.* (The questions begin on page 379.) This will give you a clear idea of what is required. Then read each selection thoroughly, formulating your own questions as necessary, and marking, as you go, the sentences containing main ideas. Then proceed to answer the questions; you may refer to the selections as you do so.

A

From *The History of the Peloponnesian War,* Book I[3]
by THUCYDIDES

1   Thucydides, an Athenian, wrote the history of the war between the Peloponnesians and the Athenians, beginning at the moment that it broke out, and believing that it would be a great war and more worthy of rela-
2 tion than any that had preceded it. This belief was not without its grounds.
3 The preparations of both the combatants were in every department in the last state of perfection; and he could see the rest of the Hellenic race taking sides in the quarrel; those who delayed doing so at once having it
4 in contemplation. Indeed this was the greatest movement yet known in history, not only of the Hellenes, but of a large part of the barbarian
5 world—I had almost said of mankind. For though the events of remote antiquity, and even those that more immediately precede the war, could not from lapse of time be clearly ascertained, yet the evidences which an inquiry carried as far back as was practicable leads me to trust, all point to the conclusion that there was nothing on a great scale, either in war or in other matters. . . .
6   Having now given the result of my inquiries into early times, I

grant that there will be a difficulty in believing every particular detail.
7 The way that most men deal with traditions, even traditions of their own country, is to receive them all alike as they are delivered, without applying any critical test whatever.

8   So little pains do the vulgar take in the investigation of truth, ac-
9 cepting readily the first story that comes to hand. On the whole, however, the conclusions I have drawn from the proofs quoted may, I believe,
10 safely be relied on. Assuredly they will not be disturbed either by the lays of a poet displaying the exaggeration of his craft, or by the compositions of the chroniclers that are attractive at truth's expense; the subjects they treat of being out of the reach of evidence, and time having robbed most of them of historical value by enthroning them in the region
11 of legend. Turning from these, we can rest satisfied with having proceeded upon the clearest data, and having arrived at conclusions as exact
12 as can be expected in matters of such antiquity. To come to this war; despite the known disposition of the actors in a struggle to overrate its importance, and when it is over to return to their admiration of earlier events, yet an examination of the facts will show that it was much greater than the wars which preceded it.

13   With reference to the speeches in this history, some were delivered before the war began, others while it was going on; some I heard myself, others I got from various quarters; it was in all cases difficult to carry them word for word in one's memory, so my habit has been to make the speakers say what was in my opinion demanded of them by the various occasions, of course adhering as closely as possible to the general sense
14 of what they really said. And with reference to the narrative of events, far from permitting myself to derive it from the first source that came to hand, I did not even trust my own impressions, but it rests partly on what I saw myself, partly on what others saw for me, the accuracy of the report being always tried by the most severe and detailed tests possible.
15 My conclusions have cost me some labour from the want of coincidence between accounts of the same occurrences by different eye-witnesses, arising sometimes from imperfect memory, sometimes from undue par-
16 tiality for one side or the other. The absence of romance in my history will, I fear, detract somewhat from its interest; but if it be judged useful by those inquirers who desire an exact knowledge of the past as an aid to the interpretation of the future, which in the course of human things
17 must resemble if it does not reflect it, I shall be content. In fine, I have written my work, not as an essay which is to win the applause of the moment, but as a possession for all time.

B

From the Preface to *The Rise of the Dutch Republic*
by JOHN LOTHROP MOTLEY

1   History has few so fruitful examples of the dangers which come from superstition and despotism, and the blessings which flow from the

maintenance of religious and political freedom, as those afforded by the struggle between England and Holland on one side, and Spain and Rome

2 on the other, during the epoch which I have attempted to describe. It is for this reason that I have thought it necessary to reveal, as minutely as possible, the secret details of this conspiracy of king and priest against the people, and to show how it was baffled at last by the strong self-helping energy of two free nations combined.

3   The materials for the volumes now offered to the public were so abundant that it was almost impossible to condense them into smaller

4 compass without doing injustice to the subject. It was desirable to throw full light on these prominent points of the history, while the law of historical perspective will allow long stretches of shadow in the succeeding portions, in which less important objects may be more slightly indicated.

5 That I may not be thought capable of abusing the reader's confidence by inventing conversations, speeches, or letters, I would take this opportunity of stating — although I have repeated the remark in the foot-notes — that no personage in these pages is made to write or speak any words save those which, on the best historical evidence, he is known to have written or spoken.

C

From the Introduction to *The Outline of History*[4]
by H. G. WELLS

1   This *Outline of History* is an attempt to tell, truly and clearly, in one continuous narrative, the whole story of life and mankind so far as

2 it is known to-day. It is written plainly for the general reader, but its aim

3 goes beyond its use as merely interesting reading matter. There is a feeling abroad that the teaching of history considered as part of general education is in an unsatisfactory condition, and particularly that the ordinary treatment of this "subject" by the class and teacher and examiner is too

4 partial and narrow. But the desire to extend the general range of historical ideas is confronted by the argument that the available time for instruction is already consumed by that partial and narrow treatment, and that therefore, however desirable this extension of range may be, it is in prac-

5 tice impossible. If an Englishman, for example, has found the history of England quite enough for his powers of assimilation, then it seems hopeless to expect his sons and daughters to master universal history, if that is to consist of the history of England, plus the history of France, plus

6 the history of Germany, plus the history of Russia, and so on. To which the only possible answer is that universal history is at once something more and something less than the aggregate of the national histories to which we are accustomed, that it must be approached in a different spirit

7 and dealt with in a different manner. This book seeks to justify that

8 answer. It has been written primarily to show that *history as one whole* is amenable to a more broad and comprehensive handling than is the history

of special nations and periods, a broader handling that will bring it within the normal limitations of time and energy set to the reading and education 9 of an ordinary citizen. This outline deals with ages and races and nations, where the ordinary history deals with reigns and pedigrees and campaigns; but it will not be found to be more crowded with names and dates, 10 nor more difficult to follow and understand. History is no exception amongst the sciences; as the gaps fill in, the outline simplifies; as the outlook broadens, the clustering multitude of details dissolves into general 11 laws. And many topics of quite primary interest to mankind, the first appearance and the growth of scientific knowledge for example, and its effects upon human life, the elaboration of the ideas of money and credit or the story of the origins and spread and influence of Christianity, which must be treated fragmentarily or by elaborate digressions in any partial history, arise and flow completely and naturally in one general record of the world in which we live.

12   The need for a common knowledge of the general facts of human history throughout the world has become very evident during the tragic 13 happenings of the last few years. Swifter means of communication have 14 brought all men closer to one another for good or for evil. War becomes a universal disaster, blind and monstrously destructive; it bombs the baby in its cradle and sinks the food-ships that cater for the non-com- 15 batant and the neutral. There can be no peace, now, we realize, but a common peace in all the world; no prosperity but a general prosperity. 16 But *there can be no common peace and prosperity without common* 17 *historical ideas.* Without such ideas to hold them together in harmonious co-operation, with nothing but narrow, selfish, and conflicting nationalist traditions, races and peoples are bound to drift towards conflict and 18 destruction. This truth, which was apparent to that great philosopher Kant a century or more ago—it is the gist of his tract upon universal 19 peace—is now plain to the man on the street. Our internal policies and our economic and social ideas are profoundly vitiated at present by wrong and fantastic ideas of the origin and historical relationship of social 20 classes. A sense of history as the common adventure of all mankind is 21 as necessary for peace within as it is for peace between the nations. Such are the views of history that this *Outline* seeks to realize.

D

From *The Whig Interpretation of History*[5]
by HERBERT BUTTERFIELD

1   It has been said that the historian is the avenger, and that standing as a judge between the parties and rivalries and causes of bygone generations he can lift up the fallen and beat down the proud, and by his exposures and his verdicts, his satire and his moral indignation, can punish 2 unrighteousness, avenge the injured or reward the innocent. One may be forgiven for not being too happy about any division of mankind into good

and evil, progressive and reactionary, black and white; and it is not clear that moral indignation is not a dispersion of one's energies to the great

3 confusion of one's judgment. There can be no complaint against the historian who personally and privately has his preferences and antipathies, and who as a human being merely has a fancy to take part in the game that he is describing; it is pleasant to see him give way to his prejudices and take them emotionally, so that they splash into colour as he writes; provided that when he steps in this way into the arena he recognises that he is stepping into a world of partial judgments and purely personal appreciations and does not imagine that he is speaking *ex*

4 *cathedra.* But if the historian can rear himself up like a god and judge, or stand as the official avenger of the crimes of the past, then one can require that he shall be still more godlike and regard himself rather as the reconciler than as the avenger; taking it that his aim is to achieve the understanding of the men and parties and causes of the past, and that in this understanding, if it can be complete, all things will ultimately be recon-

5 ciled. It seems to be assumed that in history we can have something more than the private points of view of particular historians; that there are 'verdicts of history' and that history itself, considered impersonally,

6 has something to say to men. It seems to be accepted that each historian does something more than make a confession of his private mind and his whimsicalities, and that all of them are trying to elicit a truth, and perhaps combining through their various imperfections to express a truth, which, if we could perfectly attain it, would be the voice of History itself.

7 But if history is in this way something like the memory of mankind and represents the spirit of man brooding over man's past, we must imagine it as working not to accentuate antagonisms or to ratify old party-cries but to find the unities that underlie the differences and to see all lives as

8 part of the one web of life. The historian trying to feel his way towards this may be striving to be like a god but perhaps he is less foolish than the

9 one who poses as god the avenger. Studying the quarrels of an ancient day he can at least seek to understand both parties to the struggle and he must want to understand them better than they understood themselves; watching them entangled in the net of time and circumstance he can take pity on them—these men who perhaps had no pity for one another; and, though he can never be perfect, it is difficult to see why he should aspire to anything less than taking these men and their quarrels into a world where everything is understood and all sins are forgiven.

10   It is astonishing to what an extent the historian has been Protestant, progressive, and whig, and the very model of the 19th century gentle-

11 man. Long after he became a determinist he retained his godly rôle as the dispenser of moral judgments, and like the disciples of Calvin he gave up

12 none of his right to moral indignation. Even when he himself has been unsympathetic to the movements of his own generation, as in the case of Hallam, who bitterly opposed the Great Reform Bill and trembled to think of the revolutionary ways into which the country was moving, something in his constitution still makes him lean to what might be called

the whig interpretation of history, and he refuses historical understanding to men whose attitude in the face of change and innovation was analogous
13 to his own. It might be argued that our general version of the historical story still bears the impress that was given to it by the great patriarchs of history-writing, so many of whom seem to have been whigs and gentlemen when they have not been Americans: and perhaps it is from these that our textbook historians have inherited the top hat and the pontifical manner, and the grace with which they hand out a consolation prize to the man who, "though a reactionary, was irreproachable in his private
14 life." But whether we take the contest of Luther against the popes, or that of Philip II and Elizabeth, or that of the Huguenots with Catherine de' Medici; whether we take Charles I versus his parliaments or the younger Pitt versus Charles James Fox, it appears that the historian tends in the first place to adopt the whig or Protestant view of the subject, and very quickly busies himself with dividing the world into the friends
15 and enemies of progress. It is true that this tendency is corrected to some extent by the more concentrated labours of historical specialists, but it is remarkable that in all the examples given above, as well as in many others, the result of detailed historical research has been to correct very materially what had been an accepted Protestant or whig interpretation.
16 Further, this whig tendency is so deep-rooted that even when piece-meal research has corrected the story in detail, we are slow in re-valuing the whole and reorganising the broad outlines of the theme in the light of these discoveries; and what M. Romier has deplored in the historians of the Huguenots might fairly be imputed to those in other fields of history; that is, the tendency to patch the new research into the old story even when the research in detail has altered the bearings of the whole subject.
17 We cling to a certain organisation of historical knowledge which amounts to a whig interpretation of history, and all our deference to research
18 brings us only to admit that this needs qualifications in detail. But exceptions in detail do not prevent us from mapping out the large story on the same pattern all the time; these exceptions are lost indeed in that combined process of organisation and abridgment by which we reach our general survey of general history; and so it is over large periods and in reference to the great transitions in European history that the whig view holds hardest and holds longest; it is here that we see the results of a serious discrepancy between the historical specialist and what might be called the general historian.
19   The truth is that there is a tendency for all history to veer over into whig history, and this is not sufficiently explained if we merely ascribe it
20 to the prevalence and persistence of a traditional interpretation. There is a magnet for ever pulling at our minds, unless we have found the way to counteract it; and it may be said that if we are merely honest, if we are not also carefully self-critical, we tend easily to be deflected by a first
21 fundamental fallacy. And though this may even apply in a subtle way to the detailed work of the historical specialist, it comes into action with increasing effect the moment any given subject has left the hands of the

student in research; for the more we are discussing and not merely en-
quiring, the more we are making inferences instead of researches, then
the more whig our history becomes if we have not severely repressed our
original error; indeed all history must tend to become more whig in pro-
22 portion as it becomes more abridged. Further, it cannot be said that all
faults of bias may be balanced by work that is deliberately written with
the opposite bias; for we do not gain true history by merely adding the
speech of the prosecution to the speech for the defence; and though
there have been Tory—as there have been many Catholic—partisan
histories, it is still true that there is no corresponding tendency for the
subject itself to lean in this direction; the dice cannot be secretly loaded
23 by virtue of the same kind of original unconscious fallacy. For this
reason it has been easy to believe that Clio herself is on the side of the
whigs.
24   The primary assumption of all attempts to understand the men of
the past must be the belief that we can in some degree enter into minds
25 that are unlike our own. If this belief were unfounded it would seem that
men must be for ever locked away from one another, and all generations
26 must be regarded as a world and a law unto themselves. If we were unable to enter in any way into the mind of a present-day Roman Catholic
priest, for example, and similarly into the mind of an atheistical orator
in Hyde Park, it is difficult to see how we could know anything of the
still stranger men of the sixteenth century, or pretend to understand the
process of history-making which has moulded us into the world of to-day.
27 In reality the historian postulates that the world is in some sense always
the same world and that even the men most dissimilar are never abso-
28 lutely unlike. And though a sentence from Aquinas may fall so strangely
upon modern ears that it becomes plausible to dismiss the man as a fool
or a mind utterly and absolutely alien, I take it that to dismiss a man in
this way is a method of blocking up the mind against him, and against
something important in both human nature and its history; it is really the
refusal to a historical personage of the effort of historical understanding.
29 Precisely because of his unlikeness to ourselves Aquinas is the more
enticing subject for the historical imagination; for the chief aim of the
historian is the elucidation of the unlikenesses between past and present
and his chief function is to act in this way as the mediator between other
30 generations and our own. It is not for him to stress and magnify the
similarities between one age and another, and he is riding after a whole
flock of misapprehensions if he goes to hunt for the present in the past.
31 Rather it is his work to destroy those very analogies which we imagined
32 to exist. When he shows us that Magna Carta is a feudal document in a
feudal setting, with implications different from those we had taken for
granted, he is disillusioning us concerning something in the past which
33 we had assumed to be too like something in the present. That whole
process of specialised research which has in so many fields revised the
previously accepted whig interpretation of history, has set our bearings

afresh in one period after another, by referring matters in this way to their context, and so discovering their unlikeness to the world of the present-day.

34   It is part and parcel of the whig interpretation of history that it studies the past with reference to the present; and though there may be a sense in which this is unobjectionable if its implications are carefully considered, and there may be a sense in which it is inescapable, it has often been an obstruction to historical understanding because it has been taken to mean the study of the past with direct and perpetual reference

35 to the present. Through this system of immediate reference to the present-day, historical personages can easily and irresistibly be classed into the men who furthered progress and the men who tried to hinder it; so that a handy rule of thumb exists by which the historian can select and reject,

36 and can make his points of emphasis. On this system the historian is bound to construe his function as demanding him to be vigilant for like-nesses between past and present, instead of being vigilant for unlike-nesses; so that he will find it easy to say that he has seen the present in the past, he will imagine that he has discovered a "root" or an "anticipa-tion" of the 20th century, when in reality he is in a world of different connotations altogether, and he has merely tumbled upon what could be

37 shown to be a misleading analogy. Working upon the same system the whig historian can draw lines through certain events, some such line as that which leads through Martin Luther and a long succession of whigs to modern liberty; and if he is not careful he begins to forget that this line is merely a mental trick of his; he comes to imagine that it represents

38 something like a line of causation. The total result of this method is to impose a certain form upon the whole historical story, and to produce a scheme of general history which is bound to converge beautifully upon the present—all demonstrating throughout the ages the workings of an obvious principle of progress, of which the Protestants and whigs have been the perennial allies while Catholics and tories have perpetually

39 formed obstruction. A caricature of this result is to be seen in a popular view that is still not quite eradicated: the view that the Middle Ages represented a period of darkness when man was kept tongue-tied by authority—a period against which the Renaissance was the reaction and

40 the Reformation the great rebellion. It is illustrated to perfection in the argument of a man denouncing Roman Catholicism at a street corner, who said: "When the Pope ruled England them was called the Dark Ages."

E

From *The Uses of the Past*[6]
by HERBERT J. MULLER

1   Although the practical value of a knowledge of history is commonly exaggerated, since men do not appear to learn readily from the mistakes

of their ancestors, and historians themselves are not always conspicuous for their wisdom, I suppose that few would deny the practical necessity
2 of this knowledge. When Henry Ford, in the good old boom days, said that "history is bunk," he merely illustrated the ignorance of the hard-headed industrial leaders who were leading the country straight to a
3 crash. History has also been described as a series of messes, but only by a historical analysis can we determine how we got into the latest mess,
4 and how we might get out of it. The very idea that we are in a mess involves assumptions about the "natural" course of affairs, as do all policies
5 for dealing with it. Practical men who distrust "mere theory" are especially fond of pointing out that "history shows" something or other—usually showing that they are fearful of all change and incapable of learn-
6 ing from the failures of their conservative forebears. In any event, we are
7 forever drawing upon the past. It not only constitutes all the "experience" by which we have learned: it is the source of our major interests, our
8,9 claims, our rights, and our duties. It is the source of our very identity. In an eternal present, which is a specious present, the past is all we know.
10 And as the present is forever slipping back, it reminds us that we too shall in time belong wholly to the past.
11   For such reasons our interest in history is more poetic than practical
12 or scientific. It begins as a childlike interest in the obvious pageantry and exciting event; it grows as a mature interest in the variety and complexity of the drama, the splendid achievements and the terrible failures; it ends as a deep sense of the mystery of man's life—of all the dead, great and obscure, who once walked the earth, and of the wonderful and awful
13 possibilities of being a human being. "History is neither written nor
14 made without love or hate," Mommsen wrote. The historian is inevitably an artist of a kind as he composes his narrative, selecting, shaping, color-
15 ing. The greater historians, from Herodotus to Toynbee, have generally been distinguished for their imaginative reach and grasp, not necessarily
16 the soundness of their conclusions. Gibbon remains one of the greatest, despite his apparent prejudice and his untrustworthiness in detail, because of his artistic mastery of an epic theme.
17,18   Nevertheless history must always aim at literal truth. As Trevelyan
19 said, its very poetry consists in its truth. "It is the fact about the past that is poetic"—the fact that this was the actual drama of actual men, and
20 that these men are no more. A lover of history loves it straight, without chasers of fancy; he is especially irritated by merely picturesque history,
21 or by such bastard offspring as the fictionized biography. This concern for literal truth helps to explain why historians, the lovers of the past, have been more disposed to condemn their predecessors than poets have
22 been. Over two thousands years ago Polybius noted how each successive historian "makes such a parade of minute accuracy, and inveighs so bitterly when refuting others, that people come to imagine that all other
23 historians have been mere dreamers." So the scientific historians of the

last century inveighed against the dreamers before them, and have in turn been ridiculed in this century.

24   In this view, one might wonder just where the truth comes out, and
25 why one should put any trust in the latest version of it. It is always easy to be cynical about history, as "a pack of tricks we play on the dead."
26 Yet it is impossible to deny the impressive advance that has been made
27 in the last hundred years. Historians have built up an immense body of factual knowledge, knowledge that is no less genuine because it is sub-
28 ject to different theoretical interpretations. They have systematically widened, deepened, and clarified the sources of knowledge by philo-
29 logical, paleographical, archaeological, and ethnological research. They have come to realize the importance of commonplace, everyday events, in particular the economic activities that had been neglected in favor of
30 the political and military. They have learned a great deal about the influence of both the physical and the cultural environment, what lies below
31 factual history and above it. They have become aware of evolution, of
32 origins and growths, of the history of history itself. Their very ignorance is suffused with knowledge, which at least keeps them from being ignorant of their ignorance.
33   The progress in historical knowledge, accordingly, has not been a steady advance toward absolute truth, a steady reduction in the number
34 of universal laws to be discovered. It has been a progressive clarification,
35 a fuller consciousness of what has happened, and how and why. When historians offer some fifty different reasons for the fall of the Roman Empire, we may at first be simply confused; yet we have a better understanding of the fall than if we assumed there was only one reason, or no
36 reason except Fate. In spite of all their disagreement, moreover, historians are now generally agreed in discounting the most obvious explanation, that Rome succumbed to barbarian invasions; they have a deeper insight than the great Gibbon had, and perceive the dry rot that had set in
37 during the Golden Age he celebrated. For they now have the advantage of a vast, international, co-operative enterprise, conducted in a scien-
38 tific spirit. Although every historian remains fallible and subject to bias, his work remains subject to correction and criticism by his fellows, in
39 professional journals and congresses. The relative objectivity of contemporary social science, as Karl Popper points out, is due not to the impartiality of all the social scientists, but to the publicity and community of the scientific method.

You should refer to the five passages as you answer the questions.

Phase I: main ideas.
    For each article, list here the one or more numbers of the sentences containing *main ideas.*

    A: Thucydides _____

B: Motley _____

C: Wells _____

D: Butterfield _____

E: Muller _____

Phase II: questions.

For each article, write out here the *question* that the author seems, in effect, to be most concerned to answer in the passage you read.

A: Thucydides _____

_____

_____

_____

B: Motley _____

_____

_____

_____

C: Wells _____

_____

_____

_____

D: Butterfield _____

_____

_____

_____

E: Muller _____

_____

_____

_____

Phase III: point-by-point comparison and evaluation.

1. For each article write in its answer space the numbers of the sentences where the author discusses the *general* question of the usefulness or value of a knowledge of history. If he does not discuss this, mark "X" in the answer space.

   A: Thucydides _____   **D:** Butterfield _____

   B: Motley _____   **E:** Muller _____

   C: Wells _____

2. For each article, write in its answer space the numbers of the sentences where the author discusses his *immediate purpose* in writing his work of history. If he does not state his historical purpose, mark "X" in the answer space.

   A: Thucydides _____   **D:** Butterfield _____

   B: Motley _____   **E:** Muller _____

   C: Wells _____

3. For each article, write in its answer space the numbers of the sentences where the author shows most clearly *how he feels* (as opposed to *what he thinks*) about history and/or his particular subject. If he gives you no indication of this, mark "X."

   A: Thucydides _____   **D:** Butterfield _____

   B: Motley _____   **E:** Muller _____

   C: Wells _____

4. For each article, write in its answer space the numbers of the sentences where the author states *how he has selected and evaluated* the events he reports. If he does not say, mark "X."

   A: Thucydides _____   **D:** Butterfield _____

   B: Motley _____   **E:** Muller _____

   C: Wells _____

5. For each article, write in its answer space the numbers of the sentences where the author states or implies the *opinion or point of view* about his historical subject which he would presumably wish to persuade you to share by the time you completed reading his work. If you really cannot find any such persuasive purpose, mark "X."

   A: Thucydides _____   **D:** Butterfield _____

   B: Motley _____   **E:** Muller _____

   C: Wells _____

6. For each article, write in its answer space the numbers of the sentences where the author lets you know his views on the *general* question of how one can know the truth in history. If he does not touch on this question, mark "X."

A: Thucydides _____   **D:** Butterfield _____

B: Motley _____   **E:** Muller _____

C: Wells _____

Phase IV: summarizing.

Read each article through again quickly, to clear your head after the previous cross comparisons, and then write a short summary of it.

A: Thucydides _____

_____

_____

_____

B: Motley _____

_____

_____

_____

C: Wells _____

_____

_____

_____

D: Butterfield _____

_____

_____

_____

_____

E: Muller _____

_____

_____

_____

_____

Phase V: overall comparison and contrast.

1. Which *two* authors make the most similar statements about the scope or range of their *particular historical* subject?

   ANSWER _____ and _____

2. Which *two* authors make the most similar claims about the validity of their historical evidence?

   ANSWER _____ and _____

3. Which *two* authors are in *most disagreement* about the general nature of historical understanding?

   ANSWER   A: _____

   B: _____

   Which of the others, if any, most closely agrees with A?

   ANSWER _____

   Which, if any, most closely agrees with B?   ANSWER _____

   Justify your groupings: why do you say so? _____

   _____

   _____

   _____

4. Which *two* authors are *least* likely to strive to keep their work accurate and free from bias, as far as you can judge from these passages?

   ANSWER _____ and _____

   Justify your choices: why do you say so? _____

   _____

   _____

_____

_____

5. Which *two* authors are most alike in their view about the usefulness or value of historical understanding and the study of history?

ANSWER _____ and _____

Justify your choices: why do you say so? _____

_____

_____

_____

_____

6. The five articles are reprinted in chronological order, though the last four were written during the past hundred years, while the first author, Thucydides, wrote nearly twenty-four centuries ago. What do the four recent articles suggest about the growth or change in historical thought over the past hundred years? Are they evolving closer to, or away from, Thucydides?

_____

_____

_____

_____

_____

_____

_____

_____

Integrated Exercise 2: A Biologist Reports an Experiment

In the following article, a noted biologist describes the method and results of an experiment he has conducted on the nerves and muscles of the heart of the king crab. This article is not a recent one; the experiment is, rather, a classic of its kind. The article is written for an audience of specialists; though it is clear and succinct, it is technical.

Your purpose in reading the report will be to understand it thoroughly and to perceive some of the possible implications of the results. To do so, you are to pre-read, formulate questions, read thoroughly with special attention to vocabulary, and prepare a brief general outline.

Step 1. Pre-read the report. As part of your pre-reading, examine the diagram that accompanies the report. Then turn to page 389 and do the pre-reading and question technique parts of the exercise, without looking back.

Step 2. Read the report thoroughly. Then answer the thorough-reading questions on page 390. This is not a timed exercise; you should refer to the report while answering the thorough-reading questions.

Vocabulary will probably give you difficulty in reading this article. Check in the margin the unfamiliar words whose meanings you cannot deduce from the context or with the aid of the diagram. A glossary at the end of the article briefly defines the most important technical terms.

Begin here.

"The Heart-beat in Limulus"[7]
by A. J. CARLSON

1. In taking up the study of the physiology of the heart-muscle and the heart-nerves in Limulus in order to compare the heart of arachnids with that of crustaceans, I was rewarded by finding that in this animal the relation of the cardiac ganglia and the cardiac nerves to the heart-muscle is such that the questions of the origin of the heart-beat and the nature of the process of conduction in the heart can be settled once and for all by simple and conclusive experiments. It can now be stated as a fact that in Limulus the origin of the heart-beat is nervous, not muscular, and that conduction of the impulse or the co-ordination of the different parts of the heart takes place through the nerves, not through the muscular tissue.

2. The structure and innervation of the Limulus heart are shown in Fig. I. In large specimens the length of the heart is from fifteen to twenty centimetres. When empty and collapsed it measures about two and one-half centimetres from side to side at its widest portion. The heart is plainly segmental in its makeup as indicated by the eight pairs of ostia (5) leading into the cavity of the heart on the dorsal side. These ostia are probably located between the segments, in which case the heart is composed of nine segments. Four pairs of arteries (2) are given off laterally from the corresponding four anterior segments. The main arteries (1) (two, lateral and one, median) take their origin from the anterior end of the heart. No arteries are given off from the posterior end. The heart is held in position in the pericardial sinus by systems of suspensory elastic tissue fibres essentially the same as in the crab or the lobster, the suspensory ligaments being connected with the heart by means of elastic tissue fibres which run longitudinally on the surface of the heart. Below this layer of longitudinal elastic fibres is, according to Patten and Redenbaugh, a homogeneous membrane (basement membrane) to which the strands of the heart-muscle are attached.

The muscle bands are arranged circularly, branching and anastomosing the one with the other. The walls of the heart are thickest at the lateral angles. The muscle is of the ordinary transversely striated type like that in the heart of all arthropods (with the exception of Peripatus). According to Patten and Redenbaugh, there is no endothelium lining the cavity of the heart, and the blood circulates freely between the muscular strands making up the walls.

3. The cardiac nervous complex, confined mainly to the dorsal and lateral side of the heart, is represented in Fig. I. It is composed of three longitudinal nerve-trunks, one (4) in the dorso-median line, and one (3) at each lateral angle, and an almost segmental system of anastomoses between the median and the lateral nerves. The median nerve is in reality a nerve-cord or elongated ganglion, as it is composed of longitudinal nerve-fibres and ganglion cells. The ganglion cells also extend for some distance into the main lateral branches of the nerve-cord. Patten and Redenbaugh state that there are no ganglion cells in the two lateral nerves. The median nerve-cord is thickest in the fourth, fifth, and sixth segments, diminishing in size both anteriorly and posteriorly. Ganglion cells are distributed throughout its whole length. The lateral nerves are also of largest size in the middle region of the heart. The median nerve is relatively large and of grayish white color, which makes it readily distinguished from the adjoining connective tissue in the living specimen. The lateral nerves are much smaller and branch

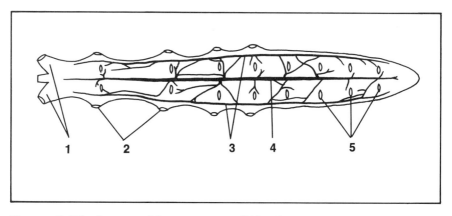

FIGURE I. The heart and heart-nerves of Limulus (the king crab), top view. The heart is shown one-half the natural size of a large specimen. (1) Anterior artery; (2) lateral (side) arteries; (3) lateral (side) nerves; (4) median nerve-cord; (5) ostia (the openings indicating the segmental makeup of the heart).

considerably, and are, in addition, of nearly the same color and transparency as the surrounding connective tissue; nevertheless they can be isolated in the living heart without the aid of a lens, and without injury to the heart-muscle. Both the lateral nerves and the dorso-median nerve-cord are separated from the heart-muscle by the ectocardium or basement membrane of

Patten and Redenbaugh, and can therefore, by careful dissection, be isolated for experimental purposes without the slightest injury to the heart.

4. The first thing about the heart-beat that arrests the attention of the observer is the apparently simultaneous contraction of all the parts of the heart. We have here a tubular or segmental heart half a foot in length, yet in the fresh specimens no difference in the beginning of contraction or relaxation of the foremost and the hindmost segments can be made out with the unaided eye. This is in striking contrast with the exceedingly slow propagation of the contraction wave in the tubular heart of the tunicates. The contraction of the Limulus heart must either begin practically at the same time in all the segments, or else the conduction of the contraction from segment to segment is much more rapid than the conduction even in the vertebrate heart. When the empty heart has been beating for several hours, or till nearly exhausted, and the rate of pulsation is in consequence much reduced, it can be made out even with the unaided eye that the contractions start in the posterior third of the heart and travel anteriorly. This is evidently also the condition in the fresh and vigorous heart. The processes which effect co-ordination in this heart are therefore conducted at a very rapid rate from one end of the heart to the other. Is it a conduction in the nerve-fibres or in the heart-muscle itself? Two simple experiments decide the question. Lesion of the median nerve-cord and the two lateral nerves in any segment of the heart destroys the co-ordination of the two ends of the heart on either side of the lesion; and, conversely, cross-section of the heart in any segment, leaving the longitudinal nerves intact, does not interfere with the co-ordination, the portions of the heart on either side of the cross-section keeping perfect unison. As the nerves are separated from the heart-muscle by the basement membrane, every muscle-fibre can be severed in the cross-section without injury to the nerves. Whatever co-ordination or conduction that is effected between the two ends of the heart after such a lesion must, therefore, be brought about by means of the nerves alone. The abolition of co-ordination by sectioning the longitudinal nerves is immediate and permanent. Both ends of the heart continue to beat, but with independent rhythm, the contraction not passing the region of the lesion either in the postero-anterior or in the reverse direction. There is no exception to these reactions. The experiments are so simple that any beginner in physiology can perform them. The only conclusion to be drawn from these reactions is that *conduction in the heart of this animal takes place in the nervous and does not take place in the muscular tissue.*

5. From the fact that in this animal the conduction or co-ordination is concerned with nervous and not with muscular elements we may not conclude that the condition is the same in all hearts, invertebrate as well as vertebrate. Engelmann's classical "zigzag experiment" on the amphibian heart argues so strongly in favor of the view that the conduction takes place through the muscle substance that I believe the majority of physiologists to-day accept that theory. But it seems to me that the purely muscular nature of conduction is not yet an established fact for the heart of any animal,

for even the great amount of work done to determine the nature of the processes of co-ordination in the vertebrate heart has not yielded a demonstration of the purely muscular nature of conduction approaching the decisiveness of the proof of the purely nervous nature of the conduction in the heart of Limulus.

6. Having found that the co-ordination of the heart is effected solely by means of the nervous elements, it was but a step to extirpate the median nerve-cord and the lateral nerves in order to determine whether without these the heart beats at all. It has already been stated that the complete removal of the median nerve-cord, together with the main lateral branches, as well as the lateral nerves, can be accomplished without the least injury to the heart, so that any effects following the extirpation of these nervous elements cannot be ascribed to injury to the heart-muscle. The results of this line of experiments are just as conclusive as those proving the nervous nature of the co-ordination. A heart or part of a heart that will beat with perfect rhythm for from twelve to fifteen hours, when the median nerve-cord is left intact, ceases to beat immediately and permanently on extirpation of the nerve-cord. The heart or part of the heart from which the nerve-cord has been removed may be made to contract by mechanical or electrical stimulation, but the contraction always ceases with the cessation of the stimulation. I have never observed a spontaneous contraction in a heart or part of the heart deprived of the nerve-cord. The presence of the lateral nerves is not sufficient to maintain the rhythm in the absence of the median nerve-cord. And removing these nerves, leaving the median nerve-cord intact, greatly diminishes the strength and regularity of the contraction in the different segments, but the rhythm and co-ordination are still maintained. *The heartbeat in Limulus is, therefore, of purely nervous origin, the result of rhythmic nervous impulses sent out from the median nerve-cord.*

7. It is not within the scope of this paper to review the arguments for and against the theory of the purely muscular origin of the beat of the vertebrate heart. The rhythm of the embryonic heart, prior to the appearance of nervous elements in it, appears to me the most conclusive fact in favor of that view. Nevertheless, the presence of ganglion cells in all hearts, vetebrate as well as invertebrate, in which a thorough search for them has been made, renders a mechanism of the cardiac rhythm and co-ordination similar to that in Limulus at least possible.

After pre-reading, answer the pre-reading questions on page 389.

After reading thoroughly, answer the remaining questions.

GLOSSARY

anastomosis — communication between vessels; meeting of the nerves
arachnid — individual of the class that includes spiders, scorpions, ticks, etc.

arthropod—individual of one of the great divisions of the animal kingdom, the one that includes insects, arachnids, crustaceans, etc.

cardiac—having to do with the heart

conduction—in this article, the transmission through the heart of the wave of contraction which is the heart "beat"

crustacean—individual of the class of animals that includes lobsters, shrimp, crabs, etc.

endothelium—membrane which lines a closed cavity

extirpate—to remove completely

ganglia—masses of gray nervous substance which serve as centers of nervous influence

innervation—here, the supply and organization of the nerves of the heart

lateral—pertaining to a side, rather than top or bottom

lesion—wound, cut

limulus—a king crab

median—middle

ostia—mouths or openings

pericardial sinus—the cavity around the heart

striated—the streaked appearance of ordinary muscle tissue; in many animals, the hearts are not composed of ordinary muscle tissue

tunicate—type of marine animal

vertebrate—backboned

Pre-reading questions. (Please do not look back.)

1. What is the problem considered in this paper? (a) How the heart of the crab is constructed; (b) comparison of the structures of arachnid hearts with those of crustaceans; (c) the origin and conduction of the heartbeat in Limulus; (d) the nervous origin of the heartbeat in vertebrates; (e) none of the above.

ANSWER _____

2. Does the author think his findings can be applied to other animals than those he worked with? (a) Definitely; (b) tentatively: he warns that his findings prove nothing for other animals, but he believes that they reopen a question that many had thought settled; (c) tentatively: he thinks that his demonstration, plus the presence of nerve tissue (ganglia) in all hearts, goes far toward proving his case; (d) no: he warns that we cannot conclude that conditions are the same in all hearts; (e) no: he specifically warns that the presence of ganglion tissue in all hearts does not prove his case.

ANSWER _____

3. Formulate here two questions to bear in mind while reading thoroughly.

a. _____

_____

b. _____

_____

Now return to the article and read it thoroughly.

Thorough-reading questions. (You may look back.)

1. Which of the following describes the organization of the report? (a) Problem-solution; (b) problem, description of experimental subject, description of experiment; (c) problem, experiments, conclusion; (d) problem, theoretical analysis, description of confirming experimental observations; (e) none of the above.

ANSWER _____

2. After pre-reading, you formulated two questions of your own. What are the answers to those?

   a. _____

   _____

   b. _____

   _____

3. List here the numbers of any paragraphs where the author is concerned with possible "experimental interference"; that is, interruption of the natural functioning of the organism through the carrying out of the experiment.

ANSWER _____

4. Why was the heart of Limulus an ideal choice for the author's experiment? (a) It is large; (b) its nerves and muscles can be separated easily from each other, without harm to the heart action; (c) its musculature is striated; (d) experimental specimens are readily available; (e) none of the above.

ANSWER _____

5. For what purpose were Patten and Redenbaugh cited? (a) This article repeats experiments of their previous research; (b) this article repeats their earlier experiments, but comes to different conclusions because of improved experimental methods; (c) Patten and Redenbaugh supplement and confirm, independently, the author's own description of the features of the heart of Limulus that are most important to the author's experiments; (d) this article supplements and extends the anatomical findings of the previous investigators; (e) none of the above.

ANSWER _____

6. List the three most important terms used by the author—the ones that are central to the theory he advances.

ANSWER a. _____ b. _____ c. _____

7. List here the numbers of all paragraphs where the author describes the actual experiments he performed.

ANSWER _____

8. Outline here the steps in the experimental procedures followed.

_____

_____

_____

_____

_____

_____

9. The author states (at the ends of paragraphs 4 and 6) two different sets of conclusions about the heart of Limulus. One of the following may *not* be true of the two conclusions. If so, which is it? (a) The second conclusion is an application of the first to the origin, as well as the conduction, of the heartbeat; (b) in establishing each conclusion, the author disposes of the possible objection that his experiments injure the heart so severely that his conclusions are invalid; (c) both conclusions are possible because of the particular construction of the Limulus' heart; (d) both conclusions are limited in their applicability to the hearts of other animals; (e) choose this answer if all of the above *are* true.

ANSWER _____

10. Besides direct experimental evidence, the author mentions observations of the exhausted heart (paragraph 4) and evidence from embryology (paragraph 7). Observations of these sorts are often important in biology, but they are sometimes dangerous to use. Why should they be used with care? (a) The embryonic (not completely developed) state and the exhausted state are both abnormal conditions; (b) normal, healthy, adult functioning may not be the same as abnormal, undeveloped, or exhausted functioning; (c) the embryonic heart has no nerves; (d) it is not always correct to argue from the structure of an organ to its function; (e) the experiments themselves, interfering with the normal functions of the organ, produce abnormal states.

ANSWER _____

Outlining.

After completing the questions above, prepare here a brief structural outline of the report, with emphasis on overall organization of the material.

_____

_____

_____

_____

CHAPTER 14

Introduction to Critical Reading: Development Analysis

Pre-read this chapter as your first step in reading. As your second step, list below the questions you expect the chapter to answer.

_____

_____

_____

_____

_____

We defined practical prose at the beginning as material you read in the first place for information. Even when you read strictly for information, however, a process of evaluation goes on. A piece of the most narrow informational reading might provoke judgments like these: _This doesn't tell me all I need to know; This is nonsense; I don't understand;_ or, _This doesn't fit in with such-and-such I remember reading three weeks ago._

Such evaluations are the simplest form of critical reading. Other more difficult and more interesting evaluations are necessary, if only because even the most practical of prose includes more than facts. The author is likely to offer opinions based on the facts, or perhaps not based on the facts. He is likely to offer reasoning and conclusions that may or may not be valid. Often enough an author will have a rhetorical purpose; that is, he will try to persuade you to believe or act in some way. What he urges may, of course, be in such obviously rhetorical areas as politics and public policies. (What do you imagine might be the rhetorical purpose of an article titled, "The Population Explosion in the United States"? Of a book about legal aid for poor people titled *A Lawyer When Needed*?) Recommendations for belief and action are also plentiful in writing about more everyday matters (article title: "The Large Corporation and Today's College Graduate"). A rhetorical purpose may be plain to see, or it may be hidden. Example of obvious rhetorical purpose: an article titled "LSD and Heredity: Birth Defects Proved." Example of less obvious rhetorical purpose: the articles which in fact appeared in the business section of a major national magazine, not many years ago, praising the economic prospects of small companies in which the business editor happened to own stock. Examples like the last certainly support the cynical view that all rhetoric is to be distrusted; yet, to complicate still further the task of critical reading, rhetorical purposes are sometimes fully justified and to one's best advantage. (Citing a previous example, suppose the scientific facts were entirely correct in that article about LSD and heredity?)

Thus, even when you read to "get the facts, only the facts," you have the problem of distinguishing just what the facts are. Almost always your purpose goes beyond facts. You want opinions and conclusions. You want to change your mind if you are shown to be wrong. You want advice if it is good advice. You want to decide how you should act. Thus, for your purpose in reading practical prose, not only information but also reasoning, even the persuasive, rhetorical purpose, may be perfectly relevant — *if the author is right.* But how are you to know?

You know, as far as you *can* know, by reading critically. To read critically is to disentangle — as best you can — fact from fallacy, truth from falsity, right action from wrong. As best you can; for although the brief examples are simple enough, much writing will give your developing critical skills a thorough workout, with no assurance that you will always be correct in your evaluation.

How are you to read critically? This book — or indeed any book — can only begin to show you. To take just one reason for this limitation, critical reading of any work depends to a considerable extent on the knowledge and critical skill you have gained with other works. But at least we can be sure that all the comprehension skills you have learned from this book will come into play — for clearly, until you understand, you have no right to criticize. "I don't know what you mean, but you're wrong!" This is the remark of the dunce, yes, but it sums up — including the note of aggressive egotism — all that many people have in mind when they disagree with a work.

Critical reading, then, is founded on understanding. Here, as always, you will find that understanding of organization is a first requirement: organization of whole books, chapters, and articles; and organization of key passages and paragraphs. Pre-reading, summarizing, and the ability to spot topic statements within the structure of a passage — all these skills are immediately pertinent. You will also find it important to answer the questions you formulated for thorough reading, particularly those that direct your attention to the author's thesis or problem, and to his main sequence of ideas.

Two of these skills can be carried considerably farther, to become two of the most powerful techniques you can use to attain complete and critical understanding of any nonfiction.

One of these is an extension of the technique of formulating questions. In addition to those questions for comprehension suggested in Chapter 7, we will discuss in the next chapter a group of what can be called *critical questions.* They are widely applicable because they help you to know whether or not you agree with an author, and if you disagree, what your basis for criticism is.

The other technique for critical reading, discussed in *this* chapter, is an additional approach to analysis of paragraphs and longer passages. Whereas Chapter 5 discussed paragraphs primarily in terms of organization, this next technique gets more directly at content, by discovering the methods the author has used to develop his statements. This technique has had several names over the 2,000 years of its history. We shall call it, awkwardly but accurately, *development analysis.* It is an instrument for close understanding of significant passages, and difficult ones. When you have mastered it, you will find that it applies especially to really hard reading and really important reading, to practical prose, and also to great books — even to fine fiction and much poetry, if you care to take an analytical approach to the appreciation of beauty.

This book has proposed, throughout, workable and specific things you can do to meet reading problems. As you gather from the last several paragraphs, that is also the aim of this discussion of critical reading. However, in two chapters we cannot be as detailed as we would like; indeed, whole books have been written about critical reading (several of them are suggested in the Bibliography on page 473). Nonetheless, for the requirements of practical prose at least, the sketch in these two chapters of two aspects of critical reading should fulfill the promise of the chapter titles: an *introduction* to critical reading.

Seven Categories of Development

With so many authors writing so many articles and books each year on a limitless variety of subjects, you may be surprised to learn that there are very few methods any author can use to develop his ideas. In fact, no matter what or how much any writer may have to say, as he sets it all down in words he is limited to some six or eight methods of development. *Development analysis* strives to recognize and follow out the author's use of these methods. The result for the reader is increased comprehension and sharpened ability to detect flaws or weaknesses — and strengths as well — in the presentation.

These are the seven categories of development:

Quotation or citation of other writers

Narration and description

Classification and division

Definition

Comparison and contrast

Example

Cause and effect

You have met one of these already. *Definition* was treated early, in Chapter 5, because it is so often indispensable to comprehension.

If we were concerned with writing, a detailed study would be necessary to show you how to *use* each method of development. Your problem in reading is simpler: how to *recognize* the methods. The presentation of the methods of development can be brief and immediately practical for reading.

Quotation or citation of other writers is not often mentioned in writing courses these days as a separate category of development along with definition, comparison, and the others. Yet when rhetoric was taught in medieval or Renaissance times, at the head of the list of categories was an item called *authority* or *testimony,* which meant the kind of evidence that pursues a thesis or line of thought with quotations or references to other writers on the subject. When one reads today a treatise from those times, it can seem so loaded down with scraps of ancient authors as to suggest that *authority* was the only method of development some writers learned. Yet even then it was recognized that to quote somebody else's reasoning or facts is usually weaker than to demonstrate the facts or work out the argument oneself. It could be for these two reasons, overuse and unoriginality, that citation of authorities ceased to get equal standing with other methods of development. Yet quotations and citations from others inescapably continue to be used. Every college student learning to paste together his first research paper is taught to search the library for relevant sources and is drilled in the forms for citing them correctly. A scientific report in *Brain Research* or *Physical Review Letters* next week will very likely have more, not fewer, citations and references for its length than any comparable passage in the Renaissance anatomist Vesalius or the physicist Newton. And as usual, what is important for the writer to be able to do skillfully, is important for you as a reader to learn to recognize.

For the reader, quotations or citations can give rise to problems of accuracy and problems of relevance. At the simplest level, accuracy is, of course, no more than: are the words quoted correctly? are the facts right? is the source identified clearly and correctly? From your work with the tools of library research in Chapter 11, you are trained to judge these questions. But accuracy also involves the more difficult question of *context*: even if the words are accurately quoted, do they really represent what the author meant? Or, taken out of the larger setting in which the author originally used them, do they now seem to mean something different?

Questions of relevance can be subtle. At the simplest level, a quotation or citation is not relevant unless it genuinely advances the line of argument, clarifies the meaning, establishes the facts or reasoning the writer claims. Quotation can also be used, of course, not to establish the writer's view but to establish what exactly it is that the writer is arguing against, so that the quote is set up and then knocked down. The question of relevance can become tricky here: it is easy for a writer to quote a weak statement of the opposition, or to quote something that is not central to the true viewpoint of his opponent—but to knock down such straw men (as they are often called) is hardly valid. Still another aspect of relevance is whether the quotation or citation is central to the writer's thesis, or not; obviously the more essential it is, the more cautiously the reader must treat it. These questions of accuracy and relevance can reinforce each other, too: when a writer presents you with a quotation from his opponent which is central to the thesis, and which you suspect may be out of context or a straw man, then surely you should check the source for yourself.

Narration and description both recount details in sequence: respectively details of *events,* in time sequence, and details of *things* or *places,* in a spatial or other sequence. A narrative tells a story, and any writing (from "Hickory-Dickory-Dock" to the *History* of Herodotus) that answers the question *what happened?* is narrative. Description presents an object or scene as it would be perceived by the senses, and any writing (from a newspaper story about an oil-polluted beach to Shakespeare's evocation of an army encampment on the eve of battle) that answers the question *what is it and how does it appear?* is description.

To perceive the sequence can be essential to understanding narration and description. Sequence in narrative seems obvious, yet we have terms like *flashback* to describe intentional complications of narrative line, while on the other hand careless writers quickly snarl up the reader by recounting details out of their correct order. Sequence in description is not so self-evident. You may never have stopped to notice it; yet in writing of any length or intricacy, the writer's careful control of sequence is what makes a description come to life in your understanding. Sequence in description can be as simple as left-to-right, or as rich as the superb opening page of E. M. Forster's novel, *A Passage to India,* describing an Indian town in its setting, which begins with the hills at the far horizon, leaps forward to the river in the foreground, then sweeps from river upwards and back, through the Indian quarter, to European houses on the high ground, and again to the horizon — and in that complex sequence, prefigures the entire story to follow.

Narration and description are often mingled in the same passage; for example, a vivid narrative must have descriptive detail so the reader can visualize what's happening, as in this example:

After a brief stop at Ceuta our boat went on around the corner of Africa to Tangier. The authorities in Madrid had not looked with a favorable eye upon my idea of visiting Morocco, and to escape their censorious attentions it seemed a good plan to make my headquarters in the international zone.	Narration
There (at least in theory) an American was on the same basis as any Spaniard or Frenchman, since Tangier belonged to all nations.	Interpolated explanatory sentence
As we came near the city, a confusion of white, cream, and yellow houses on a hill, there was firing to be heard from the black mountainous country of Angeras at the left.	Narration and description
The excitement of the moment came back whenever I thought of it again for years afterwards: the white city on the hill, demure and peaceful, with the long white beach beneath, and the vague thunder of Spanish guns off to the left, in mysterious mountains where no guns should have been.	Brief description of a series of objects
French and British gunboats bobbed harmlessly up and down on the spar-	

kling water far out in front of the town. To
meet our boat every turbaned rapscallion in   Narration
Tangier had taken to the water; in ten minutes
we were offered an infinite variety of rugs,
worked leather, embroidery, beaded objects,
guidance, and advice . . .[1]

Narrative and descriptive passages are, because of their concern with the
specific and concrete, usually easier and faster to read than abstract passages
in practical prose. Narration and description in scientific writing are important
exceptions to this rule. In practical prose, narration and description often perform a special function: they provide examples or illustrations of what the
author is saying. (*Example* as a method of development is discussed below.)

Classification and division are as closely related as *up* is to *down*. The
words themselves explain, about as far as we will go into it, what the author
does. To classify something is to place it in a class or group to which it belongs.
Classification develops the author's subject by showing what it relates to, where
it fits among things or ideas you may already be familiar with. One can classify
even the simplest thing in a variety of ways: as a part in relation to some whole
(*the sun is part of the solar system, the tongue is part of the body*); or as one of
a group of similar things (*the sun is a star*); or functionally (*the tongue is an
organ of speech*); and so on. For example, a geologist's report on a previously
unexplored island might begin by stating to which general type of island formation this particular island belongs: he classifies his subject as volcanic, coral, or
other, and by this classification he quickly tells scientific readers a great deal
about that island. The advertising man, writing an analysis of the problems of
a new client, follows the same procedure: he classifies the client's business as
industrial or consumer; as cosmetics, appliances, supermarket merchandise,
or other; and his recommendations vary accordingly.

To divide, on the other hand, is to take a subject or a group apart, to
analyze it into its components. For example, we are right now dividing our subject by listing and exploring six different methods of development. The sociologist follows the same procedure when he examines, for instance, metropolitan
New York City: he may divide it geographically, into central and suburban
counties; he may divide it according to the distribution of residents by economic
and social level; or perhaps by types of businesses and industries. Understanding the author's division of his subject is extremely important to comprehension; indeed, when you pre-read a table of contents, what else are you doing
but studying the author's own list of the general divisions he makes?

Such, in brief, are the natures of classification and division as methods of
development; classification being an "upward" movement of something into a
class or group, division the reverse, "downward," movement of something into
its various parts or aspects. When you see that an author is developing his subject by classification and division, for critical reading keep two test questions
in mind:

Is the classification or division accurate, and in particular, is it *not
overlapping*?

Is it *complete*—are all the pertinent classes, or all the parts, considered?

Classification or division can provide the organizational basis for an entire article or chapter of a book; the example familiar to everyone who has studied beginning Latin is, of course, Julius Caesar's opening sentence of his *Gallic Wars,* "All Gaul is divided into three parts; the first . . ." A classification or division is often the point of a transitional paragraph. Either of the two methods is also to be found used on a small scale, intermingled with other methods of development. An example of a division that organizes a subject, and is closely interwoven with a definition, follows the brief review of definition, below.

Definition was explored in Chapter 5; please reread pages 119–20 now. There we said that:

A precise definition states what something is, and how it differs from anything else with which you might confuse it.

On the basis of our discussion of classification and division above, we can now put the same statement in its more correct technical form:

A precise definition first *classifies* the subject. Then it proceeds to *differentiate* the subject from all others in the same class.

Classification alone does not complete a definition; without the second step it leaves you confused. For example, *an apple is a fruit* is classification but not definition, since it does not tell you how to know the differences between apples and pears, plums, and so forth. Whether the definition be short or book-length, these two steps are what you look for; and an important flaw or failure in either step will provide a basis for critical questioning of the definition.

The following example of a definition shows how inescapably this method of development relates to classification and division. The passage is drawn from one of the most famous and still fascinating textbooks ever written, the *Principles of Psychology,* which William James prepared in 1890 for his undergraduate students at Harvard.

The Empirical Self of each of us is all that he is tempted to call by the name of *me.* But it is clear that between what a man calls *me* and what he simply calls *mine* the line is difficult to draw. We feel and act about certain things that are ours very much as we feel and act about ourselves. Our fame, our children, the work of our hands, may be as dear to us as our bodies are, and arouse the same feelings and the same acts of reprisal if attacked. And our bodies themselves, are they simply ours, or are they *us?* Certainly men have been ready to disown their very bodies and to regard them as mere vestures, or even as prisons of clay from which they should some day be glad to escape.

We see then that we are dealing with a fluctuating material. The same object being sometimes treated as a part of me, at other times as simply mine, and then again as if I had nothing to do with it at all. *In its widest possible sense,* however, *a man's Self is the sum total of all that he* can *call his,* not only his body and his psychic powers, but his clothes and his house, his wife and children, his ancestors and friends, his reputation and works, his lands and horses, and yacht and bank-account. All these things give him the same emotions. If they wax and prosper, he feels triumphant; if they dwindle and die away, he feels cast down, — not necessarily in the same degree for each thing, but in much the same way for all. Understanding the Self in this widest sense, we may begin, by dividing the history of it into three parts, relating respectively to —

1. Its constituents;
2. The feelings and emotions they arouse, — *Self-feelings;*
3. The actions to which they prompt, — *Self-seeking and Self-preservation.*

1. *The constituents of the Self* may be divided into two classes, those which make up respectively —

(*a*) The material Self;
(*b*) The social Self;
(*c*) The spiritual Self; and
(*d*) The pure Ego.

(*a*) The body is the innermost part of *the material Self* in each of us; and certain parts of the body seem more intimately ours than the rest. The clothes come next. The old saying that the human person is composed of three parts — soul, body and clothes — is more than a joke. . . .

Comparison points out similarities; *contrast* points out differences. An author frequently clarifies by comparing or contrasting his subject with something familiar to the reader. Usually an author deals with only the one or two similarities or differences that concern him, even though two subjects may be similar or different in other ways as well. Therefore, when you notice that an author is comparing or contrasting his subject with other subjects, be sure that you understand the basis of the comparison or contrast.

For either comparison or contrast to be possible, there must be a basic similarity. Once that similarity is established, comparison proceeds to establish other similarities, while contrast proceeds to establish differences. Because there is no basic similarity between the North Pole and a wheelbarrow, comparison or contrast of these two subjects would be farfetched and probably meaningless. Comparison or contrast may occur on a large or a small scale. Of course comparison and contrast are often used together. Indeed, because two subjects must have some similarity to be contrasted or compared, and because on the other hand no two subjects are identical, it is difficult to use one of these methods of development without the other.

Here is an entirely everyday example of comparison, where the author explains a relatively less familiar subject (the extraordinary rise of Louis Napoleon) with the help of something more familiar.

The first coups of Louis-Napoleon, at Strasbourg in 1836 and at Boulogne in 1840, were miserable failures, like Hitler's Munich *Putsch* of 1923. Both men were treated with humane and neglectful forbearance, and in the enforced leisure of their comfortable prisons they composed their programmatic works — *Des Idées Napoléoniennes* and *Mein Kampf.* Not even at a later stage did the political leaders realize the full gravity of the situation—thinking in terms of their own and not in those of the masses, they could not descry either in Louis-Napoleon or in Hitler a possible ruler or dictator. Louis-Napoleon escaped from his prison at Ham in 1846, and settled in London. On the outbreak of the February Revolution . . .[2]

And at that point the author abandons the comparison with Hitler to pursue Louis Napoleon's career.

Examples develop and amplify a general subject. The author points to particular instances of what he means and shows how the instances are relavant to his purpose. Examples may be confined to a sentence or two within a paragraph, but they often take up entire paragraphs. Examples, as previously mentioned, may be used to establish or support a definition. Frequently in practical prose, narrative or descriptive passages are intended to be examples.

When you come across an example, several questions will often help your critical understanding. What seems to be the *purpose* of the example? What general subject does the example *represent*? What is the *connection* between the example and the general subject? And, very importantly, are there *enough* examples to establish the author's point?

Cause and effect: again, the words themselves very largely explain this last method of development. In using this method, obviously enough, the author attempts to explain in what way one thing is the result of something else. To take a simple example: *The stonemason slipped on the icy sidewalk and broke his leg.* The cause of the broken leg is apparently the fall, and the cause of the fall is apparently the icy sidewalk. Working in the opposite direction in the sequence of events, the effect of the icy sidewalk is apparently the fall, and the effect of the fall is apparently the broken leg. Of course, few effects can actually be chained to their causes so simply. For instance, the stonemason in the example above may have been drunk and unsteady, or he may have been on a diet that had too little calcium, thereby leaving his bones brittle. Thus the chains of cause and effect may be extended infinitely, and each event may have many causes and many effects.

Without opening up the grave philosophical difficulties of the question, *how does something cause something else?* we can say that the search to understand causes is a major concern of much writing. The scientist's chief aim is to set up conditions for observing facts in such a way that he limits the number of possible causes. The historian, who has no controlled experiments, still debates at book length such questions as the causes of the World War I. One of the worst forms of faulty reasoning is to assert a causal relation where there is really only a coincidence of timing, so that the author makes a narration into a cause and effect: this fallacy even has a name to remember as you watch for it, *post hoc ergo propter hoc*—"*after* this, therefore *because* of this." In sum, for critical reading remember that cause and effect are usually so complex that any analysis based on them must necessarily be tentative, probabilistic, not certain.

Our final demonstration of an author's development to be analyzed shows once again how several methods can be blended in the same passage. In the following paragraphs from *The City in History,* Lewis Mumford begins with

comparison and goes on to contrast, both supported by examples; but fundamentally the argument of the passage is about cause and effect. As you read it,
note the way your new awareness of how the author is reasoning sharpens
your understanding of what he is saying.

If one holds to the isolationist premises of the older generation of
American anthropologists and archaeologists, one must treat the forms of
Mayan, Aztec, and Peruvian cultures as a completely independent invention of the New World. This is possible, but there are many facts that keep it
from being wholly plausible. If cultures were in fact as different as biological
species, these resemblances might be as unrelated as the no less striking
resemblances between the termitary and the anthill. But what one finds in
the New World is not just a collection of houses and buildings, which might
have had the same common ancestor in the mesolithic hamlet. One dis-
covers, rather, a parallel collection of cultural traits: highly developed fertility ceremonies, a pantheon of cosmic deities, a magnified ruler and central
authority who personifies the whole community, great temples whose forms
recall such functionally different structures as the pyramid and the ziggurat,
along with the same domination of a peasantry by an original hunter-warrior
group, or (among the early Mayas) an even more ancient priesthood. Likewise the same division of castes and specialization of vocational groups,
and the beginnings of writing, time-measuring, and the calendar—including
an immense extension of time perspectives among the Mayas, which sur-
passes in complexity and accuracy even what we know of the cosmic periods
of the Babylonians and the Egyptians. These traits seem too specific to have
been spontaneously repeated in a whole constellation.

Admittedly, there are many contrasts between the cities of Sumer and
Egypt and those of the Mayas a millennium of two later, as there are, for
that matter, between those of Peru and Mexico. But these differences are
precisely what one would expect in cultures remote in space and time, connected only through a passage of ideas borne by traders, explorers, even
religious missionaries, rather than by any wholesale immigration or invasion
in force. The vehicles of this passage, boats and even islands, may well have
sunk out of sight long before the ideas themselves reached the New World.
If the cultural dispersion began very early, it might well have included the
archetypal form of the pyramid or ziggurat, but not the plow or the wheel:
it might bring the memory of the city without transporting the ox or the ass.
If Mesopotamian writing prompted the Egyptians to develop writing, as
many archaeologists believe, the form of the Egyptian hieroglyphs is no
farther removed from its immediate exemplar than Mayan signs are from
either. Thus one may account for the many differences between Egyptian,
Sumerian, Indian, Chinese, Cambodian, Mayan, Peruvian, and Aztec urban
centers, without denying their underlying similarities, and without setting
any arbitrary barrier, not even the Pacific Ocean, against the possibility of
their slow diffusion from a few points. That the pyramid form would be used

as a tomb and would represent the mountain of creation among the Egyptians, and would be transformed into a temple for collective religious ceremonies among the Mayas and the Aztecs, is no more implausible than the transformation of the gridiron street system from an original Etruscan symbol of cosmic order to a convenient pattern for creating American pioneer towns – or speculating in real estate.[3]

EXERCISES FOR CHAPTER 14

Reading Journal

Integrated Exercise 3: A Historian Offers an Extended Definition
   "On the Unpopularity of Intellect," from *Anti-Intellectualism in American Life,* by Richard Hofstadter

Integrated Exercise 4: A Philosopher Explains the Methods of Science
   "Characteristics of Scientific Method," by Bertrand Russell

Reading Journal

You should still be carrying out the assignment from Chapter 13: a coördinated attack on a single book, to which you apply, as needed, any or all of the reading techniques you have learned, recording your progress in your separate notebook. Now, as you go on, also collect and write down examples of the different methods of development. You will find it fairly easy to spot three examples of definition, and two each of narration and description, and of course many uses of example and of quotation. But the other topics – classification and division, comparison and contrast, cause and effect – may prove somewhat more elusive, both because they are used less often and less clearly, and because you are not usually aware of them as modes of thinking, while you read. Nevertheless, try to find at least three examples of each of these methods, too; for only by hunting them down actively at first will you develop the habit of noting them in your day-to-day reading.

Integrated Exercise 3:
A Historian Offers an Extended Definition

Is it true that Americans distrust and dislike intellectuals? To put the question somewhat less sweepingly, is it true that one dominant strand in American life, since the earliest days, has been a widespread anti-intellectualism? Richard Hofstadter, the noted historian, believes the answer is *yes*. He has written a book, *Anti-Intellectualism in American Life*, that examines the roots and consequences of this attitude. He recounts the chief examples of anti-intellectualism in our history to the present day, shows how and why it has erupted from a simple cultural bias (one of many sometimes conflicting attitudes) into a powerful force in education, religion, and politics. He considers the arguments and justifications that have been advanced for anti-intellectualism; he itemizes the damage this attitude has done.

But before Hofstadter can go into these questions, he must pause to define his key terms: as introduction to his book, the author offers an extended definition of intellect itself. The major portion of that extended definition forms the following article.

Pre-read the article. Go on to answer the pre-reading questions that follow, page 411. Then formulate questions to be answered during thorough reading. Come back to read the article thoroughly, and go on to answer the remaining questions.

Begin pre-reading here.

"On the Unpopularity of Intellect"[4]
from *Anti-Intellectualism in American Life*
by RICHARD HOFSTADTER

Before attempting to estimate the qualities in our society that make intellect unpopular, it seems necessary to say something about what intellect is usually understood to be. When one hopes to understand a common prejudice, common usage provides a good place to begin. Anyone who scans popular American writing with this interest in mind will be struck by the manifest difference between the idea of intellect and the idea of intelligence. The first is frequently used as a kind of epithet, the second never. No one questions the value of intelligence; as an abstract quality it is universally esteemed, and individuals who seem to have it in exceptional degree are highly regarded. The man of intelligence is always praised; the man of intellect is sometimes also praised, especially when it is believed that intellect involves intelligence, but he is also often looked upon with resentment or suspicion. It is he, and not the intelligent man, who may be called unreliable, superfluous, immoral, or subversive; sometimes he is even said to be, for all his intellect, unintelligent.*

Although the difference between the qualities of intelligence and intellect is more often assumed than defined, the context of popular usage makes it possible to extract the nub of the distinction, which seems to be almost universally understood: intelligence is an excellence of mind that is employed within a fairly narrow, immediate, and predictable range; it is a manipulative, adjustive, unfailingly practical quality—one of the most eminent and endearing of the animal virtues. Intelligence works within the framework of limited but clearly stated goals, and may be quick to shear away questions of thought that do not seem to help in reaching them. Finally, it is of such universal use that it can daily be seen at work and admired alike by simple or complex minds.

Intellect, on the other hand, is the critical, creative, and contemplative side of mind. Whereas intelligence seeks to grasp, manipulate, re-order, adjust, intellect examines, ponders, wonders, theorizes, criticizes, imagines. Intelligence will seize the immediate meaning in a situation and evaluate it. Intellect evaluates evaluations, and looks for the meanings of situations as a whole. Intelligence can be praised as a quality in animals; intellect, being a unique manifestation of human dignity, is both praised and assailed as a quality in men. When the difference is so defined, it becomes easier to understand why we sometimes say that a mind of admittedly penetrating intelligence is relatively unintellectual; and why, by the same token, we see among minds that are unmistakably intellectual a considerable range of intelligence.

This distinction may seem excessively abstract, but it is frequently illustrated in American culture. In our education, for example, it has never been doubted that the selection and development of intelligence is a goal of central importance; but the extent to which education should foster intellect has been a matter of the most heated controversy, and the opponents of intellect in most spheres of public education have exercised preponderant power. But perhaps the most impressive illustration arises from a comparison of the American regard for inventive skill as opposed to skill in pure science. Our greatest inventive genius, Thomas A. Edison, was all but canonized by the American public, and a legend has been built around him. One cannot, I suppose, expect that achievements in pure science would receive the same public applause that came to inventions as spectacular and as directly influential on ordinary life as Edison's. But one might have expected that our greatest genius in pure science, Josiah Willard Gibbs, who laid the theoretical foundations for modern physical chemistry, would have been a figure of some comparable acclaim among the educated public. Yet

*I do not want to suggest that this distinction is made only in the United States, since it seems to be common wherever there is a class that finds intellectuals a nuisance and yet does not want to throw overboard its own claims to intelligence. Thus, in France, after the intellectuals had emerged as a kind of social force, one finds Maurice Barrès writing in 1902: "I'd rather be intelligent than an intellectual." Victor Brombert: *The Intellectual Hero: Studies in the French Novel, 1880–1955* (Philadelphia, 1961), p. 25.

Gibbs, whose work was celebrated in Europe, lived out his life in public and even professional obscurity at Yale, where he taught for thirty-two years. Yale, which led American universities in its scientific achievements during the nineteenth century, was unable in those thirty-two years to provide him with more than a half dozen or so graduate students who could understand his work, and never took the trouble to award him an honorary degree.*

A special difficulty arises when we speak of the fate of intellect in society; this difficulty stems from the fact that we are compelled to speak of intellect in vocational terms, though we may recognize that intellect is not simply a matter of vocation. Intellect is considered in general usage to be an attribute of certain professions and vocations; we speak of the intellectual as being a writer or a critic, a professor or a scientist, an editor, journalist, lawyer, clergyman, or the like. As Jacques Barzun has said, the intellectual is a man who carries a brief case. It is hardly possible to dispense with this convenience; the status and the role of intellectuals are bound up with the aggregate of the brief-case-carrying professions. But few of us believe that a member of a profession, even a learned profession, is necessarily an intellectual in any discriminating or demanding sense of the word. In most professions intellect may help, but intelligence will serve well enough without it. We know, for instance, that all academic men are not intellectuals; we often lament this fact. We know that there is something about intellect, as opposed to professionally trained intelligence, which does not adhere to whole vocations but only to persons. And when we are troubled about the position of intellect and the intellectual class in our society, it is not only the status of certain vocational groups which we have in mind, but the value attached to a certain mental quality.

A great deal of what might be called the journeyman's work of our culture — the work of lawyers, editors, engineers, doctors, indeed of some writers and of most professors — though vitally dependent upon ideas, is not distinctively intellectual. A man in any of the learned or quasi-learned professions must have command of a substantial store of frozen ideas to do his work; he must, if he does it well, use them intelligently; but in his professional capacity he uses them mainly as instruments. The heart of the matter — to borrow a distinction made by Max Weber about politics — is that the professional man lives *off* ideas, not *for* them. His professional role, his professional skills, do not make him an intellectual. He is a mental worker, a technician. He may *happen* to be an intellectual as well, but if he is, it is because he brings to his profession a distinctive feeling about ideas which is not required by his job. As a professional, he has acquired a stock of mental skills that are for sale. The skills are highly developed, but we do not think of him as being an intellectual if certain qualities are missing from his work —

---

* The situation of Gibbs is often mentioned as a consequence of American attitudes. For the general situation it symbolized, see Richard H. Shryock: "American Indifference to Basic Science during the Nineteenth Century," *Archives Internationales d'Histoire des Sciences,* No. 5 (1948), pp. 50–65.

disinterested intelligence, generalizing power, free speculation, fresh observation, creative novelty, radical criticism. At home he may happen to be an intellectual, but at his job he is a hired mental technician who uses his mind for the pursuit of externally determined ends. It is this element—the fact that ends are set from some interest or vantage point outside the intellectual process itself—which characterizes both the zealot, who lives obsessively for a single idea, and the mental technician, whose mind is used not for free speculation, but for a salable end. The goal here is external and not self-determined, whereas the intellectual life has a certain spontaneous character and inner determination. It has also a peculiar poise of its own, which I believe is established by a balance between two basic qualities in the intellectual's attitude toward ideas—qualities that may be designated as playfulness and piety.

To define what is distinctively intellectual it is necessary to be able to determine what differentiates, say, a professor or a lawyer who is an intellectual from one who is not; or perhaps more properly, what enables us to say that at one moment a professor or a lawyer is acting in a purely routine professional fashion and at another moment as an intellectual. The difference is not in the character of the ideas with which he works but in his attitude toward them. I have suggested that in some sense he lives for ideas —which means that he has a sense of dedication to the life of the mind which is very much like a religious commitment. This is not surprising, for in a very important way the role of the intellectual is inherited from the office of the cleric: it implies a special sense of the ultimate value in existence of the act of comprehension. Socrates, when he said that the unexamined life is not worth living, struck the essence of it. We can hear the voices of various intellectuals in history repeating their awareness of this feeling, in accents suitable to time, place, and culture. "The proper function of the human race, taken in the aggregate," wrote Dante in *De Monarchia,* "is to actualize continually the entire capacity possible to the intellect, primarily in speculation, then through its extension and for its sake, secondarily in action." The noblest thing, and the closest possible to divinity, is thus the act of knowing. It is only a somewhat more secular and activist version of the same commitment which we hear in the first sentence of Locke's *Essay Concerning Human Understanding:* "It is the *understanding* that sets man above the rest of sensible beings, and gives him all the advantage and dominion which he has over them." Hawthorne, in a passage near the end of *The Blithedale Romance,* observes that Nature's highest purpose for man is "that of conscious intellectual life and sensibility." Finally, in our own time André Malraux puts the question in one of his novels: "How can one make the best of one's life?" and answers: "By converting as wide a range of experience as possible into conscious thought."

Intellectualism, though by no means confined to doubters, is often the sole piety of the skeptic. Some years ago a colleague asked me to read a brief essay he had written for students going on to do advanced work in his field. Its ostensible purpose was to show how the life of the mind could be cultivated within the framework of his own discipline, but its effect was to give an intensely personal expression to his dedication to intellectual work. Although it was written by a corrosively skeptical mind, I felt that I was reading a piece of devotional literature in some ways comparable to Richard Steele's *The Tradesman's Calling* or Cotton Mather's *Essays to Do Good,* for in it the intellectual task had been conceived as a *calling,* much in the fashion of the old Protestant writers. His work was undertaken as a kind of devotional exercise, a personal discipline, and to think of it in this fashion was possible because it was more than merely workmanlike and professional: it was work at thinking, work done supposedly in the service of truth. The intellectual life has here taken on a kind of primary moral significance. It is this aspect of the intellectual's feeling about ideas that I call his piety. The intellectual is *engagé* — he is pledged, committed, enlisted. What everyone else is willing to admit, namely that ideas and abstractions are of signal importance in human life, he imperatively feels.

Of course what is involved is more than a purely personal discipline and more than the life of contemplation and understanding itself. For the life of thought, even though it may be regarded as the highest form of human activity, is also a medium through which other values are refined, reasserted, and realized in the human community. Collectively, intellectuals have often tried to serve as the moral antennae of the race, anticipating and if possible clarifying fundamental moral issues before these have forced themselves upon the public consciousness. The thinker feels that he ought to be the special custodian of values like reason and justice which are related to his own search for truth, and at times he strikes out passionately as a public figure because his very identity seems to be threatened by some gross abuse. One thinks here of Voltaire defending the Calas family, of Zola speaking out for Dreyfus, of the American intellectuals outraged at the trial of Sacco and Vanzetti.

It would be unfortunate if intellectuals were alone in their concern for these values, and it is true that their enthusiasm has at times miscarried. But it is also true that intellectuals are properly more responsive to such values than others; and it is the historic glory of the intellectual class of the West in modern times that, of all the classes which could be called in any sense privileged, it has shown the largest and most consistent concern for the well-being of the classes which lie below it in the social scale. Behind the intellectual's feeling of commitment is the belief that in some measure the world should be made responsive to his capacity for rationality, his passion for justice and order: out of this conviction arises much of his value to mankind and, equally, much of his ability to do mischief.

The very suggestion that the intellectual has a distinctive capacity for mischief, however, leads to the consideration that his piety, by itself, is not enough. He may live for ideas, as I have said, but something must prevent him from living for *one idea,* from becoming obsessive or grotesque. Although there have been zealots whom we may still regard as intellectuals, zealotry is a defect of the breed and not of the essence. When one's concern for ideas, no matter how dedicated and sincere, reduces them to the service of some central limited preconception or some wholly external end, intellect gets swallowed by fanaticism. If there is anything more dangerous to the life of the mind than having no independent commitment to ideas, it is having an excess of commitment to some special and constricting idea. The effect is as observable in politics as in theology: the intellectual function can be overwhelmed by an excess of piety expended within too contracted a frame of reference.

Piety, then, needs a counterpoise, something to prevent it from being exercised in an excessively rigid way; and this it has, in most intellectual temperaments, in the quality I would call playfulness. We speak of the play of the mind; and certainly the intellectual relishes the play of the mind for its own sake, and finds in it one of the major values in life. What one thinks of here is the element of sheer delight in intellectual activity. Seen in this guise, intellect may be taken as the healthy animal spirits of the mind, which come into exercise when the surplus of mental energies is released from the tasks required for utility and mere survival. "Man is perfectly human," said Schiller, "only when he plays." And it is this awareness of an available surplus beyond the requirements of mere existence that his maxim conveys to us. Veblen spoke often of the intellectual faculty as "idle curiosity"—but this is a misnomer in so far as the curiosity of the playful mind is inordinately restless and active. This very restlessness and activity gives a distinctive cast to its view of truth and its discontent with dogmas.

Ideally, the pursuit of truth is said to be at the heart of the intellectual's business, but this credits his business too much and not quite enough. As with the pursuit of happiness, the pursuit of truth is itself gratifying whereas the consummation often turns out to be elusive. Truth captured loses its glamor; truths long known and widely believed have a way of turning false with time; easy truths are a bore, and too many of them become half-truths. Whatever the intellectual is too certain of, if he is healthily playful, he begins to find unsatisfactory. The meaning of his intellectual life lies not in the possession of truth but in the quest for new uncertainties. Harold Rosenberg summed up this side of the life of the mind supremely well when he said that the intellectual is one who turns answers into questions.

This element of playfulness infuses products of mind as diverse as Abelard's *Sic et Non* and a dadaist poem. But in using the terms *play* and *playfulness,* I do not intend to suggest any lack of seriousness; quite the contrary. Anyone who has watched children, or adults, at play will recognize that there is no contradiction between play and seriousness, and that some forms of play induce a measure of grave concentration not so readily called forth by work. And playfulness does not imply the absence of practicality. In American public discussion one of the tests to which intellect is constantly submitted when it is, so to speak, on trial is this criterion of practicality. But in principle intellect is neither practical nor impractical; it is extra-practical. To the zealot overcome by his piety and to the journeyman of ideas concerned only with his marketable mental skills, the beginning and end of ideas lies in their efficacy with respect to some goal external to intellectual processes. The intellectual is not in the first instance concerned with such goals. This is not to say that he scorns the practical: the intrinsic intellectual interest of many practical problems is utterly absorbing. Still less is it to say that he is impractical; he is simply concerned with something else, a quality in problems that is not defined by asking whether or not they have practical purpose. The notion that the intellectual is inherently impractical will hardly bear analysis (one can think so readily of intellectuals who, like Adam Smith, Thomas Jefferson, Robert Owen, Walter Rathenau, or John Maynard Keynes, have been eminently practical in the politician's or businessman's sense of the term). However, practicality is not the essence of his interest in ideas. Acton put this view in rather an extreme form when he said: "I think our studies ought to be all but purposeless. They want to be pursued with chastity, like mathematics."

An example of the intellectual's view of the purely practical is the response of James Clerk Maxwell, the mathematician and theoretical physicist, to the invention of the telephone. Asked to give a lecture on the workings of this new instrument, Maxwell began by saying how difficult it had been to believe, when word first came about it from America, that such a thing had actually been devised. But then, he went on, "when at last this little instrument appeared, consisting, as it does, of parts, every one of which is familiar to us, and capable of being put together by an amateur, the disappointment arising from its humble appearance was only partially relieved on finding that it was really able to talk." Perhaps, then, this regrettable appearance of simplicity might be redeemed by the presence somewhere of "some recondite physical principle, the study of which might worthily occupy an hour's time of an academic audience." But no; Maxwell had not met a single person who was unable to understand the physical processes involved, and even the science reporters for the daily press had almost got it right!* The thing was a disappointing bore; it was not recondite, not difficult, not profound, not complex; it was not *intellectually* new.

Maxwell's reaction does not seem to me to be entirely admirable. In looking at the telephone from the point of view of a pure scientist, and not as a historian or a sociologist or even a householder, he was restricting the range of his fancy. Commercially, historically, humanly, the telephone was exciting; and its possibilities as an instrument of communication and even of torture surely might have opened vistas to the imagination. But within his self-limited sphere of concern, that of physics, Maxwell was speaking with a certain stubborn daring about the intellectual interest in the matter. For him, thinking as a physicist, the new instrument offered no possibilities for play.

One may well ask if there is not a certain fatal contradiction between these two qualities of the intellectual temperament, playfulness and piety. Certainly there is a tension between them, but it is anything but fatal: it is just one of those tensions in the human character that evoke a creative re-

* W. D. Niven, ed.: *The Scientific Papers of James Clerk Maxwell* (Cambridge, 1890), Vol. II, p. 742.

sponse. It is, in fact, the ability to comprehend and express not only different but opposing points of view, to identify imaginatively with or even to embrace within oneself contrary feelings and ideas that gives rise to first-rate work in all areas of humanistic expression and in many fields of inquiry. Human beings are tissues of contradictions, and the life even of the intellectual is not logic, to borrow from Holmes, but experience. Contemplate the intellectuals of the past or those in one's neighborhood: some will come to mind in whom the note of playfulness is dominant; others who are conspicuously pious. But in most intellectuals each of these characteristics is qualified and held in check by the other. The tensile strength of the thinker may be gauged by his ability to keep an equipoise between these two sides of his mind. At one end of the scale, an excess of playfulness may lead to triviality, to the dissipation of intellectual energies on mere technique, to dilettantism, to the failure of creative effort. At the other, an excess of piety leads to rigidity, to fanaticism, to messianism, to ways of life which may be morally mean or morally magnificent but which in either case are not the ways of intellect.*

Historically, it may be useful to fancy playfulness and piety as being the respective residues of the aristocratic and the priestly backgrounds of the intellectual function. The element of play seems to be rooted in the ethos of the leisure class, which has always been central in the history of creative imagination and humanistic learning. The element of piety is reminiscent of the priestly inheritance of the intellectuals: the quest for and the possession of truth was a holy office. As their legatee, the modern intellectual inherits the vulnerability of the aristocrat to the animus of puritanism and egalitarianism and the vulnerability of the priest to anticlericalism and popular assaults upon hierarchy. We need not be surprised, then, if the intellectual's position has rarely been comfortable in a country which is, above all others, the home of the democrat and the antinomian.

It is a part of the intellectual's tragedy that the things he most values about himself and his work are quite unlike those society values in him. Society values him because he can in fact be used for a variety of purposes, from popular entertainment to the design of weapons. But it can hardly understand so well those aspects of his temperament which I have designated as essential to his intellectualism. His playfulness, in its various manifestations, is likely to seem to most men a perverse luxury; in the United States the play of the mind is perhaps the only form of play that is not looked upon with the most tender indulgence. His piety is likely to seem nettlesome, if not actually dangerous. And neither quality is considered to contribute very much to the practical business of life.

---

* It was part of the indictment by Julien Benda in *La Trahison des Clercs* (1927) that so many modern intellectuals had given themselves over to this kind of messianic politics to the grave loss of intellectual values: "Today, if we mention Mommsen, Treitschke, Ostwald, Brunetière, Barrès, Lemaître, Péguy, Maurras, d'Annunzio, Kipling, we have to admit that the 'clerks' now exercise political passions with all the characteristics of passion — the tendency to action, the thirst for immediate results, the exclusive preoccupation with the desired end, the scorn for argument, the excess, the hatred, the fixed ideas." (Translated by Richard Aldington as *The Betrayal of the Intellectuals* [Boston, 1955], p. 32.)

Pre-reading questions. (Do not look back at this article while answering.)

1. What steps did you take in pre-reading the article? _____

   _____

   _____

   _____

2. After pre-reading, one is sometimes able to formulate a tentative statement of what the author is saying in general. After pre-reading *this* article, what can you say about the author's subject, his thesis, and his point of view?

   _____

   _____

   _____

   _____

   _____

   _____

3. In particular, what does the author's attitude seem to be toward the thing he is defining, *intellect,* and toward intellectuals? Does he believe that intellect is justifiably unpopular? Or should it be defended? or what? And what, in

   your pre-reading, makes you think so? _____

   _____

   _____

   _____

   _____

4. The chief method of development used in this article is, of course, *definition.* But the author pursues his extended definition with the aid of several other methods of development. Which of the other methods of development did

   you discover in your pre-reading? _____

   _____

   _____

   _____

5. One of those additional methods of development is extremely important for the author's definition. Which is it, and how does he use it? _____

_____

_____

_____

6. On the basis of pre-reading, how difficult is the article? Why do you think so?

_____

_____

_____

7. Listed below are the chief points in the article that you could discover by pre-reading. But they are not in the correct order, and two of them are not part of the article at all. Please number the statements in the spaces provided to show their correct order; mark the fake statements with an "X."

_____ Society may value intellectuals; but even when it does, the reasons are tragically different from what the intellectual is likely to value in himself and his work.

_____ We can begin to understand what intellect is, and how it is generally viewed and valued, by contrasting it to another quality that is highly valued and without question, in America, namely intelligence.

_____ Intellect is not simply a matter of vocation, though we must often speak of it in vocational terms.

_____ Part of the unpopularity of intellectuals comes from their intrusion, as experts, into public affairs.

_____ Intellectualism, though by no means confined to doubters, is often the sole piety of the skeptic.

_____ Besides piety, a second aspect of the intellectual attitude towards ideas is playfulness.

_____ Intellect is the critical, creative, contemplative state of mind.

_____ Much of the work of our culture, work by lawyers, educators, editors, doctors, etc., though dependent on ideas is not distinctively intellectual.

_____ It would be a mistake to suppose that anti-intellectualism is commonly found in a pure and unmixed state.

Question technique.

Write out here the questions you will keep in mind while reading the article thoroughly. You may want to review the basic questions recommended in Chapter 7, besides formulating questions that are specific to Hofstadter's definition of intellect and intellectuals.

1. _____

    ANSWER _____

    _____

    _____

2. _____

    ANSWER _____

    _____

    _____

3. _____

    ANSWER _____

    _____

    _____

4. _____

    ANSWER _____

    _____

    _____

Thorough-reading questions. (You may look back.)

A. After reading the article thoroughly, go back to fill in the answers to your own questions, above.

B. Now, outline the article by writing a one-sentence summary of each of the nineteen paragraphs. As you consider each paragraph, begin by locating its topic sentence.

    1. _____

    _____

2. _____

_____

3. _____

_____

4. _____

_____

5. _____

_____

6. _____

_____

7. _____

_____

8. _____

_____

9. _____

_____

10. _____

_____

11. _____

_____

12. _____

_____

13. _____

_____

14. _____

_____

15. _____

16. _____

17. _____

18. _____

19. _____

C. Methods of development
1. In developing his definition, Hofstadter begins with a comparison and contrast that takes up at least the first six paragraphs. What is that contrast? How does he begin it? How does he carry it on into the subject of the relation between intellect and vocation? _____

2. In the course of that comparison, Hofstadter offers a one-sentence miniature definition of *intellect.* What is it? Is it logically complete? _____

3. How does Hofstadter use example to further the development of the contrast he has set up? _____

4. Hofstadter quotes Jacques Barzun's definition of the *intellectual* as a man who carries a briefcase. Why? (a) As a straw man; (b) for a touch of comic relief; (c) as a quip which carries a serious point, identifying the intellectual

with certain professions; (d) as a quip which carries a point that Hofstadter wants to disagree with, or at least go beyond, as he does in the last sentence of that paragraph; (e) as an example of the popular misunderstanding and distrust of intellectuals.

ANSWER _____

5. After the important contrast that begins his definition, Hofstadter goes on by setting up a division, which he describes also as a balance, between two basic qualities in the intellectual's attitude toward ideas. What are

those two qualities? _____

6. In discussing the first of the two basic qualities, Hofstadter uses a quick series of five citations or quotations from Socrates, Dante, Locke, Hawthorne, and André Malraux. What do those five quotations do? How does

he use them? _____

_____

_____

_____

7. In developing the first of those two basic qualities, Hofstadter moves from considering it in relation to the life of thought in itself, to considering it also in relation to other things, as a "medium." What does that enable

Hofstadter to say about the role of the intellectual in the world? _____

_____

_____

8. But then Hofstadter speaks of the intellectual's "ability to do mischief."

What is that ability contrasted with? _____

_____ How does that relate to the qualities of the intellectual which were discussed in the immediately

preceding paragraphs? _____

_____

_____

9. How does the idea of "mischief" provide a means of transition to the second half of Hofstadter's division of the basic qualities of the intellectual attitude

to ideas? _____

_____

10. This second basic quality is itself defined in a brief sentence; what is this

    definition? _____

    _____

11. This second basic quality is then developed, in part by another contrast.

    What is it? _____

    _____

12. What is the purpose of the reference to Harold Rosenberg? _____

    _____

    of the quotation from Acton? _____

    _____

13. What is the function of the anecdote and quotation from Maxwell? _____

    _____

    _____

    _____

14. At the end of the article, Hofstadter brings the two basic qualities together.
    What does that enable him to develop about the relation of the intellectual
    to American society, and about his subject—the unpopularity of intellect?

    _____

    _____

    _____

    _____

Integrated Exercise 4:
A Philosopher Explains the Methods of Science

In the following article, an eminent philosopher writes on a subject that
every educated man needs to understand: scientific method and why it works.
The article is written for a nonspecialist audience, in a style that is famous for
its clarity; nonetheless, the subject is difficult and is treated carefully, not
oversimplified.

Your purpose in reading the article will be to understand it as thoroughly
as possible. To do so, you will pre-read; formulate your own questions with

special attention to definitions of key terms; read thoroughly; analyze the paragraphs closely; and prepare a combined summary and outline.

Step 1. Pre-read the article; then, without looking back, answer the pre-reading questions that follow.

Step 2. Read the article thoroughly, at a comfortable but *brisk* pace for material of this kind. Then answer the thorough-reading questions starting on page 425. Answer those questions *without* looking back; but when you finish all of them, check your own answers by reviewing the article.

Step 3. Then, according to the detailed instructions that you will find after the thorough-reading questions, analyze the paragraphs, and outline the article by summarizing each paragraph. Finally, summarize the entire article.

Begin here.

"Characteristics of Scientific Method"[5]
by BERTRAND RUSSELL

1 Scientific method has been often described, and it is not possible, at this date, to say anything very new about it. Nevertheless, it is necessary to describe it if we are to be in a position later to consider whether any other method of acquiring general knowledge exists.

2 In arriving at a scientific law there are three main stages: the first consists in observing the significant facts; the second in arriving at a hypothesis, which, if it is true, would account for these facts; the third in deducing from this hypothesis consequences which can be tested by observation. If the consequences are verified, the hypothesis is provisionally accepted as true, although it will usually require modification later on as the result of the discovery of further facts.

3 In the existing state of science, no facts and no hypotheses are isolated; they exist within the general body of scientific knowledge. The significance of a fact is relative to such knowledge. To say that a fact is significant in science, is to say that it helps to establish or refute some general law; for science, though it starts from observation of the particular, is not concerned essentially with the particular, but with the general. A fact, in science, is not a mere fact, but an instance. In this the scientist differs from the artist, who, if he deigns to notice facts at all, is likely to notice them in all their particularity. Science, in its ultimate ideal, consists of a set of propositions arranged in a hierarchy, the lowest level of the hierarchy being concerned with particular facts, and the highest with some general law, governing everything in the universe. The various levels in the hierarchy have a twofold logical connexion, travelling one up, one down; the upward connexion proceeds by induction, the downward by deduction. That is to say, in a perfected science, we should proceed as follows: the particular facts, A, B, C, D, etc., suggest as probable a certain general law, of which, if it is true, they are all instances. Another set of facts suggests another general law, and so on. All these general laws suggest, by induction, a law of a higher order of gen-

erality of which, if it is true, they are instances. There will be many such stages in passing from the particular facts observed to the most general law as yet ascertained. From this general law we proceed in turn deductively, until we arrive at the particular facts from which our previous induction had started. In textbooks the deductive order will be adopted, but in the laboratory the inductive order.

4   The only science which has, as yet, come anywhere near this perfection is physics. The consideration of physics may help us to give concreteness to the above abstract account of scientific method. Galileo discovered the law of falling bodies in the neighbourhood of the earth's surface. He discovered that, apart from the resistance of the air, they fall with a constant acceleration, which is the same for all. This was a generalization from a comparatively small number of facts, namely, the cases of actual falling bodies which Galileo had timed; but his generalization was confirmed by all subsequent experiments of a like nature. Galileo's result was a law of the lowest order of generality, as little removed from the crude facts as a general law could be. Meanwhile, Kepler had observed the motions of the planets, and formulated his three laws as to their orbits. These, again, were laws of the lowest order of generality. Newton collected together Kepler's laws and Galileo's law of falling bodies, and the laws of the tides, and what was known as to the motions of comets, in one law, namely, the law of gravitation, which embraced them all. This law, moreover, as usually happens with a successful generalization, showed not merely why the previous laws were right, but also why they were not quite right. Bodies near the earth's surface do not fall with an acceleration which is quite constant: as they approach the earth, the acceleration is slightly increased. Planets do not move exactly in ellipses: when they approach near to other planets, they are pulled a little out of their orbits. Thus Newton's law of gravitation superseded the older generalizations, but could scarcely have been arrived at except from them. For over two hundred years no new generalization was found to swallow up Newton's law of gravitation, as it had swallowed up Kepler's laws. When, at last, Einstein arrived at such a generalization it placed the law of gravitation in the most unexpected company. To everybody's surprise, it was found to be a law of geometry rather than of physics in the old sense. The proposition with which it has most affinity is the theorem of Pythagoras, to the effect that the squares on the two shorter sides of a right-angled triangle are together equal to the square on the longest side. Every schoolboy learns the proof of this proposition, but only those who read Einstein learn the disproof. To the Greeks — and to the moderns until a hundred years ago — geometry was an *a priori** study like formal logic, not an empirical science based upon observation. Lobachevsky, in the year 1829, demonstrated the falsehood of this opinion, and showed that the truth of Euclidean geometry could only be established by observation, not by reasoning. Although this view gave rise to important new branches of pure mathematics, it did not

---

* *a priori:* theoretical, without observation of experimental evidence.

bear fruit in physics until the year 1915, when Einstein embodied it in his general theory of relativity. It now appears that the theorem of Pythagoras is not quite true, and that the exact truth which it adumbrates contains within itself the law of gravitation as an ingredient or consequence. Again, it is not quite Newton's law of gravitation, but a law whose observable consequences are slightly different. Where Einstein differs from Newton in an observable manner it is found that Einstein is right as against Newton. Einstein's law of gravitation is more general than Newton's, since it applies not only to matter, but also to light and to every form of energy. Einstein's general theory of gravitation demanded as a preliminary not only Newton's theory, but also the theory of electro-magnetism, the science of spectroscopy, observation of light pressure, and the power of minute astronomical observation, which we owe to large telescopes and the perfecting of the technique of photography. Without all these preliminaries, Einstein's theory could not have been both discovered and demonstrated. But when the theory is set forth in mathematical form we start with the generalized law of gravitation, and arrive at the end of our argument at those verifiable consequences upon which, in the inductive order, the law was based. In the deductive order, the difficulties of discovery are obscured, and it becomes hard to be aware of the immense extent of preliminary knowledge required for the induction which led to our major premise. The same sort of development has happened with a rapidity which is truly astonishing in regard to quantum theory. The first discovery that there were facts necessitating such a theory was made in 1900, yet already the subject can be treated in an utterly abstract way which scarcely reminds the reader that a universe exists.

5   Throughout the history of physics, from the time of Galileo onward, the importance of the *significant* fact has been very evident. The facts that are significant at any one stage in the development of a theory are quite different from those that are significant at another stage. When Galileo was establishing the law of falling bodies, the fact that in a vacuum a feather and a lump of lead fall equally fast, was more important than the fact that, in air, a feather falls more slowly, since the first step in understanding falling bodies consisted in realizing that, so far as the earth's attraction alone is concerned, all falling bodies have the same acceleration. The effect of the resistance of the air must be treated as something superadded to the earth's attraction. The essential thing is always to look for such facts as illustrate one law in isolation, or at any rate, only in combination with laws whose effects are well known. This is why experiment plays such an important part in scientific discovery. In an experiment the circumstances are artificially simplified, so that some one law in isolation may become observable. In most concrete situations, what actually happens requires for its explanation a number of laws of nature, but in order to discover these one by one it is usually necessary to invent circumstances such that only one of them is relevant. Moreover, the most instructive phenomena may be very difficult to observe. Consider, for example, how much our knowledge of matter has been enhanced by the discovery of X-rays and of radio-activity; yet both of these

would have remained unknown but for the most elaborate experimental technique. The discovery of radio-activity was an accident due to the perfecting of photography. Becquerel had some very sensitive photographic plates, which he was meaning to employ; but as the weather was bad, he put them away in a dark cupboard in which there happened to be some uranium. When they were taken out again they were found to have photographed the uranium, in spite of the complete darkness. It was this accident which led to the discovery that uranium is radio-active. This accidental photograph affords another illustration of the significant fact.

6   Outside physics, the part played by deduction is much less, while the part played by observation, and by laws immediately based upon observation, is much greater. Physics, owing to the simplicity of its subject matter, has reached a higher stage of development than any other science. I do not think it can be doubted that the ideal is the same for all sciences; but it can be doubted whether human capacity will ever be able to make physiology, for example, as perfect a deductive edifice as theoretical physics is now. Even in pure physics the difficulties of calculation swiftly become insuperable. In the Newtonian gravitation theory it was impossible to calculate how three bodies would move under their mutual attractions, except approximately when one of them was much larger than the other two. In the theory of Einstein, which is much more complicated than Newton's, it is impossible to work out with theoretical exactness even how two bodies will move under their mutual attraction, though it is possible to obtain a sufficiently good approximation for all practical purposes. Fortunately for physics there are methods of averaging, by which the behaviour of large bodies can be calculated with a quite sufficient approximation to the truth, although a wholly exact theory is utterly beyond human powers.

7   The part played by measurement and quantity in science is very great, but is, I think, sometimes overestimated. Mathematical technique is powerful, and men of science are naturally anxious to be able to apply it whenever possible; but a law may be quite scientific without being quantitative. Pavlov's laws concerning conditioned reflexes may serve as an illustration. It would probably be impossible to give quantitative precision to these laws; the number of repetitions required to establish conditioned reflexes depends upon many conditions, and varies not only with different animals, but with the same animal at different times. In the pursuit of quantitative precision we should be driven first to the physiology of the cortex and the physical nature of nerve-currents, and we should find ourselves unable to stop short of the physics of electrons and protons. There, it is true, quantitative precision may be possible, but to pass back by calculation from pure physics to the phenomena of animal behaviour is beyond human power, at any rate at present, and probably for many ages to come. We must, therefore, in dealing with such a matter as animal behaviour, be content in the meantime with qualitative laws which are none the less scientific for not being quantitative.

8   All scientific laws rest upon induction, which, considered as a logical process, is open to doubt, and not capable of giving certainty. Speaking

crudely, an inductive argument is of the following kind. If a certain hypothesis is true, then such and such facts will be observable; now these facts are observable; therefore the hypothesis is probably true. An argument of this sort will have varying degrees of validity according to circumstances. If we could prove that no other hypothesis was compatible with the observed facts we could arrive at certainty, but this is hardly ever possible. In general, there will be no method of thinking of all the possible hypotheses, or, if there is, it will be found that more than one of them is compatible with the facts. When this is the case, the scientist adopts the simplest as a working hypothesis, and only reverts to more complicated hypotheses if new facts show that the simplest hypothesis is inadequate. If you had never seen a cat without a tail, the simplest hypothesis to account for this fact would be: "all cats have tails"; but the first time that you saw a Manx cat, you would be compelled to adopt a more complicated hypothesis. The man who argues that because all cats he has seen have tails, therefore all cats have tails, is employing what is called "induction by simple enumeration." This is a very dangerous form of argument. In its better forms, induction is based upon the fact that our hypothesis leads to consequences which are found to be true, but which, if they had not been observed, would seem extremely improbable. If you meet a man who has a pair of dice that always throw double sixes, it is possible that he is lucky; but there is another hypothesis which would make the observed facts less astonishing. You will therefore be well advised to adopt this other hypothesis. In all good inductions, the facts accounted for by the hypothesis are such as would be antecedently improbable, and the more improbable they would be, the greater becomes the probability of the hypothesis which accounts for them. This is one of the advantages of measurement. If something which might have any size, is found to have just the size that your hypothesis had led you to expect, you feel that your hypothesis must at least have something in it. As common sense this seems evident, but as logic it has certain difficulties.

9   There is one remaining characteristic of scientific method about which something must be said, namely, analysis. It is generally assumed by men of science, at any rate as a working hypothesis, that any concrete occurrence is the resultant of a number of causes, each of which, acting separately, might produce some different result from that which actually occurs; and that the resultant can be calculated when the effects of the separate causes are known. The simplest examples of this occur in mechanics. The moon is attracted both by the earth and by the sun. If the earth acted alone, the moon would describe one orbit; if the sun acted alone, it would describe another; but its actual orbit is calculable when we know the effects which the earth and the sun separately would produce. When we know how bodies fall in a vacuum, and also the law of the resistance of the air, we can calculate how bodies will fall in air. The principle that causal laws can, in this way, be separated, and then recombined, is in some degree essential to the procedure of science, for it is impossible to take account of everything at once,

or to arrive at causal laws unless we can isolate them one at a time. It must be said, however, that there is no reason *a priori* to suppose that the effect of two causes, acting simultaneously, will be calculable from the effects which they have severally; and in the most modern physics, this principle is found to have less truth than was formerly supposed. It remains a practical and approximate principle in suitable circumstances, but it cannot be laid down as a general property of the universe. Undoubtedly, where it fails, science becomes very difficult; but, so far as can be seen at present, it retains sufficient truth to be employed as a hypothesis, except in the most advanced and delicate calculations.

Pre-reading questions. (Do not refer to the article while answering.)

1. What is the purpose of this article? (a) To explain scientific method; (b) to describe the limitations of scientific method; (c) to show the importance of mathematics in science; (d) to show that scientific method is the only way to arrive at general knowledge; (e) none of the above.

ANSWER _____

2. What assumption has science almost always found it necessary to make about causes? (a) That the effect of two causes acting simultaneously is not necessarily calculable from the effects they have severally; (b) that most effects have only one cause; (c) that all causes can be isolated by experiment so that the effects of each cause can be detected separately; (d) that all causes are ultimately explainable in terms of those causes with which physics is concerned; (e) none of the above.

ANSWER _____

3. Which *one* of the following subjects or topics does pre-reading *not* discover to be treated in the article? (a) Evaluation of the importance of measurement and quantity in science; (b) the special question of scientific method in the study of human physiology; (c) the use of induction and deduction in sciences; (d) causal analysis in science; (e) the importance of the "significant fact."

ANSWER _____

4. What does pre-reading tell you about the level of reading difficulty of this article? Answer in terms *both* of the difficulty of the *subject matter* and of

the *style of writing.* _____

_____

_____

5. There are five, perhaps six, key terms the author uses in the article. All of them can be discovered by pre-reading. List three key terms here.

a. _____

b. _____

c. _____

6. *One* question you should have in mind while reading is: What are the author's key terms and how does he use them? Now formulate here one *additional*

question you expect the article to answer for you. _____

_____

Now go back to the article and Step 2 of the instructions.

Thorough-reading questions. (Do not look back at the article while answering. When you have completed *all* the questions, however, review and correct your answers by checking them against the article itself.)

1. What is the difference between *induction* and *deduction?*

_____

_____

_____

2. The most reliable form of induction is (a) induction by simple enumeration; (b) induction from as many cases as possible; (c) induction which accounts for unusual facts; (d) induction from which seemingly improbable consequences can be deduced and verified.

ANSWER _____

3. When is a fact "significant" in modern science? (a) When it can be used as a new instance of an existing theory; (b) when it can be used as an instance of a new theory; (c) when it helps to establish or refute some general law; (d) when it can be deduced from a theory and then discovered by experiments.

ANSWER _____

4. The author says that there are three main stages in arriving at a scientific law. The first of them is given below. Fill in the other two.
   a. The observation of significant facts

   b. _____

   c. _____

5. The author does not explicitly consider the role of experimentation in scientific method. But in which of the three stages of the scientific method would experiments be of value? (a) The first; (b) the second; (c) the first and second; (d) the first and third; (e) the second and third.

ANSWER _____

6. One step in the threefold process which the author calls scientific method has been called by others the "hunch" stage. Which of the following would that be? (a) Observing the significant facts; (b) arriving at a tentative hy-

pothesis; (c) deducing the observed facts from the hypothesis; (d) deducing new facts from the hypothesis, and then discovering them to be true.

ANSWER _____

7. Define *hypothesis.* _____

_____

_____

8. How is a *scientific law* related to a hypothesis?

_____

_____

_____

9. Which of the following is the best summary of the author's statements about the role of measurement and quantity in science? (a) Quantitative exactness adds credibility to a scientific law; (b) though they are desirable, because they lend credibility to a theory, the lack of quantitative exactness and mathematical techniques does not necessarily make a theory unscientific; (c) quantitative exactness is required before a theory can be accepted; (d) exact measurement and the application of mathematical techniques are desirable, but not always possible.

ANSWER _____

10. Would the author agree that eventually all sciences can be quantitatively precise? (a) Yes, for, as in physics, the fundamental subject matter of all sciences is ultimately simple; (b) yes, for in pursuit of quantitative precision we are driven to the physics of electrons and protons, where quantitative precision is possible; (c) possibly, but at present the difficulties of calculation are impossibly complex if the scientist wishes to move from the precision of physics into such fields as animal behavior; (d) no, because quantitative precision is not necessary to science, even though its presence makes a theory more likely to be true for the facts the theory is concerned with.

ANSWER _____

Now review the article and correct your answers before going on to the next step.

Analysis and summary. (For these questions you will, of course, refer to the article.)

A. There are nine paragraphs in the article. List here the sentence number for the topic sentence *or sentences* of each.

Paragraph 1. _____ 2. _____ 3. _____

4. _____ 5. _____ 6. _____

7. _____ 8. _____ 9. _____

B. Now, for the last seven paragraphs (the first two are succinct to the point of summary, already), write out here your own summary.

3. _____

_____

_____

4. _____

_____

_____

5. _____

_____

_____

6. _____

_____

_____

7. _____

_____

_____

8. _____

_____

_____

9. _____

_____

_____

C. There is *one sentence* in the article that is very close to being a summary of the whole. Which is it? Write it out here.

_____

_____

_____

_____

Two major topics of the article are *not* mentioned explicitly in that sentence, though they are perhaps implied. What are the topics that would have to be added to complete the summary?

1. _____

2. _____

CHAPTER 15

Introduction to Critical Reading: Four Critical Questions

Pre-read this chapter as your first step in reading it. As your second step, list below the questions you expect the chapter to answer.

_____

_____

_____

_____

Critical reading is many things; but its ultimate aim is to convert your relation with a book from a monologue, where you are simply the recipient of the author's words, into a dialogue. All monologues are much alike, however interesting, because you the audience are more or less passive, unselective, too easily inattentive. There can be many forms of dialogue with a book—as between strangers, between eager new acquaintances, between opponents in a controversy, between student and respected teacher, between policeman and suspect, between old friends. Yet all dialogue is based on questions. "With all these questions," as one student has complained, "it gets so I can't read a paragraph without feeling _suspicious._" But if you modify that complaint only by changing the word _suspicious_ to _skeptical_ or _alert,_ you will come up with a good description of the skilled reader. He is alert when he reads, alert to bad logic, prejudgments and prejudices, and incomplete or one-sided statements. He is skeptical of the author's methods and motives when necessary. And sometimes he is even suspicious. The skilled reader is alert, skeptical, and sometimes suspicious, not only of the passage he is reading, but also of _himself_—of the prejudices, one-sided views, and inadequate information that he, the reader, brings into the dialogue he is conducting with the writer.

This chapter begins where Chapter 7 left off, developing the question technique into an instrument for critical reading. The four master questions that Chapter 7 introduced were:

What is the thesis or problem here?

What is your purpose in reading this particular work?

What is the main sequence of ideas?

What particular information or ideas can you now say you will be hunting for as you read thoroughly?

To review: the purpose of those questions you ask before thorough reading is to direct your attention, to highlight certain essentials, during thorough reading. Although you will sometimes be able to sketch out answers on the basis of pre-reading alone, such a sketch is provisional, no more, until amplified, corrected, and confirmed during thorough reading. (The last of those four questions, you will remember, is used to develop further questions of your own.)

Now here are the critical questions we shall examine:

What is the rhetorical (that is, persuasive) purpose of the work?

What prejudgments and prejudices do you, the reader, bring to the work?

What are the author's key terms, and how does he use them?

How well does the work prove its thesis or resolve its problem?

What Is the Rhetorical Purpose of the Selection?

Compare those two sets of four questions above. You will note that they are closely related, the critical four developing logically from the earlier ones. Thus, an author's rhetorical, or persuasive, purpose is in most cases closely related to his thesis or problem. Yet the two are not the same. The thesis or problem, you will recall, is the central subject the author treats and the main thing he has to say about it. You know what the thesis or problem is if you can give a brief but comprehensive answer to the question: *What is he trying to say?* Once you know this, however, there follows another question: *Why is he saying it?* Answer this, and you know the author's rhetorical purpose.

However straightforward the stated thesis may seem, and however neutral its author may appear to be about the conclusions you draw, most writers intend ultimately to influence your thoughts in some way. You will not usually find this persuasive purpose explicitly stated; often you must infer it from the tone, direction, assembly of facts in the selection as a whole. For example, even when such purpose is at its simplest and most unobtrusive, an author hopes that if he gives you what he considers the right information, you will draw what he considers to be the right conclusions. The most objective scientific report, for example, attempts to give you all the data necessary for you to judge the correctness of the theory advanced; and the author, of course, hopes that upon examination you will accept the theory. This is persuasive purpose at its most rudimentary level. But consider for a moment the various scientific reports over the last several years on the relation of cigarette smoking to lung cancer; consider also the way the press treated these reports. What is likely to be the persuasive purpose of the American Cancer Society in issuing a statement to the press explaining one of these scientific reports? On the other side, the cigarette manufacturers have issued "scientific reports" of their own; what is likely to be persuasive purpose of these? (What is the persuasive purpose of the quotation marks in the last sentence?) The smoking controversy is by no means an isolated example. Persuasive purposes are very often found in scientific reports, and frequently in the publicity releases and news stories based on them. You need only recall the controversies over fluoridation of drinking water and over radioactive fallout from atomic weapons tests.

Clearly, if rhetorical purposes are frequent in the relatively objective, fact-oriented area of scientific writing, then they are always to be found in politics, history, business and practical affairs, and so forth.

Yet it is time to repeat that rhetorical purposes may not necessarily be reprehensible in any way. Advertising, "hidden persuasion," propaganda, ideological conflict—these features of our modern age have generated a widespread and often justified resentment of persuasive efforts. But if rhetorical purposes are present everywhere, then blind resistance to them leaves you no better off than blind acceptance. Some works do indeed try to persuade you in ways that you may decide are wrong or against your best interests; others have rhetorical purposes that are necessary, useful, even admirable. A classic example is *The Federalist Papers,* written in 1787–88 to win votes for the Constitution of the United States, and still regarded today as a superb example of both political analysis and persuasive reasoning. An honorable modern instance is the book *Silent Spring,* in which Rachel Carson warned at graphic and moving length of the grave dangers to wildlife, to man, and to the balance of nature, from DDT and other chemical insecticides and weedkillers, ten years before they were widely recognized as a worldwide menace of epidemic proportion. You will find other examples of contemporary writing with strong rhetorical purposes among the integrated exercises following the chapters of this section of this book.

Why is he saying it? That, we suggested, is the test question for determining rhetorical purpose; it can break down into other questions:

What is the *audience* the writer has in mind for his work? What is the *occasion*—the event, the situation, the immediate reason, what journalists often call the "peg"—for his writing to that audience?

What seem to be the author's own sentiments on his subject?

Does the author have any detectable special interest? That is, does he stand to gain or lose, and how, if his suggestions are acted on?

What conclusions does he want the reader to draw, and why?

Discovery of purpose must sometimes be tentative or provisional; even so, it helps you to evaluate a work, to weigh its possible bias and probable accuracy, to judge its practical value to you, and ultimately to judge its ethical or moral validity.

What Prejudgments and Prejudices Do You, the Reader, Bring to the Work?

A true dialogue cannot be one-sided: just as you have the right, and the necessity, to question the writer's motives, he has the right to have you question your own fairness, examine your possible unacknowledged preconceptions. Yet an open mind is not the same as an empty one. Of course, you will have opinions on subjects you know something about. The problem is being able to hold those opinions consciously and reasonably, and based on knowledge, rather than on blind prejudice. The importance of questioning your own pre-judgments in order to appraise the work fairly, is obvious; yet no criticism is more difficult to apply. Whereas the book, no matter how difficult or obscure, at least has specific statements formulated in print, your own ideas and atti-tudes are rarely thought out in explicit, complete statements. For this reason it is often easier to understand what the author says, and to know where you agree or disagree, than it is to know exactly what you yourself think about the matter. What you think may be right or wrong; it is a prejudgment in either case, and the problem is to get it into the open so that it can be fairly tested against what the author has to say. When your prejudgments have not been examined, they may be thoroughly in error, and yet influence your thinking strongly.

Now, of course, no reader can have a thoroughly worked out, balanced, correct view on the subject of every book he picks up. What you must do is to use your reading to develop a clearer understanding of your own views as well as the author's. This is one of the great benefits of critical reading. It is also one of the important reasons for taking notes as you read, for only in this way can you get your own views down in black and white to compare them thoroughly with the author's.

The problem of prejudgment is compounded by the problem of prejudice —the natural human tendency to be emotionally committed to your own view because it is yours. "I think this, and I've argued and studied to arrive at this; therefore it must be the truth—and you are a fool, or worse, if you disagree." The only remedy, but an effective one, is to have an even greater commitment to the truth wherever it may lead. Then it will be clear that a strong reaction to an author's statement—a reaction in favor, just as much as a reaction against— is a clear sign that prejudice may be fogging your view and dulling your wits.

Your developed reading skills obviously reduce the influence of prejudg-ment and prejudice. Without listing them all again, we can say that the whole thrust of the techniques of reading is to make you more analytical, reasoning, controlled, and self-aware. The more you use these techniques, the more you will be able to understand what a work is really trying to tell you, without reading your own notions into it; and the more you will be able to judge it on its own merits.

So without prejudgment and without prejudice, what can you decide about an author's work, particularly about his thesis, conclusions, rhetorical purpose, recommendations? You may decide to agree, in whole or in part; or you may decide to disagree, in whole or in part. Often, however, the most reasonable decision is *to reserve judgment:* in other words, to decide that you lack the information or understanding to be able to say surely that you agree or disagree. On what basis do you decide? That brings us to the next two critical questions.

What Are the Author's Key Terms, and How Does He Use Them?

When the college bull session or the executive luncheon gets into an argument about politics, economics, religion, or another "big" subject, almost always at some point a peacemaker will try to calm the contestants by urging, "We've got to define our terms!" The peacemaker is usually right, but have you ever noticed how rarely a serious effort is made to follow his suggestion? Reading is a quieter form of discussion, and if only for that reason it should be more conducive to orderly thought. Yet it is dismaying to discover how few readers are able to list, let alone explain, the most important terms and expressions of a work they have just finished reading. They have not done their part of the job of defining terms in their dialogue with the author.

Without clarity about key terms, thorough and critical understanding is impossible. To be sure, in much practical prose this understanding is relatively automatic because words are used in generally accepted ways. For example, in a business or technical field if you have the vocabulary at all you should not often be seriously troubled by misunderstanding key terms. Whenever critical reading becomes necessary, however, questions of terminology are likely to come up.

In some areas, problems of definition are immediately obvious. For example, the word *socialism* is a different term to a Soviet Communist than to a member of the British Labour Party; for the first, democracy as we mean it is ruled out, while for the second, it must be included in the meaning of the term. Confusion over terms, however, also occurs in more everyday areas. Examples can be found almost anywhere. In the fine arts, the term *media* includes watercolors, pen-and-ink, oils, lithography, and so forth. In the advertising trade press, the term means television, radio, outdoor billboards, magazines, and so forth. The psychologist who writes about visual perception of words, objects, colors, and so forth, uses the term *fixation* in the sense we have used it in this book; the psychologist who gives advice to neurotics may mean, by the same term, "a very strong emotional attachment to a particular person."

You run into some of the most important questions of definition when one book uses the same word or phrase to mean several different things. This happens often, and is a rich source of confusion when the terms are among the most important in the book.

In this book, *reading* is a key term. It is used with several different shades of meaning.

Early chapters use *reading* with emphasis on the physical process — what your eyes do as they move across the page.

As the word is used in relation to comprehension, understanding, and criticism, it has to do with mental, thinking activities — activities quite different from the physical, eye-movement process, and not nearly so well understood.

As the book progresses the term stretches to take in study, note-taking, research—areas that some people might not immediately associate with the word as used in the book's title.

As used in connection with poetry, fiction, drama, and philosophy, the term changes again, and even excludes some of the "techniques of reading."

Any serious, lengthy work will almost unavoidably contain such shifts in meaning of key terms. To chart them can prove one of the subtlest problems of critical reading. The thoughtful man who nonetheless misses those distinctions in the use of the term *reading* might well recoil, because he sees this as a book that treats reading "simply" as a mechanical process, one that would mutilate his appreciation of great novels by making him read the last chapter first. Just such misunderstandings of this book do indeed occur. And if they occur in a subject so straightforward, you can see how essential it is for critical understanding of difficult and important works, to analyze the author's key terms and to keep coming back to them to see how his use of them may be changing.

How Well Does the Work Prove Its Thesis or Resolve Its Problem?

To answer this—to decide whether you agree, disagree, or reserve judgment—you must hold one principle firmly in mind. It is one of the chief points of critical reading, indeed one of the principles of clear thought, that *if an exposition really is persuasive, you must allow yourself to be persuaded.* You have no right to disagree with an author unless you can prove that his view is wrong or that yours is better. If you *cannot prove* that he is wrong or that you know better, then it is nonsense to suppose that you have any right to your own different opinion. You must either agree, or reserve judgment until you have more information or more complete understanding. And if the new information or understanding does not give you your proof, then eventually you must agree.

This principle sounds stern and uncompromising, and so it is. You must remember, after all, that an author may very well know more about his subject than you do. In that case you have no choice but to learn from him, modifying your own thoughts and abandoning prejudices if necessary. But on the other hand, the author may be wrong:

His facts may be incorrect;

his facts may be incomplete;

his reasoning may be faulty.

If you can show that an author has made one of these errors—in a way that is *essential* to his thesis, problem, or conclusions—then you have proved him wrong. Of course, it is not fair to pick up some trivial misstatement: any error that could be corrected, without changing the main thesis or conclusions, is not by itself enough to establish your case. Suppose the author gives facts that you can prove to be incorrect. If, and only if, the correct facts would upset his conclusions, can you rightly disagree with him. Suppose all his facts are correct, as far as they go; but you know something more that is important and pertinent and upsets his conclusions; then, too, you can rightly disagree. Finally, suppose his essential facts are accurate and complete; then you can disagree only if you can catch him in an error of reasoning that cannot be corrected without upsetting the conclusions.

Those, then, are the ways you prove your right to disagree. This brief outline will make it obvious that there will be cases where you are convinced that an author is wrong, but where you cannot identify the incorrect fact, supply the missing fact, or detect the misstep in reasoning. In these cases, and when you are sure your resistance is not mere prejudice, you must suspend judgment until you either find the error or are obliged to agree.

EXERCISES FOR CHAPTER 15

Reading Journal

Integrated Exercise 5: An Essay with Direct Rhetorical Purpose
"An Unteachable Generation," from *Compulsory Mis-Education,* by Paul Goodman

Integrated Exercise 6: A Memoir, Also with a Rhetorical Purpose
"The Sellout," by Freeman J. Dyson

Reading Journal

As you approach the end of the project assigned in Chapter 13 — the coordinated attack on a single book with all the applicable techniques of reading — you should apply the critical questions we have just discussed. To the written record you have been making of your reading of that book, therefore, add now your estimate of the author's persuasive purpose. Stop also to think out your own reactions to the book, especially your possible prejudgments. Then go back over what you have read, to extract and list the author's key terms with brief definitions and notes about the ways their meanings may have shifted or grown as the author went on. Finally, go back to your notes for your original questions after pre-reading. In them, you raised the question of the author's thesis or problem; by now you should be able to answer succinctly what that thesis or problem is, and then, as you finish the book, to decide and discuss how well it has proved the thesis or settled the problem.

Integrated Exercise 5:
An Essay with Direct Rhetorical Purpose

Everybody writes about youth; about its supposed problems, its supposed needs, its apathy, its rebelliousness, and its new consciousness or new culture. The writings purport to be rhetorical in the best sense, to analyze and exhort to constructive reforming action; too often they are rhetorical in the worst sense—windy, hysterical, irrelevant, unhelpful, self-inflating, opportunistic, or simply silly. But long before the current wave of writing about youth, Paul Goodman was writing about youth with cool, sensible precision and loving sympathy. Goodman is a psychologist, novelist and poet, anarchist, city-dweller and writer on urban affairs, professor and writer about education—and an old campaigner for practical ways to give young men and women more worthwhile opportunities and choices. The essay that follows is from Goodman's book about what's wrong with present-day compulsory education, from kindergarten through college. This part of the book is an analysis of what happens to youth after high school. Though analytical in form and calm in tone, the essay is intensely rhetorical in purpose, as you will discover.

Please pre-read it; then go on to answer the pre-reading questions; formulate your own questions for thorough reading; then return to read the article thoroughly and answer the remaining questions.

Begin pre-reading here.

"An Unteachable Generation"[1]
from *Compulsory Mis-Education*
by PAUL GOODMAN

At 17 and 18, nearly half go off to something called college, and the others go to work, if there are jobs. We shall see that college is not a very educative environment, but by and large the world of work is even less so.

For most poor urban youth, the strongest present reason to go to work is family pressure; to bring in some money and not be a drag on the hard-working parents who are supporting them. Needless to say, such a reason springs from a complex of problematic emotions: resentment, spite, need for dependency and independence; and from conditions of poverty often at a crisis just at this juncture. As an incentive for finding a job, finding the right job, or preparing oneself for a job, these are unhappy auspices, and they often operate in reverse, toward balkiness and truancy.

But the more objective social form of this reason—"You ought to pull your oar as a member of society; by the sweat of thy brow shalt thou eat bread"—is nowadays much less telling. We do not have, in America, an economy of scarcity, only an enormous number of poor people. To expand the economy still further might well be politically expedient, to diminish unemployment and keep up the rate of profit, but the facts are pretty plain that there is a synthetic demand and an absurd standard of living. Every kid jeers at the ads. And the prestigious flashy desirable goods are not such as poor youth beginning in jobs are going to get. In poor neighborhoods the men who do get them — on credit — are not usually models for modest labor.

Nor do the idle actually starve. For political and humanitarian reasons the affluent society doles out a subsistence, although stingy in this as in other public goods such as education, neighborhood beauty, and care for the delinquent and insane. And we can hardly expect a youth to have a sense of responsibility to his community when every force in modern urban life tends to destroy community sentiment and community functioning.

Perhaps most important of all is that the moral ideology and the dominant economic behavior are entirely inconsistent. Managers adopt as many labor-saving machines as possible, but the saving of labor is *not* passed on to society as a whole in shorter work hours, or even cheaper prices. And even in service-operations where there is no automation, such as restaurants, there is a cutback of employment: bigger crowds, and fewer people to serve them. Yet there is political excitement about unemployment.

Add, finally, that at least 25% of the gross national product is rather directly devoted to the 1,000 overkill.*

It is hard to know how much these philosophical considerations weigh with simple folk and children. In a profound sense, people are not fools, and they sniff the atmosphere correctly. In any case, the argument, "If you work, you can hold your head up with self-respect" does not have the overpowering force among our poor youth that it once did. Hipster notions of finding a racket seem also to satisfy the community ethic. And there is even the ethic that to work for a mere living is to be a fool.

There is an evident and sickening disproportion between the money that people work hard for, whether as dish-washer, hospital orderly, stenographer, schoolteacher, or artist, and the "soft" money that comes from expense accounts, tax-dodge foundations, having "made it" as a personality. I have referred to the disproportionate cut of the pie that falls to the academic monks in any welfare operation. Then why should those who are not going to be in the Establishment *work* for money, rather than look for an angle or wait for luck? And it does not help when kids see an immense part of their parents' hard-earned money go on usurious installment payments for high-priced hardware, and rent swallowing up more than a quarter of income.

My guess is that many poor kids are in the cruel dilemma of feeling guilty about not working, and yet uneasy among their peers and even in their own better judgment if they do try to get jobs — especially when trying to get a job has its own degrading humiliations, of confronting prejudice,

---

* That is to say, spent more or less directly on armaments. [Ed.]

bureaucratic callousness, and gouging agencies, and often when the young are frustrated by sheer ignorance of how to look for a job at all.

And there is another philosophical aspect, usually overlooked, that is obviously important for these young. I have mentioned it before. So far as they can see—and they see clearly—the absorbing satisfactions of life do *not* require all this work and rat-race. In societies where it is possible to be decently poor, persons of superior education and talent often choose to be poor rather than hustle for money.

In the inflationary American economy, however, decent poverty is almost impossible. To be secure at all, one has to engage in the competition and try to rise; and the so-called "education" is geared to economic advancement. Thus, a common-sensible youth—and especially a poor one whose opportunities for advancement are limited and whose cultural background is unacademic—might reasonably judge that games, sex, and the gang are *preferable* to school and work, but he will then get not independence but misery. He will be so out of things that he will have nothing to occupy his mind. He is disqualified for marriage. He is inferior, out-caste.

As it is, the only ones who can afford the absorbing and simple satisfactions that do not cost much money are those who have succeeded economically and are by then likely unfit to enjoy anything. From this point of view, the chief blessing that our copious society could bestow on us would be a kind of subsistence work that allowed spirited people to be decently poor without frantic insecurity and long drudgery.

If we turn to the deeper human and religious answers to the question "Why should I work?"—for example, work as fulfillment of one's potentialities, work as the vocation that gives justification—our present economy has little to offer to poor youth.

Unskilled and semi-skilled jobs are parts of elaborate enterprises rationalized for their own operation and not to fulfill the lives of workmen. Work processes are rarely interesting. Workmen are not taught the rationale of the whole. The products are often humanly pretty worthless, so there is no pride of achievement or utility. Craft and style are built into the machines, lost to the workmen. Labor unions have improved the conditions and dignity of the job, but they have also become bureaucratized and do not give the sense of solidarity.

It is only in the higher job brackets, beyond most poor youth, that there begins to be a place for inventiveness and art; and independent initiative belongs only to top management and expert advisors. There are fewer small shops. Neighborhood stores give way to centralized supermarkets where the employees have no say. There is a great increase in social services, but these require official licenses and are not open to those otherwise qualified who wish to work in them.

The total background of poor youth, including the inadequacies of the schools, conduces to dropping out; but the simplest worthwhile jobs require diplomas.

Here again, it may be asked if these considerations, of vocation, job-interest, job-worthiness, weigh with poor youth. They weigh with every-body. Indeed, the hard task of a youth worker is to find some objective activity that a youth might be interested in, and proud of achieving, that will save him from recessive narcissism and reactive hostility or withdrawal, and give him something to grow on. Further, as I argued in *Growing Up Absurd,* the high premium that workmen put on "Security" is largely a substitute for the feeling of being needed, fully used, indispensable.

Some of the human deficiencies in the jobs can be ameliorated – at least until automation makes the whole matter nugatory by vanishing the jobs. For example, with elementary thoughtfulness, a big plant that has many positions can allow a prospective employee to visit and try out various stations, rather than making an arbitrary assignment. Work processes can be efficiently designed on psychological grounds; for instance, a small group assembling a big lathe from beginning to end, so they have something to show for their day, as the crane carries the product away. In a form of "collective contract" or gang-system used in Coventry, England, fifty workers contract with the firm on a piece-work basis, and then settle among themselves the particular assignments, personnel, schedule, and many of the processes; there must be many industries where this humanizing procedure is feasible. With technical education paid for by industry in cooperation with the schools, we could have more understanding workmen.

The important point is that job-worthiness, the educative value of the job, must be recognized by managers and labor-unions as a specific good.

But of course this is part of the much larger need, to make our whole environment more educative, rather than rigidly restricting the concept of education to what happens in schools.

Socially useful work is probably an indispensable element in the education of most adolescents. It provides an objective structure, a bridge of norms and values, in the transition from being in the family to being oneself. This is the rationale of a good Youth Work Camp, as I described it in *Utopian Essays;* a community of youth democratically directing itself, and controlling itself, to do a job. Many colleges have adopted the Antioch plan of alternating academic periods with periods of work in the economy, which are then made the subject of further academic criticism. But what a pity that precisely the poor youth, who *have* to go to work, get no value from the jobs they work at!

Finally, let me say a word about the miserable job induction at present. I have already mentioned the degrading and humiliating conditions that accompany looking for scarce jobs. Again, we do not appreciate the terrors and hang-ups for the semi-literate and socially paranoiac in filling out personnel forms. Often young human beings are tormented and talent is lost simply for the convenience of business machines. And naturally, for those disposed to feel rejected and inferior, each further frustration rapidly accumulates into an impassable block. A lad soon turns in the form not filled out, or even turns back outside the door. Or, pathetically, there is manic excitement at landing a job which he soon quits or cannot do anyway. The entire process is hopelessly and irrelevantly charged with emotion. And the pitiful and anxious lies that are written on those forms!

Certainly the current proposals to make the school the employment agency are reasonable; the school is at least familiar, even if the kid hates it and has dropped out.

Our classical ideology is that the job should be looked for with resolution and ambition. But how are these possible on the basis of ignorance and alienation? Here as elsewhere, our problem is lapse of community. Our society has less and less community between its adults and its youth. Traditional and family crafts and trades no longer exist, and a youth has few chances to form himself on model workmen in his neighborhood and learn the ropes and opportunities. The difficulties of getting into a union seem, and often are, insuperable. Middle class academic youth in their colleges have at least some contact with the adults who belong to the ultimate job-world, and placement is pretty good. But poor urban youth in schools whose culture is quite alien to them and whose aims fit neither their desires nor their capacities, are among jailers, not models.

These remarks are not optimistic toward solving the problems of employment, and unemployment, of youth. By and large, I think those problems are insoluble, and *should* be insoluble, until our affluent society becomes worthier to work in, more honorable in its functions, and more careful of its human resources.

But this is also a hard generation to teach in colleges what I think ought to be taught. I do not mean that the students are disrespectful, or especially lazy, or anything like that; in my experience, they pay us more respect than we usually deserve and they work as earnestly as could be expected trying to learn too much on too heavy schedules. Of course, as I have been arguing, many of the students, probably the majority, ought not to be in a scholastic setting at all, and their presence causes dilution and stupefying standardization as well as overcrowding. But let us here concentrate on several other difficulties that are in the very essence of present-day higher education. (a) The culture we want to pass on is no longer a culture for these young; the thread of it has snapped. (b) These young are not serious with themselves; this is a property of the kind of culture they do have. (c) And as with the lower schools, the auspices, method and aims of the colleges themselves are not relevant to good education for our unprecedented present and foreseeable future.

The culture I want to teach—I am myself trapped in it and cannot think or strive apart from it—is our Western tradition: the values of Greece, the Bible, Christianity, Chivalry, the Free Cities of the twelfth century, the Renaissance, the heroic age of Science, the Enlightenment, the French Revolution, early nineteenth century Utilitarianism, late nineteenth century Naturalism.

To indicate what I mean, let me mention a typical proposition about each of these. The Greeks sometimes aspire to a civic excellence in which mere individual success would be shameful. The Bible teaches that there is a created world and history in which we move as creatures. Christians have a spirit of crazy commitment because we are always in the last times. Chivalry is personal honor and loyalty, in love or war. Free Cities have invented social corporations with juridical rights. The Renaissance affirms the imperious right of gifted individuals to immortality. Scientists carry on a disinterested dialogue with nature, regardless of dogma or consequence. The Enlightenment has decided that there is a common sensibility of mankind. The Revolution has made equality and fraternity necessary for liberty. Utilitarian economy is for tangible satisfactions, not busy-work, money, or power. Naturalism urges us to an honest ethics, intrinsic in animal and social conditions.

Needless to say, these familiar propositions are often in practical and theoretical contradiction with one another; but that conflict too is part of the Western tradition. And certainly they are only ideals—they never did exist on land or sea—but they are the inventions of the holy spirit and the human spirit that constitute the University, which is also an ideal.

Naturally, as a teacher I rarely mention such things; I take them for granted as assumed by everybody. But I am rudely disillusioned when I find that both the students and my younger colleagues take quite different things for granted.

For instance, I have heard that the excellence of Socrates was a snobbish luxury that students nowadays cannot afford. The world "communicated" in the mass media is, effectually, the only world there is. Personal loyalty leaves off with juvenile gangs. Law is power. Fame is prestige and sales. Science is mastering nature. There is no such thing as humanity, only patterns of culture. Education and ethics are what we program for conditioning reflexes. The purpose of political economy is to increase the Gross National Product.

These are not foolish propositions, though I state them somewhat sarcastically. They make a lot of theoretical sense and they are realistic. It is far better to believe them than hypocritically to assert ancient clichés. The bother with these views, however, is that they do not structure enough life or a worthwhile life; that is, as ideals they are false. Or, if they do not pretend to be ideals, what will one do for ideals?

I think that this lack of structure is felt by most of the students and it is explicitly mentioned by many young teachers. They regard me, nostalgically, as not really out of my mind but just out of time and space—indeed, I am even envied, because, although the traditional values are delusions, they do smugly justify, if one believes them and tries to act them. The current views do not mean to justify, and it is grim to live without justification.

There is not much mystery about how the thread of relevance snapped. History has been too disillusioning. Consider just the recent decades, overlooking hundreds of years of hypocrisy. During the first World War, Western culture already disgraced itself irremediably (read Freud's profound expression of dismay). The Russian revolution soon lost its utopian élan, and the Moscow Trials of the thirties were a terrible blow to many of the best youth. The Spanish Civil War was perhaps the watershed—one can almost say that Western culture became irrelevant in the year 1938. Gas chambers and atom bombs showed what we were now capable of, yes our scientists. The Progress of the standard of living has sunk into affluence, and nobody praises the "American Way of Life." Scholars have become personnel in the Organization. Rural life has crowded into urban sprawl without community or the culture of cities. And the Cold War, deterrence of mutual overkill, is normal politics.

In this context, it *is* hard to talk with a straight face about identity, creation, Jeffersonian democracy, or the humanities.

But of course, people cannot merely be regimented; and we see that they find out their own pathetic, amiable, or desperate ideals. Creatureliness survives as the effort to make a "normal" adjustment and marriage, with plenty of hypochrondria. The spirit of apocalypse is sought in hallucinogenic drugs. There is para-legal fighting for social justice, but it is hardly thought of as politics and "justice" is not mentioned. On the other hand, some poor youth seem to have quite returned to the state of nature. Art regains a certain purity by restricting itself to art-action. Pragmatic utility somehow gets confused with doing engineering. Personal integrity is reaffirmed by "existential commitment," usually without rhyme or reason.

Unfortunately, none of this, nor all of it together, adds up.

I can put my difficulty as a teacher as follows: It is impossible to convey that Milton and Keats were for real, that they were about something, that they expected that what they had to say and the way in which they said it made a difference. The students can (not brilliantly) tell you about the symbolic structure or even something about the historical context, though history is not much cultivated; but, if one goes back more than thirty years, they don't have any inkling that these poets were writers and *in* a world. And, not surprisingly, young people don't have ancient model heroes any more.

Since there are few self-justifying ideas for them to grow up on, young people do not gain much confidence in themselves or take themselves as counting. On the other hand, they substitute by having astonishing private conceits, which many of them take seriously indeed.

The adults actively discourage earnestness. As James Coleman of Johns Hopkins has pointed out, the "serious" activity of youth is going to school and getting at least passing grades; all the rest—music, driving, 10 billions annually of teen-age commodities, dating, friendships, own reading, hobbies, need for one's own money—all this is treated by the adults as frivolous. The quality or meaning of it makes little difference; but a society is in a desperate way when its music makes little difference. In fact, of course, these frivolous things are where normally a child would explore his feelings and find his identity and vocation, learn to be responsible;

nevertheless, if any of them threatens to interfere with the serious business —a hobby that interferes with homework, or dating that makes a youth want to quit school and get a job—it is unhesitatingly interrupted, sometimes with threats and sanctions.

At least in the middle class, that fills the colleges, this technique of socializing is unerring, and the result is a generation not notable for self-confidence, determination, initiative, or ingenuous idealism. It is a result unique in history: *an élite that has imposed on itself a morale fit for slaves.*

The literature favored by youth expresses, as it should, the true situation. (It is really the last straw when the adults, who have created the situation for the young, then try to censor their literature out of existence.) There are various moments of the hang-up. Some stories simply "make the scene," where making the scene means touring some social environment in such a way that nothing happens that adds up, accompanied by friends who do not make any difference. Such stories do not dwell on the tragic part, what is *missed* by making the scene. Alternatively, there are picaresque adventure-stories, where the hipster heroes exploit the institutions of society which are not their institutions, and they win private triumphs. More probingly, there are novels of sensibility, describing the early disillusionment with a powerful world that does not suit and to which one cannot belong, and the subsequent suffering or wry and plaintive adjustment. Or alternatively, the phony world is provisionally accepted as the only reality, and the whole apocalyptically explodes. Finally, there is the more independent Beat poetry of deliberate withdrawal from the unsatisfactory state of things, and making up a new world out of one's own guts, with the help of Japanese sages, hallucinogens, and introspective physiology. This genre, when genuine, does create a threadbare community—but it suits very few.

In order to have something of their own in a situation that has rendered them powerless and irresponsible, many young folk maintain through thick and thin a fixed self-concept, as if living out autobiographies of a life that has been already run. They nourish the conceit on the heroes of their literature, and they defend it with pride or self-reproach. (It comes to the same thing whether one says, "I'm the greatest" or "I'm the greatest goof-off.") They absorbedly meditate this biography and, if vocal, boringly retell it. In this action, as I have said, they are earnest indeed, but it is an action that prevents becoming aware of anything else or anybody else.

It is not an attitude with which to learn an objective subject-matter in college.

After pre-reading, go on to the pre-reading questions below.

Pre-reading questions. (Please do not refer to the article as you answer.)

1. In general terms, what is Goodman's thesis or problem in this passage?

_____

_____

_____

2. What can you say, after pre-reading but before reading thoroughly, about the general direction of the author's rhetorical or persuasive purpose?

_____

_____

_____

3. The essay splits neatly into halves; what are they, and what is the overall sequence of ideas within those halves?

   a. _____

      (1) _____

      (2) _____

      _____

      _____

      _____

   b. _____

      (1) _____

      _____

      _____

      _____

      _____

4. What do you now think, before reading thoroughly, about Goodman's overall subject, and about his approach to it as far as you can tell from pre-reading?

_____

_____

_____

_____

5. Now formulate here the questions you will bear in mind while reading thoroughly. After reading thoroughly, you will return to these to fill in answers.

Q: _____

A: _____

_____

_____

Q: _____

A: _____

_____

_____

Q: _____

A: _____

_____

_____

Q: _____

A: _____

_____

_____

Now go back to read the article thoroughly.

Thorough-reading questions. (You may refer to the article as you answer these.)

1. What are your answers to your own questions, above?
2. The title of the essay, as reprinted here, was originally the title of the second

half only. What does Goodman mean by it? _____

_____

_____

3. Summarize the first half of the essay: _____

_____

_____

_____

4. And now summarize the second half: _____

_____

_____

_____

5. Goodman starts out by analyzing a set of problems; but explicitly, and even more by implication, these problems demand solutions, that is steps to be taken to correct them. In part, these solutions are found elsewhere in the book from which this essay is excerpted, so that it is not entirely fair to take this passage out of its context; but allowing for that, what sorts of solutions

   does Goodman seem to be urging, and what do you think of them? _____

_____

_____

_____

_____

_____

_____

6. How well does what Goodman describes agree with your own experience?

   Do you think he is right? wrong? In what ways and why? _____

_____

_____

_____

_____

_____

_____

Integrated Exercise 6:
A Memoir, Also with a Rhetorical Purpose

The following article first appeared in *The New Yorker*. Certainly *The New Yorker's* audience is likely to be finished with formal education and established in professions, financially well-off, and in large part Eastern and urban. *The New Yorker* gives that audience a variety of kinds of writing, from entertainment through serious fiction to concerned, liberal comment on current affairs; criticism which has sometimes been distinguished; and journalism which has sometimes been among the best published anywhere. Thus, if you came to the following article as it originally appeared, you might not know exactly what to expect. Would it be a short story? Would it be humorous? or what? And how should you read it; what techniques would be appropriate or inappropriate?

Decide for yourself, then, the most fitting way to read the article. Read it. Then go on to the questions. They are about how you decided to read the article, and then about the article itself.

Begin here.

"The Sellout"*
by FREEMAN J. DYSON

In England in November, it gets dark early. I walked home, as usual, after my music lesson, groping my way through the War Cloister. I was thirteen, and already I could understand why people said that our Cloister, in the Hampshire town of Winchester, was the finest war memorial in Europe. It is a square colonnade built of white stone and enclosing a plot of grass with a plain white cross in the center. The wall surrounding it is unbroken except for three gates for people to pass through. All round the wall the names are carved—the names of six hundred boys from our school who were killed in the 1914–18 war, the war that for us was simply The War. Architecturally, the War Cloister is a masterpiece. Although we walked through it every day, its atmosphere of quietness, dignity, and tragedy never weakened. That evening, as I came through the War Cloister alone, I saw a soldier kneeling. I saw him quite clearly—a young man in the familiar uniform of The War. Then I looked again, and he wasn't there. I found this not particularly surprising. Later, I told my friends about it and we agreed that it was not surprising. Most of us preserved an agnostic attitude concerning the existence of ghosts. Maybe I had had an ordinary hallucination, induced by the solemnity of the War Cloister. Or maybe I had actually seen one of the six hundred, paying his respects there to the living as we did to the dead. If one of the six hundred was still restlessly haunting the earth, it would be a natural thing for him to come to find peace in the War Cloister.

The older generation had fought The War and built the War Cloister. They were determined that we should be constantly reminded of their tragedy. And, indeed, our whole lives were overshadowed by it. Every year, on November 11th, there was the official day of mourning. But much heavier on our souls weighed the daily reminders that the best and the brightest of a whole generation had fallen. English life had sunk into sloth and mediocrity, we were told, because none were left of those who should have been our leaders. Everywhere, tired men of sixty-five were doing the work that vigorous men of forty-five should have done. The arithmetic was simple. Our school put out each year a graduating class of eighty boys. Our six hundred dead were more than seven complete years. The classes of 1914, 1915, and 1916 were wiped out. Few survived from the eight years between 1910 and 1917.

We of the class of 1941 were no fools. We saw clearly in 1937 that another bloodbath was approaching. We knew how to figure the odds. We saw no reason to expect that the next round would be less bloody than the one before. We expected that the fighting would start in 1939 or 1940, and we observed that our chances of coming through it alive were about the same as if we had belonged to the class of 1915 or 1916. We calculated the odds to be about ten to one that we would be dead in five years. Feeling ourselves doomed, we found it comforting to believe that the whole society in which we lived was doomed equally. The coming war would certainly bring large-scale bombing of civilian populations. And we expected bombing not with old-fashioned high explosives but with poison gas, such as the Italians had recently been using in Ethiopia, or with the anthrax bombs that Aldous Huxley described in *Brave New World*. We expected biological weapons to be used more and more recklessly, until some new Black Death got out of control and destroyed half the population of Europe. Gas had been used recklessly by both sides in the First World War, and there was no reason to hope that germ warfare would lend itself to any greater restraint. We then expected the Second World War to end with man-made plagues destroying our civilization, just as, thirty years later, we expect thermonuclear weapons to do the job in the Third World War.

In 1937, we of the younger generation had absorbed from our elders this profoundly tragic view of life, and we had not yet asserted our independence. We read and reread *The Ascent of F6,* the play by Auden and Isherwood, and I used to know long stretches of it by heart. It appeared in 1936, and marvellously expressed the mood of the time—especially one of the hero's opening speeches:

> O, happy the foetus that miscarries and the frozen idiot that cannot cry 'Mama!' Happy those run over in the street today or drowned at sea, or sure of death tomorrow from incurable diseases! They cannot

be made a party to the general fiasco. For of that growth which in maturity had seemed eternal it is now no tint of thought or feeling that has tarnished, but the great ordered flower itself is withering; its life-blood dwindled to an unimportant trickle, stands under heaven now a fright and ruin, only to crows and larvae a gracious refuge.

We who were pacifists all enjoyed digging the air-raid shelter. This was in the days of crisis before the Munich agreement. Sporting activities were suspended, and the boys were put to work with shovels digging a long trench. It was obvious to anybody of the meanest intelligence, we said, that the thing would never be of any use. It was a quarter of a mile away from the nearest school building, across an open field. It was in a low-lying spot, where any lethal gas was most likely to collect. And after the first good rain it would be full of water anyway. So we set to work with a will, digging this hole in the ground and enjoying the autumn sunshine. The enterprise was so demonstrably useless that we could take part in it without compromising our pacifist principles. We looked with satisfaction at the completed trench, regarding it as a monument to the total bankruptcy of the military mind.

By that time, we had made our break with the establishment and were fierce pacifists. We saw no hope that any acceptable future would emerge from the coming war. We had made up our minds that we would at least not be led like sheep to the slaughter, as the class of 1915 had been. Our mood was no longer tragic resignation but anger and contempt for the older generation, which had brought us into this mess. We raged against the hypocrisy and stupidity of our elders in the same way the young rebels are raging today, and for very similar reasons. We were not so naïve as to blame our predicament upon Hitler. We saw Hitler as only a symptom of the decay of our civilization, not as the cause of it. To us, the Germans were not enemies but fellow-victims of the general insanity. The first book I read in German was Remarque's *All Quiet on the Western Front,* describing the German class of 1914 torn to pieces by The War in the same way as their English contemporaries. Remarque's book is as powerful a memorial to them as our War Cloister is to our six hundred. My tears stained the pages of my German dictionary as I came to the end of the story. We did not bother to read *Mein Kampf.*

We looked around us and saw nothing but idiocy. The great British Empire visibly crumbling — and the sooner the better, as far as we were concerned. Millions of men unemployed, and millions of children growing up undernourished in dilapidated slums. A king mouthing patriotic platitudes none of us believed. A government that had no answer to any of its problems except to rearm as rapidly as possible. A military establishment that believed in bombing the German civilian economy as the only feasible strategy. A clique of old men in positions of power, blindly repeating the mistakes of 1914, having learned nothing and forgotten nothing in the intervening twenty-four years. A population of middle-aged nonentities, caring only for money and status, too stupid even to flee from the wrath to come. We looked for one honest man among the political leaders of the world. Chamberlain, our Prime Minister, we despised as a hypocrite. Hitler was no hypocrite, but he was insane. Nobody had any use for Stalin or Mussolini. Winston Churchill was our arch-enemy—the man personally responsible for the Gallipoli campaign, in which so many of our six hundred had died. He was the incorrigible warmonger, already planning the campaigns in which we were to die. We hated Churchill as our American successors in 1968 hated Lyndon Johnson. But in 1938 we were lucky enough to find one man whom we could follow and admire—Mahatma Gandhi. We loved him for three things. First, he was against the Empire. Second, he was against wealth and privilege. Third, his gospel of non-violent resistance gave us hope. We seized upon non-violence as the alternative to neverending bombs and death. We were not sure whether Hitler could be successfully opposed with non-violence and turned from his evil ways, but at least there was a chance. With bombs and guns, we were convinced, there was no chance. If the worst came to the worst, if we opposed Hitler nonviolently and he killed us, we should be dying in a good cause. That would be better than dying for Mr. Churchill and the Empire.

Brian was our leader. He was sixteen, and Welsh. He had the eloquence of a Welsh preacher, and we loved to listen to him talk. He claimed that he could make even the stupidest and stubbornest person believe in non-violence if only he could talk to him for six hours. "Talking to them for six hours" was Brian's answer to all problems. His ultimate purpose was to talk to Hitler for six hours, or die in the attempt. The school had an O.T.C., corresponding in function to the American R.O.T.C. Brian decided that we should non-violently resist taking part in the O.T.C. The school authorities amiably put us to work growing cabbages instead. Some time later, the colonel in charge of the O.T.C. shot himself, and this we considered very reasonable. We subscribed to *Peace News,* the organ of the Peace Pledge Union, and spent our small savings on quantities of propaganda leaflets that the Union supplied. We soon found that leaflets did not make converts to our cause. Nothing short of a six-hour session with Brian seemed to be effective. It was uphill work. In the end, Brian had about ten wholehearted disciples, in a school of four hundred boys. The worst of it was that nobody bothered to oppose us. We were just ignored. The rotten society around us blundered along to its inevitable doom, heedless of our warnings.

We had grand visions of the redemption of Europe by non-violence. The goose-stepping soldiers marching from country to country and meeting no resistance, finding only sullen non-coöperation and six-hour lectures. The leaders of the non-violence being shot and others coming forward fearlessly to take their places. The goose-stepping soldiers, sickened by the cold-blooded slaughter, one day refusing to carry out the order to shoot. The massive disobedience of the soldiers disrupting the machinery of military occupation. The soldiers, converted to non-violence, returning to their own country to use on their own government the tactics that we had taught them. The final impotence of Hitler, confronted with the refusal of his own soldiers to hate their enemies. The collapse of military institutions everywhere, leading to an era of worldwide peace and sanity. These visions were to us perfectly real. We knew that we faced a long struggle to make them real to even a minority of our countrymen. But we were not discouraged. After all, Gandhi had struggled for twenty-five years to make such visions real in India, and he had succeeded. Our self-confidence was sustained by the knowledge that if our program did not make sense in terms of immediate practical politics, the idea of fighting the Second World War in order to save the Czechs or the Poles or the European Jews made even less sense. We could see clearly that, however much we might suffer in the coming war, the Czechs and the Poles and the Jews would suffer worse. In this, as in many of our judgments of that time, history has proved us right. Above all, we were strengthened by the certainty that our program was moral and the society around us was immoral. Whether or not we had a chance of succeeding, we must stand up for the right as we saw it. In 1938, we were no longer responsive to the Oriental fatalism of Auden's and Isherwood's *F6*. In that year, Cecil Day Lewis published a volume of poems called "Overtures to Death." His robust pessimism suited our new mood much better:

> And, if the truth were told,
> You'd count it luck, perceiving in
> what shallow
> Crevices and few crumbling grains
> of comfort
> Man's joy will seed, his cold
> And hardy fingers find an eagle's hold.

My father had built a small house on a swampy piece of land, a mile from the nearest village, on the south coast, in Hampshire. We came home one fine day in September, 1940, after spending a night in London, and found our road barricaded, with a big sign saying, "Danger. Unexploded Bomb." A number of serious men in tin hats were inspecting the property. They had discovered on our lot eight neatly drilled holes, exactly straddling the house. Each hole was round, and so deep that one could not see the bottom. We were informed that in each there was sitting a hundred-kilogram time bomb, ready to explode at any moment. It was out of the question for us to live in the house until the bombs had been disarmed. The bomb-disposal squads had plenty of pressing business to attend to in London and elsewhere before they could be expected to come to our help; in fact, it was unreasonable to ask anybody to risk his life digging these bombs out, since they inconvenienced nobody except us. The bombs had been dropped during the night by some bewildered Germans who had failed to find their way to London. Perhaps they had mistaken the Solent for the Thames. At its narrowest, the Solent is two miles wide, and from twenty thousand feet it would be much easier to see. While we were still wondering what to do, a bomb-disposal expert drove up to our lot and asked to be shown the holes. As soon as he saw the first hole, he knelt down and sniffed into it. Then he laughed. He rapidly went round to the seven others and took a good sniff at each. "You can take down the sign," he said before he drove away. The bombs had all exploded when they landed. Our ground was so soft and sticky that they exploded deep underneath, without even making a crater. When we went into the house, we found not a plate broken.

So this was the war against which we had raged with the fury of right-eous adolescence. It was all very different from what we had expected. Gas masks that had been issued to the civilian population before the war began were gathering dust in closets. Nobody spoke of anthrax bombs anymore. London was being bombed, but the streets of our village were not choked with maimed and fear-crazed refugees. All our talk about the collapse of civilization began to seem a little irrelevant. Mr. Churchill had now been in power for four months, and he had carried through the Socialist reforms that the Labour Party had failed to achieve in twenty years. War profiteers were unmercifully taxed, unemployment disappeared, and the children of the slums were, for the first time, being adequately fed. It began to be difficult to despise Mr. Churchill as much as our principles demanded.

Our little band of pacifists was dwindling. Brian had left the school in 1939, and without him we made no new converts. Those of us who were still faithful continued to grow cabbages and boycott the O.T.C., but we felt less and less sure of our moral superiority. For me, the final stumbling block was the establishment of the Pétain-Laval government in France. This was in some sense a pacifist government. It had abandoned violent re-sistance to Hitler and chosen the path of reconciliation. Many of the Frenchmen who supported Pétain were sincere pacifists, sharing my faith in non-violent resistance to evil. Unfortunately, many were not. The worst of it was that there was no way to distinguish the sincere pacifists from the opportunists and collaborators. Pacifism was destroyed as a moral force as soon as Laval touched it. Gradually, it became clear to me that what had happened in France would also happen in England if ever our pacifist prin-ciples were put into practice. Supposing that we succeeded in converting Mr. Churchill and a majority of the British public to the gospel of non-violence, what then? We should nobly lay down our arms and impress our moral superiority upon the German invaders by silent non-coöperation. But the English equivalent of Laval would soon appear, to make a deal with the Germans and make us contemptible in their eyes. Quite soon, a few of us would forget our pacifism and begin an armed resistance in the Scottish Highlands. After that, Englishmen would have to choose between a col-laborationist government in London and a heroic fight in the Cairngorms. Any honest pacifist would choose the Cairngorms. By the end of 1940, the only members of our group whose faith remained alive were the religious pacifists—boys who believed in non-violence as a matter of individual con-science, independent of political considerations. Sadly, I parted company with them. For me, pacifism had been not a religion but a political program, and Laval had tarnished it irremediably.

Those of us who abandoned Gandhi and reënlisted in the O.T.C. did not do so with any enthusiasm. We still did not imagine that a country could fight and win a world war without destroying its soul in the process. If anybody had told us in 1940 that England would survive six years of war against Hitler, achieve most of the political objectives for which the war had been fought, suffer only one-third of the casualties we had had in the First World War, and finally emerge into a world in which our moral and humane values were largely intact, we would have said, "We do not believe in fairy tales." Having been brought up to take a tragic view of life, we were pleasantly surprised by every small rebirth of hope. The ludicrous incompetence with which the Germans conducted their bombing campaign made the war almost enjoyable. We did not need Churchill's oratory to tell us that we could take it. We liked much better the quiet rhythms of T. S. Eliot, whose "East Coker" appeared in September, 1940, and sold out five printings by February, 1941:

> There is only the fight to recover
>   what has been lost
> And found and lost again and again:
>   and now, under conditions
> That seem unpropitious. But per-
>   haps neither gain nor loss.
> For us, there is only the trying.
>   The rest is not our business.
>
> Home is where one starts from. As
>   we grow older
> The world becomes stranger, the
>   pattern more complicated
> Of dead and living.[2]

I arrived at the headquarters of the Royal Air Force Bomber Command in July, 1943, just in time for the big raids against Hamburg. On the night of July 27th, we killed forty thousand people and lost only seventeen bombers—by far the best we had ever done. For the first time in history, we had created a fire storm, which killed people even inside shelters. The casualties were about ten times as numerous as in a normal attack of the same size, without a fire storm. Nobody understands to this day why or how fire storms begin. In every big raid, we tried to raise a fire storm, but we succeeded just twice—once in Hamburg and once, two years later, in Dresden. Probably the thing happens only when there is a preëxisting instability in the local meteorology, which the bombs trigger off. The big slaughter in Hamburg and Dresden was not the result of a political decision to attack those places in any special way. It was a technological accident. Berlin and the Ruhr cities received many attacks of the same size as the one on Dresden but never had a fire storm. The Americans later had the same experience in Japan. They raised two fire storms—in the conventional bombing of Tokyo and the nuclear bombing of Hiroshima—and each killed about a hundred thousand people. Their other raids, including the nuclear attack on Nagasaki, were less destructive.

My office at Bomber Command was in a low wooden building in the middle of a forest. Thick beech trees were growing right up to the windows, so the room was dark summer and winter. The idea was to make it invisible from the air. I do not know whether it was in fact invisible, but certainly the Germans never disturbed us. I had come to this place after an interview with C. P. Snow, who at that time was responsible for putting technically trained people into the appropriate jobs. I was nineteen and had finished two years at the university, so I counted as a trained mathematician. Snow explained to me that my job, which was called operational research, would require very little mathematics but a lot of common sense and political tact. I went to it willingly.

In a short time, I became the Bomber Command expert on collisions. Since we bombed at night and did not fly in formation, collisions occurred from time to time. The crews who returned had many experiences of narrowly avoided collisions. They also frequently reported seeing fatal collisions over Germany, but it was impossible to trust these reports, because a single bomber hit by a shell and falling in two pieces would look just like a collision. The crews were understandably resentful. They were willing to risk being shot down by German fighters, feeling that they at least had a chance to shoot back, but to die in collisions seemed utterly pointless. The Command had a difficult decision to make. On the one hand, we disliked losing bombers in collisions. On the other hand, we knew that the preponderant cause of bomber losses, then running at the almost unendurable rate of four per cent per operation, was the German night fighters. By bunching the bombers closer together, we reduced the losses caused by fighters—the same principle that made the convoying of ships a good tactic against submarines. Each time we ordered the bombers to fly closer together, we cut down the total losses and increased the crews' anxiety about collisions. The Command had to decide how far we could go in concentrating the bomber stream before we would begin to lose more to collisions than we would save from fighters. The first essential in making a sound decision was to know how high the collision rate was.

I collected whatever information I could find about collisions. About the collisions we were ultimately interested in, lethal collisions over Germany, I found no information that I could trust. But I had good information about non-lethal collisions over Germany, since all damage to returning bombers was regularly reported to us in detail. With more difficulty, I collected evidence concerning non-lethal and lethal collisions in night flying over England. The numbers of each kind were small but reliable. The ratio of lethal to non-lethal collisions over England proved to be about three to one. In this ratio, I had already allowed for the fact that some non-lethal collisions over England would have been lethal if they had occurred over Germany. So in the end I told the Command that our best guess at the number of lethal collisions over Germany was to multiply the number of non-lethal collisions by three. That was all the mathematics I had to do. In practical terms, my information meant that we were losing only about one bomber to collisions in a thousand sorties. I told the Command that this was not nearly enough. I told them to increase the density of the bomber force five-fold, so that the collision losses would come up to one-half per cent. I told them that they would save much more than one-half per cent in losses to fighters. The Command followed my advice, and the crews reluctantly obeyed. This decision confirmed the crews' belief that Air Chief Marshal Sir Arthur Travers Harris, their commander-in-chief, familiarly known as Bert Harris or Butcher Harris, was as callous toward them as he was toward the Germans.

Bert Harris was a man of the same stamp as General Curtis LeMay and General Thomas S. Power. Strategic bomber forces seem to require such men to command them. Secure in his personal relationship with Churchill, Harris ran his show as he saw fit, frequently ignoring or over-riding his nominal superiors at the Air Ministry. At one time, I had on my desk a lengthy memorandum addressed to Harris by Air Chief Marshal Sir Norman Howard Bottomley, Deputy Chief of the Air Staff, entitled "On the Proper Use of a Bomber Force." Underneath the title was pencilled in Harris's neat hand, "A lesson for Grandma on how to suck eggs. A. T. H." Unfortunately, we had in those days no Xerox machines to preserve such indiscretions for the enjoyment of future historians.

I was in a highly privileged position at Bomber Command. I knew much more than most of the operational officers about the general course of the campaign. I knew much more than the Cabinet Ministers in London about the details of our operations. I was one of a very few people who knew what the objectives of the campaign were, how miserably we were failing to meet these objectives, and how expensive this was for us in money and lives. The bombing campaign represented roughly one-quarter of the total British war effort. It was costing the Germans less than this to defend themselves against the bombing and to repair the industrial damage it caused. Their defenses were so effective that the Americans had to give up daylight bombing over most of Germany from the fall of 1943 until the summer of 1944. We stubbornly refused to give up when the Americans did, but the defenses made it impossible for us to bomb accurately. We stopped trying to hit precise military objectives. Burning down cities was all we could do, so we did that. Even in killing the civilian population, we were inefficient. The Germans had killed one person for every ton of bombs that they dropped on England. To kill a German, we dropped three tons. I felt my responsibility deeply, being in possession of all this information that was so carefully concealed from the British public. Many times, I decided I owed it to the public to run out into the streets and tell them what stupidities were being committed in their name. But I never had the moral courage to do it. I sat in my office until the end, carefully calculating how to murder another hundred thousand people most economically.

After the war ended, I read reports of the trials of men who had been high up in the Eichmann organization. They had sat in their offices writing memoranda and calculating how to murder people efficiently, just like me. The main difference was that they were sent to jail or hanged as war criminals and I went free. I felt a certain sympathy for these men. Probably many of them had loathed the S.S. as much as I loathed Bomber Command, but they, too, had not had the courage to speak out. Probably many of them, like me, had lived through the whole six years of the war without ever seeing a dead human being.

Already, by 1943, the war had made us all insensitive. Poetry did not heighten our feelings then as it had done earlier. In 1943, Cecil Day Lewis spoke for us in a short poem entitled "Where Are the War Poets?"

> It is the logic of our times,
> No subject for immortal verse —
> That we who lived by honest dreams
> Defend the bad against the worse.

In August, 1945, I was all set to fly to Okinawa. We had defeated the Germans, but Mr. Churchill had still not had enough. He persuaded President Truman to let him join in the bombing of Japan with a fleet of three hundred bombers, which he called Tiger Force. We were to be based in Okinawa, and since the Japanese had almost no air defenses, we were to bomb, like the Americans, in daylight. I found this new slaughter of defenseless Japanese even more sickening than the slaughter of well-defended Germans. Still I did not quit. By that time, I had been at war so long that I could hardly remember peace. No living poet had words to describe that emptiness of the soul which allowed me to go on killing without hatred and without remorse. But Shakespeare understood it, and he gave Macbeth the words:

> I am in blood
> Stepp'd in so far, that, should I
>   wade no more,
> Returning were as tedious as go o'er.

I was sitting at home eating a quiet breakfast with my mother when the morning paper arrived with the news of Hiroshima. I understood at once what it meant. "Thank God for that," I said. I knew that Tiger Force would not fly, and I would never have to kill anybody again.

You will need to refer to the article as you answer the questions.

1. How, precisely, did you read the article? (With what techniques, in what

sequence?) _____

_____

_____

_____

_____

_____

2. What questions did you have in mind while reading? _____

_____

_____

_____

3. The article is organized in five sections; the last is very short. Summarize each section briefly, so that you establish the main sequence of ideas.

   a. ''War Cloister''— _____

   _____

   b. _____

   _____

   c. _____

   _____

   d. _____

   _____

   e. _____

   _____

4. What is the overall thesis or problem and the overall persuasive purpose— insofar as you can identify one with any exactitude—of the article? (In relation to this, what is the point of the title?) _____

   _____

   _____

   _____

   _____

5. In relation to that overall thesis and purpose, what is the function of each of those five parts you distinguished in question 3, above? How does the development progress from each of these parts to the next, in a way that

serves the author's purpose? _____

_____

_____

_____

_____

_____

6. Each of the parts of the article contains a fragmentary quotation of poetry.

Why? _____

_____

_____

What does each fragment establish or suggest?

a. _____

b. _____

c. _____

d. _____

e. _____

7. One way to say what the author does is that he presents five different attitudes towards war which he himself felt at five moments of his young manhood. Which of those five do you yourself normally agree with most closely: in other words, what is your usual judgment of the complex issues

Freeman Dyson is raising? _____

_____

_____

_____

8. The author makes several comparisons of events or opinions from his past

to present-day events or opinions. What are those, and why does he make

them? _____

_____

_____

_____

9. What is the *tone* or *feeling* of the work, and how does that contribute, if it

   does, to the author's persuasive purpose? _____

   _____

   _____

   _____

   _____

10. What is the point of Dyson's comparison of himself with war criminals high
    up in Eichmann's command? How does he now regard his own part in

    World War II? _____

    _____

    _____

    _____

11. What does Dyson seem to think of Churchill, Roosevelt, and Truman? Why

    is he indirect rather than direct in making his opinions apparent? _____

    _____

    _____

    _____

12. One of Dyson's most important points, though presented with character-
    istic quietness, is the comparison of what he knew at Bomber Command
    about the effectiveness of bombing, and the information available to leaders
    like Churchill and the generals; part of that point is what he says about
    how information was kept from reaching Churchill. What is the relation of

    all that to the rhetorical purpose of the article? _____

    _____

_____

_____

13. How well does Dyson establish his thesis? _____

_____

_____

_____

14. In a paragraph or two, compare Dyson's article with Paul Goodman's essay, beginning page 436.

_____

_____

_____

_____

_____

_____

_____

_____

_____

_____

_____

_____

_____

_____

_____

_____

_____

CHAPTER 16

A Lifetime of Reading

Pre-read this chapter as your first step in reading. As your second step, list here the questions you expect the chapter to answer.

_____

_____

_____

_____

_____

Practical prose: the notion has served us well. It has provided a strategy for talking about efficiency in reading, without getting stuck in the problems raised by those types of reading for which efficiency — in the obvious sense, anyway — is not the chief aim. But in the last few chapters, treating critical reading, we have quietly moved away from any strict limitation of the discussion to practical prose. Is it now time to go beyond that limitation altogether? Practical prose we defined as material of a factual nature read primarily for information; we said that practical prose would probably make up 70 to 90 per cent of your reading over the next fifty years; we disclaimed the attempt to apply the techniques of reading to "that all-important 10 to 30 per cent" of your lifetime of reading that will be fiction, poetry, philosophy, the best of history and criticism, and so forth. But what about that reading, after all? Is it, except in conventional piety, so all-important? Is it so impractical? Should the trained reader, who when he reads practical prose is to be so relentlessly questioning, analytical, purposeful, self-aware, tense, and so on, suddenly lapse into stumbling undirected incoherence when he picks up a book that is really subtle, perhaps difficult, maybe even beautiful? What, after all this talk about reading, can the trained reader do to make reading those subtle, difficult, maybe beautiful works not a tiresome chore but fully as enjoyable, stimulating, and enriching as the conventional piety—and all one's hopes, as well—insist they should be?

In your dialogue with this book, with any book that is serious about reading, you should raise such questions. In my dialogue with you, I have the obligation to suggest answers. Some will be obvious and undisputable from what has gone before. Some must be more tentative and personal.

To begin with the obvious, many of the techniques of reading apply to all reading matter; especially applicable are those techniques that get at organization and those that raise questions appropriate to what you are reading. Often, when you apply a technique to other than practical prose, your chief problem is one of *tact.* How do you use the method like a surgeon not a butcher? One technique, in particular, will prevent you from making tactless applications of other techniques: this is *the habit of being precisely aware of your purpose* in reading, so that you read at the appropriate speed—perhaps at 60 words per minute and aloud, if it's a poem—and choose comprehension techniques sensibly and sensitively. Awareness of purpose will also suggest new variations in the way you apply some of the techniques. For example, when someone brings up the banal observation that you don't apply pre-reading to detective novels, my answer is that surprisingly enough you may want to apply, to some great fiction, a sequence of steps like those of pre-reading—but with the difference that you make your structural analysis, first and last chapters and all the rest of it, not before reading thoroughly but afterwards.

Thus, when reading works of imagination or high seriousness, the first essential is flexibility, directed by your clarity of purpose. Here, as we can see yet again, it is the untrained reader who is most likely to approach all reading in the same unimaginative and unvarying way. For the trained reader, the possible variations in use of his techniques are as extensive as the variety of reading problems he may face. In the nature of the case, then, this chapter can do no more than illustrate some of the possible applications and variations. Let us begin with problems of structure and organization, go on to problems of meaning, and conclude with what we can call problems of judgment.

Problems of Structure

Pick up the program of any concert of classical music, or read the sleeve of many a recording: the notes that introduce a piece of music naturally rely heavily on structural analysis. ". . . After the even flow of the exposition, the return of the introduction, in G major, is very dramatic in effect. . . . On its last appearance the introduction is reduced from six bars to four. . . ." Music may well be the most emotional of all the arts. If such emphasis on analysis of structure is important to show you how to get the most from listening to music, surely structural analysis may have place in understanding and enjoying literature. If that detective novel was a really clever one, you won't have extracted all the enjoyment possible from reading it until you have gone back from its last sentences to reconstruct exactly how beautifully the author misled you. But something similar is true of certain novels, for instance, *War and Peace*. Part of the beauty of that novel is not perceived until you have understood the relation between the majestic sweep and rhythms of the entire work, and the individual moments of character portrayal and events; and to understand that relation, at some point you must step back from your reading to think about the construction of the whole novel. What better time than towards the end, or even at the end?

This leads us to the simple possibility suggested above: when reading a work that normal pre-reading might spoil, if you remain uncertain of its structure and overall meaning when you reach the end of normal reading, *then* may be the time to apply the steps of pre-reading. In effect you review the work by applying the approach of pre-reading (just as Chapter 10 suggested you might review any work as a step in studying it).

If some such attempt to understand structure is desirable for enjoying a novel like *War and Peace,* there are other works of imagination that demand extensive structural analysis in any serious attempt to understand them at all. Take an extreme case: James Joyce's *Ulysses* is a novel of extraordinary interest and beauty, and undeniably of difficulty as well. Many of its allusions, references, and verbal devices will not yield much to an overall structural analysis; but I defy anyone to approach the simplest understanding (or enjoyment) of the work without at some point pondering the complex sequence of its parts. To understand that sequence requires that the reader go back and figure it out; what is such an organized reexamination but a flexible form of pre-reading after the fact?

Structures are perhaps more laborious to dig out in long works than in short ones, but they can be just as important even in a short story or a short poem. You may recall that when you read the fourteen lines of a sonnet, one of the things you read for is the relation of the last six lines (the structural unit called the sestet) to the first eight lines (or octave); and then the internal structure of the sestet itself, particularly the functioning of the final two lines of the poem. Again, so lyrical, spontaneous an outpouring as an ode by Keats in fact will be found to have an internal organization of great precision and skill; to discern that organization does not harm but rather enhances one's sense of the beauty of the ode. Similarly, I recall reading for the first time a new short story by Samuel Beckett. No more than a page in length, it was so strangely, densely written that it took me over an hour to read it through. I came nowhere near understanding it until, weeks later, someone pointed out some of its structural peculiarities: the first half and the last half contained the identical words in the identical phrases, but the phrases were arranged in a different sequence; the total number of phrases was limited, repeated in a complex cycle; and so on. Of course, I should have taken pencil and paper to figure those things out for myself after my first reading.

Questions of structure, the architectural plan of the whole work, are essential in reading great history books, helpful even in reading well-written criticism; but where structural analysis comes into its own is with serious philosophy, and this on the simplest of grounds that great philosophical works are often difficult to understand. Any aid to understanding philosophy is also essential to enjoyment—after all, the enjoyment of philosophy *is in* the understanding of it. But the most important point about reading philosophy is that structural analysis works: in combination with other methods, analyzing a philosopher's organization of ideas is often profoundly revealing. To keep to a simple but central example, consider the application to a work of philosophy of one of the questions suggested for critical reading in the last chapter: *What are the author's key terms and how does he use them?* To distinguish among the several shades of meaning with which a philosopher employs a key term, and to establish the sequence in which he introduces those meanings and the function of the meaning in relation progressively to each section of the work — these, taken together, often make up one of the most essential problems in reading a work of philosophy; the problem is in great part one to be attacked through the organization.

Analysis of structure, since it is central to so many kinds of difficult serious reading, may use not only flexible versions of the steps of pre-reading, but will often call on subsidiary skills. Summarizing is one of these. Paragraph analysis, in its various forms, is another. The most important is outlining. Hardly any other approach can focus your understanding, not just of organization but of the meanings the author has organized, so effectively as the labor of going back over a work or part of it to construct a careful outline. A truly important work, and this I think includes many works of imagination, can only grow in your mind as, by outlining it, then correcting and improving your outline, you come to understand it and to learn it thoroughly.

Structural analysis is, of course, particularly important to students, and especially to students of literature. One problem that often afflicts English majors, at some point in their studies, is a kind of literary indigestion, too many novels or plays or long poems to read in too short a time. The symptoms of the problem are restlessness, boredom, concentration difficulties, and trouble keeping all the different works straight in the mind. The best remedy I know is to concentrate intensively on structural analyses, including outlining: sharp focus on organization allows both details and overall significance to fall more effortlessly into place.

Problems of Meaning

When you are actually reading, of course, you don't use any one method or technique all by itself, and you use every method with the understanding of meaning as your controlling aim. Thus, organization is important to you, finally, because it shows you how an author's various particular meanings fit together into his overall meaning. As you know, the two techniques that get at meaning most powerfully are questions, particularly the critical questions, and development analysis. Although some people find detailed examination of organization too clinical a method for imaginative writing, no such reservations seem ever to be raised about reading with questions in mind. If you consider any lecture or book that claims to introduce a kind or period of literature, or to guide your appreciation of it, you will quickly find that the useful parts are either straightforward factual background (*Who was Molière? What kinds of people did he write his plays for?*), or else can be summarized as a series of questions that you are urged to ask of works of imagination as you read them. Examples can be found on almost any page of almost any book about literature; consider these observations about Sir Thomas Browne that Basil Willey makes in *The Seventeenth Century Background*:

The peculiar irony of Browne, his wistfulness, the air of compassion with which he ponders all time and all existence, proceed from his detachment from each and all of the worlds he contemplates; so that he can indulge his whim in fitting together what patterns he pleases from the fragments. . . . It is a romantic falsification to "relish" Browne for his "quaintness." It is more valuable, in reading him, to try to recover some of his own inclusiveness, in virtue of which his juxtapositions are *not* quaint, but symbols of his complex vision. . . . In thinking of Browne as a "metaphysical" we must not forget that he had in him a large infusion of the Baconian experimentalist. In the *Pseudodoxia Epidemica* he makes as it were an amateur contribution to what I have called the main intellectual problem of the seventeenth century, the separation of the "true" from the "false."[1]

The purpose of such observations is to guide your actual reading of Sir Thomas Browne. Do you see how each observation tells you something of what Willey thinks you should read for, in effect what questions to bear in mind as you read?

About philosophy it can be said that what the questions of Socrates established about the philosophical methods of the classical Greeks, is still true today: a central concern, sometimes it might seem the only concern, of philosophers has been to consider what kinds of questions can be asked, what kinds of statements can and cannot significantly be made. Ponder, for example, Alfred J. Ayer, in his *Language, Truth and Logic*:

> The question that must be asked about any putative statement of fact is not, Would any observations make its truth or falsehood logically certain? but simply, Would any observations be relevant to the determination of its truth or falsehood? And it is only if a negative answer is given to this second question that we conclude that the statement under consideration is nonsensical.[2]

Ayer is establishing the question we must ask if we want to know whether a statement — any statement whatever — is sense or nonsense. He is thus at the same time identifying the most important problem for his philosophy and for the whole modern English school of philosophy of which he has been a leader. Susanne Langer makes a similar point with wider application, in *Philosophy in a New Key*:

> The intellectual treatment of any datum, any experience, any subject, is determined by the nature of our questions, and only carried out in the answers. . . . A philosophy is characterized more by the *formulation* of its problems than by its solution of them. Its answers establish an edifice of facts; but its questions make the frame in which its picture of facts is plotted. They make more than the frame; they give the angle of perspective, the palette, the style in which the picture is drawn — everything except the subject. In our questions lie our *principles of analysis*.[3]

The problem in reading beyond the limits of practical prose, then, is not that the question technique does not apply, but rather that questions are too important and too variable to be applied mechanically. Once again, the first requirement is tact. To that must be added patience and imagination, for clearly the critical questions this book has suggested are only the beginning of what some kinds of serious reading may require.

Similarly, with development analysis, your need will be to deepen and extend your understanding of the various categories, from definition through cause and effect, so that you can use your ability to spot them as a means of thinking along with an author — whether he be a philosopher, a historian, or a poet. Nobody denies that writers use the modes of development introduced in Chapter 14. Even the subtlest imagery of poetry can be shown to have its roots in such modes of development. But to define metaphor as a kind of compressed comparison is one thing; it is something much more intricate to elucidate the varieties of metaphor in even a single act from a play by Shakespeare, and to trace them to their roots in those modes. Entire books have been written about that kind of reading; yet what they demonstrate is that such reading is not mastered by abandoning techniques like development analysis, but rather by pushing them further.

Problems of Judgment

We said at the end of the last chapter that *it is one of the chief points of critical reading, indeed one of the principles of clear thought, that if an exposition really is persuasive, you must allow yourself to be persuaded.* That point is itself an introduction to the problems of judgment in reading. It applies with redoubled force to the reading of many great works, as do the questions about facts and reasoning as tests of an author's persuasiveness. For such serious reading, beyond the bounds of practical prose, that first principle of judgment is joined by many others. Here are two.

The point about persuasiveness applies of course to works that reason from a base of facts and assumptions, whether the work is a textbook like this one, a business memorandum, a governmental position paper, a scientific report, a historical essay, or an original work in philosophy. When we reach out to works of imagination, however, that principle must be joined by its twin: *Is it persuasive?* has as its counterpart something very simple indeed, *Do I like it?*

But of course it isn't so simple. That question introduces at last what most people think is the main point about critical reading — that is, *criticism.* We have kept away from criticism in this sense, until now, because it is of all aspects of reading the most difficult without thorough understanding, without a thorough grounding in the other techniques of reading, and without grave risk from prejudgment and prejudice. If you can correct those conditions, it is of course necessary and proper that you react to a work of imagination; it is not necessary that your reaction agree with the conventional piety of the defenders of the great tradition. There are reasons for disliking Dickens, or at least some of his novels; there are reasons for disliking Henry James, and so on. But there are no reasons for disliking any work because it is unfamiliar, in language or background, or because it is difficult. To take a trivial example, the person who "doesn't like Shakespeare" because the vocabulary is unfamiliar, can only be told that he has no right to a critical judgment until he has mastered that difficulty. In sum, the most absurd prejudgment about works of imagination is the one that dismisses them before they are understood — that dismisses them unread.

The best precaution has already been suggested: suspension of judgment. This means, applied to works of imagination, that you cannot really answer the question, *Do I like it?* until you are sure you can satisfy other requirements, such as, *Do I understand it? Have I analyzed its structure? Do I know how the work relates to the time and place where it was written? Do I perceive what the author is really trying to do, so that I am not taking his work for something it isn't, not condemning him for failing to do something he never intended?*

Such questions grow naturally out of the critical questions you have already worked with. They evidently deserve elaboration, beyond what we can do here. Some of them clearly apply to any great work, not just to works of the imagination. They also lead to another kind of judgment, which is the subject of the final section of this final chapter.

Your Next Fifty Years of Reading

When is a work a great work? Have there been many really great works written in man's history? With all the unimportant reading that crowds into a lifetime, how can one be sure of getting to the reading that is more important, if less obviously and immediately relevant?

To judge from the book review section of any magazine or Sunday news-paper, important books are published every week; dozens and scores of them every year. Ask any serious critic, "When was the last good novel published?" and he may cite some work of the last twelve months. Ask him again, "When did you last read a *really* great novel?" and he will pause before he mentions so many as two published in the past decade. The same is true for history, philos-ophy, plays and poetry, and so on: one's judgment of greatness depends in part on context, so that what appears excellent compared to the run of the press from week to week, is hardly outstanding when considered in a longer view. Thus the editor of the scientific magazine *Nature* publishes a dozen articles each week, but would cheerfully admit that in the exciting, fast-breaking field of molecular biology there are perhaps two really important papers a year; and when asked for the most important papers in the last twenty years, could easily hold his list to eight or so. Similarly the eminent critic F. R. Leavis some years ago would admit that hardly more than three or four novelists of all those who have ever written belong to what he called "the Great Tradition" of the English novel. George Eliot, Henry James, Joseph Conrad, and D. H. Lawrence com-prised Leavis' list, though he has since admitted at least Dickens and Jane Austen to candidate membership.

Such stringent limitations seem excessive, yet they have a point: truly great works of any kind are rare. They can be defined as *those that have made a difference,* those whose publication has changed the way people think or feel. Defined like that, there are few great works indeed. Defined like that, they are obviously the ones that you owe it to yourself to read, firsthand and with all the skill you can bring to them, at some point in your next fifty years of reading.

The most ambitious, even arrogant attempt to define the great works was one I happened to grow up with—the idea of the "great books."* By this notion,

---

* Sometimes called the "100 great books," though the suggested lists rarely got lower than about 115. The idea has since been commercialized as "the great ideas of the west-ern world with Syntopicon," a publishing venture where complete works and snippets are reprinted in bright bindings together with an index to the 100 or so "great ideas," all to be sold like encyclopedias. Another instance of a good idea vulgarized.

the works that have made a difference can be narrowed down to very few. At the fringes of the list there can be endless argument: Stendhal's *The Red and the Black* included, but no Turgenev? Kant, but no Hegel? Copernicus and Kepler, but no Galileo? Livy's history of Rome, and Gibbon's *Decline and Fall of the Roman Empire,* but no modern historians? The discussion quickly becomes a parlor game, an intellectual version of Twenty Questions. Yet even this illustrates and develops something of the principles of judgment that are at the heart of the definition of great works. There are many works that nobody would doubt should be included. But the definition says more. It says that it ought to be the mark of an educated man that he has read most of them, the mark of a thoughtful reader that in preference to less important works he returns to these repeatedly, and for pleasure, in his lifetime.

EXERCISES FOR CHAPTER 16

Reading Journal

Integrated Exercise 7: An Experiment with Impractical Prose

Reading Journal

There is a Zen Buddhist question-and-answer that goes like this:

"What is infinity?" asks the student.
The master replies, "Have you eaten your rice?"
"Yes," says the student.
"Then wash your bowl."

Just so: no mathematician would disagree, for it may be that the best working definition of infinity is simply, "a number higher than any you can mention," or "the process of keeping-on-counting." And so: "The next fifty years of reading?" asks the student. "What is the *next book* you want to read?"
The rest of the journal is yours. Enjoy it!

Integrated Exercise 7: An Experiment with Impractical Prose

Here is a list of short stories, ranging from three or four pages to ten times that in length; all are widely regarded as excellent. The stories chosen can easily be found in paperback collections or college textbooks. For this exercise, choose *two* of these stories; or substitute others by the same authors. Read these two as stories, to understand them, hopefully to enjoy them. You will also be reading them to see how a judicious application of reading methods, and above all an eye for structure and a sense for such questions as theme and point of view, can help you to understand and enjoy them.

Read the first story you choose at your normal reading speed, whatever seems comfortable. Then answer the questions that follow the list of stories, below. Put your answers into the pages of your Reading Journal. Then read the second story you have chosen; and apply the same questions to it in turn.

While reading the stories and answering the questions, remember that this is not a test, that these questions do not attempt to give you some system for reading fiction, for that is an aim to which many authors have devoted anthologies or texts as long as this one. Rather, this is simply an initial exploration and a set of tentative suggestions.

The list

"Death in the Woods," by Sherwood Anderson
"A Shower of Gold," by Donald Barthelme
"The Guest," by Albert Camus
"The Darling," by Anton Chekhov
"The Portable Phonograph," by Walter Van Tilburg Clark
"The Secret Sharer," by Joseph Conrad (long)
"King of the Bingo Game," by Ralph Ellison
"Barn Burning," by William Faulkner
"My Kinsman, Major Molineux," by Nathaniel Hawthorne
"On the Road," by Langston Hughes
"The Beast in the Jungle," by Henry James
"An Encounter," by James Joyce
"The Rocking-Horse Winner," by D. H. Lawrence
"Prologue: The Man Who Studied Yoga," by Norman Mailer (long)
"The Magic Barrel," by Bernard Malamud
"Greenleaf," by Flannery O'Connor
"My Oedipus Complex," by Frank O'Connor
"The Forks," by J. E. Powers
"Don't Call Me by My Right Name," by James Purdy
"Matryona's House," by Alexander Solzhenitsyn (long)
"The Catbird Seat," by James Thurber
"Lifeguard," by John Updike
"Death of a Travelling Salesman," by Eudora Welty
"The Man Who Lived Underground," by Richard Wright

The questions

1. Not because it is necessarily the most important way to understand fiction, but simply because it is a familiar tool by now, review first the *structure* of the story you have just read. Without looking back at the story, write out in your Reading Journal whatever you can recall about the progression, sequence, organization, growth of the story from beginning to end. Then go back to the story, skim it carefully in the pre-reading "after the fact" suggested in this chapter. Revise and add to your notes in your Reading Journal.

2. What kinds of questions do you find are appropriate to ask about this story?

   You will recall that the four master questions introduced in Chapter 7, and the four critical questions of Chapter 15, inquired into *the thesis or problem* of the work, *your purpose in reading, the main sequence of ideas, the rhetorical or persuasive purpose* of the work, your own *prejudgments and prejudices,* the author's *key terms, how well the thesis is proved,* and your own, more specific, questions about the selection. Which of those questions can be asked sensibly about the story you have just read? Which can be adapted? In answering the previous question about the story's structure, for example, you have gone into the equivalent, for a piece of fiction, of the main sequence of ideas. In the same way, the thesis or problem of a piece of nonfiction has as its fictional equivalent the *theme* of the story. What is the theme of the story you have just read? Then again, your purpose in reading is clearly worth focussing by a brief restatement; and the possibility that the story has a persuasive or rhetorical effect can turn out to be a very powerful critical consideration indeed. Similarly, it can prove very revealing to raise the question of your own prejudices, for much of the best fiction today, or indeed in the past, has the power to touch intensely personal emotions, arouse passion, or provoke hostility. And even when you find a story tedious or hard, that reaction, too, may be a product of your own prejudgments.

   Therefore, in your Reading Journal, write out the list of questions that can be applied or adapted to the story you have read. Then answer each question.

3. Clearly, fiction has questions which are particular to it, questions that have no exact equivalents for nonfiction. Traditionally, since Aristotle, the most important categories where questions can be asked have been:

   Plot, or action (which you will have approached in analyzing the structure of the story).

   Character, which is so important for many short stories that their plot can almost be defined as the sequence of development of character—either change in that character or progressive growth of our understanding of it.

   Thought, under which we can include not only what the characters may think about the situations they are in and the world as they experience it, but more importantly the point of view and conclusions of the author, sometimes stated openly, more often hinted and implied.

   Diction, or the words and language of the story, which include its style, its effectiveness in catching character traits through speech, and the elusive but important question of the *tone* of the story.

   To these traditional questions, we can perhaps add these days the question of *relevance.* As has been recognized for thousands of years, imaginative writing has a remarkable and paradoxical truthfulness of its own that goes deeper than the truthfulness of ordinary reporting. The best history makes us say, merely, "Oh, so that's the way it was." The best imaginative writing makes us assent gladly — "Yes! That's the way it is!" The best fiction in America today is deeply concerned with the way it is, here, today. By its very concern with the fine-grained detail and particularity, it evokes the human condition generally.

Plot, character, thought, diction, and relevance — these are basic questions. Work through them in your Reading Journal, with their variations and subquestions that we have sketched in, and you will be well started as a critical reader of impractical prose.

4. Finally, of course, two more questions: How well does the story do what it sets out to do — that is how good is it? And then, how did you like it?

BIBLIOGRAPHY

Manuals for Reading Development

A College Developmental Reading Manual, by S. Vincent Wilking and Robert G. Webster. Boston, Houghton Mifflin Company, 1943.
Developing College Reading, by Lee A. Jacobus. New York, Harcourt Brace Jovanovich, Inc., 1970.
Improving College Reading, second edition, by Lee A. Jacobus. New York, Harcourt Brace Jovanovich, Inc., 1972.
Learning to Learn, Donald P. Smith, general editor, *et al.* New York, Harcourt Brace Jovanovich, Inc., 1961.

Vocabulary

Harbrace Vocabulary Guide, second edition, by Donald W. Lee. New York, Harcourt Brace Jovanovich, Inc., 1970.
The Vocabulary of Science, by Lancelot Hogben. New York, Stein & Day, 1970. London, William Heinemann Ltd., 1969.

Paragraph Development and Sentence Structure

Harbrace College Handbook, seventh edition, by John C. Hodges and Mary E. Whitten. New York, Harcourt Brace Jovanovich, Inc., 1972.
Writer's Guide and Index to English, fourth edition, by Porter C. Perrin, revised by Karl W. Dykema and Wilma R. Ebbitt. Chicago, Scott-Foresman, Lothrop, 1965.

Critical Reading

How to Read a Book, by Mortimer J. Adler. New York, Simon and Schuster, Inc., 1940.
Language in Thought and Action, third edition, by S. I. Hayakawa. New York, Harcourt Brace Jovanovich, Inc., 1972.

Research

The Modern Researcher, revised edition, by Jacques Barzun and Henry F. Graff. New York, Harcourt Brace Jovanovich, Inc., 1970.

INSTRUCTIONS FOR TIMING

Several kinds of exercises in this book require that you time your reading so that you can measure your progress in speed. But unless you time your reading very accurately, you will not get a significant measure of speed. Here is the best method for timing yourself when you are not in a classroom, and when you have no stop watch or stop clock.

1. Use a watch or clock with a sweep second hand. With pencil and paper handy, wait until the second hand is about ten seconds before the 60-second mark. Then write down the exact time in minutes. When the second hand crosses 60, begin the timed reading.

2. As soon as you have finished reading, note the position of the second hand. Then write down the exact time in minutes and seconds. Your paper will look something like this:

> Start: 38 min.
> Stop: 42 min. 22 sec.

Subtract the starting time from the stopping time, and you have your reading time in minutes and seconds. (In our example, of course, the reading time is 4 minutes and 22 seconds.)

3. Record your reading time in the space provided on the exercise sheet. Then answer the questions. When you have finished, check your score by rereading the timed material and comparing it with your answers.

4. With the Reading Speed exercises, use the conversion table on page 475 to change your reading time into words-per-minute speed. Then enter your score on the Progress Profile, page vii. With Skimming exercises, enter your score on the score sheet provided on page 482.

Reading Speed Conversion Table

For Reading Speed exercises, use this table to convert your reading time in minutes and seconds, to words-per-minute speeds. Move across the top row to find the particular exercise; then read down that column to entry that is opposite your reading time for the exercise. When your reading time falls between two of the times listed, you must estimate your speed between the two corresponding entries. For example, a reading time of 1:58 (one minute and fifty-eight seconds) is $8/10$ of the way between 1:50 and 2:00; on Reading Speed Exercise Average Level 6, that would be $8/10$ of the way between 638 w.p.m. and 585 w.p.m. — or 596 w.p.m. (Remember, as your reading time goes up, your speed goes down.)

Time in min:sec	Average Level Exercises							Difficult Level Exercises			
	1	2	3	4	5	6	7	1	2	3	4
1:10									681		
1:20	922	990	903		1132	877	935	732	596		922
1:30	823	880	803	1178	1008	779	831	650	530	925	823
1:40	738	792	722	1062	906	701	748	585	477	831	738
1:50	671	721	657	963	825	638	680	532	434	757	671
2:00	615	660	602	884	756	585	624	488	398	694	615
2:10	568	609	556	816	698	540	576	450	367	638	568
2:20	527	570	516	759	648	501	534	418	341	594	527
2:30	492	528	482	708	605	468	499	392	318	554	492
2:40	461	492	452	663	566	439	468	366	298	519	461
2:50	434	466	425	624	534	413	440	343	281	490	434
3:00	410	440	401	589	504	390	416	325	265	462	410
3:10	388	418	380	558	477	369	394	308	251	438	388
3:20	369	396	361	531	454	351	374	293	239	416	369
3:30	351	380	344	506	432	334	356	278	227	396	351
3:40	335	360	328	482	412	319	340	266	217	378	335
3:50	321	344	314	461	394	305	325	254	207	362	321
4:00	308	330	301	442	378	292	312	244	199	347	308
4:10	295	317	289	424	363	281	299	234	191	333	295
4:20	284	305	278	408	349	270	288	225	183	319	284
4:30	273	294	268	393	336	260	277	216	177	308	273
4:40	263	285	258	379	324	251	267	209	170	297	263
4:50	254	273	249	365	313	242	258	201	164	287	254
5:00	246	264	241	354	302	234	249	195	159	277	246
5:20	231	246	226	332	284	219	234	183	149	260	231
5:40	217	233	212	312	267	206	220	172	140	245	217
6:00	205	220	201	294	252	195	208	163		231	205
6:20	194	209	190	279	239	185	197	152		219	194
6:40	185	198	181	265	227	175	187	145		208	185
7:00	176	190	170	253	216	167	178			198	176
7:30	164	176	161	235	202	156	166			185	164
8:00	154	164	151	221	189	146	156			173	154
8:30	145	155	142	208	178		147			163	145
9:00		147		196	168					154	
10:00				177							

PHRASE FLASHING

This material has been designed to help you develop the quick and accurate perception of *phrases as units* upon which efficient reading speeds depend. In the groups of phrases below, the phrases start short, and become progressively longer. The object is to look at each phrase for the briefest possible fraction of a second so that you must read it completely in only one glance, if you are to read it at all. To flash the phrases very briefly requires that you follow carefully the precise directions in the next paragraph. Start with group A; if you can complete it without difficulty, go on to group B, and so on. Work with phrase flashing for only five to seven minutes at one time, but at least four times a week, and preferably every day. Each time, begin with the last group you completed successfully the previous day and progress to the next. When you finish each practice session, enter on the score sheet that follows the number of phrases you read correctly.

Cover with a sheet of paper the columns to the right of the one you are working with. Use a 3 × 5 card in your left hand. Cover the column of phrases with the card and move the card down and up again with the quickest possible flick of your wrist, so that the first phrase in the column is exposed for an instant. Write down what you think you saw. If you are not certain, make a guess. Then check yourself and cross off on your answer sheet any words you missed. As you check each phrase, keep the rest of the column covered. Move right down the column this way and continue with the next column. Work quickly, and expose each phrase *for the shortest possible time,* even if you make frequent mistakes.

Group A

iconoclastic	a success story	the coal miners
on this spot	more and more	her purple dress
out on strike	get out of hand	strange question
beat them all	the grim reaper	It's not worth it.
ignorant of it	savage repartee	in the same boat
at high speed	once and for all	student rebellion
miss the boat	the other media	old acquaintance
came too late	bright and early	musical evenings
a key witness	being in fashion	lead him a dance
money orders	ulterior motives	He's impractical.
vital statistics	five months ago	not my fair share
thunderstruck	notwithstanding	source of income
the spare tires	before and after	far from accurate
along that line	better than ever	do the impossible
afraid to think	What time is it?	unusual endeavor
as they do say	in the meantime	graduate students
bacteriological	free information	an optical illusion
vegetable crop	finished product	whiskey and soda
our way of life	beyond question	They don't know.
old comic strip	He had seen me.	as clear as crystal

Group B

under suspicion?	The sky is clear.	take another look?
bigger and better	be that as it may	in the final analysis
largest molecules	get along without	acts like a chimney
I don't believe it.	as a matter of fact	a million and a half
basic significance	of real importance	relative instabilities
legal professional	the Panama Canal	world trouble spots
in the first quater	it stands to reason	fencing instructions
incomprehensible	almost as much as	Start all over again.
no brighter future	from bad to worse	good administration
a perfect example	freedom of speech	molecular biologists
for the time being	a new lease on life	over and over again
so greatly in need	under construction	We are not amused.
the political scene	staggering problem	5 barrels of gasoline
a patent absurdity	extremely valuable	crude oil production
a flying laboratory	a standard practice	at your convenience
Council of Europe	inferiority complex	few and far between
the primary lesson	another application	at this time last year
bone of contention	a college education	a sharp straight nose
balance the budget	Second World War	will not be permitted
turn back the clock	theory and practice	to settle the question

Group C

effective operations
crude oil drilling rig
dissatisfied customer
partly for this reason
Take my word for it.
perfunctory applause
What a brilliant idea!
to explain these facts
manipulate the media
precision instruments
vote of no confidence
to add insult to injury
it now seems possible
It's too much trouble.
setting out poinsettias
unpolluted waterways
Estimate your results.
no fluorescent lighting
coal and iron reserves
psychological moment
He said nothing at all.
by the end of the year
change in temperature
three remarkable facts
the nineteenth century
of all the requirements
He bets on the horses.
It goes without saying.
unhappily disorganized
the local representative

Is he a reliable man?
millions of Europeans
based upon experience
How much did it cost?
devastating earthquake
produce the best result
overwhelming majority
throughout the country
a necessary adjustment
to play into their hands
It's not very important.
important contributions
make enough to live on
circumstantial evidence
It's a matter of custom.
a presidential candidate
because of bad weather
if the truth were known
throughout the universe
a serious miscalculation
big electrical appliances
in what has gone before
a problem of nationality
He rose from the ranks.
How fast can you read?
a reciprocal relationship
you simply can't impose
Roman Catholic Church
three different languages
You know what I mean.

Group D

first virus crystallized
a dramatic monologue
we lack the incentives
training and experience
this anarchistic outlook
What splendid animals!
an awkward disposition
the humanistic tradition
I shall be most grateful.
our analysis has implied
That accusation is false.
a rapid circulation of air
really needs overhauling
a personal responsibility
in international relations
under the circumstances
that you follow this plan
They can easily be seen.
a functional arrangement
great financial difficulties
take it into consideration
attorneys for the defense
no foreign correspondent
Supreme Court decisions
no mechanical difficulties
engineering achievements
noncommissioned officers
eighteenth-century novels
House of Representatives
United Nations Assembly

running around in circles
happily playing the piano
try to discover new ways
when all is said and done
it brings in the whole line
at the end of four months
This need not prevent us.
many years of experience
started moving cautiously
due to prior commitments
for some special comment
We have great confidence.
bewildered and withdrawn
the Union of South Africa
The verdict was "Guilty."
in three different countries
underground storage tanks
The whole thing is absurd.
many-branched candelabra
we may approach the work
an alternative interpretation
no hospitalization insurance
a Constitutional amendment
two political representatives
Governor of South Carolina
about the fifteenth of March
three wars in one generation
Mutual Broadcasting System
We may have made an error.
resume the military operation

ANSWERS TO EXERCISES

Answers to the multiple-choice questions are arranged by chapters.

CHAPTER 1: READING SKILLS SURVEY

Summarizing   A:2   B:3   C:1   D:1   E:3   Entire passage:1
Pre-reading   1:a   2:Ch. 1, Ch. 23, possibly Ch. 2, Ch. 3   3:p. 579   4:c
    5:Ch. 23   6:c   7:c   8:b
Reading Speed: Average Level 1   1:F   2:F   3:T   4:T   5:c   6:c
    7:d   8:c   9:c   10:d
Reading Speed: Difficult Level 1   1:c   2:d   3:a, c, e, d, b (in that order)
    4:e   5:a   6:b   7:b   8:a   9:c   10:d

CHAPTER 2

Summarizing   A:2   B:3   C:2   D:1   E:1   F:3   Entire passage:2
Reading Speed: Average Level 2   1:F   2:F   3:T   4:T   5:a   6:e
    7:c   8:c   9:b   10:d

CHAPTER 3

Pre-reading   1:Ch. 1, Ch. 7; possibly Ch. 2, Ch. 3; not necessarily Ch. 14
    2:c   3:b   4:Ch 1   5:c   6:d   7:b   8:a
Summarizing   A:3   B:1   C:3   D:2   E:1   F:3   Entire passage:3
Reading Speed: Average Level 3   1:T   2:F   3:T   4:F   5:b   6:a
    7:b   8:b   9:c   10:d

CHAPTER 4

Pre-reading   1:c   2:c, f   3:b   4:c   5:b   6:d   7:c
Reading Speed: Difficult Level 2   1:c   2:d   3:b   4:d   5:e   6:d
    7:d   8:c   9:c   10:f, c, a, (in that order)

CHAPTER 5

Pre-reading   1:c   2:f   3:a   4:d   5:Ch. IX   6:a, e   7:b
    8: Conclusion, Ch. IX; What particular listeners did, Ch. IV, Ch. VIII; What was actually broadcast . . . and what . . . public reaction was, Ch. I, Ch. II; General conditions, Ch. VII; The true role of intelligence and/or education, Ch. V (or "none"); Why the panic was not foreseen, "none"; Specific situations or problems, Ch. VI, Ch. VIII; The essential differences, Ch. V, Ch. VI, Ch. VIII, possibly Ch. IX; What individual listeners thought they heard, Ch. III; The role of neurosis, "none."
    9:d
Summarizing   A:2, sentences 1, 2   B:3, sentence 1   C:1, sentence 1

D:1, sentences 1, 6   E:3, sentences 1, 2   F:2, sentences 1, 2   G:1, sentence 1   Entire passage: 1

Reading Speed: Average Level 4   1:T   2:T   3:F   4:F   5:b   6:d
7:a   8:c   9:d   10:c

CHAPTER 6

Pre-reading   1:Ch. I, Ch. II, Ch. XVI   2:c   3:d   4:c   5:c   6:d
7:a   8:d   9:b   10:b

Summarizing   A:1, sentences 1, 2   B:3, sentences 1, 4   C:2, sentences 1, 6   D:1, sentences 1, 9   E:3, sentences 1, 4   Entire passage: 2

CHAPTER 7

Reading Speed: Average Level 5   1:F   2:T   3:T   4:F   5:c   6:d
7:a   8:b   9:b   10:b

CHAPTER 8

Summarizing   A:2   B:3   C:1   D:1   E:2   Entire passage: 2
Reading Speed: Difficult Level 3   1:d   2:c   3:a, b   4:b, d   5:a
6:e, d, b, c, a (in that order)   7:c   8:d   9:a   10:d

CHAPTER 9

Pre-reading   1:Ch. I, Ch. X, Ch. XXIV   2:c   3:b   4:b   5:c   6:c
7:(essay answer)   8:Ch. V and Ch. VI   9:Ch. XX and Ch. XXI

CHAPTER 10

Reading Speed: Average Level 6   1:F   2:T   3:T   4:F   5:b   6:d
7:a   8:d   9:c   10:b

CHAPTER 11

Reading Speed: Difficult Level 4   1:b   2:b   3:d   4:a   5:a   6:e
7:b   8:d   9:d   10:c

CHAPTER 12

Reading Speed: Average Level 7   1:F   2:F   3:F   4:T   5:c   6:c
7:a   8:c   9:d   10:c

CHAPTER 13

Integrated Exercise 2   Pre-reading questions: 1:c   2:c   Thorough-reading questions: 1:e   3: 3 and 4   4:b   5:c   6: a. *conduction* b. *nervous* c. *muscular* (in any order)   7:4 and 6   9:e   10:b

CHAPTER 14

Integrated Exercise 4   Pre-reading questions: 1:a   2:c   3:b
5: *induction, deduction, hypothesis, significant fact, analysis* (and, arguably, *observation, consequence, general law*) (in any order) Thorough-reading questions: 2:d   3:c   5:d   9:b   10:c

Score Sheet

Phrase Flashing

Enter here the number of phrases you got *completely* correct. Punctuation and capital letters count. Since the difficulty of the exercise material increases greatly from the beginning to the end of the series, you should not expect your score to improve markedly from one group to the next. There are sixty phrases in each group. If you get fewer than fifty correct on any one group, you should repeat that group the next day before going on to the more difficult groups. However, repeat no group more than twice before going on to the next; you can come back to it a third time after going ahead one group.

	Group A	Group B	Group C	Group D
First trial				
Second trial				
Third trial				

Score Sheet

Skimming Exercises

Enter your time and the number correct. Enter the result below, and work to *decrease* your time score.

	Set 1 Page 23	Set 2 Page 151	Set 3 Page 174	Set 4 Page 204	Set 5 Page 234	Set 6 Page 292	Set 7 Page 326
Time in sec.							
Number correct							

Copyrights and Acknowledgments

The author thanks the following publishers and copyright holders for their permission to use the selections reprinted in this book. The number in parentheses following each acknowledgment refers to the chapter in which the selection occurs; the superior figure corresponds to that found at the end of the title or the selection paragraph.

GEORGE ALLEN & UNWIN, LTD., for selections from *The Kon-Tiki Expedition*, by Thor Heyerdahl, 1950 (1[8], 12[9]); and for "Characteristics of Scientific Method," from *The Scientific Outlook*, by Bertrand Russell, 1931 (14[5]).

THE AMERICAN PHYSIOLOGICAL SOCIETY, for material adapted from "The Nervous Origin of the Heart-Beat in Limulus," by Anton J. Carlson, in the *American Journal of Physiology*, Vol. XII, 1904 (13[7]).

APPLETON-CENTURY-CROFTS, INC., for selection from *International Law*, 3rd Edition, by Charles G. Fenwick. Copyright, 1948, Appleton-Century-Crofts, Inc. (7[3]).

BARRIE & JENKINS, LTD., for material from *The Economics of Taste*, by Gerald Reitlinger, The Cressett Press (11[4]).

G. BELL & SONS, LTD., for pp. 1–14 from *The Whig Interpretation of History*, by Herbert Butterfield (13[5]).

W. A. BENJAMIN, INC., for "A Chemist's Look at the Bacterial Cell." Reprinted by permission from James D. Watson, *Molecular Biology of the Gene*, Second Edition, © 1970, W. A. Benjamin, Inc., Menlo Park, California (12[7]).

BRITISH MEDICAL JOURNAL, for heading of article, from *British Medical Journal*, March 28, 1970. From the paper "Cardiovascular State of Newly Discovered Diabetic Women," by J. A. Weaver, S. K. Bhatia, D. Boyle, D. R. Hadden, and D. A. D. Montgomery (3[1]).

THE CLARENDON PRESS, for material on p. 268 from *Bibliography of British History, Tudor Period*, 2nd edition, edited by Conyers Read, 1959. Reprinted by permission of The Clarendon Press, Oxford (11[1]).

J. M. DENT & SONS, LTD., for material from the Everyman's Library edition of *History of the Peloponnesian War*, by Thucydides, translated by Richard Crawley, revised by R. Feetham (13[3]).

E. P. DUTTON & COMPANY, INC., for material from the Everyman's Library edition of *History of the Peloponessian War*, by Thucycides, translated by Richard Crawley, revised by R. Feetham (13[3]).

THE ECONOMIST NEWSPAPER LTD., for selection from *The Economist*, March 22, 1969 (12[3]).

FORTUNE MAGAZINE, for paragraph from "How the Japanese Mount That Export Blitz" from *Fortune*, September 1970 (8[4]); for paragraph from p. 32, *Fortune*, December, 1968 (1[6]). Courtesy of *Fortune Magazine*.

W. H. FREEMEN AND COMPANY, for introductory material to the article "Giant Brain Cells in Mollusks" by A. O. D. Willows, from *Scientific American*, February 1971, p. 69. © 1971 by Scientific American, Inc. All rights reserved (3[2]).

Crash, by John Kenneth Galbraith, 1955 (4[1]); for paragraph from *The Theory and Practice of American National Government,* by Carl B. Swisher, 1951 (1[5]).

LUND HUMPHRIES, for extract from *Painting in the Twentieth Century,* Vol. I, by Werner Haftmann. Reprinted by permission of the publisher (11[3]).

LITTLE, BROWN AND COMPANY, for material from *How to Buy Stocks,* by Louis Engel, copyright 1953, © 1957, 1962 by Louis Engel, by permission of Little, Brown and Company (8[5]).

LONGMAN GROUP LIMITED, for table of contents and preface, pp. vii–x and xiii–xvi from *The War for America, 1775–1783,* by Piers Mackesy. Reprinted by permission of the publishers (12[6]).

MC GRAW-HILL BOOK COMPANY, for table of contents from *Anthropology: The Study of Man,* by E. Adamson Hoebel. Copyright 1966 by McGraw-Hill, Inc. (3[4]).

THE MACMILLAN COMPANY, for "In Defense of Contemporary Fiction" from *How We Live* by Penny Chapin Hills and L. Rust Hills. Reprinted with permission of the Macmillan Company from *How We Live* by Penny Chapin Hills and L. Rust Hills. © Rust Hills and Penny Hills, 1968 (7[7]).

G & C MERRIAM COMPANY, for the entry on osmosis. By permission. From *Webster's Third New International Dictionary,* copyright 1961 by G. & C. Merriam Co., publishers of the Merriam-Webster Dictionaries (13[2]).

NATURE, for article "Spaced Receiver Observations of Radio Pulses" from *Nature,* October 24, 1970. Reprinted by permission of *Nature* (13[1]).

THE NEW YORK TIMES COMPANY, for the following articles: "U. S. Trade Moves Back to Surplus" by Edwin L. Dale, Jr., April 29, 1969 (8[3]); "Navy Considering Plan to Mothball 6 to 18 Carriers" by William Beecher, October 21, 1970 (12[1]); © 1969, 1970 by the New York Times Company. Reprinted by permission; "Governor Asks $1.40-an-Hour Minimum Farm Pay," February 4, 1969 (12[4]).

THE NEW YORKER, for "The Sellout" by Freeman Dyson. From *The New Yorker,* February 21, 1970. Reprinted by permission; © 1970 The New Yorker Magazine, Inc. (15*).

W. W. NORTON & COMPANY, INC., for "Characteristics of Scientific Method" reprinted from *The Scientific Outlook,* by Bertrand Russell. By permission of W. W. Norton & Company, Inc. Copyright 1931, 1959 by Bertrand Russell (14[5]); for pp. 1–14 from *The Whig Interpretation of History,* by Herbert Butterfield. By permission of W. W. Norton & Company, Inc. 1954. All rights reserved by W. W. Norton & Company, Inc. (13[5]).

OXFORD UNIVERSITY PRESS, INC., N. Y., N. Y., for selection from *The Uses of the Past,* by Herbert J. Muller. Copyright 1952 by Oxford University Press, Inc. Reprinted by permission (13[6]); for selection from pp. 17–18 of *Handel's Dramatic Oratorios and Masques,* by Winton Dean, 1959 (11[5]).

FREDERICK A. PRAEGER, INC., for paragraph from *Painting in the Twentieth Century,* Vol. I, Werner Haftman, p. 350 (11[3]); for paragraph from *The Schoolhouse in the City,* edited by Alvin Toffler. For the selection "The Community Centered School" by Preston R. Wilcox (1[1]).

PRINCETON UNIVERSITY PRESS, for material from *The Invasion from Mars* by Hadley Cantril and associates by permission of Princeton University Press. Copyright, 1940, © 1968 by Princeton University Press (5[6]).

PUTNAM AND COMPANY, LTD., for material on p. 69 from *Kobbes' Complete Opera Book,* edited and revised by the Earl of Harewood, London, 1966 (11[2]).

RANDOM HOUSE, INC., ALFRED A. KNOPF, INC., for selection from pp. xxiv–xxvii from *The Children of Sanchez,* by Oscar Lewis. Copyright © 1961 by Oscar Lewis. Reprinted by permission of Random House, Inc. (8[9]); for selection from *Society: An Introduction to Sociology,* by Ely Chinoy. Copyright © 1961 by Ely Chinoy. Reprinted by permission of Random House, Inc. (1[9]); for selection from pp. 24–33 from *Anti-Intellectualism in American Life,* by

Richard Hofstadter. Reprinted by permission of Alfred A. Knopf, Inc. (14⁴); for selection from *Democracy in America*, by Alexis de Tocqueville. (Reeve/Bowen/Bradley trans.) Copyright 1945 by Alfred A. Knopf, Inc. Reprinted by permission of the publisher (5⁷).

RAND McNALLY & COMPANY, for selections from *Kon-Tiki: Across the Pacific by Raft*, by Thor Hyerdahl. Published in the U. S. by Rand McNally & Company (1⁸, 12⁹).

THE READING LABORATORY, INC., for adapted material copyrighted 1953 by The Reading Laboratory, Inc., New York (5⁴).

THE REPORTER, for "The Morning After," by Otto Friedrich, in *The Reporter*, April 30, 1959. Copyright 1959 by The Reporter Magazine Company (7⁸).

VINCENT SHEEAN, for selections from *Personal History*, by Vincent Sheean. Modern Library edition (3⁷, 14¹).

SIMON AND SCHUSTER, INC., for selection from *How to Read a Book*, by Mortimer J. Adler. Copyright 1940 by Mortimer J. Adler. Reprinted by permission of Simon and Schuster, Inc. (10³).

STEIN AND DAY/PUBLISHERS, for seven-line excerpt from *The Vocabulary of Science*. Copyright © 1969 by Lancelot Hogben. Reprinted with the permission of Stein and Day/Publishers (8¹).

STUDIO VISTA LIMITED PUBLISHERS, for paragraph from *Victorian Painting*, by Graham Reynolds. By permission of the publisher (11⁶).

THAMES AND HUDSON, LTD., for "Aspects of Ceramic Technology in Archaeology" from *Science In Archaeology*, by Brothwell and Higgs © Thames and Hudson 1969 (8⁸).

TIME: THE WEEKLY NEWSMAGAZINE, for selection from "The Great Glass Battle" from *Time*, February 7, 1969 (8²); for "Mental Illness" from *Time*, March 14, 1969 (12²). Reprinted by permission from *Time, The Weekly Newsmagazine;* Copyright Time Inc. 1969.

TIME NEWSPAPERS LIMITED, for selections from article "Adams to meet LSE students" by Brian MacArthur from *The Times*, May 3, 1969; for Science Report from *Times*, October 1970 (12⁵).

D. VAN NOSTRAND COMPANY, INC., for selection from White's *Classical and Modern Physics* (1940) D. Van Nostrand Company, Inc., Princeton, N. J. (6¹).

A. P. WATT & SON, for material from *The Outline of History*, 1929, published by Doubleday & Co., Inc., and Cassell & Co., Ltd. Copyright H. G. Wells 1920. Reprinted by permission of Professor G. P. Wells (13⁴).

WAYNE STATE UNIVERSITY PRESS, for selection from Leonard Bloomfield's Preface to *Let's Read: A Linguistic Approach*, by Leonard Bloomfield and Clarence L. Barnhart. Copyright © 1961 by Clarence L. Barnhart. Philippines Copyright 1961, by Clarence L. Barnhart. International Rights Reserved (2¹).

JOHN WILEY & SONS, INC., PUBLISHERS, for preface, table of contents, and introductory chapter from *Social Class and Mental Illness*, by August B. Hollingshead and Frederick C. Redlich (11⁷).

Additional Sources

"The David J. Adams" excerpt from United States–Great Britain Claims Arbitration, 1921 (7⁶).

Economic Concentration and World War II, Similar War Plants Corporation, U. S. Government Printing Office, 1946 (1²).

Effects of Atomic Weapons, Atomic Energy Commission, 1950 (6³).

"The Grace and Ruby" excerpts from decision of U. S. District Court, District of Massachusetts, 1922. 283 F. 475 (7⁴).

Monthly Report of the Military Governor (for Germany), August 1948 (7²).

National Resources Committee, Gardiner C. Means, *et al., The Structure of the American Economy,* Vol. I, U. S. Government Printing Office, 1939 (1³).

"The Navemar" excerpts from decision of District Court, E.D.N.Y., 1937. 18 F.S. 153 (7⁵).

Selection of Lumber for Farm and Home Building, Farmers' Bulletin No. 1756, U. S. Department of Agriculture (5¹).

Henry D. Smyth, *Atomic Energy for Military Purposes,* Princeton University Press, 1946 (6²).

U. S. Bureau of the Census, *Statistical Abstract of the United States: 1962.* (Eighty-third edition.) Washington, D. C., 1962, p. 46 (8⁶).